Government and Society in Colonial Peru

History: Bloomsbury Academic Collections

This Collection of 23 reissued titles from The Athlone Press and Leicester University Press offers a distinguished selection of titles that showcase the width and breadth of historical study, as well as the interdisciplinary nature of the subject. Crossing over into politics, linguistics, economics, politics, military and maritime history, and science, this Collection encompasses titles on British, European and global subjects from the Early Modern period to the late 20th Century.

The collection is available both in e-book and print versions.

Titles in History are available in the following subsets:

History: British History

History: European History

History: History of Latin America

History: History of Medicine

Other titles available in History: History of Latin America include:

José Martí: Revolutionary Democrat, Ed. by Christopher Abel and Nissa Torrents

British Railways in Argentina 1857-1914: A Case Study of Foreign Investment, Colin M. Lewis

Latin America, Economic Imperialism and the State: The Political Economy of the External Connection from Independence to the Present, Ed. by Christopher Abel and Colin M. Lewis

The Rise and Fall of the Peruvian Military Radicals 1968-1976, George D.E. Philip

Government and Society in Colonial Peru

The Intendant System 1784-1814

J. R. Fisher

History: History of Latin America
BLOOMSBURY ACADEMIC COLLECTIONS

Bloomsbury Academic
An imprint of Bloomsbury Publishing Plc

B L O O M S B U R Y
LONDON · NEW DELHI · NEW YORK · SYDNEY

Bloomsbury Academic
An imprint of Bloomsbury Publishing Plc

50 Bedford Square
London
WC1B 3DP
UK

1385 Broadway
New York
NY 10018
USA

www.bloomsbury.com

BLOOMSBURY and the Diana logo are trademarks of Bloomsbury Publishing Plc

First published in 1970 by The Athlone Press

This edition published by Bloomsbury Academic 2015

© John R. Fisher 2015

John R. Fisher has asserted his right under the Copyright, Designs and Patents Act, 1988, to be identified as Author of this work.

All rights reserved. No part of this publication may be reproduced or transmitted in any form or by any means, electronic or mechanical, including photocopying, recording, or any information storage or retrieval system, without prior permission in writing from the publishers.

No responsibility for loss caused to any individual or organization acting on or refraining from action as a result of the material in this publication can be accepted by Bloomsbury or the author.

British Library Cataloguing-in-Publication Data
A catalogue record for this book is available from the British Library.

ISBN: HB: 978-1-4742-4117-5
ePDF: 978-1-4742-4118-2
Set: 978-1-4742-4119-9

Library of Congress Cataloging-in-Publication Data
A catalog record for this book is available from the Library of Congress

Series: Bloomsbury Academic Collections, ISSN 2051-0012

Printed and bound in Great Britain

University of London Historical Studies

XXIX

GOVERNMENT AND SOCIETY
IN COLONIAL PERU
THE INTENDANT SYSTEM 1784–1814

This volume is published with the help of
a grant from the late Miss Isobel Thornley's
Bequest to the University of London

Government and Society in Colonial Peru
The Intendant System
1784-1814

by

J. R. FISHER

UNIVERSITY OF LONDON
THE ATHLONE PRESS
1970

Published by
THE ATHLONE PRESS
UNIVERSITY OF LONDON
at 2 Gower Street London W C 1
Distributed by Tiptree Book Services Ltd
Tiptree, Essex

Australia and New Zealand
Melbourne University Press

U.S.A.
Oxford University Press Inc
New York

© *J. R. Fisher* 1970

ISBN 0 485 13129 3

Printed in Great Britain by
WESTERN PRINTING SERVICES LTD
BRISTOL

PREFACE

The viceroyalty of Peru was an inevitable victim of the imperial reform programme of Charles III. The introduction of freer trade within the empire completed the destruction of the old commercial structure on which the prosperity of Lima had depended, while the incorporation of Upper Peru in the new viceroyalty of the Río de la Plata diverted the flow of most of Potosí's silver away from Lima to Buenos Aires. Despite the depressing effects of these changes in Peru, however, the crown believed that the viceroyalty could be made more prosperous and more profitable, and was determined to provide it with better government and improved financial and judicial administration. But conservative groups in Peru stubbornly and effectively resisted the efforts of the *visitador general* who arrived in 1777 to implement this programme. His work was brought to a complete halt by the outbreak of the rebellion of Túpac Amaru in 1780.

Many historians have turned their attention to the rebellion of Túpac Amaru, although few have resisted the temptation to see it as an expression of Peruvian nationalism rather than a demand for reform within the imperial structure. The conflict between the *visitador general* and the viceregal establishment has been analysed clearly by Palacio Atard, while the important work of Céspedes del Castillo covers the economic and financial aspects of the separation of Upper Peru. Relatively little attention has been paid, however, to the period after the suppression of the Indian rebellion, when the crown made a renewed effort to provide Peru with a radically reformed structure of government. The *visita general* was revived and reached its peak in 1784, when the system of provincial administration by intendants— already operating in the neighbouring viceroyalty of the Río de la Plata—was extended to Peru. This development was in part a response to the rebellion of Túpac Amaru, which had focused attention upon the abuses suffered by the Indians at the hands of the *corregidores*, but it also reflected the wider aims of stimulating economic development in Peru, increasing the yield of royal revenues and generally making crown authority more effective.

The recent work of Deustua Pimentel provides a useful introduction to the creation of the Peruvian intendancies, but deals largely with royal intentions rather than the consequences of reform in the provinces. The basic questions about the effects of the introduction of the intendant system—dealt with for the viceroyalty of the Río de la Plata by the outstanding work of Dr John Lynch—have remained unanswered for the viceroyalty of Peru. The aims of this work are to explore the background to and the effects—social, political and administrative—of administrative reform in Peru in the late colonial period, and to examine the achievements of the intendants in relation to their aims and duties as defined in the Ordinance of Intendants.

The Archivo General de Indias in Seville provided much of the manuscript material on which the book is based. The detailed documentation of the *visita general* in the section *Audiencia de Lima* was particularly valuable. Both this section and *Audiencia de Cuzco* contain important material on the policies of the crown and the Council of the Indies, and correspondence with viceroys, intendants, *cabildos* and *audiencias*. The Archivo Nacional in Lima yielded important information on the functioning of the machinery of government within the viceroyalty, while the section *Cabildo* of this archive, together with the *Libros de Cabildo* and the *Libros de Cédulas y Provisiones Reales* in the Archivo Histórico Municipal of Lima, proved indispensable for the study of relations between the intendants and the municipal corporations. Material on financial administration was obtained from the Archivo Histórico del Ministerio de Hacienda y Comercio in Lima, while the city's Biblioteca Nacional provided valuable documents on administration in general. The manuscript section of the Archivo General del Ministerio de Relaciones Exteriores in Lima contains some interesting material for the late colonial period. Several unpublished contemporary studies on Peruvian commerce were consulted in the British Museum, together with a fine set of maps, many of which were prepared under the auspices of the intendants.

PREFACE

I wish to express my gratitude to the directors and staffs of these libraries and archives—and to those of the Institute of Historical Research in London and the Escuela de Estudios Hispanoamericanos in Seville—for their kind assistance and co-operation. I am grateful to Félix Denegri Luna, who allowed me to consult rare printed sources in his private library in Lima, and to Pablo Macera Dall'Orso for his expert advice on Peruvian archives. I am particularly indebted to Professor R. A. Humphreys and Dr John Lynch for their encouragement, advice and assistance, and for their patient scrutiny of the book's first draft—the defects of course are my responsibility. A grant from the University of London Central Research Fund aided my researches in Spain. Finally, I should like to thank my wife for her unfailing support and co-operation.

University of Liverpool,   J. R. F.
October 1969

CONTENTS

	Abbreviations	xii
I.	The Decadent Viceroyalty	1
II.	Administrative Reorganization	29
III.	Intendants and Viceroys	54
IV.	Intendants, Subdelegates and Indians	78
V.	Intendants and the Exchequer	100
VI.	Intendants and the Economy	124
VII.	Intendants and Public Administration	156
VIII.	Intendants and *Cabildos*	174
IX.	Administration on the Eve of Revolution	201
X.	Conclusion	233
	Appendices	
	1. List of intendants with biographical notes	239
	2. Population of the viceroyalty of Peru in 1795	251
	3. Product of the *Casa de Moneda* of Lima, 1776–1820	254
	4. Tribute revenue, 1780–1811	256
	5. Production of mercury at Huancavelica, 1759–1812	257
	Glossary of Spanish Terms	258
	Bibliography	261
	Index	275

MAP
Intendancies of the Viceroyalty of Peru   273

ABBREVIATIONS

A.G.I.	Archivo General de Indias, Seville
A.G.M.R.E.	Archivo General del Ministerio de Relaciones Exteriores, Lima
A.H.M.	Archivo Histórico Municipal, Lima
A.H.M.H.	Archivo Histórico del Ministerio de Hacienda y Comercio, Lima
A.N.P.	Archivo Nacional del Perú, Lima
B.M.	British Museum, London
B.N.P.	Biblioteca Nacional del Perú, Lima
H.A.H.R.	*Hispanic American Historical Review*
Ord. Ints.	*Real Ordenanza para el establecimiento e instrucción de intendentes de exército y provincia en el virreinato de Buenos-Ayres*

CHAPTER I

The Decadent Viceroyalty

THE SECOND HALF of the eighteenth century witnessed the application in Spanish America of the Bourbon programme of administrative, economic and financial reform. The aims of the programme were to centralize and improve the structure of government, to create more efficient economic and financial machinery, to defend the empire from other powers, and in general to restore integrity and respect for law at all levels of administration. The comprehensive overhaul of the imperial structure was initiated in 1763 by Charles III and his enlightened ministers after the humiliating defeat of Spain in the Seven Years War. Yet, although military defeat provided the immediate stimulus for imperial reform, the programme was neither hasty nor ill-prepared; it was part of a continuing process inaugurated at the beginning of the century by Philip V, the first Spanish Bourbon, and continued by Ferdinand VI. During the reigns of the first two Bourbons the emphasis lay on reform in Spain itself; during the reign of Charles III reform continued in the peninsula, but the main emphasis shifted to the empire.

The seventeenth century had been for Spain an era of catastrophic decline, characterized by a drain of wealth and manpower, territorial loss, political confusion and economic stagnation.[1] The end of the War of the Spanish Succession in 1713 saw further territorial contraction, with the loss of Milan, Naples, Sardinia, Luxembourg and Flanders. Spain was left militarily and economically exhausted, but she was left too with a new monarchy. The Bourbon, Philip V, aided by French advisers and encouraged by a long period of comparative peace

[1] E. J. Hamilton, 'Money and economic recovery in Spain under the first Bourbon, 1701–46', *Journal of Modern History*, xv (1943), 192–3.

in Europe, devoted his reign to the task of reviving and reforming the decadent country which he had inherited. Progress was slow but steady. In the economic sphere, for example, Philip's reign was marked by the consistent application of mercantilist theories and policies.[1] Internal barriers to trade were eliminated, model factories were created, protection was introduced for domestic agriculture, industry and commerce, and sweeping reforms were made in public finance.

One of the most powerful incentives to reform was the need to unify the country, economically and politically, and to impose central control and direction over provincial government. Under French inspiration the solution adopted was to introduce a system of administration by intendants, provincial governors with a mixture of military, financial, economic and judicial authority, directly responsible to the king's ministers in Madrid.[2] The first intendants were appointed in 1711 and provision was made for the introduction of this new system of administration on a more comprehensive basis in 1718. It was not, however, until 1749, with the provision of a new instruction or ordinance, that the system began to operate effectively throughout the peninsula.[3] By 1749 the intendant system had proved its worth in those provinces where it had operated on a permanent basis throughout the reign of Philip V, and with the encouragement of persuasive reformist ministers, such as José Patiño and José de Campillo, Ferdinand VI felt justified in formally recognizing it as the basis for the provincial administration of the country.

Campillo, Minister of Finance under Philip V, had risen to high office from the lower ranks of the administrative hierarchy, serving for four years as intendant of Zaragoza.[4] His approach to political and administrative problems was indicative of the general attitude of the early Bourbons and their ministers—reform must be based upon the application of reason, and must

[1] M. Artola, 'Campillo y las reformas de Carlos III', *Revista de Indias*, xii (1952), 687-90.
[2] H. Kamen, 'El establecimiento de los intendentes en la administración española', *Hispania*, xxiv (1964), 374-8.
[3] W. W. Pierson, 'The establishment and early functioning of the *Intendencia* of Cuba', *The James Sprunt Historical Studies*, xix (Chapel Hill, 1927), 78.
[4] Kamen, op. cit., 385.

be preceded by inspection and the collection of accurate information. In his *Nuevo sistema de gobierno para la América*, written in 1743, Campillo turned his attention from the peninsula to the empire, which he saw as a market for Spanish manufactures and as a source of raw materials for Spanish industry.[1] His work fell into two parts: a critical analysis of the defects of the economic and administrative structure of the empire, and proposals for reform. His main proposals, for general inspections, or *visitas generales*, the creation of intendancies and the introduction of 'free trade', became the basis for the reform programme of Charles III.

The capture of Havana by the British in 1762 dramatically demonstrated to Spain the strategic weaknesses of the imperial structure; the commercial boom which resulted from the British decision to open the port indicated the economic and financial benefits which a general relaxation of trade restrictions might bring.[2] Peace in 1763 was followed by the rapid implementation of a four-pronged programme of reform. In Spain a special committee was appointed to consider the defects of the imperial commercial system and to suggest remedies.[3] The result was a gradual relaxation of the old restrictionist pattern, beginning in 1765 with the grant of permission for various Spanish ports to trade with the major Caribbean islands. The experiment worked, and the concessions were gradually extended to other parts of the empire, until in 1778 the new system was applied to all the empire except New Spain and Venezuela, an exception which lasted until 1789.[4] Restrictions still applied, but thereafter the major ports of Spain were free to trade directly with the major ports of the empire, and the latter were free to trade with each other.

The policy of removing barriers to imperial communication was accompanied by an even more radical process of reforming the empire from within. A rapid *visita* of Cuba in 1763-4

[1] Artola, op. cit., 690–713.
[2] Pierson, op. cit., 81.
[3] Ibid., 83. For a thorough examination of the whole process of reform see J. Lynch, *Spanish colonial administration 1782–1810* (London, 1958), 46–61.
[4] J. Muñoz Perez, 'La publicación del reglamento de comercio libre de Indias de 1778', *Anuario de Estudios Americanos* iv (1947), 640–3. R. Vargas Ugarte, *Historia del Perú. Virreinato (Siglo XVIII) 1700–1790* (Lima, 1956), 395–7.

established the need for drastic reform of the island's administration, and provoked the decision to create an intendancy there.[1] In the following year, 1765, final preparations were made for the famous *visita general* of José de Gálvez to New Spain.[2] His inspection of the viceroyalty confirmed that attempts to improve its defence, prosperity and government must be based upon territorial reorganization and the creation of a new system of administration.[3]

The outline of Gálvez's scheme for the creation of a system of intendancies in New Spain was ready by 1768.[4] Discussion of it occupied the attention of ministers in Madrid for nearly twenty years, but practical progress in its application was slow, due as much to ministerial caution in Madrid as to viceregal obstruction in Mexico.[5] When Gálvez was appointed Minister of the Indies in 1776 further intendancies had been created only in Louisiana and Sonora, but in that year the reform programme entered a new phase, with the creation of the new viceroyalty of the Río de la Plata.[6] This step provided the stimulus for the introduction of the intendant system in the new viceroyalty in 1782, and for its extension to the viceroyalties of Peru and New Spain in 1784 and 1786.

The immediate reason for the creation of the new viceroyalty was a desire to ensure the success of the expedition sent to the Río de la Plata to repel Portuguese infiltration.[7] Its commander, Pedro de Cevallos, argued convincingly that if his military authority was to be effective it should be reinforced by political control of the Plate area. Consequently he was named head of a new viceroyalty, with its capital in Buenos Aires, ostensibly on a temporary basis. The apparent impermanence of the arrangement was merely an insurance against failure, and the viceroyalty was made permanent in 1777. There were many

[1] Pierson, op. cit., 82.

[2] L. Navarro García, *Don José de Gálvez y la comandancia general de las Provincias Internas del norte de Nueva España* (Sevilla, 1964), 143.

[3] A.G.I., Indif. General 1713, 1714, for full *expedientes* of discussions on Gálvez's proposals.

[4] A.G.I., Indif. General 1713, 'Informe y plan de Intendencias que conviene establecer en las provincias de este reyno de Nueva España', 15 Jan. 1768.

[5] L. Navarro García, *Intendencias en Indias* (Sevilla, 1956), 22–40. For an example of viceregal resistance see A.G.I., Indif. General 1713, Bucareli to Arriaga, 27 July 1772.   [6] Lynch, op. cit., 39–40.   [7] Ibid.

arguments to support this decision, and the idea of creating a new viceroyalty for the Río de la Plata area had been advocated previously. A major obstacle, however, had always been the apparent inability of the area to function without economic assistance from Peru. To solve this problem, and to provide funds for the expedition, it was decreed in 1776 that the new unit should include the rich mining area of Upper Peru. This decision made the new viceroyalty economically viable. For the viceroyalty of Peru, however, it was destructive and harmful since it disrupted a commercial pattern in existence for over two hundred years.

The separation from Peru of the rich mining provinces of Upper Peru did not entirely halt the flow of silver from Potosí to Lima but there was a significant fall in the volume of trade between the two areas.[1] Moreover, the opening of the port of Buenos Aires in 1778 accelerated the decline of Lima as the centre of commercial activity for the Spanish empire in South America. It is true that before 1778 the Lima monopoly was already being undermined from within, as much contraband traffic went directly to Buenos Aires and other ports, but the formal removal of Lima's privileges inevitably made the situation worse and produced an atmosphere of extreme pessimism there.[2] The double blow of commercial and territorial reorganization threatened the interests of the powerful merchant and office-holding groups, as well as the general prosperity of the viceroyalty. The provinces of Upper Peru and those further south, such as Salta and Tucumán, had a long-established commercial relationship with the Peruvian provinces of Arequipa and Cuzco; now they were forced, perhaps unwillingly, to turn to Buenos Aires. At the same time imported manufactures brought ruin to the domestic industries of Arequipa and Cuzco, as well as to those of the interior provinces of the new viceroyalty.[3] Peruvian agriculture also suffered. Sugar producers, for example, found their formerly profitable

[1] G. Céspedes del Castillo, *Lima y Buenos Aires* (Sevilla, 1947), 139–46.

[2] S. Villalobos R., *Comercio y contrabando en el Río de la Plata y Chile* (Buenos Aires, 1965), 19–22. R. Vargas Ugarte (ed.), 'Informe del tribunal del consulado de Lima, 1790', *Revista Histórica* (Lima), xxii (1955–6), 266–310.

[3] M. Burgin, *The economic aspects of Argentine federalism 1820–1852* (Cambridge, Mass., 1946), 3–18.

markets in the Río de la Plata and Chile undercut by cheaper Brazilian sugar imported through Buenos Aires.[1] Peru possessed tremendous economic potential, with a wide range of animal, vegetable and mineral resources, but in 1778 her prospects were gloomy. The future seemed to offer continuing commercial and economic depression, unless the crown could provide the means of stimulating the exploitation of resources and bring about general economic revival.

There was clearly scope for internal economic development, but the possibilities of the domestic market of the reduced viceroyalty, with a total population of a little over one million, were limited. Statistics for colonial population are notoriously suspect, but those for the late eighteenth century can certainly be accepted as more reliable than the varied estimates available for the sixteenth and seventeenth centuries. The census of viceroy Gil, completed in 1792, showed a total population of 1,076,122.[2] The majority, 608,894, were classified as Indians, a further 244,436 as *mestizos*, 81,592 as free coloureds and slaves, and only 135,755 as *españoles* (plus 5496 clergy). A further census, completed in 1795, produced a higher total figure, 1,115,207, the increase depending largely on an increase in the Indian population to 648,615.[3] The upward trend was maintained. Although no further census was taken before independence, it seems that the total population in the early years of the nineteenth century was about 1,400,000.[4] The further increase was due in part to territorial readjustment. According to the estimates of Hipólito Unanue, the celebrated geographer of colonial Peru, the addition to the viceroyalty of the intendancy of Puno in 1795 and of Mainas and Guayaquil in 1802 and 1803 added 200,000 to the population. Expansion within the areas included in the 1792 census accounted for the remainder of the increase.

[1] A.G.I., Aud. de Lima 1100, Escobedo to Gálvez, no. 181, 16 Jan. 1784. See below, 128.
[2] M. A. Fuentes (ed.), *Memorias de los virreyes que han gobernado el Perú* (6 vols, Lima, 1859), vi, 1–353, Gil, *Memoria de Gobierno*, appendix 6–9, table 3.
[3] A.G.I., Indif. General 1525, *estado* with Bonet to Gil, 29 Dec. 1795. See below, 251–3.
[4] A. Rosenblat, *La población indígena y el mestizaje en América* (2 vols., Buenos Aires, 1954), i, 199. The population of Mainas was estimated at 25,641 in 1814—A.G.I., Indif. General 1525, 'Censo de la población de la provincia de Maynas'.

The vast majority of the Indians and many of the *mestizos* were rural inhabitants, concentrated in farming and mining villages in the *sierra*. The *españoles*—a definition which includes creoles as well as peninsular-born Spaniards—were predominantly town and city-dwellers. The censuses of 1792 and 1795 showed that over forty per cent of their number lived in the cities of Lima, Cuzco and Arequipa alone.[1] Further nuclei were to be found in other centres of provincial administration, such as Tarma and Trujillo, in mining centres, such as Huaylas and Huánuco, and in coastal towns such as Ica and Moquegua.

This pattern reflected the traditional urban character of Spanish settlement in America. Many of the city-dwellers were rural landowners who chose for social reasons to live in urban centres. The focus of Spanish society in Peru was, of course, Lima. Here were to be found noble families, many of whom could trace their ancestry, if not their titles, to the conquistadores, forming a powerful, interwoven hierarchy of wealth and prestige.[2] Lima was also the home of great merchant families, who were often related by ties of kinship or economic interest to the titled nobility. The two groups are difficult to separate. There were nobles without commercial interests and merchants without titles, but in the middle there was a complex overlapping. José Antonio de Lavalle Cortés, for example, *prior* of the *consulado*, was in 1782 granted the title conde de Premio Real.[3] Through his wife, Mariana de Sugasti Ortiz de Foronda, he was already related to the powerful family whose head held the title conde de Vallehermoso.[4] The first conde de Premio Real had served as *alcalde* of Lima in 1779, and was appointed a lifetime *regidor* in 1784.[5] His son, Juan Bautista, served as *alcalde* in 1814.[6] This was an example of a single family linking the titled nobility with the merchant hierarchy and the municipal oligarchy.

[1] 56,548: 135,755 (1792); 59,524: 140,890 (1795).
[2] R. Vargas Ugarte, *Títulos nobiliarios en el Perú* (Lima, 1965), 19-74.
[3] Ibid., 49.
[4] J. Bromley, 'Alcaldes de la ciudad de Lima en el siglo xviii', *Revista Historica*, xxv (1960-1), 322.
[5] Ibid., 346. A.G.I., Aud. de Lima 619, Escobedo to Gálvez, no. 321, 20 Aug. 1784.
[6] A.H.M., Libro de Cabildo 43, ff. 86-7, *acta cap.*, 19 Dec. 1813.

The third important segment of the upper class of Peruvian society consisted of the powerful office-holders: the *oidores*, members of the viceregal court, treasury ministers, officials of the mint, the tribunal of accounts and other financial offices, army and naval commanders, and Church dignitaries. Again it is impossible to define this as a separate group, since the ties of friendship and family which linked the office-holders to the titled nobility, the landowners and the merchants were complex and intricate. It is true that some leading offices—that of viceroy, for example—were reserved for *peninsulares*, but many creole families formed part of the upper structure of administration and government. The example of the Manrique de Lara family illustrates this.

The family was descended from the conquistadores of Peru, in particular from Nicolás de Rivera, one of the founders of the city of Lima.[1] The title, marqués de Lara, was granted in 1739 to Nicolás Manrique de Lara, who, although a native of Lima, reached the upper ranks of the administrative hierarchy in the peninsula, serving as a minister of both the Council of the Indies and the Council of Castile.[2] The title was inherited in 1754 by his brother, Francisco, whose wife, Rosa María Carrillo de Albornoz y Bravo de Lagunas, was a sister of the conde de Montemar, head of another great Lima family. Their son, Nicolás, served as *alcalde* of Lima in 1769, and was appointed first intendant of the province of Huamanga in 1784.[3] In 1779 he inherited from his father not only the family title, but the important office of *contador mayor* of the tribunal of accounts of Lima, which, after his return from Huamanga in 1785, he continued to serve until his retirement in 1798.[4]

The idea that creoles were excluded from government is a misleading oversimplification. They were excluded from some posts and they increasingly sought a larger share of offices in general, but in this period they monopolized minor offices and also procured a number of higher appointments. If creoles had been excluded from office, administration might have been less

---

[1] A.N.P., Superior Gobierno 33, *cuaderno* 1085, description of family's history.
[2] Ibid. See also Vargas, *Títulos nobiliarios*, 38.
[3] Bromley, op. cit., 338. See below, 37–42.
[4] See below, 243–4.

corrupt. As it was, Lima society, embracing merchants, landowners and office-holders, formed a tightly knit sector or group, riddled with self-interest and impregnable to all but the most determined investigators and reformers. Administrators arriving from Spain tended to merge into this structure of power, rather than to challenge it. According to Juan and Ulloa, even the most honest viceroys, who arrived in Peru with good intentions, succumbed to the all-pervasive system of bribery, corruption, influence and maladministration for which Peru had become notorious by the middle of the eighteenth century.[1]

Reform of administration in the viceroyalty of Peru offered perhaps the most daunting challenge to Charles III and his ministers. In their report on conditions in Peru Juan and Ulloa emphasized the fact that all groups and officials in positions of authority—the viceroys, the *audiencias*, the *oficiales reales*, the *corregidores*, the *cabildos*—simply ignored any royal orders which they found inconvenient or detrimental to their private interests.[2] They noted that this lack of respect for justice and order began at the top of the administrative structure, with over-powerful viceroys. The extensive personal powers which they enjoyed sometimes prevented absurdities and mistakes in the adaptation of rigid general laws to local conditions, but on other occasions this authority was abused.[3] Moreover the *audiencia*, in theory a counterweight to the viceroy, co-operated in this process of holding up or failing to apply royal orders which threatened the interests of its ministers or of their influential friends.[4] For example, Juan and Ulloa complained that the sale of merchandise brought to Lima by specially-registered ships in 1743 was held up while the *cédula* granting permission for the voyages was examined and considered by the *audiencia*. Meanwhile, the monopolist merchants, closely linked with the *oidores* by family and personal ties, sold off their previous stocks.[5]

---

[1] J. Juan y Santacilla and A. de Ulloa, *Noticias Secretas de América* (Buenos Aires, 1953), 355–9.

[2] Ibid., 341. There is evidence that their report was known not only in Madrid but also in Cuzco in 1783. See D. Valcárcel, *Las Noticias Secretas en 1783* (Lima, 1965).

[3] Juan and Ulloa, op. cit., 351–2.

[4] Ibid., 352, 357.   [5] Ibid., 366–7.

A further aspect of viceregal authority which offered scope for abuse and corruption was the power to appoint district officers, or *corregidores*, and treasury officials.[1] The sale of *corregimientos* seems to have been a regular occurrence, and, although complaints against the practice were sometimes upheld, a viceroy was usually able to avoid censure.[2] When evidence was collected for the *juicio de residencia* of viceroy Manuel de Amat (1761–76) he was charged with irregularity in making these appointments. Despite the fact that the charges were known widely to be justified, Amat was exonerated by the *juez de residencia*, on the grounds that the evidence presented to support the charge was contradictory and ill-prepared.[3] The *residencia*, or official review of an official's record at the end of his term of office, was in theory a valuable check on viceregal misrule, but, according to Juan and Ulloa, a viceroy usually ensured lenient treatment by carefully cultivating the friendship of the senior *oidor*, who would be in charge of the process.[4]

Individual administrators who attempted to root out corruption found themselves frustrated by the strength of the vested interests ranged against them. After his visit to Spanish America in the 1740s Antonio de Ulloa served in a number of administrative posts until, in 1758, he was appointed governor of Huancavelica.[5] Since Huancavelica was the major source of mercury for the American silver miners, efficiency and honesty in the operation of the mine was essential. Ulloa found instead a network of interlocking interests, including the *corregidor* and the treasury officials, preoccupied with personal gain, at the expense of the treasury and the miners, rather than with the mine's efficient operation. His attempts to improve administration failed, since each level of authority was, in turn, involved in corruption. Thus, the miners bribed the treasury officials and the *corregidor*. These were protected by minor officials of

[1] Ibid., 349.
[2] See Vargas, *Historia del Perú. Virreinato (Siglo XVIII) 1700–1790*, 55, for details of sale of office by viceroy Castell dos Rius.
[3] See E. Dunbar Temple, 'Un informe del obispo don Baltasar Jaime Martínez de Compañon en el juicio de residencia del virrey Amat', *Documenta* (Lima), año 2, no. 1 (1949–50), 654.
[4] Juan and Ulloa, op. cit., 362.
[5] See A. P. Whitaker, 'Antonio de Ulloa', *H.A.H.R.*, xv (1935), 179.

the viceregal court, who were themselves secure from censure due to the bribes which they paid to the *fiscal*. In Ulloa's view the office of the *fiscal*, or attorney-general, was 'a marketplace where he who has no substance to contribute is an object of contempt'.[1] As a last resort Ulloa appealed to Amat for support in his attempts to reform administration at Huancavelica. Instead of support he met resistance from a viceroy who had no desire to challenge the accepted standards of the structure which he headed.[2]

The problem of getting to the root of bad government was complicated by the fact that individual authorities, although prepared to acknowledge the existence of maladministration, were concerned merely with passing the responsibility for it to other groups or individuals. Amat, for example, participated in corruption, but repeatedly complained that the responsibility for bad administration in Peru lay with others. In 1762, shortly after his arrival in Lima, he claimed that 'the source and origin of all the political ills of the country' was the *audiencia* of Lima, whose ministers, with the exception of the dean, were interested only in trade.[3] He alleged that the sub-dean, in particular, was fit only for the conduct of trade, 'which is the sole object of his attention'. The prologue to Amat's *Memoria de Gobierno* also dwelt upon the deficiencies of the viceroyalty's administration, describing Peru as 'a kingdom governed by the caprice of an insatiable greed of those who command the provinces'.[4] He was referring to the *corregidores*, and there is no doubt that the government of Peru was at its worst outside of the capital, at a provincial level. The ultimate responsibility for corruption lay in Lima, but the practical consequences of maladministration were most damaging in the provinces.

The need to reform local government was one of the chief

[1] Ibid., 180, Ulloa to Arriaga, 15 Aug. 1762.
[2] For a discussion of Ulloa's relations with Amat see V. Rodríguez Casado and F. Pérez Embid, 'Estudio preliminar' to *Memoria de gobierno del virrey Amat* (Sevilla, 1947), xciii–cvii.
[3] See 'El virrey del Perú, Manuel de Amat, informa al rey del estado de las audiencias del virreinato y en especial de la de Lima...', *Revista de la Biblioteca Nacional* (Buenos Aires), 24 (1942), 349–50.
[4] See 'Prólogo de la Memoria del virrey Amat', *Revista chilena de historia y geografía*, 117 (1951), 44. The prologue was probably written by Miguel Feyjóo, who served as *corregidor* in Quispicanches and Trujillo.

motives for Gálvez's desire to introduce an intendant system in New Spain. He described the district officers there as: 'two hundred wretches, who, with their empty title of judges, have come to constitute an independent judicial sphere, wherein, driven by their greed, they work out their own fortunes at the expense of the royal treasury and the ruin of the people'.[1] In Peru conditions were even worse. One of Gálvez's most experienced subordinates during the *visita* to New Spain was Antonio de Areche, who began a separate *visita* to Peru in 1777.[2] Shortly after his arrival, he wrote to a former colleague in Mexico:

This land bears no comparison with that of Your Excellency in any respect. In Mexico there is usually justice; here tyranny is common. . . . Peru is being ruined by the lack of honest judges, forced Indian labour and the forced trade conducted by the district officers. The *corregidores* are concerned solely with their own interests. . . . Oh dear friend! how close we are to losing everything here, unless these disgusting abuses are corrected, because they have already continued far too long, and a tragic end can be forseen if a remedy is not provided. Here everything is private interest, nothing public good.[3]

There is a mass of documentary evidence to support the claim that the *corregidores* were greedy and rapacious officials.[4] To a certain extent they were victims of circumstances in that their official salaries were utterly inadequate for their subsistence and expenses of government. For example, the *corregidor* of Chancay received an annual salary of 1250 pesos, the *corregidor* of Huamachuco 1000, and the *corregidor* of Cañete 962 pesos 4 reales.[5] However, the official salary was usually irrelevant

[1] Quoted in C. E. Castañeda, 'The corregidor in Spanish colonial administration', *H.A.H.R.*, ix (1929), 448.
[2] V. Palacio Atard, *Areche y Guirior. Observaciones sobre el fracaso de una visita al Perú* (Sevilla, 1946), 7.
[3] Vargas, *Historia del Perú. Virreinato (Siglo XVIII) 1700–1790*, 379–80, Areche to Mangino, 17 Dec. 1777.
[4] See for example L. A. Eguiguren (ed.), *Guerra separatista. Rebeliones de Indios en Sur America. La sublevación de Túpac Amaru. Crónica de Melchor de Paz* (2 vols., Lima, 1952).
[5] A.G.I., Indif. General 1713, Areche to Gálvez, no. 195, 20 Aug. 1780. The equivalent value of the peso in contemporary English money varied, according to the exchange rate of silver, but was usually between 4s and 5s.

when the value of a *corregimiento* was assessed. The significant factors were the number of Indians in the province and the value of goods laid down for the *repartimiento*. Thus, the *corregimiento* of the *cercado* of Lima was considered to be of little value, because the *arancel* of the *repartimiento*, or forced sale of goods to the Indians, was fixed at the relatively low figure of 10,000 pesos.[1]

The abuses made possible by the trade of the *corregidores* were described in great detail by Juan and Ulloa and other contemporaries, and were well known to the central government.[2] In defence of the system it was often argued that, despite abuses, it was the only means of providing the Indians with essential items, such as cloth, iron and mules, and of making them take an active part in the economic life of the viceroyalty.[3] But one of the disturbing features of the *repartimiento* system was that the goods forced upon the Indians were often completely useless. Baltasar de Arandia, the *corregidor* of Chichas in the period immediately before the Túpac Amaru rising, found in the warehouse of his predecessor a number of books to be distributed to the Indians, including eleven volumes of *The Christian Year*, two of *The Spiritual Discourses*, the fourteen volumes of Feijóo and two volumes of an economic dictionary.[4]

The chief function of the *corregidores* was judicial, but the fair application of justice was made difficult by the fact that the *corregimientos* were 'diphthongs of Merchants and Justice, so that in them the staff of commerce is joined with that of justice'.[5] The *corregidor* distributed his merchandise, he disposed of the public force necessary for the collection of debts due to him, while at the same time he was the judge who dealt with the complaints of the Indians, including those against his commercial activities. In practice there were no real checks upon abuse of this authority. The *residencia* which the *corregidor*

[1] B.M., Eg. MS 1810, f. 78v.
[2] Juan and Ulloa, op. cit., 189, 193–6, 198–9. See also B.N.P., MS C4129, for detailed reports on *repartimientos* in the diocese of Arequipa in 1778.
[3] This was Escobedo's reason for wishing in 1784 to retain some form of official distribution. See below, 89–90.
[4] B. Lewin, *La rebelión de Túpac Amaru y los orígenes de la emancipación americana* (Buenos Aires, 1957), 293.
[5] Amat, *Memoria*, ii, 186. The same phrase is used in B.M., Add. MS 13981.

had to face on completion of his term of office was a theoretical deterrent against bad government; in fact this deterrent was ineffective because the process had become a mere monetary transaction between judge and judged.[1] The alternative legal recourse for aggrieved Indians—appeal to the *audiencia* of Lima—was equally ineffective, partly because of cost and distance, and partly because the *audiencia* tended to support the authority of the *corregidor*.[2] Legal remedies denied, the Indians came to see rebellion as the only effective means of opposition to an oppressive *corregidor*. The chief cause of the rebellion of Juan Santos Atahualpa, which broke out in the provinces of Tarma and Jauja in 1742 and lasted until 1756, was the tyranny of the *corregidores*.[3]

Although tolerated by the *audiencia* of Lima, the commerce of the *corregidores* was strictly illegal and remained so until the middle of the eighteenth century.[4] Complaints were frequently made to the crown, and during the government of the viceroy conde de Superunda it was decided to authorize and regulate the *repartimientos*, partly in an attempt to remove their worst features, but with the chief aims of reducing the constant distraction caused to the viceroys and of exploiting a useful potential source of crown revenue.[5] A *cédula* of 15 June 1751 ordered the formation of a special *junta* in each viceregal capital to prepare lists of the quantity, quality and prices of the goods which each *corregidor* was to be allowed to distribute to the Indians of his province. The *aranceles* for Peru were approved in 1756, when it was ordered that copies should be posted at the doors of the *ayuntamientos* and outside the houses of the *corregidores*. A *corregidor* who exceeded the limits laid down was to be fined and removed from office.

The value of the *aranceles* for the whole of Peru amounted to 5,429,000 pesos. The *corregidor* of Ica, for example, was allowed a *repartimiento* to the value of 100,000 pesos during his five-year

[1] Juan and Ulloa, op. cit., 200.
[2] B.M., Add. MS 20986, f. 143, edict of Túpac Amaru for the province of Carabaya, 15 Nov. 1780.
[3] Juan and Ulloa, op. cit., 196. See also C. D. Valcárcel, 'Perú borbónico y emancipación', *Revista de Historia de América*, 50 (Dec. 1960), 335–9.
[4] Amat, *Memoria*, ii, 186.
[5] Ibid., ii, 186–9.

term of office; for Cañete the figure was 124,000; for Huanta 112,000.[1] Each *corregidor* paid an *alcabala* duty of four per cent on the total of the *arancel* for his province. The value of this tax for the viceroyalty amounted to the considerable sum of 217,160 pesos, and it seems that this might have been the chief factor inducing Superunda, who had the reputation of being an efficient administrator of financial affairs, to attempt to reform the structure.[2] On this point Amat commented: 'the tariffs formed serve only for the charge of *alcabalas*, but in no way for the control of the *corregidores*' conduct, for each distributes what he wants, and at prices determined by his uncontrolled authority and desires'.[3] The old problem of the lack of an adequate administrative machinery to enforce the law persisted.

Amat wished to abolish completely the *repartimiento* system, and to provide the *corregidores* with larger salaries, the cost of which would be met by general economy and by an increase in the rate of tribute. He rejected the commonly-held view that, without the *repartimientos*, the Indians would decline into laziness and idleness, pointing out that in Lima the Indians who exercised the mechanical arts, or who were employed on estates around the city, worked well, 'for no other reason except that in this city they see the fruit of their work'.[4] Indians who fled from their villages or from estates did so not to avoid work, but to escape from ill-treatment, 'and this is what those who are thus unable to persecute them call laziness and indolence...'.

During the years between the Santos rebellion and the great Indian rising led by Túpac Amaru in 1780, there were frequent local disturbances originating in Indian discontent with their *corregidores*. Amat described the desperate and unorganized rioting against the *corregidor* of Sicasica (1770–1), when the *teniente* was murdered, and he reported on the murder of the *corregidor* of Pacajes in 1771 and the riots at Huamachuco in 1773 and 1774.[5] His successor, Manuel de Guirior, described

[1] B.M., Eg. MS 1810, ff. 78–155, gives a description of each *corregimiento*, including details of the salary, the *arancel* and the *alcabala* to be paid.
[2] Vargas, *Historia del Perú. Virreinato (Siglo XVIII) 1700–1790*, 236–7.
[3] Amat, *Memoria*, 189.
[4] Ibid., 194–5.
[5] Ibid., 292–304.

similar outbreaks at Chumbivilcas and Urubamba in 1776, and at Huamalíes in 1777.[1]

In its unreformed state local government not only harassed the Indians with the *repartimientos*; it also failed to protect them from abuses committed by white property-owners. It is clear that the excessive labour demands of the owners of *obrajes* (textile workshops to which the Indians were sent to work), of the miners and *hacendados*, and even the misdeeds of the local clergy, were tolerated by the *corregidores*, 'who, preoccupied with their own trade and business, not only fail to check the violence and corruption which they discover, afraid themselves of being accused of greater crimes, but in order to protect their own interests, quietly ignore and tolerate all abuses'.[2]

A practice which provided considerable scope for abuse was the *mita*, or forced labour recruitment of the Indians. The most notorious example was the *mita* of Potosí to which seventeen provinces were subject.[3] In provinces which contained few or no mines the Indians were sent to work on *haciendas*, or in *obrajes*, *cocales* and *cañaverales* (plantations). In all of these cases regulations carefully prescribed the number of Indians to be sent, the length of service, the maximum distance to be travelled, the wage rates, and other details. However, these laws were often ignored because, as Amat pointed out,

> the guardians of the laws and ordinances provided for the benefit of the Indians are the *corregidores*. . . . They are the very men who sell them to the *obrajes*, who send them to work in the mines, *cocales* and *cañaverales*, thus making the profits which are the sole aims of their operations.[4]

Legally, the Indians recruited for the *mita* were to return to their homes after the completion of their period of work, but it was common for them to accept goods in advance of their wages, thus gradually falling into a state of hereditary debt-peonage. Similarly, it was a practice for *corregidores* to send

---

[1] See J. H. Rowe, *The Incas under Spanish colonial institutions*, H.A.H.R., xxxvii (1957), 168.
[2] Amat, *Memoria*, 194.
[3] See *Mercurio Peruano* (Lima), 212, 13 Jan. 1793, for a critical account of the *mita* by Baquíjano.
[4] 'Prólogo de la Memoria del virrey Amat', loc. cit., 50.

Indians, who had not paid their tribute, to local *obrajes*. Half of their wages would go to the *corregidor* to meet the arrears; the remaining half would be insufficient for subsistence. Thus, food and clothing would have to be accepted on credit, and these Indians, too, would become tied to the *obrajes*.[1]

One point at which the social interests of the Indians coincided with the financial interests of the crown was in the collection of tribute. The laws governing liability to, and collection of, this tax were, in themselves, not excessive. It had been established in 1579 that Indians between the ages of eighteen and fifty-five should pay; from 1618 women were exempt, as were chiefs, and the blind, crippled and insane.[2] Once again, however, these qualifications were ignored by *corregidores*, who, with the connivance of *caciques* who were encharged with collection within the villages, prepared and applied double tribute lists.[3] One, for their own use, included many Indians who were supposedly exempt, while the second, for presentation to the treasury officials, listed far fewer Indians. Thus, the Indians suffered and the treasury suffered, since the tribute of able-bodied Indians went to the *corregidor*'s own pocket.

Reform of this corrupt system of local government was clearly one of the major tasks facing the visitor to Peru, Areche. Part of his instructions, issued by Gálvez in 1776, looked forward to the introduction of a system of administration by intendants, ordering Areche to carry out the preliminary studies and to suggest how the scheme might be implemented.[4] Until this could be achieved, however, it was necessary to purge the existing system of administration. Areche was to undertake a close investigation of the *repartimiento* system and take immediate steps to reform the collection of tribute, eradicating fraud and making *revisitas* to the provinces for the purpose of preparing more accurate tribute lists.[5] The aims of the *visita* went beyond correcting the abuses suffered by the Indians. Social problems formed only one aspect of the general

[1] Juan and Ulloa, op. cit., 216.
[2] See J. M. Ots de Capedqui, *Manual de historia del derecho español en las Indias* (Buenos Aires, 1945), 245–6.
[3] Juan and Ulloa, op. cit., 184–5.
[4] Palacio, op. cit., 12. Instructions issued 20 June 1776.
[5] Ibid., 10.

decadence of the viceroyalty. Equally important, in the view of the crown, was the need to purify the administration of justice and the general structure of government in Lima, to rationalize the tax structure and improve its yield, and to take radical measures to stimulate mining and encourage agriculture.[1] In short, the *visita* was intended to play a key part in the Bourbon programme of imperial reform, reflecting its chief aims of overhauling administration and increasing revenue.

The story of what has been accurately described as 'el fracaso de una visita' is well known.[2] Although in the long term these basic aims were fulfilled, the *visita* was hopelessly ineffective while Areche controlled it. One of his basic problems was an inability to work with viceroy Guirior. At first they clashed over relatively minor matters, such as the viceroy's obstruction of Areche's creation of a *Colegio de Abogados*.[3] Matters took a more serious turn when Guirior resisted the increase of the *alcabala* on Peruvian goods from four to six per cent, a measure bitterly opposed by the circle of influential *hacendados* around the viceroy.[4] In Areche's view, the viceroy's sole aim was: 'to be loved by these Americans because they believe in him and worship him as the protector of their ... liberties and privileges'.[5] By 1779 Areche began to demand repeatedly that either Guirior be removed or the *visita* be brought to an end.[6] Clearly, personal animosities were serious, but the real problem was a basic disagreement about the fundamental nature and function of viceregal authority in Peru. Areche recognized this, going beyond personal criticism of Guirior to attack the viceregal institution in general. He declared 'my judgement will always be that it is never suitable to have such a powerful authority in provinces as distant from Spain as these'.[7]

Early in 1780 disturbances broke out in Arequipa, Cuzco and a number of smaller towns, directed partly against the innovations of the *visita*.[8] In Arequipa in particular there was a direct relationship between the discontent and the decision to

[1] Ibid., 14.
[2] The best general study of the *visita* is Palacio's. For further details of financial aspects see below, 100–7.
[3] Palacio, op. cit., 25. [4] Ibid., 27–8.
[5] Ibid., 32, Areche to Gálvez, 20 Jan. 1779. [6] Ibid., 35.
[7] Ibid., 32. [8] Ibid., 39–43.

THE DECADENT VICEROYALTY 19

transfer the collection of the *alcabala* from the inefficient control of local treasury ministers to a newly-created *aduana*, or customs house. Moreover the tax was collected at the new rate of six per cent, and resentment was caused by the administrator's decision to levy it on grain and foodstuffs.[1] A further source of unrest, which helps account for the popular support for the disturbances, was the belief that *mestizos* and other castes were to pay tribute when the new lists were completed.[2] The proximity of these protests to the general Indian rising which broke out later in the year has led some historians to conclude that the two movements were connected.[3] In fact, as Areche reported to Gálvez, the Indians had neither desire nor reason to be involved in the troubles of the first half of 1780.[4] Those opposed to the payment and efficient collection of taxes were 'only these described here as of the class of the nobility', namely landowners and merchants, supported by the viceroy, whose material interests would suffer from an improved collection of the *alcabala*.

In fact, before news of these events reached Spain, the crown had already decided, as a result of Areche's earlier demands, to relieve Guirior, replacing him with Agustín de Jáuregui.[5] The new accusations were readily believed. In 1783, when instructing the newly-nominated viceroy, Teodoro de Croix, of recent events in Peru, Gálvez informed him that the riots had been encouraged by Guirior's weak government.[6] His immoderate support for the interests of the rich *hacendados* had caused a general crisis of authority for Areche. When Guirior further attempted to have Areche recalled to Spain, 'His Majesty decided to remove D. Manuel Guirior from the viceroyalty to prevent him continuing his aid and immoderate support for the conflagration caused by his defamations against the measures of this Ministry. . .'.

Areche also believed that there was a connexion between

[1] See F. A. Loayza, *Preliminares del incendio. Documentos del año de 1776 a 1780. . .* (Lima, 1947), 62, report of *corregidor*, Sematnat, to viceroy, 11 Jan. 1780.
[2] Lewin, op. cit., 156–7.
[3] See, for example, Loayza, op. cit., 42.
[4] Ibid., 128, Areche to Gálvez, 12 May 1780.
[5] A.H.M., Libro de Cabildo 30, f. 232, Jáuregui to *cabildo* of Lima, 17 Aug. 1780.
[6] A.G.I., Aud. de Lima 640, Gálvez to Croix, 28 March 1783.

the riots of 1780 and his efforts to impose stricter controls over the *repartimientos*.[1] He had insisted that, before taking merchandise into his province, a *corregidor* must receive a licence from the *aduana* and that, where possible, local receptories should be established to check these permits. The motives for the decision were twofold: to provide some protection for the Indians by ensuring that the legal limits were not exceeded, and to avoid evasion of the *alcabala*. Both these aims were contrary to the *corregidores'* personal interests, and Areche's conclusion was: 'the *corregidores* . . . secretly have made and are making war upon the *aduanas* and the receptories. . .'.[2] Other aspects of administration by the *corregidores* displeased Areche, notably the inefficiency and fraud associated with tribute collection. By 1780 *revisitas* were completed for the provinces of Ica, Cajamarca and Huamachuco.[3] The new lists revealed an increase in the number of contributors from 11,753 to 15,854, and an increase in the value of tribute from 59,231 pesos to 81,693 pesos. He had found the system of collection in great confusion, with several different classes of contributors and, according to the old lists, too many Indians exempt as nobles —'made noble by the will of those who count them'.[4]

Areche was convinced that it was the dependence of the *corregidores* upon *repartimientos* which was the root of their maladministration. Following receipt in Spain in 1776 of warnings from the bishop of Arequipa of the dangers of the existing system, both the visitor and the viceroy were ordered in January 1777 to review the situation.[5] Similar orders were sent to the bishops, asking for information on the defects of local administration and suggestions for alternative methods of financing local government.[6] Guirior recognized that defects existed, and that the frequent local disturbances in the viceroyalty were caused by the failure of the *corregidores* to observe the *aranceles* and by other irregularities.[7] His general attitude,

---

[1] Palacio, op. cit., 45, Areche to Gálvez, 12 April 1780.
[2] Ibid. [3] Ibid., 25.
[4] Vargas, *Historia del Perú. Virreinato (Siglo XVIII) 1700–1790*, 380.
[5] A.G.I., Indif. General 1713, *informe* of bishop of Arequipa, 10 April 1776; royal order, 12 Jan. 1777.
[6] B.N.P., MSS c4014 and c4129, for reports of *curas* in diocese of Arequipa, 1778.
[7] A.G.I., Indif. General 1713, Guirior to Gálvez, no. 196, 20 Aug. 1777.

however, was one of complacency, and he claimed in October 1778 that most of the abuses reported by the bishop of Arequipa no longer existed.[1] In any case, he believed that the presence in Arequipa of a *protector*, to whom the Indians could complain, provided them with sufficient protection.

Areche was less complacent than Guirior.[2] His opinion was that the *repartimientos* should be abolished, and the *corregidores* be provided with increased salaries, ranging from 3000 to 5000 pesos a year.[3] In the meantime, from the end of December 1779, he continued to pay salaries, at the old rates, to only ten of the *corregidores*—those for the provinces of Lima (*cercado*), Huánuco, Trujillo, Chachapoyas, Santa, Angaraes, Huamanga, Cailloma, Tarapacá and Cuzco (*cercado*), where profits from the *repartimientos* were small, or even non-existent.[4] Areche saw the need to abolish the system as a key part of his general reform programme. He argued that only with the abolition of the *repartimientos* would free trade be introduced to the provinces, and only then would the *corregidores* withdraw their opposition to his financial reforms. As long as they had an interest in commerce, they would resist his efforts to create provincial *aduanas* and to collect the *alcabala* and other taxes more efficiently.[5]

The *repartimientos* were abolished in December 1780, by a proclamation of viceroy Jáuregui, on the grounds of 'the injuries and wrongs which they caused the Indians, whose complaints flooded the tribunals'.[6] The measure was a response to the Túpac Amaru rising, which had broken out in the previous month; but it came too late to prevent the general Indian rebellion which had long appeared inevitable to many observers. Everywhere the *corregidores* were the principal targets of attack, and the rebellion began with the capture and execution of Antonio Arriaga, the *corregidor* of Tinta.[7] It was alleged that Arriaga had distributed goods worth more than 300,000

---

[1] A.G.I., Indif. General 1713, Guirior to Gálvez, no. 207, 20 Oct. 1777.
[2] Palacio, op. cit., 44–5.
[3] A.G.I., Indif. General 1713, Areche to Gálvez, no. 195, 20 Aug. 1780.
[4] Ibid., enclosure with letter no. 195.
[5] Ibid.
[6] A.H.M.H., Colección Santamaría, MS 00126, Jáuregui to *cabildo ecclesiástico* of Huamanga, 20 Dec. 1780, enclosing proclamation of 18 Dec.
[7] B.M., Add MS 20986, f. 159, for list of *corregidores* attacked and killed by rebels.

pesos, although the *arancel* for the *repartimiento* of the province was fixed at 112,000 pesos.[1] Similar excesses had been committed in other provinces, and José Gabriel Túpac Amaru explained that, as the most distinguished Indian of Inca blood, he felt compelled to lead a rising, because of 'the repeated complaints which the inhabitants of this province have incessantly made to me of the wrongs inflicted on them by various persons, such as the *corregidores* and Europeans. Although complaints were made to the various tribunals no remedy was found to stop them.'[2]

While beseiging Cuzco, in January 1781, the Indian leader informed the city's *cabildo* of his reasons for rising and of his aims. He explained:

My desire is that this class of officials should be completely removed; that their *repartimientos* should end . . . that in this city there should be founded a royal *audiencia* . . . so that the Indians will have the recourses of justice nearer to them. This is for now the whole object of my undertaking . . . leaving direct dominion to the king of Spain . . . and maintaining the obedience due to him. . . .[3]

Túpac Amaru repeatedly proclaimed that he was not rebelling against the monarch, but acting in his name to keep the Indians loyal to the crown, despite their ill-treatment by immoral judges, who perverted a benevolent king's wise laws and good intentions. This idea was emphasized especially when he tried to secure the support of influential creoles for a combined effort to improve administration. For example, his edict for the province of Chichas, issued on 23 December 1780, assured creoles that he had no intention of harming them, nor did he plan any attack on 'our sacred catholic religion'.[4] He planned to take only those measures which would secure 'the aid, protection and conservation of the Spanish creoles, *mestizos*, *zambos* and Indians, because all are our countrymen and compatriots, they are born in our lands, are of the same origin as the natives, and all have suffered equally from oppressions and tyrannies of the Europeans'.

---

[1] Lewin, op. cit., 475.   [2] B.M., Add MS 20986, f. 143.
[3] Lewin, op. cit., 465, Túpac Amaru to *ayuntamiento* of Cuzco, 3 Jan. 1781.
[4] Ibid., 402.

His complaints against the Spaniards included proposals which were more likely to be attractive to creoles than to Indians. A letter sent to the inhabitants of Arequipa in December 1780 demanded the 'total abolition of the *aduanas*' and of all other innovations made by the *visita*.[1] Despite these inducements, the creoles failed to support Túpac Amaru, and as the rebellion progressed they actively opposed him. The social dangers of encouraging a rising of the Indian masses were obvious. At a purely economic level, their interests would not be served by the withdrawal of cheap Indian labour from the mines and *haciendas*. The decree of Túpac Amaru of 16 November 1780, freeing the negro slaves of Tungasuca, alienated the creole sugar planters.[2] Moreover, most of the *obrajes* which the rebels destroyed were creole-owned, and influential creole merchants had a direct interest in the restoration of some type of *repartimiento* system.

Despite creole hostility towards the movement and despite Túpac Amaru's limited aims, some historians have been tempted to see the rebellion as an attempt to achieve independence, or to re-create the Inca empire.[3] Had creole support been forthcoming, it might have developed into a separatist movement. However, seen in the light of conditions in 1780, it makes more sense as a story of fruitless attempts to secure the legal redress of grievances, followed by a sudden, unplanned, violent outburst.[4] Its aims were the creation of an *audiencia* in Cuzco, the removal of the *corregidores*, and an end to the *repartimiento* system. Túpac Amaru sought, too, an improvement in working conditions in the mines and *obrajes*, and, more specifically, the end of the obligation of the Indians in his home province of Tinta to provide men for the *mita* of Potosí. These were social aims in response to harsh conditions.

The reaction of the Spanish authorities was mixed. On the

[1] Ibid., 422, 461.
[2] See E. Choy, 'Sobre la revolución de Túpac Amaru', *Revista del Museo Nacional* (Lima), xxiii (1954), 264.
[3] See J. J. del Pino, 'Significado de la revolución de Túpac Amaru frente al estudio de la causa de la independencia', *La causa de la emancipación del Perú* (Lima, 1960), 28.
[4] See D. Valcárcel, 'Túpac Amaru, fidelista y precursor', *Revista de Indias*, xvii, 68 (1957), 242.

one hand it was fully recognized that the rebellion was caused by oppressive social conditions which resulted from an unsatisfactory system of provincial administration. Gabriel de Avilés, the commander of the army which quelled the rebellion, complained strongly to Gálvez, while still engaged with the pacification of the interior provinces, about the evils and weaknesses of the existing administration by *corregidores*.[1] Because of Avilés's official position his testimony must be considered to have been well-informed and certainly not biased towards the Indians. Although he rejected the view that all the *corregidores* were evil, Avilés was convinced that the existing system of administration was bad, since it provided far too much scope for abuse. His two years of command in the interior provinces had confirmed his view, formed after twelve years residence in the viceroyalty, that 'the majority of the *corregidores*, blinded by greed and carried away by the incentive of usurious profits, believe it just to enforce a tyrannical slavery of the Indians'.[2] He recognized that in theory there were sound economic arguments to support the *repartimiento* system, but insisted that in practice the *corregidores* distributed useless goods at excessive prices. These views on the social problems of the Indians were remarkably similar to those put forward by Túpac Amaru in his various edicts and proclamations. Avilés's advice and opinions were readily accepted by Gálvez, not only as an explanation of the meaning of the rebellion, but as guidelines for future policy. When reviewing recent events in Peru in 1783, for the benefit of Croix, Gálvez informed him: 'In Peru attention was paid only to the extortion from the poor Indian of all possible temporal gain, without the provision of religion, manners, civility, understanding, or obedience to and love of the king. Around them they saw only tyrants, *corregidores* and similar *curas*. . .'.[3]

Thus the grievances of the Indians were recognized and appreciated. The rebellion had succeeded in bringing them to the direct attention of the Minister of the Indies, and it was clear that means would be sought to meet Túpac Amaru's

[1] A.G.I., Aud. de Lima 618, Avilés to Gálvez, 30 Sept. 1782.
[2] Ibid.
[3] A.G.I., Aud. de Lima 640, Gálvez to Croix, 28 March 1783.

demands. However, for political reasons, it was decided that the rebellion should be decisively crushed by military force. In this respect the policy of viceroy Jáuregui was strongly criticized as too mild and conciliatory.[1] Jáuregui's period of office had proved extremely difficult. He had hardly had time to settle into his position when the rebellion had broken out, and his task had been made no easier by Areche's lack of effort to work amicably with him. Early in 1781 a number of disputes broke out between them over relatively minor matters, causing undesirable division at a time of crisis.[2] Since the beginning of the *visita* the weight of the central government had been thrown behind Areche, but this attitude began to change in the middle of 1781. Areche had been in Peru for four years, but was still complaining about the gloomy prospects of fulfilling the *visita*'s aims, and about the people with whom he had to work.[3] In the hope that a change of personnel might revive the whole operation, it was ordered in September 1781 that Areche should return to Spain, and that the *visita* be taken over by Jorge Escobedo, who had very successfully fulfilled his commission of subdelegate of the *visita* in Potosí.[4]

The removal of Areche did not, however, imply increasing confidence in Jáuregui. In January 1783 Avilés insisted that all the efforts to quell the rising would be wasted, unless the administration of the viceroyalty were immediately improved and firm steps were taken to remove from Peru the surviving leaders of the rising.[5] In his view there could be no security in the interior as long as Diego Túpac Amaru (the brother of José Gabriel, the leader) and his nephews, Mariano (the son of José Gabriel) and Andrés, were allowed to remain, since they would provide stimuli for future disturbances. Avilés admitted that the amnesty declared by Jáuregui had helped calm the viceroyalty, but doubted the wisdom of allowing Diego to return to Tungasuca, where he enjoyed a large personal following. Avilés had wanted their arrest and expulsion, but failed to obtain the support of Jáuregui for this policy. The viceroy not

---

[1] A.G.I., Aud. de Lima 618, Avilés to Gálvez, 28 Jan. 1783.
[2] Palacio, op. cit., 50–1.
[3] Ibid., 54.   [4] Ibid., 55.
[5] A.G.I., Aud. de Lima 618, Avilés to Gálvez, 28 Jan. 1783.

only set Diego and his nephews free but also provided them with pensions.[1]

Gálvez replied that he and the king were fully aware of the weaknesses of Jáuregui's policy, and had supported his declaration of amnesty only out of necessity and to avoid breaking an undertaking given in the king's name.[2] He seems, in fact, to have relied heavily upon the advice of Avilés for the formulation of his policy. He informed Croix in March 1783 that Jáuregui was to be removed for his 'ineptitude'.[3] Gálvez repeated the criticism made by Avilés that the viceroy's policy towards the rising had been too moderate, adding that Jáuregui, like Guirior before him, had allowed himself to be over-influenced by the opinions of influential creoles in Lima.

Avilés was particularly concerned in 1783 about the dangers of a fresh rising since, in the extremely difficult economic conditions which followed the rebellion, some *corregidores* were beginning to undertake fresh *repartimientos*.[4] Against his wishes a number of *corregidores*, forced to flee in 1780, were being allowed to return to their provinces. Two in particular, Pedro Zenteno of Calca and Josef Ignacio Campino of Chumbivilcas, had begun to distribute goods. Similarly, in the province of Quispicanches, Josef Alvarado, former *habilitador* (supplier) of the dead *corregidor*, Fernando Cabrera, was attempting to collect money owing for goods distributed before the rising. Such activities were extremely dangerous, since the Indians were even less able than usual to bear this burden. As a result of the war many villages were devastated, fields were uncultivated, herds and flocks had been destroyed, and many Indians were starving. Avilés pointed out that the culprits were not only the *corregidores*. Behind them, encouraging their activities, were the *habilitadores*, merchants resident in Lima and other urban centres, who either supplied the goods to be distributed, or the capital for their purchase. They were now putting pressure on the *corregidores*, insisting that they collect money for goods issued on credit before the rebellion began. Avilés felt

---

[1] A.G.I., Aud. de Lima 640, Gálvez to Croix, 28 March 1783.
[2] A.G.I., Aud. de Lima 640, Gálvez to Avilés, 22 Sept, 1783.
[3] A.G.I., Aud. de Lima 640, Gálvez to Croix, 28 March 1783. For more details of suppression of rising, see below, 29–30.
[4] A.G.I., Aud. de Lima 618, Avilés to Gálvez, 28 Jan. 1783.

that their selfish demands would lead to a fresh rising, particularly since one of the conditions on which the Indians had laid down their arms was that the *repartimientos* should not be renewed. He recommended that this promise should be kept, and that no exceptions should be made even for essential items, such as iron and mules, since he was convinced that these and other commodities could be supplied in sufficient quantities by normal trade.[1]

Avilés believed, too, that the security of Peru would be improved by the implementation of another of Túpac Amaru's demands, the creation of an *audiencia* in Cuzco.[2] Such a tribunal, with jurisdiction over the bishoprics of Cuzco, Huamanga and Arequipa, would, he believed, provide quicker, more accessible justice for the viceroyalty's interior provinces. Its ministers would be in a better position to supervise the activities of the *corregidores*, and their very presence in the interior would act as an effective deterrent against maladministration.

Not only did Gálvez accept this recommendation. He went further, informing Avilés in September 1783 that royal policy to improve administration aimed to get to the very root of the viceroyalty's problems, 'by means of the effective and unique measure of abolishing the *corregimientos*, and appointing to the provinces selected magistrates with adequate salaries'.[3] The letter was accompanied by a copy of the Ordinance of Intendants for Buenos Aires, to illustrate to Avilés the lines which reform would now follow, and he was informed, confidentially, that immediate steps were to be taken to extend the intendant system to Peru. The aim of the decision was that Peru should 'be delivered in one stroke from her former anarchy, confusion and disorder'. Avilés was promoted to the rank of brigadier and made commander-general of the province of Cuzco, as a reward for his services and as a sign of confidence in him.[4] It

[1] Ibid. A marginal note says this information 'deve tenerse pres'te q'do se trata de aprobar el proyecto del visitador Escovedo s're que subsista el repartimiento de mulas y de otros efectos q'e llama de prim'a necesidad a cargo del consulado de Lima...'. See below, 89–91.
[2] A.G.I., Aud. de Lima 618, Avilés to Gálvez, 30 Sept. 1782.
[3] A.G.I., Aud. de Lima 640, Galvez to Avilés, 22 Sept. 1783.
[4] Ibid.

was hoped, too, that his presence in the city would assist the task of restoring it to its former splendour. A key part of this effort would be the king's decision to follow Avilés's advice and create an *audiencia* there.

Thus, the decision to abolish the *repartimientos*, the introduction of the intendant system in 1784 and the creation of the *audiencia* of Cuzco in 1787 were all part of an official programme to reform administration in Peru. The creation of the viceroyalty of the Río de la Plata and the commercial reforms of 1778 emphasized the need to stimulate the Peruvian economy; the general programme of imperial reform made it essential to increase the yield of crown revenues in the viceroyalty; the difficulties encountered in Lima by Areche underlined the need for a radical reorganization of authority and administration in the viceregal capital; the rebellion of Túpac Amaru focused attention upon the social consequences of the unreformed structure of administration, and the threat of a second rising emphasized that remedies were urgently required. The decision to tackle all of these problems together, by the introduction of the intendant system, was, as Gálvez wrote, not a mere tinkering with the situation, but an attempt to get to the very heart of the problems of the decadent viceroyalty.

CHAPTER II

Administrative Reorganization

THE ESTABLISHMENT of the intendant system in the viceroyalty of Peru was, in the view of Areche's successor, Jorge de Escobedo, the 'final perfection' of the *visita*, the key to the general programme of financial and administrative reform which he directed, first as *visitador* and then as superintendent, between 1782 and 1787.[1] His first task on succeeding Areche was simply to restore order, and to tackle the viceroyalty's critical economic and financial situation. As a result of the Túpac Amaru rising commerce, agriculture and mining were at a standstill in many areas, and the exchequer receipts were consequently falling, at a time when the expenses of government were abnormally high.[2] It was imperative to restore order, since without it constructive work was impossible. Escobedo's attitude to the Indian rebellion was similar to that of Avilés. Understanding that their discontent stemmed from corruption and maladministration, he sympathized with their demands for reform, but, as a royal servant, he saw his first task as the need to end the rebellion, by taking decisive action against its surviving leaders. Despite the amnesty which Jáuregui had granted to Túpac Amaru's family, Escobedo anticipated the contents of the royal order of 5 April 1782 and had Diego Túpac Amaru and other members of the family arrested. Some were executed in Cuzco by Benito de la Mata Linares, the future intendant of the province; others were sent to Spain, to life imprisonment.[3] It was only after their removal from the

[1] A.G.I., Aud. de Lima 1102, Escobedo to Gálvez, no. 561, 20 Oct. 1785. A published copy of this general account of the visita is in S. Lorente (ed.), *Relaciones de los virreyes y audiencias que han gobernado el Perú* (3 vols, Lima and Madrid, 1867–72), iii, 369–444.   [2] Ibid.
[3] See Inca Juan Bautista Túpac Amaru, *Las memorias de Túpac Amaru* (Lima, 1964).

scene that Escobedo was able to turn his attention to the more constructive aims of the *visita*.

Areche had been a firm supporter of the general aim of introducing the intendant system to Peru.[1] He was particularly attracted by the prospect of reforming the exchequer structure by replacing the existing *cajas reales* with provincial subtreasuries, over which the intendants would exercise supervision. He was aware, however, that radical administrative reorganization of this type must be preceded by a careful examination of regional conditions in Peru, and, in accordance with his instructions, he confined himself to suggesting the lines along which future changes might be made. He proposed in 1778 that, as a first stage, three intendancies be established, with their capitals in Lima, Trujillo and Tarma or Jauja.[2] If the experiment proved a success, he envisaged a second stage, with two further intendancies centred in Arequipa, in Lower Peru, and Oruro in Upper Peru. A third, and final, stage would see four more intendancies for Upper Peru, with their capitals in La Paz, Chucuito, Potosí and Charcas.

In fact, the establishment of intendancies in Upper Peru, which Areche had envisaged as the final stage in the process, preceded by two years the introduction of the new system in Lower Peru. The creation of the viceroyalty of the Río de la Plata, in which Upper Peru was included, was rapidly followed by the introduction of the intendant system there in 1782.[3] In July 1782 Gálvez sent Escobedo a copy of the new Ordinance for Buenos Aires, asking for his views on its suitability for application in Peru.[4] When he received the *visitador*'s suggestions in the second half of 1783, his correspondence with Avilés had already convinced him of the need for rapid implementation of the reform programme.[5]

Escobedo's response to Gálvez's original inquiry was enthusiastic, but cautious.[6] He emphasized that he believed the

[1] A.G.I., Aud. de Lima 606, Areche to Gálvez, 19 Feb. 1778.
[2] Ibid.   [3] Lynch, op. cit., 40–3.
[4] A.G.I., Aud. de Lima 1117, royal order, 29 July 1782. Escobedo's work is examined briefly in: C. Deustua Pimentel, *Las intendencias en el Perú (1790–1796)* (Sevilla, 1965), 5–8.
[5] See above, 31–6.
[6] A.G.I., Aud. de Lima 1117, Escobedo to Gálvez, 16 June 1783.

introduction of the intendant system to be not only desirable, but essential, if the viceroyalty was to be saved from complete ruin. He was careful, however, to consider the aims of the Ordinance in the light of actual conditions in Peru, and to suggest the problems and difficulties which its application might bring. The extent of the viceroyalty and the difficulties of communication would clearly pose serious problems, preventing intendants from making the required annual inspections of their provinces.[1] Escobedo feared, too, that the intendants might have difficulty in fully asserting their authority outside of the provincial capitals. In smaller, more remote towns and cities the removal of the *corregidores* might leave power in the hands of *cabildos*, causing irregular municipal activity, intrigue and faction. Partly because of this fear, and partly because of an anticipated difficulty in obtaining subdelegates and *alcaldes ordinarios*, he believed that it might be advisable to retain some *corregidores* to act as auxiliaries of the intendants in the interior towns.

Escobedo foresaw that the greatest problems caused by the proposed administrative reorganization would be not at a local level, but at the centre, in the viceregal capital, where there would be an inevitable clash of authority between the viceroy and the superintendent. The intendants would be subject to the general authority of the viceroy and the *audiencia*, but in financial and economic matters to the superintendent, who, as well as being intendant in his own province, was to exercise executive authority for these matters throughout the viceroyalty.[2] Escobedo emphasized that the superintendent would need to be an exceptional man if he were to tolerate the inevitable clashes of jurisdiction with the viceroy. He forecast, in fact, that, if the stability of the new system of administration was to be assured, at some time in the future the powers and duties of the superintendent would need to be transferred to the viceroy.[3] An additional problem in establishing the system

[1] Ibid. See, too, 'Real Ordenanza para el establecimiento e instrucción de intendentes de exército y provincia en el virreinato de Buenos Aires', 28 Jan. 1782 (hereafter referred to as *Ord. Ints.*), arts. 21–2. The Ordinance is published in *Documentos referentes a la guerra de la independencia y emancipación política de la República Argentina*, Archivo General de la Nación (3 vols, Buenos Aires, 1914–26), i, 31–95.

[2] *Ord. Ints.*, art. 6.   [3] See below, 60–1.

would be that of vice-patronage. Escobedo had not worked out the details of the boundaries of the future intendancies by 1783. Consequently he did not elaborate this point, but emphasized that the existing ecclesiastical divisions were unsuitable for the superimposition of intendancies.[1]

Some of Escobedo's doubts were resolved by the circular royal order of 5 August 1783. The first of its seventeen declarations, for example, insisted that no *corregimientos* should remain.[2] Thereafter, stimulated by the urgency felt in Spain for rapid reorganization, Escobedo made speedy progress. In February 1784 he reported that work was proceeding satisfactorily.[3] By then the intendancy of Cuzco had been established in all but name, with the delegation of authority to Mata, who had acquired considerable knowledge of the area since his arrival in the previous year to deal with the aftermath of the Túpac Amaru rising. Mata had already made considerable progress with the preparation of more accurate tribute lists for some *partidos*. While praising his work, Escobedo pointed out that it was unfortunate that it had not been possible to complete this process at an earlier stage of the *visita*. Since it had not been possible, one of the first duties of the new intendants would be to have the new lists prepared, and Escobedo feared that this might associate administrative reform, in the minds of the public, with 'the idea of oppression'.[4]

When viceroy Croix reached Lima in April 1784, with instructions to co-operate with Escobedo in the process of creating the intendancies, he found that the work of adapting the Ordinance to the needs of Peru was almost complete.[5] Early in July Escobedo gave him a detailed report and his final proposals for the division of the viceroyalty into intendancies.[6] The *visitador* believed that, as far as possible, the intendancies should conform to the boundaries of the bishoprics, in the hope

[1] The dioceses were: Lima (archdiocese), Huamanga, Cuzco, Trujillo and Arequipa.
[2] A.G.I., Aud. de Buenos Aires 354, Gálvez to viceroy and intendant of Buenos Aires, 5 Aug. 1783, 'declaración primera'.
[3] A.G.I., Aud. de Lima 1099, Escobedo to Gálvez, no. 218, 16 Feb. 1784.
[4] Ibid. See below, 111–13.
[5] A.G.I., Aud. de Lima 640, instruction of government to Croix, 19 June 1783, art. 57. See Croix, *Memoria de Gobierno*, 70–1, in Fuentes, op. cit., v, 1–393.
[6] A.G.I., Aud. de Lima 1117, Escobedo to Croix, 1 July 1784.

that complications in the exercise of vice-patronage could be avoided. The bishoprics of Trujillo and Arequipa covered extensive areas, but, since neither was large enough to be divided, each should form a separate intendancy.[1] Three *partidos* of the diocese of Cuzco had been transferred to the viceroyalty of the Río de la Plata. The remaining eleven were to form the intendancy of Cuzco. This, too, would be large but not, in Escobedo's view, unmanageable, since the city of Cuzco was conveniently located at the centre of the area. The diocese of Huamanga was the smallest in the viceroyalty, but Escobedo proposed to divide it into two intendancies, since he wanted one intendant to be able to give his undivided attention to the mercury mine of Huancavelica. Thus, the intendancy of Huancavelica was to consist of the *partidos* of Angaraes, which contained the mine, Tayacaja, which supplied the mine with wood, and Castrovirreina. The five remaining *partidos* of the diocese were to form the intendancy of Huamanga. In this way five intendancies were to be formed from the four provincial dioceses. The greatest problem was posed by the archdiocese of Lima. It was clearly too large for one intendancy, a point illustrated by the fact that the archbishop needed a year simply to tour it for the purpose of confirmations. Its proposed division into two intendancies, one with its capital in Lima, the other at Tarma, promised to bring difficulties, since the archbishop, accustomed to dealing with the viceroy in matters of vice-patronage, would almost certainly resent dealing with a mere intendant in Tarma. Yet Escobedo saw no other solution, and he emphasized to Croix that it was imperative to put the new system into operation, ignoring its obvious problems until a later date.

Croix agreed. A decree of 7 July approved Escobedo's scheme, in all its details, and ordered that immediate steps be taken to put it into practice.[2] As soon as the intendants reached their capitals the *corregidores* were to relinquish office, with the exception of those for Santa, Huarochirí, Arica and Cajamarca,

[1] Although part of the diocese of Arequipa, the island of Chiloé was excluded from the intendancy. Instead a separate intendancy was founded there as part of the programme for Chile—A.G.I., Aud. de Lima 1105, Escobedo to Gálvez, no. 605, 20 Jan. 1786.
[2] A.H.M.H., leg. 51, no. 90, decree of Croix, 7 July 1784.

who, having been recently appointed, were to remain as subdelegates.[1] The remainder deserved to be removed, in Escobedo's view; not only had they continued their *repartimientos*, but also they had intensified them in an attempt to make the maximum profit before administrative change was completed. Escobedo was aware, however, that it might be difficult to obtain subdelegates, and repeated to Gálvez his conviction of the need to provide them with adequate salaries.[2] In practice *corregidores* remained in office, in some areas, as temporary subdelegates.[3]

The first *junta superior de real hacienda*, a powerful committee with the duty of assisting the superintendent with the control of the viceroyalty's financial and economic affairs, met on 13 July 1784.[4] The selected intendants swore oaths of allegiance on the same day. They were unable, however, to leave immediately for their provinces, since Escobedo had only one copy of the Ordinance of Intendants. Until further copies arrived he could not give the new officials this vital set of instructions, which was to guide all their activities.[5] Since no separate ordinance was issued for Peru, the intendants there were governed by the Ordinance of Intendants for Buenos Aires. But Escobedo also prepared a special instruction for each of the six intendants under his jurisdiction: besides summarizing their duties in the four main branches of administration, these attempted to interpret the articles of the general Ordinance in the light of the particular needs of each province.[6] Each instruction contained descriptions of the resources of the various *partidos* of the respective intendancies. The intendant of Trujillo, for example, was given a detailed account of the mines of Hualgayoc and Callana, while the attention of the intendant

[1] A.G.I., Aud. de Lima 1117, Escobedo to Croix, 1 July 1784.
[2] A.G.I., Aud. de Lima 1117, Escobedo to Gálvez, no. 306, 16 July 1784.
[3] B.N.P., MS C3024, decree of intendant of Huancavelica, 24 Dec. 1784, ordering that *corregidores* in his province remain in office until subdelegates can be appointed.
[4] A.G.I., Aud. de Lima 1117, Escobedo to Gálvez, no. 306, 16 July 1784. For more detail on *junta superior* see below, 103.
[5] A.G.I., Aud. de Lima 1098, Escobedo to Gálvez, no. 322, 20 Aug. 1784.
[6] A.G.I., Aud. de Lima 1098, 'Instrucción práctica que para adaptar la nueva R'l Ordenanza se da por el Tribunal de Visita al Señor don ... que va a servir...' Copies of the individual instructions, dated 4 Oct. 1784, were enclosed with Escobedo to Gálvez, no. 368, 20 Nov. 1784.

of Tarma was drawn to the vast potential agricultural and vegetable resources of his province. The emphasis throughout was upon the need to stimulate exploitation of the viceroyalty's resources and to encourage agriculture, industry and commerce. Only in a few cases did an element of contradiction appear. The intendant of Cuzco, for example, was informed that the manufacture of cloth was an important source of trade in the *partido* of Paruro.[1] Since this provided, by way of taxation, revenue for the crown, manufacture was to continue, but not to be expanded, lest the market for textiles imported from Spain be damaged. Similarly the intendant of Arequipa was told that the basic industry of the *partido* of Moquegua was the production of wine and *aguardiente,* and these were the major items in the province's trade with Upper Peru.[2] Production had been banned in the past, to prevent competition with Spanish wines and because of the ruinous effects of alcoholism among the Indians. Despite this, production had continued, and provided a valuable source of revenue for the *alcabala.* The intendant was instructed, therefore, to maintain the industry at its existing level, but discreetly to discourage any attempts to expand it.

The intendant of Huancavelica received two sets of instructions, the first dealing with the whole range of his duties, the second more specifically with the mercury mine.[3] Escobedo provided him with all the relevant information he possessed on the past and present workings of the mine, emphasizing that the need to exercise a close supervision over it was the basic reason for the founding of an intendancy in Huancavelica. The intendant was warned that the town was notoriously difficult to govern, and was specifically informed that its inhabitants disliked the existing system of direct working of the mine by the crown. Escobedo believed that the alternative, private enterprise by individual miners, would lead to a fall in production, but left it to the intendant's discretion to adopt this system if he thought it necessary.

The preparation of these detailed instructions by Escobedo

[1] A.G.I., Aud. de Lima 1098, Instruction to Mata, art. 18.
[2] A.G.I., Aud. de Lima 1098, Instruction to Menéndez, art. 19.
[3] A.G.I., Aud. de Lima 1100, Escobedo to Gálvez, no. 368, 20 Nov. 1784.

illustrates the thoroughness of his approach to the introduction of the intendant system. He attempted to anticipate the problems which might arise, and then to issue orders or advice to forestall them. In 1783 he had warned Gálvez that he feared disputes between the intendants and the bishops, and between the intendants and the *cabildos*. These fears persisted in 1784. All the bishops had been sent copies of article six of the Ordinance, conferring vice-patronage on the intendants, so that on arrival in their provinces the new officials would be received with the appropriate ceremony.[1] Doubts, however, remained. The bishop of Cuzco had complained that he was uncertain how he should receive the intendant, and asked for more detailed guidance. The intendants, most of them still in Lima, made similar requests. The basic problem was that in the past the vice-patron had been the viceroy. It was difficult to determine, therefore, whether rights, such as that of kissing the missal after the gospel, had been enjoyed by the viceroy as vice-patron, or in his civil capacity. If the former, they would be transferred to the intendants. Questions of protocol of this kind were treated with great seriousness. Consequently, in an attempt to introduce the new system of administration as peacefully as possible, Escobedo had a further set of instructions prepared, for the benefit of bishops and intendants, describing in minute detail the ceremonies and rules to be observed.[2] Copies were distributed to all concerned on 15 November 1784. On the same date copies of a similar document, regulating the details of protocol to be observed between the intendants and the *cabildos*, were also distributed.[3] The intention was the same, to avoid the emergence of disputes which might mar the assumption of authority by the intendants.

The selection of the first intendants was a task shared between Escobedo and the crown, although all appointments

[1] A.G.I., Aud. de Lima 1098, Escobedo to Gálvez, no. 371, 15 Nov. 1784. Aud. de Lima 598, summary of Croix to Gálvez, 5 Dec. 1784.

[2] A.G.I., Aud. de Lima 1098, 'Ceremonial que en las Provincias de Obispado deberá practicarse en las Iglecias Cathedrales, Colegiatas o Parroquiales con los S'res Intendentes, Gov'res Vice Patronos', 23 Oct. 1784.

[3] A.G.I., Aud. de Lima 1098, 'Prevenciones de Ceremonias y Cortesía recíproca de los S'res Intendentes con los Cavildos Seculares a q. presiden, y de estos en el Recivimiento, concurrencias y asistencias con aquellos Magistrados', 23 Oct. 1784.

made were dependent upon ultimate royal approval. The intendancy of Lima was filled by Escobedo himself.[1] He was also appointed superintendent-subdelegate, with control over economic and financial affairs throughout the viceroyalty, and intendant of the army, with jurisdiction over the financial and administrative aspects of military matters. Escobedo believed that the post of superintendent alone was more than enough for him to handle, and had suggested in August 1784, that, while he remained in Lima in this office, exercising a general supervision over the intendants, a separate intendant of Lima should be appointed to deal with municipal affairs in the capital and with general administration in the rest of the province.[2] The response to this urgent request was a mere assurance that the king would appoint a separate intendant of Lima if and when he saw fit to do so.[3]

For two of the remaining six intendancies *títulos* were received from Spain in July 1784, confirming the selection of Mata for Cuzco, and appointing Fernando Márquez de la Plata to Huancavelica.[4] Both were well qualified—Mata was an *oidor* of the *audiencia* of Lima and Márquez *alcalde del crimen*—and Escobedo agreed fully with their appointment.[5] For the other four he made his own selection. José Menéndez Escalada, whose office of director-general of *alcabalas* had been abolished as part of the reform of financial administration, was appointed to Arequipa, despite the fact that his advanced age and delicate constitution raised doubts about his ability to manage such an extensive province. The intendant of Trujillo was to be Fernando Saavedra, who had come to Peru with Areche as *contador* of the *visita*, a post he had continued to hold under Escobedo. For Tarma Juan María Gálvez, the viceregal secretary, was selected. These five, like Escobedo, were *peninsulares*. The only creole selected was Nicolás Manrique de Lara, who was to go to Huamanga. The nomination of this leading member of Lima's creole society was a deliberate attempt to encourage creole support for the intendant system. Escobedo informed

[1] A.G.I., Aud. de Lima 646, royal order, 24 Jan. 1785.
[2] A.G.I., Aud. de Lima 1098, Escobedo to Gálvez, no. 322, 20 Aug. 1784.
[3] A.G.I., Aud. de Lima 1117, royal order, 21 May 1785.
[4] A.G.I., Aud. de Lima 1117, Escobedo to Gálvez, 16 July 1784.
[5] A.G.I., Aud. de Lima 1117, Escobedo to Croix, 1 July 1784.

Croix that his selection was 'based upon the political motives of which your excellency is aware', and confirmed that it was received with much joy in Lima.[1]

The crown, or rather the Minister of the Indies, was apparently less conscious of the need to appease creole opinion. In January 1785 royal approval was given to Escobedo's work in establishing the intendancies.[2] The appointments of Juan María Gálvez and of Saavedra were confirmed, but confirmation was withheld from Menéndez and Manrique. The intendant of Arequipa was to be Antonio Álvarez y Jiménez, a Spanish army officer who had previously been to America with the expedition of Cevallos. Menéndez, it was promised, would be appointed to one of the intendancies to be created in Chile. Manrique was to return to Lima, to the post of *contador mayor* of the tribunal of accounts, since in September 1784 the *título* to the intendancy of Huamanga had been granted to Juan de la Piedra, the superintendent of the Patagonian coast.[3] Piedra, in fact, died while on the way to Peru, and Manrique, who had taken up his post in Huamanga in November 1784, remained in command there for most of 1785. By the middle of 1785 Escobedo and Croix had received news of both the appointment and the death of Piedra, but, instead of awaiting further instructions from Spain, had decided to recall Manrique, as previously ordered, and to appoint Menéndez temporary intendant of Huamanga.[4] The same decision had been reached independently in Spain, the *título* appointing Menéndez to Huamanga having been issued in June.[5]

The urgency felt by Escobedo and Croix to recall Manrique is explained by their anxiety to bring to an end a serious clash of authority between the intendant and the bishop of Huamanga. Despite Escobedo's precautions, a number of intendants found themselves involved in disputes with the bishops. Patronage, the power to appoint to benefices and to supervise clerical discipline and general ecclesiastical administration, had been granted to the Spanish crown by the papacy during

[1] Ibid.
[2] A.N.P., Superior Gobierno 33, *cuaderno* 1071, Gálvez to Escobedo, 24 Jan. 1785.
[3] A.G.I., Aud. de Lima 630, *título*, 27 Sept. 1784.
[4] A.G.I., Aud. de Lima 1117, Croix to Gálvez, no. 256, 20 July 1785.
[5] A.G.I., Aud. de Lima 1117, Gálvez to Croix, *reservada*, 26 Oct. 1785.

the early years of colonization. Many of these powers were then delegated to the crown's representatives in America, the viceroys and presidents, and they remained in their hands for two hundred and fifty years. The transfer of vice-patronage to the intendants not only offended the viceroys, but disturbed the bishops, who considered it beneath their dignity to have to deal with these lower officials. Escobedo informed Gálvez in 1785 that even in provinces where the bishops had made no open attempts to challenge the intendants' authority in ecclesiastical affairs there was a possibility of future trouble.[1] As it was, disputes had already broken out in Huamanga and Arequipa and, 'a little less openly' in Cuzco and Trujillo.[2] Of these the most serious was that in the intendancy of Huamanga, where the conflict was complicated by the failure to confirm the nomination of Manrique as intendant.

The arrival in Huamanga in April 1783 of a new bishop, Francisco López Sánchez, had seen the beginning of a zealous campaign to improve the conduct and standards of the corrupt clergy. In many cases, however, the bishop acted hastily and clumsily, arousing the hostility of not only some clergy but also the *corregidor* and other officials.[3] When Manrique took up his post in November 1784 deep divisions and factions already existed. Huamanga, in fact, was so notoriously difficult to govern that, according to Escobedo, it was the least desirable of the intendancies.[4] He warned Manrique of the need for caution, informing him of the hostility towards the bishop of both the *corregidor* and the *cabildo secular*.[5]

The *cabildo*'s hostility stemmed from the bishop's interference in its elections for 1784. By means which are not clear he had succeeded in imposing his candidates as *alcaldes ordinarios*.[6] As a consequence they became, in the words of Croix, 'mere executors of his commands'. When Manrique arrived the bishop showed an immediate lack of courtesy, motivated, in Croix's

[1] A.G.I., Aud. de Lima 1103, Escobedo to Gálvez, no. 462, 20 April 1785.
[2] A.G.I., Aud. de Lima 1106, Escobedo to Sonora, no. 740, 5 Aug. 1786.
[3] A.G.I., Aud. de Lima 1103, Escobedo to Gálvez, 20 April 1785. This long *informe* is accompanied by nineteen enclosures.
[4] Ibid.
[5] A.G.I., Aud. de Lima 1098, Instruction to Manrique, art. 8.
[6] A.G.I., Aud. de Lima 599, Croix to Gálvez, no. 306, 16 Nov. 1785.

view, 'by the desire that nobody but himself should exercise superior authority'.[1] A specific case occurred when, on the bishop's orders, the two submissive *alcaldes*, accompanied by soldiers, broke down the door of the house of the administrator of tobaccos to arrest a priest who had taken refuge there in an attempt to evade trial before the ecclesiastical court.[2] Manrique did not question the bishop's jurisdiction over the priest, but did challenge his right to have him forcibly removed from a private house without the intendant's permission. A more serious clash of jurisdiction occurred when the Indians of the village of Pausa, in the *partido* of Parinacochas, having failed to convince the ecclesiastical court that their *cura* was charging excessive parochial dues, locked the church and refused to admit him.[3] Ignoring the intendant's jurisdiction, and without notifying him, the bishop attempted to bring the Indians before the ecclesiastical court. The intendant subsequently insisted that the case came within his jurisdiction and claimed that the bishop's investigation had been inadequate and disorderly.

Escobedo attributed responsibility for the growing discord to the bishop.[4] He was anxious to find a solution because he saw ominous similarities with the dispute which had occurred a few years earlier between bishop Moscoso of Cuzco and the *corregidor* Arriaga.[5] The whole issue was still under discussion in Lima when, in February 1785, it was complicated by the receipt of requests from the intendant and his *asesor*, José Muñoz, that they be allowed to resign.[6] Manrique complained that his position had been undermined by a rumour that he was to be replaced by Piedra. The little prestige he had enjoyed had disappeared, while the bishop's faction, led by Ignacio Leguanda, the *contador* of the provincial treasury, had been encouraged by the rumour, and had begun to threaten the security of the *asesor*, whose only crime had been to uphold the legal authority of his intendant. These requests put Escobedo in a difficult position, but he eventually decided that they should not be granted.[7] Piedra had still not reached Peru and, in any

[1] Ibid. [2] Ibid. [3] Ibid.
[4] A.G.I., Aud. de Lima 1103, Escobedo to Croix, 8 Feb. 1785.
[5] See Lewin, op. cit., 254–73.
[6] A.G.I., Aud. de Lima 1103, Manrique to Escobedo, 10 Feb. 1785.
[7] A.G.I., Aud. de Lima 1103, Escobedo to Croix, 2 March 1785.

case, Escobedo felt that Manrique should remain in Huamanga until he was aware of the reaction in Spain to his selection of intendants, since it was possible that, on hearing of Manrique's nomination, the king might confirm it, cancelling the appointment of Piedra. Moreover, to relieve Manrique would be to confirm the power of the church and of factious individuals in Huamanga over the authority of the representative of the king.

By the middle of 1785 Escobedo had received news both of the failure to confirm Manrique's appointment and of the death of Piedra. Moreover, the decision to appoint Álvarez to Arequipa meant that, as soon as he arrived, Menéndez would be free. Escobedo and Croix agreed, therefore, not only to recall Manrique and nominate Menéndez to replace him but also to remove other officials who had a close personal involvement in the disputes.[1] The *asesor* and the two chief ministers of the Huamanga treasury were the most prominent, after Manrique, to be removed.[2]

There remained, however, a further problem. Menéndez could not leave Arequipa until the arrival of Álvarez in November. Consequently Manrique remained in command in Huamanga during the second half of the year, and in that period his conflict with the bishop became even more bitter. In August the bishop issued a whole range of serious charges against the intendant's general conduct.[3] He alleged that, because of his family connexions with one of the *alcaldes* of Huamanga, Manrique was allowed to behave as he wished in his capital. He had encouraged his brother, who was suing in the ecclesiastical court for the annulment of his marriage, to write an abusive letter to the bishop. The most serious charge was that Manrique was implicated in a large *repartimiento* of mules in the *partidos* of Huanta and Cangallo by a merchant, Ramón Viton, acting under his protection. A few days after receiving these charges Croix received complementary accusations against the bishop from Manrique.[4] The intendant again asked to be relieved, announced that he had left Huamanga

[1] A.G.I., Aud. de Lima 1117, Croix to Gálvez, no. 256, 20 July 1785.
[2] A.G.I., Aud. de Lima 1109, Escobedo to Gálvez, no. 637, 5 March 1786.
[3] A.H.M.H., Casa de Moneda, MS 14-63, report of *fiscal*, 15 Sept. 1786.
[4] A.G.I., Aud. de Lima 599, Croix to Gálvez, no. 306, 16 Nov. 1785.

for the town of Huanta, and demanded that a special commissioner be appointed to examine the charges made by and against the bishop.

The commission to investigate affairs in Huamanga was given to the *alcalde del crimen*, the intendant of Huancavelica Márquez.[1] This choice displeased the bishop, since the intendancy of Huancavelica was part of his diocese, a fact which he suspected would lead Márquez to support his fellow intendant.[2] It also displeased Márquez, who attempted to evade the commission, arguing that not only was he fully occupied at Huancavelica, but that he was an intimate friend of Manrique.[3] Viceroy Croix, however, affirming his confidence in Márquez's objectivity, insisted that he undertake the investigation.[4] Márquez collected evidence during 1786 on all of the charges brought by the bishop, paying particular attention to the most serious, that concerning the *repartimiento*. His conclusion was that the bishop had not told the truth, possibly because he had been misinformed rather than because he deliberately sought to deceive, but, due to his steadfast refusal to reveal the names of his informants, he had to be held personally responsible.[5] The *real acuerdo* of the *audiencia* of Lima accepted Márquez's findings, declaring Manrique innocent of all charges.[6] It expressed its disapproval of the bishop's behaviour and in particular of his lack of co-operation and haughty attitude. This was to be reported to the Council of the Indies. If the bishop repeated his extraordinary conduct the viceroy and the *audiencia* would use their fullest powers to deal with him. The last word on the case was said by the Council of the Indies in 1793.[7] It commended Manrique for his 'prudence, zeal, tact and moderation', and expressed regret that since the offending bishop had died he could not be punished.

The death of the bishop in 1789 did not mark the end of ecclesiastical problems in Huamanga. Rather it brought

[1] A.G.I., Aud. de Lima 1103, Escobedo to Sonora, no. 854, 20 Feb. 1787.
[2] B.N.P., MS C4555, bishop of Huamanga to Croix, 5 Jan. 1786.
[3] B.N.P., MS C4555, Márquez to Croix, 22 Nov. 1785.
[4] B.N.P., MS C4555, decree of Croix, 6 Dec. 1785.
[5] A.H.M.H., Casa de Moneda, MS. 14–63, report of *fiscal*, 15 Sept, 1786.
[6] A.H.M.H., Casa de Moneda, MS 14–63, *auto* of *real acuerdo*, 2 May 1787.
[7] A.G.I., Aud. de Lima 599, report of Council, 11 March 1793.

problems of a different kind. These concerned the provision to vacant benefices, since, in the absence of episcopal supervision, the canons of the cathedral fought among themselves to have friends or relatives appointed and showed complete disrespect for Menéndez's authority.[1] The situation seems to have improved with the appointment in 1792 of a new bishop, Bartolomé Fabro Palacios.[2] At least there is no evidence of further serious clashes between episcopal and civil authorities there.

The struggle between Manrique and the bishop of Huamanga was the most serious clash of its kind to occur in Peru. It was not, however, unique; rather it reflected a general pattern, since in other provinces the arrival of intendants sparked off disputes over vice-patronage, which, as in Huamanga, decreased in both frequency and significance as time progressed. In Lima Escobedo experienced considerable difficulty with the archbishop, even though he had decided, in order to forestall opposition from both viceroy and archbishop, that the vice-patronage of the province of Lima should remain in the viceroy's hands.[3] Strained relations developed because Escobedo insisted that the vice-patronage in the intendancy of Tarma, part of the archdiocese of Lima, should be transferred from the viceroy to the intendant, since, without this authority, the intendant would be unlikely to command the respect and obedience of the province's clergy.[4] Gálvez confirmed Escobedo's decision but in 1790 the vice-patronage for the province was restored to the viceroy.[5]

Relations between intendant Álvarez of Arequipa and bishops Pamplona and Chaves were occasionally stormy. These disputes normally concerned matters of etiquette or problems which arose over the provision of clergy to vacant benefices; they were not serious affairs with political overtones.[6] The same could not be said of relations between the first intendant of Cuzco, Mata, and the city's episcopal authorities, whose

[1] B.N.P., MS c1288, Pedro de Tagle to Croix, no. 128, 6 Oct. 1790.
[2] B.N.P., MS c3558, *provisión* of *acuerdo* of *audiencia* of Lima, 24 Jan. 1792.
[3] A.G.I., Aud. de Lima 1097, Escobedo to Gálvez, no. 342, 20 Sept. 1784.
[4] A.G.I., Aud. de Lima 1103, Escobedo to Gálvez, no. 462, 20 April 1785.
[5] A.G.I., Aud. de Lima 695, Gil to Porlier, no. 23, 20 July 1790, acknowledging royal order of 5 Jan. 1790. See below, 67–8.
[6] Croix, *Memoria*, 86–8.

opposition was interpreted by the intendant as an integral part of a massive creole conspiracy against royal authority. Like other intendants Mata had grievances about matters of protocol. His complaints about details of the ceremonies conducted at his reception in the cathedral of Cuzco had been one factor influencing Escobedo's decision to issue an instruction for guidance on such matters.[1] However, the intendant's grievances against bishop Juan Manuel Moscoso y Peralta had a deeper origin. He was convinced that Moscoso had given sympathy and aid to the leaders of the Túpac Amaru rising, and that so long as he remained bishop of Cuzco he would continue to have a dangerous political influence.[2] He informed Gálvez: '... as long as *señor* Moscoso lives, or, at least, as long as he remains in this part of America, there will be plots. His heart is full of hatred for Spain'.[3] Not even the decision to summon Moscoso to Lima for investigation of his conduct satisfied Mata, since, in his absence, the bishop's influence prevailed through his vicar-general, José Pérez, who remained in charge of the diocese.[4] Connected with both Moscoso, a native of Arequipa, and Pérez, were the prominent Cuzco families of Peralta and Ugarte, whose wealth was increased by the profits from rich benefices and other ecclesiastical posts given to members of the families by the bishop.[5] Mata provided details of such appointments, insisting that both political and religious affairs would improve if Pérez and a number of other corruptly-appointed *curas* were summoned to Spain.[6] Those singled out included Bernardo Tayo, 'bosom-friend and confidant of the bishop', and Vicente Puente, 'notorious as a troublemaker and as the agent for the bishop's decisions'.

The intendant attacked the close involvement of suspect creole families with the ecclesiastical establishment in Cuzco and identified it not only as a political danger but also as a source of corruption which caused moral and spiritual abuses

[1] A.G.I., Aud. de Cuzco 35, Mata to Gálvez, no. 1, 23 Aug. 1784.
[2] A.G.I., Aud. de Cuzco 35, Mata to Gálvez, no. 24, 30 Aug. 1784.
[3] Ibid.
[4] A.G.I., Aud. de Cuzco 35, Mata to Sonora, no. 34, 17 July 1786.
[5] A.G.I., Aud. de Cuzco 35, Mata to Gálvez, no. 32, 7 July 1786, and no. 33, 9 July 1786.
[6] A.G.I., Aud. de Cuzco 35, Mata to Sonora, no. 49, 6 March 1787.

in the parishes. He protested frequently about the neglect and ill-treatment suffered by the Indians at the hands of their *curas*.[1] Greedy for profit, they made extortionate charges for the administration of the sacraments, and there were even cases of absentee priests sending vicars to the parishes, not to give the sacraments, but to collect ecclesiastical dues. Mata was aware that royal orders had frequently prohibited such abuses, but pointed out that they were ineffective.[2] The basic problem which bedevilled political affairs applied, too, in ecclesiastical matters: royal orders which conflicted with the private interests of those encharged with their enforcement were simply ignored. The creation of the intendant system had seemed likely to improve matters. Mata alleged, however, that even his presence in Cuzco had brought little improvement, since, instead of being allowed a free hand, he was subject to the control of authorities in Lima who failed to recognize the seriousness of affairs in Cuzco. He summed up the situation: 'Here they laugh at the orders of the king....'[3]

In December 1784 Mata arrested a number of *cuzqueños* and charged them with plotting a rebellion. The leaders, the Ugarte brothers, the lawyer Capetillo and the clerk Palacios, were sent to Lima, but after investigation were declared innocent and allowed to return to Cuzco.[4] The intendant was convinced of their guilt, but claimed that the passive resistance of the inhabitants of Cuzco prevented him from providing witnesses to prove it to the satisfaction of the *audiencia* of Lima. Avilés supported his demand that he be given wider powers to act against conspirators, without the need to go through a cumbersome legal process, especially when those suspected of treason were 'distinguished subjects'.[5] This appeal for the right to exercise summary justice was supported by the claim that without it satisfactory proof of plots such as that in Cuzco would never be obtained. Fear or partiality caused potential prosecution witnesses to deny what they knew to be true, while others freely provided accused creoles with whatever documents

---

[1] A.G.I., Aud. de Cuzco 35, Mata to Gálvez, no. 4, 16 Nov. 1784.
[2] A.G.I., Aud. de Cuzco 35, Mata to Gálvez, no. 10, 4 Aug. 1785.
[3] Ibid. [4] Ibid.
[5] A.G.I., Aud. de Cuzco 2, Avilés to Gálvez, 1 Jan. 1785.

they needed to prove their innocence. Moreover, the need to go through a formal legal process meant that the intendant had to disclose his sources of information to public scrutiny, thus dissuading potential informers from coming forward.

To Mata the affairs of church and state were inextricably linked. Two of the chief suspects in the alleged plot of 1784 were members of the Ugarte family, which had close links with both Moscoso and his vicar-general, as well as relatives in influential church positions. Because of the influence which Moscoso was able to exercise in Cuzco, even in his absence, Mata insisted that it should be general policy to appoint Europeans to ecclesiastical posts.[1] In his view all the bishops should be Europeans, and at least two thirds of the minor posts should be reserved for Europeans. Such a policy, he argued, would provide not only greater political security but also more honest ecclesiastical administration.

Croix was more cautious, believing the situation too delicate for him to take the drastic step of dismissing Moscoso's vicar-general.[2] Perhaps such a measure, instead of producing the effect desired by Mata, 'would inflame and revive the cry of rebellion'. He did, however, share Mata's view that it was desirable to have a trustworthy European appointed as bishop of Cuzco, 'a diplomatic and learned ecclesiastic, who with his prudence, tact and affability will calm the minds of its inhabitants'. This, in fact, was to be the solution to the problem. Moscoso sailed to Spain in April 1786 and, although never formally convicted of charges of aiding the Túpac Amaru rising, was not allowed to return to Peru. Instead he was appointed bishop of Granada in 1789, and replaced in Cuzco by Bartolomé María de las Heras, a native of Andalusia, and a future archbishop of Lima.[3] The situation in Cuzco was further eased by the decision in 1787 to appoint the sometimes over-zealous Mata to the regency of the *audiencia* of Buenos Aires.[4] Mata's successors seem to have enjoyed good relations with the ecclesiastical authorities in Cuzco. In 1791, for

[1] A.G.I., Aud. de Cuzco 35, Mata to Gálvez, no. 10, 4 Aug. 1785.
[2] A.G.I., Aud. de Cuzco 4, Croix to Gálvez, no. 23, *reservada*, 20 May 1786.
[3] See M. de Mendiburu, *Diccionario histórico-biográfico del Perú. Parte I, que corresponde a la época de la dominación española* (11 vols, Lima, 1931–5), vi, 237–9.
[4] See below, 61–2.

example, the president-intendant Carlos de Corral reported that his relationship with the bishop was good.[1] He made the observation while reporting a dispute with the bishop concerning jurisdiction over a Cuzco hospital; but it was a friendly disagreement, with none of the bitterness which marred the early establishment of the intendancy.

The conflicts which developed between intendants and bishops in these early years of the new system of administration varied in significance from one province to another. In Cuzco the conflict had some political content; in Huamanga the fact that the first intendant was a creole accounted in part for the bishop's conviction that he was involved in trade and used family connexions for his personal gain; in Lima and Tarma problems arose basically from the archbishop's belief that it was beneath his dignity to deal with mere intendants. In the viceroyalty as a whole it was this last consideration which lay behind disputes. Vice-patronage had previously been exercised by the viceroys, and bishops felt that to make them formally acknowledge in public ceremonies the ecclesiastical authority of intendants was in some way reducing the status of the Church and of themselves.

There are signs that a similar attitude prevailed among members of the *audiencia* of Lima. There is no evidence of serious clashes between the intendants and the *audiencia*, but minor disputes there were, reflecting, perhaps, a resentment of the *audiencia* at the wide powers enjoyed by the intendants in the administration of justice. In 1786, for example, intendant Gálvez of Tarma protested that the style of address used in documents sent to him by the *sala del crimen* of the *audiencia* did not show sufficient respect for his authority.[2] Moreover, the *audiencia* was delaying the administration of justice in the *partidos* of his province by insisting on sending correspondence on legal matters with the subdelegates to the intendant's office, rather than directly to the *partidos*.

The process of administrative reform, in particular the creation of the intendancies and the foundation of the *audiencia* of Cuzco, clearly caused a decline in both the authority and the

[1] A.G.I., Aud. de Cuzco 5, Corral to Porlier, no. 33, 8 Sept. 1791.
[2] A.G.I., Aud. de Lima 1117, Gálvez to Croix, no. 16, 1 July 1786.

business of the *audiencia* of Lima. In 1791 its chancellor, Juan Josef Aguero, appealed to the crown for compensation, because of the declining profits of his position.[1] He had bought the office in public sale, but, since much legal business was now dealt with elsewhere, it no longer provided him with a decent standard of living. The Council of the Indies found his complaint to be justified, and ordered that his annual salary be increased from 100 to 400 pesos.[2] Such a decision, although acknowledging the justice of the appeal, was out of character, since the normal response to requests for salary increases was either deferment or rejection. In 1786 Escobedo requested that the salaries of the Peruvian intendants be increased from 6000 to 7000 pesos, and that the 600 pesos allowed for clerical expenses and for the costs of *visitas* be doubled.[3] The request was based upon the fact that the intendants had experienced financial difficulties, especially in making *visitas*. The response from Spain was that the intendants should adjust their standards of living to conform with the salaries provided.

The creation of the *audiencia* of Cuzco was the last major step in the Bourbon programme of administrative reform in Peru. Túpac Amaru had demanded the reform; Avilés had strongly recommended it. Mata, too, was a strong supporter of the idea, for a variety of reasons. He argued, on strategic grounds, that Cuzco and the *sierra* provided the key to the Spanish empire in South America.[4] If Spain were to lose Buenos Aires and Lima to foreign invaders, the empire could remain intact if control were retained of Cuzco, 'but, with Cuzco lost, all the kingdom will be lost, since the *sierra* is the shield of all this America. . .'. It was, therefore, vital to take measures which would increase Spanish authority and maintain order in Cuzco. Mata believed that the presence of an *audiencia*, respected and obeyed by the citizens, would assist the fulfilment of these aims. It would not only provide the poor with cheaper justice but also act as a curb on the excessive influence of the ecclesiastical authorities.

[1] A.G.I., Aud. de Lima 599, *extracto* of *Mesa*, 14 Sept, 1792.
[2] A.G.I., Aud. de Lima 599, report of Council, 11 Sept. 1795.
[3] A.G.I., Aud. de Lima 612, report of *contaduría general*, 17 Dec. 1790, which contains summaries of Escobedo's letters of 20 Feb. 1786 (no. 628) and 5 Sept. 1786 (no. 975).
[4] A.G.I., Aud. de Cuzco 35, Mata to Gálvez, no. 26, 21 Feb. 1786.

Moreover, Mata saw the creation of an *audiencia* as an integral part of his general vision of bringing about a renaissance of the city.[1] Cuzco, the capital of the Incas, had remained rich and important in the second half of the sixteenth and the first half of the seventeenth centuries; but the decline of the *encomenderos* inaugurated a period of decadence which culminated in the rebellion of Túpac Amaru. The destruction of property and the abolition of the *repartimiento* system hit economic life in the province. Mata expected the creation of an *audiencia* to help to arrest this economic decline, since it would bring wealthy administrators and officials to the city. Their presence would induce rich families to return, and this, in turn, would bring increased trade and consumption and stimulate cultural life.

The creation of the *audiencia* was formally ordered by the *cédula* of 26 February 1787, which also named Josef de la Portilla as regent-intendant.[2] He reached Cuzco in June 1788, and the new tribunal, staffed by three *oidores* and a *fiscal* in addition to Portilla, began to function in November.[3] Mata had recommended that the jurisdiction of the new *audiencia* should extend over the intendancies of Cuzco, Arequipa, Huamanga and Huancavelica, and over the intendancy of Puno in the viceroyalty of the Río de la Plata.[4] The *cédula* of 26 February 1787 simply ordered that its authority cover the bishopric of Cuzco and any further area to be decided after consultation between Escobedo and Croix. Two problems immediately arose. The *audiencia* of Lima would resist the loss of any more territory under its jurisdiction. The second was more complex. The new *audiencia*'s authority covered the bishopric of Cuzco, not the intendancy, and the boundaries of the two were not identical. In fact three *partidos* of the intendancy of Puno—Lampa, Carabaya and Azángaro—formed part of the diocese. These *partidos* were subject to the control of the bishop and *audiencia*

[1] A.G.I., Aud. de Cuzco 35, Mata to Sonora, no. 54, 4 July 1787.

[2] A.G.I., Aud. de Lima 620, *cédula*, 26 Feb. 1787. Until 1791 Portilla served as both regent and intendant; in 1791, although remaining as regent, he was succeeded as intendant by Carlos de Corral. As the province's political head, Corral became president of the *audiencia*.

[3] A.H.M.H., Libro de Cédulas 1063a, ff. 51-8, three *cédulas* of 3 May 1787 and one of 10 May 1787, for appointment of *oidores*. For details of opening ceremonies see Vargas, *Historia del Perú. Virreinato (Siglo XVIII) 1700-1790*, 443-4.

[4] A.G.I., Aud. de Cuzco 35, Mata to Gálvez, no. 26, 21 Feb. 1786.

of Cuzco in ecclesiastical and judicial matters and to that of the intendant of Puno and the viceroy of Buenos Aires for political affairs and general administration. Since the authorities in Cuzco owed general allegiance to Lima, the intendancy of Puno was controlled by two superior governments, two bishops and two *audiencias*.[1] Escobedo had proposed in 1785 that a new diocese, consisting of the whole province of Puno and part of that of Arequipa, should be formed.[2] The alternative solution which he offered in 1787 was that the whole province of Puno should be made part of the diocese of Cuzco, and be transferred to the viceroyalty of Peru.[3] It would then be under the jurisdiction of the new *audiencia*. He recommended at the same time that the province of Arequipa, too, should be subject to the authority of the *audiencia* of Cuzco. Viceroy Croix, however, was more conservative, reflecting perhaps the pressure of the *audiencia* of Lima. He recommended that until further orders came from Spain the new *audiencia*'s territory should be restricted to the diocese of Cuzco.[4]

The *audiencia* of Lima supported suggestions to transfer the intendancy of Puno to the viceroyalty of Peru but, not unnaturally, was opposed to the creation of the *audiencia* of Cuzco, and even more to the idea of granting it jurisdiction over the province of Arequipa.[5] It argued, rather unconvincingly, that Cuzco had been served well by the *audiencia* of Lima during the previous two centuries. Since the old system had worked efficiently in the past, when Cuzco had been rich and flourishing, there was even less justification for separation when the city and province were in decline, unable to provide enough work for a new *audiencia*. On the question of the province of Arequipa it argued that, although Arequipa seemed to be much nearer to Cuzco than to Lima, communications with the latter were much easier. Moreover, much of Arequipa's commerce, from which many legal cases originated, was with Lima. The final argument was simply that the *audiencia* of Lima depended upon cases arising in Arequipa for much of its

[1] A.G.I., Indif. General 1713, Machado to Nestares, Madrid, 17 April 1789.
[2] A.G.I., Aud. de Lima 1101, Escobedo to Gálvez, no. 434, 20 Jan. 1785.
[3] A.G.I., Aud. de Lima 599, *resumen* of Council of the Indies, 9 Oct. 1795.
[4] Ibid.   [5] A.G.I., Aud. de Lima 599, *audiencia* to Porlier, 16 April 1788.

business. To hand this over to Cuzco would quickly bring ruin and decay to the *audiencia* of Lima. Asked by the Council of the Indies for his opinion, viceroy Fray Francisco Gil de Taboada y Lemos dismissed these objections as self-interested and inaccurate.[1] His opinion was that it would be far better for the inhabitants of Arequipa to travel sixty leagues to Cuzco for justice than the two hundred and sixty leagues to Lima. The further objection that Cuzco had insufficient ministers to deal with a sudden influx of business could, he pointed out, be easily solved by the transfer of staff from Lima.[2]

The practical defects of the existing arrangements for the administration of justice in the intendancy of Puno became apparent soon after the opening of the new *audiencia*. Portilla forwarded to Spain, in February 1789, a representation of 'various inhabitants' of Lampa and Carabaya which alleged that the subdelegates of the two *partidos*, in co-operation with treasury officials in Putiña, had made a large *repartimiento* of mules and cloth, using 60,000 pesos of royal funds as capital.[3] Croix made a similar report, explaining that the *audiencia* of Cuzco could do little to check such activities as long as accused individuals brought before it could ensure interminable delay by issuing appeals to authorities in Buenos Aires.[4] When asked for their views on the proposed transfer of Puno to Peru, the viceroy and the *audiencia* of Buenos Aires opposed it, on the grounds that it would reduce the prestige of the *audiencia* of Charcas, which had jurisdiction over those *partidos* outside the diocese of Cuzco, and that the loss of the province would have an adverse effect on the general economic prosperity of the whole viceroyalty of the Río de la Plata.[5]

Having considered the views of all interested parties, the Council produced its conclusions in 1795, recommending that the intendancy of Puno be transferred to the viceroyalty of Peru, and that the intendancy of Arequipa be transferred to the

[1] A.G.I., Aud. de Lima 599, *extracto* of Council of the Indies, 9 Oct. 1795.
[2] The *audiencia* of Lima had a regent, eight *oidores*, four *alcaldes del crimen* and two *fiscales*—A.H.M.H., Libro de Cédulas 900, f. 110, royal order, 21 April 1788.
[3] A.G.I., Aud. de Lima 599, Portilla to Council of the Indies, 27 Feb. 1789.
[4] A.G.I., Aud. de Lima 599, Croix to Council of the Indies, 31 Jan. 1790.
[5] A.G.I., Aud. de Lima 599, *extracto* of Council of the Indies, 9 Oct. 1795.

jurisdiction of the *audiencia* of Cuzco.[1] The first proposal was accepted by the governor of the Council, the marqués de Bajamar, but the second was rejected, on the grounds that no further measures should be taken which would bring about a reduction in the 'splendour' of the viceregal capital.[2] The crown accepted his advice. A *cédula* of 1 February 1796 ordered that the intendancy of Puno be transferred to Peru and to the territory of the *audiencia* of Cuzco for judicial matters, and confirmed that the province of Arequipa should remain subject to the authority of the *audiencia* of Lima.[3]

The number of intendancies in Peru was thus increased to eight. As part of his general scheme for administrative reorganization in the viceroyalty Escobedo had suggested in 1785 that the province of Guayaquil, in the viceroyalty of New Granada, be transferred to Peru.[4] He pointed out that most of Guayaquil's trade, in *cacao*, wood and tobacco, was with Lima, while even the port's trade with Acapulco was carried by Peruvian ships. The province as a whole was similar in many ways to the intendancy of Trujillo, and he believed that it would be administered more efficiently from Lima than from Santa Fé de Bogota. Above all he thought that change was necessary for strategic reasons, since Guayaquil could be far more easily defended from the Peruvian capital. For all of these reasons he suggested that a further intendancy should be established in Guayaquil and that the whole province be transferred to Peru. No immediate action was taken on this suggestion. In fact, the first change in the northern boundaries of the viceroyalty, made in 1802, dealt not with Guayaquil, but with Mainas, a vast mission area in the north east. This territory, under the command of a military governor, was transferred from the province of Quito, in the viceroyalty of New Granada, to Peru.[5] It possessed an enormous range of natural resources, but was virtually unsettled and the resources of the viceroyalty were inadequate for its exploitation. In the following year, 1803, it was finally decided to transfer Guaya-

[1] Ibid.
[2] A.G.I., Aud. de Lima 599, Bajamar to Llaguno, 10 Oct. 1795.
[3] A.G.I., Aud. de Lima 610, *cédula*, 1 Feb. 1796.
[4] A.G.I., Aud. de Lima 1101, Escobedo to Gálvez, no. 435, 20 March 1785.
[5] A.G.M.R.E., *cédula*, 15 July 1802.

quil to Peru.[1] The decision was made on the advice of a *junta de fortificaciones*, which pointed out, as Escobedo had done in 1785, that the city and province could be more easily defended from Lima, and that the defence of Peru would also be aided by the accessibility of wood and other naval supplies. The province remained, however, under the control of a governor, and Escobedo's suggestion that it should become a further intendancy was ignored.

Although readjustment continued until 1803, the basic programme of administrative and territorial reorganization was complete by 1784. From 1782 its chief architect, Escobedo, prepared the way for the creation of seven intendancies in 1784, and for the addition of an eighth in 1795. Perhaps an even greater achievement was his success in instilling a feeling of optimism into the inhabitants of a viceroyalty which had suffered considerably from other aspects of the Bourbon reform programme. It is clear that in 1784 Peruvians believed that the intendants could bring with them economic progress, advances in public administration and a less corrupt structure of local government.[2] Escobedo shared this optimism. He believed, too, that the intendants could succeed in fulfilling the equally important tasks of increasing the revenues of the crown and making its authority in the viceroyalty of Peru more effective.[3]

[1] A.G.I., Aud. de Lima 610, royal order, 8 July 1803.
[2] A.H.M., Libro de Cabildo 38, ff. 1–5, *acta cap.*, 13 July 1784, illustrates enthusiasm of *cabildo* of Lima.
[3] A.G.I., Aud. de Lima 1102, Escobedo to Gálvez, no. 561, 20 Oct. 1785.

CHAPTER III

Intendants and Viceroys

THE VICEREGAL INSTITUTION was one which, in the eyes of many reformers, had outlived much of its usefulness by the late eighteenth century. In earlier times the need to concentrate civil, military and religious authority in the hands of a single representative of the king had been clear enough; now, when reforms were urgently needed, the system seemed to produce only inefficiency and corruption. It is true that even in the sixteenth century the powers of the viceroy had been restricted, both in theory and in practice, by those of other institutions, notably the *audiencia*. Nevertheless, the viceroys, especially those of Peru, had enjoyed extensive personal authority. It was felt that the aims of achieving a greater centralization of authority in Madrid, of making absolutism more effective, and of ensuring a greater efficiency in financial and general administration would be more easily fulfilled if executive authority were distributed among a wider circle of administrators. Consequently powers previously enjoyed by the viceroy were transferred to the superintendent and the other intendants. Viceregal hostility and demands for the restoration of lost powers were natural consequences of the reforms.

Even before the formal introduction of the intendant system in 1784 it had become clear that ministers in Madrid were impatient and dissatisfied with the misuse and abuse of viceregal powers, and that within Peru viceregal prestige was in decline. Viceroy Amat had experienced considerable difficulty in obtaining *fiadores* to provide financial guarantees, when arrangements were being made for his *residencia* on the completion of his term of office in 1776.[1] His difficulty was caused

[1] See L. Durand Flores, 'El juicio de residencia en el Perú republicano', *Anuario de Estudios Americanos*, x (1953), 381.

by the widespread belief in Lima that he would be fined for irregular conduct. His successor, Guirior, entered into a trial of strength with the *visitador*, and emerged on the losing side. Areche's insistence that many of the viceroyalty's administrative problems, especially disobedience to royal orders and exchequer frauds, were caused by the abuse of viceregal powers was accepted by Gálvez. Guirior's dismissal in 1780 made it clear that the Minister of the Indies would not tolerate obstruction to the programme of reform.[1] The next viceroy, Jáuregui, also found it difficult to satisfy Gálvez. His term of office was brought to an abrupt end as a result of criticisms of his handling of the Túpac Amaru rising and of dissatisfaction with his complacent attitude towards administrative problems.[2]

When, therefore, the new viceroy, Teodoro de Croix, took up his post in April 1784, he was fully aware of the dangers of obstruction of the process of reform. Special instructions from Gálvez in the previous year had made clear the minister's dissatisfaction with the conduct of Guirior and Jáuregui and his enthusiasm for the intendant system.[3] Croix was specifically ordered to co-operate with Escobedo in the introduction of this reform, and it appears that he paid scrupulous attention to this command. Nowhere in the reports and correspondence dealing with administrative reorganization is there evidence of viceregal obstruction; on the contrary there is clear evidence of positive assistance. The complex question of vice-patronage illustrates this. Although the exercise of vice-patronage by the intendants involved a reduction of viceregal powers, Croix resisted the temptation to encourage the bishops' opposition to the new officials. Instead he helped Escobedo to produce an instruction to regulate relations between intendants and bishops, and supported the *visitador*'s decision that vice-patronage in the intendancy of Tarma should be transferred from the viceroy to the intendant.[4]

However, despite this close co-operation in 1784, disagreements between Escobedo and Croix over jurisdiction and policy were probably inevitable. The most likely cause of

[1] See above, 19.   [2] See above, 25–6.
[3] A.G.I., Aud. de Lima 640, instruction to Croix, 19 June 1783, art. 57.
[4] See above, 36, 43.

conflict was the transfer of executive authority for economic and financial affairs from the viceroy to a superintendent, resident in the viceregal capital.[1] Complaints made by the viceroy of Buenos Aires had produced the assurance in 1783 that in an emergency the viceroy would not be left without funds due to possible disagreement over policy with the superintendent.[2] In such a situation the viceroy, as military commander, could take control of finances; in normal circumstances, however, he would no longer be in control of economic and financial affairs.

Escobedo himself remained in Lima, as intendant of the province and superintendent of the whole viceroyalty, with the formal end of the *visita* in 1785.[3] His previous good relations with the viceroy probably accounts for the fact that disputes between them were never as bitter as those which broke out between the viceroy and the superintendent in Buenos Aires.[4] Nevertheless, Croix was to inform his successor in 1790: 'With my authority endangered and jurisdiction divided, my decisions were altered, or their application obstructed. . .'.[5] Preliminary skirmishing between the two authorities centred around requests for instructions from Spain about details of ceremony and protocol. Croix enquired in October 1785 whether, following the end of the *visita*, the superintendent should continue to sit at his right hand during the meetings of various committees and at public ceremonies.[6] Writing on the same day Escobedo, too, asked for the resolution of this issue, but made it clear that friction was being caused and an excessive amount of time wasted by disagreement over a number of more serious matters.[7] He referred in particular to Croix's insistence that the superintendent, although president of the *cabildo* of Lima, had no authority to issue proclamations dealing with municipal affairs and with the public administration of the city. Escobedo protested that if this authority were to be enjoyed only by the viceroy then the chief intendant of the viceroyalty

[1] *Ord. Ints.*, arts. 2–3.   [2] Lynch, op. cit., 94.
[3] A.G.I., Aud. de Lima 646, royal order, 24 Jan. 1785.
[4] For details of problems in Buenos Aires see Lynch, op. cit., 95–107.
[5] Croix, *Memoria*, 1.
[6] A.G.I., Aud. de Lima 606, summary of Croix to Gálvez, no. 299, 20 Oct. 1785.
[7] A.G.I., Aud. de Lima 606, Escobedo to Gálvez, no. 563, 20 Oct. 1785.

would be denied faculties enjoyed by his subordinates in other provinces.

This disagreement concerning jurisdiction over the *cabildo* of Lima lay behind other disputes. The basic issue was viceregal hostility to the idea that control over municipal administration in the capital should be removed from the viceroy's hands, while Escobedo insisted that he, as president of the *cabildo*, enjoyed ultimate responsibility for its activities. Escobedo had recommended the creation in Lima of a *tribunal de la acordada*, a judicial body to deal with public order not only in the city but elsewhere in the province.[1] The subdelegate of Chancay, for example, needed such assistance to deal with the armed bands of negroes who attacked *haciendas* in the Guaral valley.[2] Rejecting the basic proposal until he could obtain information about how the *acordada* of Mexico operated, Croix took the interim measure of ordering the arming of two companies of dragoons.[3] He informed the *cabildo* of his decision without consulting Escobedo, who protested that extraordinary expenditure of this nature could not be made without consideration of the matter by the superintendent, assisted by the *junta superior*, nor could the income of the *propios* be devoted to such an end without his approval.

In the wider economic field the viceroy again clashed with Escobedo. The latter believed that, as superintendent, he had control over mining in the viceroyalty and specifically of preparations for the creation of a mining tribunal.[4] Croix, on the other hand, insisted that Escobedo had enjoyed this authority only as *visitador*, and had begun to issue his own orders on mining affairs. Escobedo pointed out that if superior orders were to be issued by himself and the viceroy confusion would ensue. Moreover, miners dissatisfied with their intendants might be tempted to appeal to the viceroy against their decisions, due to the popular knowledge that Croix 'usually appears to be dissatisfied with those governors...'. The fact that the public had become aware of the confusion caused by the

---

[1] A.G.I., Aud. de Lima 979, Escobedo to Sonora, no. 835, 20 Jan. 1787.
[2] Ibid., enclosure no. 2.
[3] A.G.I., Aud. de Lima 979, Escobedo to Sonora, no. 835, 20 Jan. 1787.
[4] A.G.I., Aud. de Lima 1110, Escobedo to Sonora, no. 682, 5 May 1786.

division of authority was, in his view, a serious matter. A popular rumour had spread that the powers of the superintendent were to be transferred to the viceroy—even Escobedo suspected that there might be some truth in the story.[1]

There were, then, two aspects to the clash between superintendent and viceroy: the general desire of the latter to control economic policy throughout the viceroyalty and his specific insistence that within the capital he, and not Escobedo, should control municipal affairs. The election by the *cabildo* of a new *alcalde ordinario* for 1787 caused further problems. On the eve of the election the *cabildo* went through the formality of asking for Croix's permission to proceed.[2] The viceroy claimed, however, that the corporation had shown 'a real contempt' for his authority, by having already decided, a few days earlier, who should be elected.[3] He pointed out that he was not opposed to the principle that the power to confirm the election should remain with the intendant, but wanted it to be made clear that, in asking for his permission to hold the election, the *cabildo* was not performing a mere ceremony, but recognizing him as 'the head of the kingdom, in whom the king has deposited all his authority and complete powers'.

Escobedo saw this attitude simply as an unwarranted attempt to interefere with the *cabildo*'s newly-won electoral freedom.[4] In giving the intendants the right to confirm *cabildo* elections, the Ordinance had expressly revoked the law (*ley* 10, *tít.* 3, *lib.* 5) which had previously granted it to the viceroy.[5] Moreover, the secret instruction given to Croix by Gálvez in 1783 had warned him not to copy Jáuregui's attempts to select the *alcaldes*.[6] According to the superintendent, Croix's real desire was not simply that the *cabildo* should require his permission before proceeding to its election, but that it should present to him a short-list of several candidates, so that he might exclude those whom he thought unsuitable. In Escobedo's view the

---

[1] Ibid.
[2] A.G.I., Aud. de Lima 598, report of Council of the Indies, 11 Feb. 1788.
[3] A.G.I., Aud. de Lima 598, summary of Croix to Sonora, 5 Jan. 1787.
[4] A.G.I., Aud. de Lima 598, summary of Escobedo to Sonora, no. 829, 5 Jan. 1787.
[5] *Ord. Ints.*, art. 8.
[6] A.G.I., Aud. de Lima 640, instruction to Croix, 19 June 1783, art. 33.

implementation of such a scheme would mean that 'soon there will be a return to the former practice of appointing them arbitrarily, restricting both the freedom of the *cabildo* and the authority of the intendant, with the restoration of the law 10 which was revoked by the Ordinance'. He conceded that the viceroy should have the right to object to the election of an unsatisfactory *alcalde*, but felt that he could make his views known to the superintendent and rely upon him to take appropriate action. The specific issue was finally resolved in November 1787, with the order that the right to confirm the annual election of *alcaldes* and other officials by the *cabildos* of the viceregal capitals should be restored to the viceroys.[1] In other towns and cities the right of confirmation was to remain with the intendants, but they were to give the viceroy punctual and precise accounts of their decisions. The wider issue of the clash between the viceroy and the superintendent had already been resolved in August 1787, when it was ordered that Escobedo should return to Spain, and the powers of the superintendent be transferred to the viceroy.[2]

The immediate dispute which preceded this order was trivial. Escobedo had decided to levy a tax on the woollen and leather goods manufactured and traded by the Indians. He aroused Croix's opposition by failing to consult him on the affair. Thus, although the financial aspect was insignificant, the basic political and administrative problem remained serious. As long as executive authority in the viceroyalty was shared, there would be disagreements. The recall of Escobedo to serve as a minister of the Council of the Indies would, it was hoped, 'nip in the bud the repetition of similar nuisances'. Meanwhile, 'until more information is obtained on the matter', his powers were to be exercised by the viceroy, whose conduct was warmly praised. The formal transfer of authority took place on 15 December 1787.[3] Although Escobedo expressed gratitude to the king for 'the piety with which he has heard my repeated appeals, granting me permission to return to Spain', it is clear that the decision to recall him came not from a concern for his

[1] A.G.I., Aud. de Lima 598, royal order, 22 Nov. 1787.
[2] A.G.I., Aud. de Lima 1069, Valdés to Croix, 1 Aug. 1787.
[3] A.G.I., Aud. de Lima 639, Croix to Valdés, 16 Dec. 1787.

personal interests, but as a result of a major shift in the policy and attitudes of the Spanish government towards the intendant system.[1]

José de Gálvez, the Minister of the Indies who had been the chief architect of administrative reorganization in the empire, died on 17 June 1787.[2] In the following month the single ministry he had occupied for a decade was divided into a Ministry of Grace and Justice, headed by Antonio Porlier, former *fiscal* of the Council of the Indies, and a Ministry of War and Finance, headed by Antonio Valdés.[3] The very decision to make this adjustment in Madrid indicated a triumph for conservatives, alarmed by the gathering momentum of reform in Gálvez's later years. It was followed, not by the completion of the process of administrative reorganization, but by an abrupt halt and the repeal of some of the key measures already enforced. The creation of the superintendencies had been one of the most important aspects of the basic plan to improve the efficiency and integrity of the exchequer, by removing control of economic and financial affairs from the viceroy and placing it in the hands of an independent official. In some parts of the empire, notably in Buenos Aires, the new system had not worked well, because of acrimonious personal disputes between viceroy and superintendent.[4] In Lima, despite inevitable difficulties, the system had proved workable. But the appointment of Valdés was followed by a systematic attack on all the superintendencies.[5] Escobedo's recall had been ordered on 1 August 1787; on 2 October the superintendent of Mexico was ordered to relinquish his post; a similar order was sent to the superintendent of Buenos Aires in May 1788. Although the creation of the superintendencies had caused administrative problems, it seems that their abolition came not because the reform had proved unworkable, but because a change of personnel at the centre produced a radical change in the direction of imperial policy. The process of administrative reform came to a halt, with the cancellation of plans to extend the intendant system

[1] A.G.I., Aud. de Lima 974, Escobedo to Valdés, no. 2, 20 Dec. 1787.
[2] Navarro, *Intendencias en Indias*, 115.
[3] A.H.M.H., Libro de Cédulas 900, f. 167, royal decree, 8 July 1787.
[4] Lynch, op. cit., 104–5.
[5] Navarro, *Intendencias en Indias*, 117.

to the viceroyalty of New Granada, and a new process of restoring powers to the viceroys began.[1]

Contemporaries were aware that the death of Gálvez was the key to the administrative changes of 1787. Writing from Lima in December 1787, the *asesor* of Tarma, Bartolomé Bedoya, reported that the transfer of the superintendent's powers to the viceroy and the consequent excitement in the city originated from the death of the Minister of the Indies.[2] He added that one consequence of the change was an increase in intrigue and deceit, with everybody taking decisions and forming policies simply on the basis of self-interest, with the basic aim of improving their standing with the viceroy. The abolition of the superintendencies was hardly likely to improve either the honesty or the efficiency of government; it did, however, please the viceroys. Croix informed his successor that its effect was: 'my authority was less restricted and my decisions more effective'.[3] As far as the remaining intendants were concerned the removal of Escobedo had detrimental effects. Technically his functions would be exercised by the viceroy; in fact, the viceroy, already over-worked, found it impossible to provide the direction, guidance and efficiency in financial and economic affairs which had characterized Escobedo's command. Even more serious was the fact that, with the removal of Escobedo's restraining influence, the latent opposition of Croix towards the intendant system in general rapidly turned into open hostility.

While Escobedo remained, Croix had confined himself to criticizing individual intendants and specific aspects of their administration. Mata, intendant of Cuzco, was a favourite target. Croix believed that his uncompromising attitude to creoles and his persecution of suspected conspirators was causing dangerous unrest in Cuzco.[4] In response to the viceroy's appeals for Mata's removal, it was decided in 1787 to

[1] A.G.M.R.E., copy of Francisco Viaña to Miguel Cayetano Soler, undated but written after withdrawal of *Nueva Ordenanza*. Viaña informs Soler that a royal order of 24 April 1787 informed viceroy of New Granada that nominations of intendants for his viceroyalty were being made. The plan to extend the system came to an end, however, 'por haber fallecido poco despues el Señor Marqués de Sonora'.

[2] A.N.P., Superior Gobierno 18, *cuaderno* 480, Bedoya to Josef Domínguez, 27 Dec. 1787. [3] Croix, *Memoria*, 2.

[4] A.G.I., Aud. de Cuzco 4, Croix to Sonora, no. 26, *reservada*, 16 June 1786.

appoint him to the regency of the *audiencia* of Buenos Aires.[1] At the same time Avilés, military commander of Cuzco, who had been accused by Croix of sharing Mata's faults, was made sub-inspector of the troops of the viceroyalty and governor of Callao.[2] Both new appointments were promotions, but both were made in response to viceregal criticism. Moreover, viceregal complaints about the conduct of the intendant of Huancavelica, Márquez, were resolved by concessions to Croix. The management of Huancavelica by Márquez had been strongly criticized by both Croix and Escobedo, and it was believed that the collapse of the mine in 1786 was partly due to his negligence and inadequate supervision.[3] Consequently it was ordered in 1788 that he be replaced by Manuel Ruiz Urries de Castilla, who had recently succeeded Avilés as military commander of Cuzco.[4] Croix acknowledged the order, but recommended that it would be more satisfactory to restore overall control of the mine to the viceroy.[5] The advice was taken. In 1790 Escobedo's order that the superintendency of the mercury mine should be vested in the intendant of Huancavelica—the basic reason for the creation of an intendancy there—was revoked.[6]

Croix's criticism of individual intendants gave way in 1789 to a general attack on the whole structure of the new administration, and a recommendation that a system of *corregimientos* be restored.[7] He provided Valdés with a detailed list of his reasons for concluding that the intendant system was inadequate for the good government of Peru. The authority of the viceroy, he argued, had been reduced to a dangerously low level, with the result that the intendants showed him little respect, and even defied him openly. The problem of vice-patronage was also emphasized. When these powers had been exercised by the viceroy conflicts with the ecclesiastical authorities had been rare; now, Croix continued, there were numerous disputes, partly because the bishops resented dealing with inferior

[1] A.G.I., Aud. de Cuzco 4, royal order, 26 Feb. 1787.
[2] Ibid.
[3] See below, 141-3.
[4] A.G.I., Aud. de Lima 647, preamble to royal order, 2 March 1790.
[5] Ibid., summary of Croix to Valdés, no. 12, 16 March 1789.
[6] A.G.I., Aud. de Lima 647, royal order, 2 March 1790.
[7] A.G.I., Indif. General 1714, Croix to Valdés, 16 May 1789.

administrators, partly because the intendants meddled in ecclesiastical affairs, encouraging disobedience to episcopal authority among the lower clergy.

The viceroy claimed that the intendants had failed to stimulate agriculture, industry and commerce. Mining had not only failed to progress, but had declined, for the abolition of the *repartimientos*, by reducing the profits of merchants, had led to a fall in the amount of capital available for investment in the industry. The delegation of judicial authority to the intendants had failed to produce improvements in the administration of justice, although it had caused some poverty among lawyers and court officials in Lima. The representation continued in similar vein, criticizing almost every aspect of the work of the intendants: they interfered with the *cabildos*, antagonizing *alcaldes*; they had failed to make *visitas*, and their proposals for the reform of public administration, although impressive on paper, were rarely put into practice. Above all they had failed in the management of finance and treasury affairs. In Croix's view the increase in revenue which had occurred was a result of better book-keeping and the provision of monthly accounts, reforms which could have been carried out within the framework of administration by *corregidores*.

More detailed criticism of the management of treasury affairs was contained in a separate representation of the same date.[1] It was argued that little progress had been made in the collection of the *alcabala* and other taxes, largely because provincial treasury officials submitted general accounts to the tribunal of accounts rather than detailed accounts for individual taxes to specialists in Lima. The situation was made worse by the negligence of the intendants, who not only failed to detect fraud but were also prone to accept bribes. Croix insisted that exchequer administration in the provinces would never improve 'when it is generally known that corrupt officials have and use the opportunity to win over the intendants'.

Having demonstrated to his own satisfaction that the intendants had failed in the three main aspects of their work—the administration of justice, finance and public administration—

[1] A.G.I., Aud. de Lima 1181, Croix to Valdés, *reservada*, 16 May 1789. See below, 115–16.

Croix completed his indictment with the assertion that they were not needed for the fulfilment in the fourth branch of government, that of *guerra*, of the aims of the Ordinance.[1] There were few regular troops in the viceroyalty, and in those provinces which did have garrisons—Cuzco, Arequipa and Tarma, in addition to Lima—control by the intendants had been unsatisfactory. The viceroy's general verdict on the intendants was: 'they are not only useless, but harmful to the public interest and to the service of the king'. He proposed a return to the old pattern of government through *corregidores*. He recommended, too, the revival of the *repartimiento* system, arguing that the repetition of former abuses could be prevented by an increased centralization of authority in the hands of the viceroy.

These reports of Croix were sent to the Council of the Indies in 1790 for examination and discussion.[2] They joined a growing body of documents dealing with the problems of administrative and territorial reorganization, which grew even larger as, during the next decade, the Council's ministers debated the utility of the intendant system. Advice was obtained from many individuals and institutions, but the issue was reduced basically to a choice between the views of two viceroys. Croix was the chief opponent of the intendant system; its chief supporter was the conde de Revillagigedo, viceroy of New Spain, who in 1791 sent a number of reports proclaiming the benefits of the new system and attacking those who demanded the restoration of *corregidores*.[3]

Meanwhile in March 1790 Fray Francisco Gil de Taboada y Lemos, previously viceroy of New Granada, arrived in Lima to replace Croix. During his journey he had been corresponding with the temporary intendant of Huancavelica, Pedro de Tagle y Bracho, an *oidor* of the *audiencia* of Lima sent to investigate the causes of the mining disaster of 1786. Tagle warned him to be extremely cautious and wary of the powerful pressure-groups which awaited him at the viceregal court.[4] In reply Gil insisted that Tagle return to Lima as soon as possible, since he

[1] A.G.I., Indif. General 1714, Croix to Valdés, 16 May 1789.
[2] A.G.I., Indif. General 1714, Valdés to Francisco Moniño, 16 March 1790.
[3] Navarro, *Intendencias en Indias*, 123.
[4] A.H.M.H., Colección Santamaría, MS 00153, Gil to Tagle, 8 Feb. 1790; MS 00155, Tagle to Gil, 8 March 1790.

had powerful reasons to distrust those who surrounded him at court.[1] Neither the nature of these intrigues nor details of the business which he wished to entrust to Tagle were revealed in this correspondence. Nevertheless, the terms used indicate that Gil came to a court notorious for its intrigues, and inherited advisers whose integrity was to be doubted. Whether or not these advisers influenced his attitudes towards the intendant system is not clear. What is clear is that very soon after his arrival Gil began to repeat the criticisms made by his predecessor in 1789.

Gil complained in April 1790 that the intendants had failed to fulfil their duties in the conduct of public administration.[2] In his view this aspect of government should have been their main concern, since judicial affairs were delegated to the subdelegates and the *tenientes asesores*, treasury affairs were handled almost entirely by treasury officials, and the intendants' duties in the department of war were few. Nevertheless, he continued, during the six years of the existence of the intendant system in Peru no topographical maps had been made and no censuses had been undertaken, with the result that there was a lack of reliable information about population distribution and the general commercial, agricultural and industrial potential of the viceroyalty.[3] In an attempt to obtain information of this type, Gil sent a circular order to all the intendants, demanding prompt reports on twenty points of public administration: when and how *visitas* had been undertaken, details of population and land use, the state of mining, commerce and industry, and other matters of an economic and geographical nature.[4]

Three months later, prompted perhaps by a slow response to this order, Gil turned from an attack on one aspect of the intendants' work to a general criticism of the whole intendant system.[5] His complaints, in fact, were mere repetitions of those

[1] A.H.M.H., Colección Santamaría, MS 00154, Gil to Tagle, 14 May 1790.
[2] A.G.I., Aud. de Lima 647, Gil to Porlier, no. 7, 30 April 1790.
[3] Some of these charges were inaccurate. Maps had already been provided by the intendants of Arequipa, Cuzco, Trujillo and Tarma. See P. Torres Lanzas, *Relación de los mapas, planos, etc., del virreinato del Perú existentes en el Archivo de Indias* (Barcelona, 1906), nos. 85–104, 115.
[4] Deustua, op. cit., 201–5, circular order of Gil, 30 April 1790.
[5] A.G.I., Aud. de Lima 1118, Gil to Valdés, no. 103, 20 July 1790. See Deustua, op. cit., 22–34.

made by Croix a year earlier. Gil himself pointed this out, reporting that Croix's 'investigation and knowledge of the question oblige me to repeat his views, merely adding a few thoughts of my own...'. His proposed alternative system of administration was similar to that suggested by Croix. He advocated that the *partidos* should be controlled by military governors, independent of each other and directly dependent on the viceroy. He differed from Croix, however, over the proposal to restore the *repartimiento* system. Gil believed that such a policy would be detrimental to the interests of the Indians. But the basic reason for his hostility to the *repartimiento* system was not humanitarian concern for the masses, but the economic conviction that only free trade within Peru could provide the stimulus of competition and efficiency needed for the exploitation of the viceroyalty's resources.

By 1796, the year in which his term of office came to an end, Gil's initial hostility towards the intendant system had been modified. He maintained his view that the administration of exchequer affairs was mismanaged by some intendants, but in general appeared to be satisfied with the structure of provincial government.[1] He wrote in the report which he left for his successor: 'I have had the fortune to find, during my term of office, magistrates of credit and worth, men dedicated to the sacred functions of the judicature'.[2] The detailed work which Gil supervised on the preparation of an elaborate scheme to provide salaries for the subdelegates suggests that, although he recognized faults in the intendant system, he came to favour constructive reform rather than its abolition.[3] Moreover, his relations with individual intendants seem to have been good, although some problems arose over the appointment of subdelegates.[4] He was strongly criticized by the crown in 1795 for his methods and procedure in this aspect of administration. In the same year he was further criticized for interfering in the work of the tribunal of accounts, with the aim of protecting the interests of an intendant.[5]

[1] Gil, *Memoria*, 202.
[2] Ibid., 353.
[3] See below, 95–6.
[4] See below, 84–5.
[5] A.G.I., Aud. de Lima 612, the conde de Casa Valencia (*contador general*) to Gardoqui, 27 April 1795.

The trouble arose out of the viceroy's decision to nominate his nephew, Vicente Gil de Taboada, to the intendancy of Trujillo, which fell vacant in 1791 with the death of Saavedra. The new intendant took up his post in November of that year. When news of his nomination reached Spain the *título*, official confirmation of appointment, was issued, reaching Lima for the viceroy's countersignature in September 1792. Although it was well established that an intendant, or any other treasury or judicial official, should receive only half his salary until this procedure was completed, the treasury officials of Trujillo paid Gil his salary at the end of 1792 at the full rate of 6000 pesos from the date of his taking up office. Consequently when the accounts of the provincial treasury were scrutinized in Lima the tribunal of accounts ordered that the excess sum, almost 3000 pesos, should be refunded. Not only did the intendant object, but he was supported by his uncle, who, despite a general prohibition on viceregal interference in such matters, demanded that the tribunal provide him with a full report.[1] The reaction of the Council of the Indies was to condemn Gil's attempts to intimidate the members of the tribunal and to use his official influence for the personal benefit of his nephew.

During the term of office of his uncle's successor, Ambrosio O'Higgins, marqués de Osorno, viceroy of Peru from 1796 to 1801, Gil found viceregal authority set against him. A protracted dispute with Osorno over the appointment of subdelegates led the viceroy to threaten the intendant with imprisonment if he continued to criticize him.[2] Acrimonious disputes flared up between Osorno and other intendants, too, but they were few in number. The most serious was that caused by the perennial problem of the exercise of vice-patronage in the intendancy of Tarma, which embittered relations between the viceroy and the intendant, Ramón de Urrutia. It had been ordered in 1790 that the powers of vice-patronage in the province should be restored to the viceroy, since he already

[1] Ibid. Casa Valencia quotes *ley* 59, *tit.* 1, *lib.* 8, which orders the viceroys and *audiencias* to protect the financial tribunals, 'y no se introduscan a conocer de ningun caso tocante a su exercicio directo, ni indirecto, dexandolos usar y exercir lo que orden librem'te'.
[2] See below, 86.

exercised this authority in the province of Lima, which formed the other half of the archdiocese.[1] The situation was complicated however, by a *cédula* of 1795, issued after consideration of complaints made to the crown by viceroys Croix and Gil against the intendants' alleged mismanagement of vice-patronage.[2] It was ordered in 1795 that in exercising this authority the intendants were to be regarded as subdelegates of the viceroy, who was to be responsible for ecclesiastical appointments. But the intendants were to remain directly responsible for other aspects of ecclesiastical affairs, such as the construction and management of churches and cemeteries, the collection of *diezmos* and the general conduct of the clergy.[3] Only in the capital province of the viceroyalty was the viceroy to exercise full vice-patronage.

Urrutia argued that this *cédula* superseded the royal order of 1790 which had extended the viceroy's vice-patronal powers to the province of Tarma.[4] He produced practical arguments, too, in support of his case. Since the viceroy rarely visited Tarma, ecclesiastical affairs there were in disorder, the intendant's *visita* having revealed widespread indiscipline and fraudulent use of ecclesiastical revenues at a parochial level. These accusations of neglect of duties made against Osorno by Urrutia, like those of abuse of authority made by intendant Gil, were exceptions to the general pattern. The majority of the intendants seem to have been satisfied with Osorno and he, in turn, was satisfied with the general structure of administration in the viceroyalty. Undoubtedly the viceroy's own experience in Chile, where he had served as an intendant, gave him a greater understanding than that possessed by his predecessors of both the advantages and the problems of the intendant system.[5] Soon after his arrival in Lima he informed the intendants of his admiration for 'the excellent ideas of the Instruction of Intendants, expressed in clear and precise

[1] A.G.I., Aud. de Lima 695, Gil to Porlier, no. 23, 20 July 1790, acknowledging royal order of 5 Jan. 1790.
[2] Gil, *Memoria*, 12, quoting *cédula* of 9 May 1795.
[3] *Ord. Ints.*, arts. 66, 150–79, 195.
[4] A.G.I., Aud. de Lima 763, Urrutia to Llaguno, no. 2, 21 Feb. 1798.
[5] See R. Donoso, *El marqués de Osorno, don Ambrosio O'Higgins* (Santiago, 1941), 125.

articles, unlike the old laws, regulations and orders, which were forgotten or ignored by the majority of judges and magistrates'.[1] He suggested that the early problems which had arisen could be attributed to 'the excitement inevitably caused by every innovation', rather than to basic weaknesses in the system, and, while recognizing that problems remained, especially over the appointment and control of the subdelegates, he made it clear that he was prepared to co-operate with the intendants. In practice he enjoyed good relations with them, and his admiration for the general system completed the trend begun by Gil of modifying viceregal hostility into grudging acceptance, and then into an effort to work with the intendants in an attempt to overhaul the viceroyalty.

While the viceroys of Peru were reconciling themselves to the intendant system, the Council of the Indies was still considering the reports made to it by Croix and Revillagigedo in 1789 and 1791.[2] In December 1801, having finally reached a conclusion, it condemned 'the vulgarity, ignorance and lack of ideas with which the report of the viceroy of Peru was produced', and praised 'the understanding, learning and impartiality' of Revillagigedo.[3] Its decision to reject Croix's criticisms and to affirm its faith in the utility of the intendant system owed much to the perseverance and influence of Jorge Escobedo, who had served as one of the Council's ministers since returning to Spain from Peru. Escobedo pointed out that Croix had been unable to suggest a satisfactory alternative form of government for Peru, since the restoration of the *corregidores* would inevitably bring with it the former pattern of maladministration and abuse.[4] He conceded that individual intendants might have been guilt of dishonesty or corruption, but pointed out that this criticism could be made of any group of officials, including viceroys and bishops. Inevitably, he continued, the application of the Ordinance of Intendants had offended various groups. The viceroys resented a reduction in their powers and some *cabildos* disliked close control of their

[1] Ibid., 459–61, Osorno to the intendants, 19 July 1796.
[2] See Lynch, op. cit., 280–4.
[3] A.G.I., Aud. de Lima 1119, report of Council of the Indies, 2 Dec. 1801.
[4] A.G.I., Aud. de Lima 1119, 'Voto particular del S'or d'n Jorge Escobedo en el exp'te de Int's', 23 Nov. 1801.

funds. Clearly, however, each aggrieved group was guided merely by self-interest, and made no attempt to examine either the aims or the achievements of administrative reform from a general, detached standpoint. The worst culprits, in his view, had been the viceroys. All, including Revillagigedo, had been determined to attack certain aspects of the new system, insisting in particular on the restoration of powers of vice-patronage and the removal of the superintendents.

Escobedo recognized that the intendant system had failed to fulfil all the hopes of its creators. He pointed out, however, that, if inefficiency persisted in financial affairs, the viceroys, as superintendents, were perhaps more responsible than the intendants. Moreover, some intendants might have been reluctant and hesitant to use and assert their faculties when they knew that the abolition of the system was under consideration. His general conclusion, which the Council endorsed, was that the intendant system should be retained, but that immediate steps should be taken to remedy those defects which had come to light. It insisted that one of the most important modifications to be made should be the provision of salaries for the subdelegates.[1] The crown responded promptly to the Council's recommendations. A special committee, headed by Escobedo, was formed in March 1802 to undertake the reform of the Ordinance of Intendants.[2] The committee worked quickly and by October had formulated its chief resolutions which, after minor modifications suggested by the full Council, were incorporated in a new ordinance, approved by the king on 29 June 1803.[3] The *Nueva Ordenanza de Intendentes* confirmed that the superintendencies should be filled by the viceroys, but adopted the suggestion made by both Revillagigedo and Escobedo that separate intendants be appointed for the capital provinces of the viceroyalties.[4] A number of articles attempted to clarify the powers of the intendants in relation to the duties of exchequer

[1] See below, 96.
[2] A.G.I., Aud. de Lima 1119, Escobedo to Collar, 27 March 1802, quoting royal order of same date.
[3] A.G.I., Aud. de Lima 1119, royal order, 29 June 1803.
[4] *Ordenanza General formada de orden de S.M. para el gobierno e instrucción de intendentes, subdelegados y demas empleados en Indias* (Madrid, 1803) (Hereafter cited as *Nueva Ordenanza*), arts. 10, 34.

officials, and an important innovation was the incorporation of the scheme produced in Lima for the classification of subdelegacies into three salaried groups.[1]

While preparations were being made for the application of these measures, it was abruptly ordered on 11 January 1804 that the New Ordinance be suspended, following complaints from the Ministry of War that the articles dealing with military affairs were incompatible with recent legislation.[2] Articles 10 and 34, ordering the appointment of provincial intendants in the viceregal capitals, had already been published, however, by a separate decree, and were to be allowed to stand.[3] The intendant of the viceregal capital was to enjoy the same powers as other intendants in his province as a whole, but within the boundaries of the city was limited to the exercise of appellate jurisdiction in treasury and financial affairs, to assistance with the preparation of monthly accounts and to the presidency of the committee of auctions.[4] Control of the tribunals and financial offices of the capital, the receipt and expenditure of funds, the control of shipping, and all matters relating to the general administration of the city and to the affairs of its *cabildo* were reserved to the superintendent. This office was to be filled by the viceroy. One of his responsibilities would be to uphold the intendant's authority and to work in harmony with him.

Chosen as intendant of Lima was Juan María Gálvez, a veteran of the system, who had served as first intendant of Tarma until 1794, and then as intendant of Huancavelica.[5] He received news of his appointment in May 1804, though it was a year later before he took up his new post, because the viceroy, Gabriel de Avilés, refused to grant him permission to do so until he received orders from Spain defining the new

[1] Ibid., arts. 16, 18, 19, 96.
[2] A.G.I., Indif. General 1713, royal order, 11 Jan. 1804. Juan María Gálvez attributed the decision to Godoy's annoyance that the ordinance had been issued without his approval. This fact, asserted Gálvez, was 'generally known throughout the kingdom'. See A.G.I., Aud. de Lima 1115, Gálvez to 'V.A.', no. 2, 24 Feb. 1809.
[3] A.G.I., Indif. General 1713, royal decree, 29 June 1803.
[4] A.G.I., Aud. de Lima 613, royal order, 22 Oct. 1804. See also C. A. Romero (ed.), *Memoria del virrey del Perú, marqués de Avilés* (Lima, 1901), 66.
[5] See below, 241–2.

intendant's precise duties.[1] This initial difficulty indicated clearly that although the intention behind the appointment of an intendant for the capital was good—the basic aims were to streamline administration and to relieve the viceroy of overwork—the practical effect was more likely to be to cause a wide range of disputes and clashes of jurisdiction between intendant and viceroy.

Avilés had arrived in Lima in 1801 to succeed Osorno, who had died in office.[2] An experienced administrator, who had played a key role in the suppression of the Túpac Amaru rising and in the administrative reform which followed, the new viceroy adopted an attitude to the intendants similar to that of his predecessor, one of approval, with occasional criticism of individuals.[3] In the wider field he entered into a number of disputes over the nomination and control of subdelegates.[4] But his only general complaint against the intendants was that they failed to exercise an adequate control over the conduct of exchequer affairs.[5] The intendant of Tarma, he claimed, was particularly at fault: in his province the accumulated debt owing to the department of *azogues* alone was 327,812 pesos, but the intendant was taking no effective action against debtors, partly because of an inability to work harmoniously with the provincial treasury officials. When this complaint was considered by the Council of the Indies, Escobedo expressed the hope that the provisions of the New Ordinance would make it easier to achieve such co-operation.[6] He criticized, however, the tendency to blame the intendants for all problems, since, in financial affairs at least, ultimate responsibility rested with the viceroy, as superintendent.

With this exception, Avilés's relations with the intendants outside of Lima were good. His relations with the intendant of Lima began badly and increasingly grew worse. The arrival in Lima of Gálvez was itself marked by an ominous dispute. The intendant considered it necessary to have a *teniente asesor*, who would advise him on the administration of appellate

[1] A.G.I., Aud. de Lima 1117, Gálvez to Soler, no. 43, 18 Oct. 1804, and no. 1, 8 June 1805.   [2] Romero, op. cit., vii–xii.
[3] See above, 24–8.   [4] See below, 86–8.
[5] A.G.I., Indif. General 1713, Avilés to crown, 23 March 1803.
[6] Ibid., marginal note of Escobedo, 9 Jan. 1804.

jurisdiction in the city and on general judicial affairs for the rest of the province.[1] The viceroy agreed but, instead of accepting Gálvez's nominee, appointed to the post an official who already dealt with litigation arising from the affairs of various financial tribunals. Despite the intendant's protests, this step was upheld in Madrid, since it avoided duplication of officials, thereby saving money.[2] In itself the incident was trivial, but it was significant in the wider context, since it made clear the viceroy's determination to emphasize his authority over the intendant at an early stage.

Gálvez was clearly dissatisfied with the subservient role he was forced to play in the capital. In December 1805 he sent to Spain an account of the disorderly administration of Lima's theatres and other places of amusement, complaining that tickets for the bullring were sold at inflated prices.[3] He considered that he, as intendant, should have authority to control such matters. The reaction of the official who dealt with the complaint was to express surprise that the intendant should question the viceroy's authority merely because he found it difficult to obtain tickets to take his family to a bull fight.[4] More serious was the intendant's complaint that the viceroy was referring to him only a few of the cases involving appellate jurisdiction in exchequer affairs, while reserving the most important matters for his own jurisdiction.[5] In general it seems clear that Avilés resented the presence of an intendant in the capital and made little real effort to work amicably with him; on the other hand it seems equally clear that Gálvez took up his post with a sense of grievance. He had lost the zeal and directness of purpose displayed twenty years earlier; now he increasingly made trouble over minor matters.

The arrival in Lima in July 1806 of a new viceroy, José Fernando de Abascal y Sousa, did nothing to improve the situation. Gálvez alleged in June 1808 that, despite being overburdened with work, Abascal delegated only minor matters

[1] A.G.I., Aud. de Lima 613, Gálvez to Soler, no. 2, 23 June 1803.
[2] A.G.I., Aud. de Lima 613, Casa Valencia to Soler, 7 June 1806.
[3] A.G.I., Aud. de Lima 1117, Gálvez to Soler, no. 7, 21 Dec. 1805.
[4] Ibid., marginal note.
[5] A.G.I., Aud. de Lima 1117, Gálvez to Soler, no. 8, 23 Dec. 1805. A.N.P., Superior Gobierno 30, *cuaderno* 947, Gálvez to Avilés, no. 20, 15 June 1805.

to his jurisdiction.[1] Like Avilés, he dealt personally with important cases, such as those arising from smuggling, without consulting the intendant. Gálvez realized that formal protests to the viceroy were pointless, since they led only to disputes which were always resolved in the latter's favour. Accusing Abascal of a 'complete greed for power', he alleged that as a result of his attitude 'the intendant of this capital is a mere subdelegate'.[2] In the following year Gálvez protested that Abascal saw the very existence of his office as an insult to viceregal authority, and was determined to prevent him fulfilling any useful function.[3] The viceroy's alleged lack of co-operation meant that his presence in Lima was 'truly useless'.[4]

Gálvez's dejection increased throughout 1809. He was still dissatisfied with the *teniente asesor* forced upon him by Avilés, and pleaded that the post be given to Bartolomé Bedoya, who had served him in that capacity in Tarma.[5] By then Abascal's contempt for his presence had reached the point where he simply ignored him, refusing to answer the stream of complaints sent by the intendant. Gálvez wrote in April 1809: 'my position exists in name only. The letters which I send to the viceroy, far from having any effect, are answered only with silence'.[6] Shortly afterwards an additional grievance emerged with Abascal's decision that the governor of the *partido* of Huarochirí should no longer be subject to the intendant's authority, but instead should be directly responsible to the viceroy.[7] The step was taken because of a long-standing dispute between Gálvez and the governor over the issue of whether the intendant enjoyed jurisdiction over an area with a military governor appointed by the crown.[8] It was interpreted by Gálvez as an

---

[1] A.G.I., Aud. de Lima 1115, Gálvez to Minister of Finance, no. 20, 23 June 1808.
[2] A.G.I., Aud. de Lima 1115, Gálvez to Minister of Finance, no. 24, 23 Sept. 1808.
[3] A.G.I., Aud. de Lima 1115, Gálvez to 'V.A.', no. 3, 24 Feb. 1809.
[4] A.G.I., Aud. de Lima 1115, Gálvez to 'V.A.', no. 2, 24 Feb. 1809.
[5] A.G.I., Aud. de Lima 1115, Gálvez to crown, no. 4, 24 Feb. 1809.
[6] A.G.I., Aud. de Lima 1115, Gálvez (no addressee), no. 8, 25 Apr. 1809.
[7] A.N.P., Superior Gobierno 33, *cuaderno* 1065, decree of Abascal, 19 May 1809.
[8] A.N.P., Superior Goberno 33, *cuaderno* 1065, Gálvez to Abascal, no. 368, 25 Feb. 1809.

attempt to proceed from ignoring his authority within the city of Lima to restricting it elsewhere in the province.[1]

By royal order of 12 April 1809 Gálvez was instructed to return to Spain and his powers were assigned to the viceroy.[2] No reason was given for the decision, but one factor seems to have been that ministers in Spain drew a logical conclusion from his frequent insistence that he performed no useful function.[3] Basically, however, the order stemmed from well-meant but disruptive attempts of the *Junta Central* to improve administration by removing from office those intendants against whom complaints had been made. Gálvez was not the only one to suffer, since other intendants were similarly removed.[4] The process began, in fact, with the dismissal of Juan Vives y Echeverría, intendant of Huancavelica from 1807, who gave up his post in April 1809, on receipt of the royal order of 4 February 1809.[5] The decision to remove Vives was based in part upon the advice of Abascal, who passed on complaints of despotism and misrule made against the intendant by inhabitants of Huancavelica, with the recommendation that he be found a different post, but not as an intendant, 'because he lacks the required moderation, prudence and judgement'.[6] In both cases it was subsequently decided in the peninsula, in 1811 and 1812, that the intendants had been wrongly removed and should be restored to office.[7] The whole episode did little either to enhance the authority of the intendants or to maintain confidence in the general system of administration.

Vindicated by the Council of the Indies and the Regency, Gálvez returned to Lima in 1812, merely to continue to complain that Abascal refused to allow him to exercise his authority.[8] His attacks upon the viceroy became increasingly more vehement, and in 1815 he accused Abascal of taking advantage of the critical state of the viceroyalty to ignore the

[1] A.G.I., Aud. de Lima 1115, Gálvez (no addressee), no. 11, 23 Aug. 1809.
[2] A.G.I., Aud. de Lima 601, royal order, 12 April 1809.
[3] A.G.I., Aud. de Lima 610, report of Juan Antonio de Santelices (*contador general*), 18 Jan. 1811.
[4] See below, 206–7.
[5] A.G.I., Aud. de Lima 602, report of Council of the Indies, 26 Feb. 1812.
[6] Ibid. See below, 207–10.   [7] See below, 210.
[8] A.G.I., Aud. de Lima 602, Gálvez (no addressee), 6 March 1812.

laws and rule despotically.¹ It was, in fact, recognized in Spain that Abascal had exceeded the formal limits of his powers and was denying the intendant full use of his jurisdiction, but in view of the precarious financial and political state of Peru it was decided that it would be unwise to undermine viceregal authority.² Abascal's replacement by Joaquin de la Pezuela had no real effect upon the intendant's position, and he remained virtually powerless until his death in 1820. Reporting his death, Pezuela conceded that an intendant of Lima was required in time of war, so that the viceroy might delegate routine administration to him.³ He believed, however, that the post would be superfluous in peacetime, adding, optimistically, that its existence 'should be provisional, while the present circumstances persist'.

The history of the intendancy of Lima between 1804 and 1820 is mainly a history of continuous disputes between intendant and viceroy. Similarly between 1784 and 1787, when Escobedo served as intendant of Lima and as superintendent, viceroy Croix was unable to reconcile himself to sharing general authority within the capital and economic and financial jurisdiction in the viceroyalty as a whole. Both during and after the creation of the intendancies Croix and Escobedo were able to work together on many matters, but the growing number of disputes between them revealed increasing viceregal hostility to the new administrative structure. Despite this, the recall of Escobedo and the transfer of the superintendency to the viceroy was a consequence of changing policies in Madrid, rather than an admission that this key reform had proved unworkable in Peru. Thereafter Croix's hostility to the intendant system grew more intense, until he came to demand its total abolition. Soon after his arrival in Lima viceroy Gil repeated this demand, but, as practical experience gave a clearer picture of the administrative structure, his attitude moderated. In general subsequent viceroys were satisfied with the intendant system, although all were ready to criticize individual intendants and specific aspects

[1] A.G.I., Aud. de Lima 1116, Gálvez to Miguel de Lardizabal, no. 5, 3 Oct. 1815.
[2] A.G.I., Aud. de Lima 602, report of Council of the Indies, 16 June 1818.
[3] A.G.I., Aud. de Lima 1121, Pezuela (no addressee), no. 474, 28 March 1820.

of policy. Although they showed an uncompromising hostility to the resurrected idea of having a separate intendant in the capital, all were ready to accept the intendant system as a permanent reform. Under it viceregal authority was wider than the framers of the original Ordinance had envisaged. Nevertheless, it was more restricted than before 1784. The wide authority exercised by Abascal was a product of special circumstances; in peacetime the intendant system provided the machinery to make royal authority more effective and viceregal power less arbitrary. The viceroys recognized the greater efficiency in government which the intendants achieved, and themselves became more efficient and less corrupt.

CHAPTER IV

Intendants, Subdelegates and Indians

THE BOURBON programme of imperial reform was a many-sided process. The Ordinance of Intendants itself covered four main spheres of government, with an emphasis on financial administration. In the viceroyalty of Peru, however, the need to purify local government and to improve administration of justice at a provincial level was a particularly strong motive for reform. Indeed it might be argued that, although leading reformers never lost sight of the economic and financial aspects of the reform programme, they realized that their basic problem in Peru was to rid the viceroyalty of the social and administrative abuses for which the *corregidores* had become notorious. These abuses had provided the impetus for the Túpac Amaru rising, and it was recognized by Avilés, Escobedo and Gálvez that the danger of further Indian rebellion would persist as long as the maladministration which had caused it was tolerated by the Spanish government.[1] So strong was the effect on José de Gálvez of the insistence of his advisers in Peru and the viceroyalty of the Río de la Plata that action to deal with the *corregidores* must be prompt and decisive, that in 1783 a significant alteration was made to the Ordinance of Intendants. The original Ordinance established that *corregidores* should be allowed to complete their terms of office, so that the change to administration by intendants and subdelegates would be gradual;[2] the first of the seventeen declarations contained in the modifying royal order of 5 August 1783 ordered that all *corregidores* should be immediately removed from office.[3]

[1] See above, 23–8.
[2] *Ord. Ints.*, art. 8. A *corregidor* normally served a five-year term.
[3] A.G.I., Aud. de Buenos Aires 354, royal order, 5 Aug. 1783, 1st declaration.

This order was scrupulously obeyed in Peru, insofar as circumstances would permit. In some remote areas it was necessary for the intendants to leave *corregidores* in temporary command until suitable replacements could be found.[1] But the general policy ordered by Escobedo and applied by the intendants was to appoint new personnel, even in cases where the *corregidores* had been appointed after the prohibition in 1780 of the *repartimiento* system. For example José Antonio de Zavala, *corregidor* of Piura, was removed from office by the intendant of Trujillo, despite his pleas to be allowed to continue his five year term.[2] The *junta superior* rejected his appeal for reinstatement, on being informed by Escobedo that, although he had not occupied his post until December 1781, Zavala had undertaken 'some business' in his province.[3] In the superintendent's view this fact was the chief reason for Zavala's desire to remain in office, and the chief reason for the need to refuse his request for restoration. Escobedo's general attitude was that reform must be thorough, even if individual *corregidores* were treated harshly, and in only two cases outside of his own province did he give his permission for *corregidores* to remain as subdelegates. In the province of Arequipa the *corregidor* of Arica was to remain in office and to enjoy his salary, but with his powers restricted to those of other subdelegates.[4] Similarly in the province of Trujillo the *corregidor* of Cajamarca was to remain as subdelegate.[5]

It was recognized in the Ordinance of Intendants that the intendants would need subordinates to assist them with the government of their extensive provinces, and provision was made for the appointment of subdelegates, who were to be based in the towns previously governed by *corregidores* and *tenientes de gobernadores*.[6] Their selection was to be left to the intendants and they were to remain in office for as long as the intendants wished to retain them. The authority of each subdelegate was to extend over the whole of the *partido* in which

---

[1] This was the case in the intendancy of Huancavelica—B.N.P., MS c3024, decree of Márquez, 24 Dec. 1784.
[2] A.N.P., Superior Goberno 23, *cuaderno* 646, Zavala to Croix, 18 Jan. 1785.
[3] A.G.I., Aud. de Lima 1110, Escobedo to Sonora, no. 692, 20 May 1786.
[4] A.G.I., Aud. de Lima 1098, Instruction to Menéndez, art. 3.
[5] A.G.I., Aud. de Lima 1098, Instruction to Saavedra, art. 3.
[6] *Ord. Ints.*, art. 9.

his capital was situated, and, like his intendant, he was to enjoy jurisdiction in the four main *causas* of public administration, exchequer, justice and war.[1] It was made clear, however, that this authority was to be exercised on behalf of the intendant. Thus in judicial affairs the subdelegates' responsibility was to make preliminary investigations and prepare documents, but to pass on cases to the intendant for final decision.[2] Further provision was made for the appointment, according to the wishes of intendants, of subdelegates with powers restricted to financial and military affairs.[3]

Nearly all the subdelegates in Peru had jurisdiction in all four *causas*, governing extensive *partidos* from towns previously commanded by *corregidores*. Moreover, in most cases the boundaries of the new subdelegacies were identical with those of the former *corregimientos*. When the intendant of Arequipa applied in 1786 for permission to divide the extensive *partido* of Camaná into two, the *junta superior* rejected the request on the grounds that the profits from the Indian tribute were insufficient to support two subdelegates.[4] This consideration was significant, since the Ordinance made no provision for the payment of fixed salaries to subdelegates. Instead they were to receive three per cent of the tribute collected in their respective *partidos*.[5] In another case division of an old *corregimiento* was permitted. The intendant of Trujillo recommended in 1787 that the *partido* of Cajamarca be divided, since the subdelegate was unable to give sufficient attention to the important mining centre of Hualgayoc.[6] The intendant's inspection had revealed the need for close regulation of the provision of labour and essential materials, and he proposed the creation of a new *partido*, consisting of the mining centre and the seven surrounding villages which provided workers and food supplies. Such an innovation, he believed, would bring about greater efficiency,

---

[1] See J. Comradrán Ruiz, 'Los subdelegados de real hacienda y guerra de Mendoza 1784–1810', *Revista del Instituto del Derecho* (Buenos Aires), x (1959), 82–111.
[2] *Ord. Ints.*, arts. 38, 73.
[3] Ibid., art. 73. Comradrán, op. cit., 87–8.
[4] AGI., Aud. de Lima 1109, Álvarez to Sonora, 20 June 1786.
[5] *Ord. Ints.*, art. 38.
[6] A.G.I., Aud. de Lima 1112, Saavedra to Escobedo, 10 March 1787.

leading to an increase in silver production. Moreover, the mineowners were enthusiastic supporters of the plan, since it would be in their interests to have close at hand an official to provide speedy administration of judicial affairs, and had offered to provide up to 4000 pesos for a subdelegate's salary. The *junta superior* agreed to the creation of the new *partido*, to be called Guambas, but rejected the idea that the subdelegate should be entirely dependent upon the miners for his salary, in case this should lead to disrespect for his authority as a royal judge.[1] It was decided that he should continue to receive his percentage of tribute, and that his income from this source should be made up to 3000 pesos a year by contributions from the miners.

The intendants themselves replaced the *corregidores* of the capital *partidos* of the new provinces. In the province of Tarma, for example, Juan María Gálvez appointed subdelegates to Jauja, Conchucos and other *partidos*, but remained responsible himself for the central area commanded previously by the governor of Tarma.[2] A number of intendants soon discovered, however, that they had little time to deal with the details of administration in their seats of government, and came to the conclusion that it would be convenient to appoint subdelegates, with faculties limited to dealing with exchequer affairs, to relieve them of the burden. Thus in 1785 the intendant of Huancavelica appointed a subdelegate for the town, whose sole job would be to collect the tribute of Indians living in and around Huancavelica.[3] It was decided in 1790 to appoint a subdelegate of Cuzco for a similar purpose.[4]

The *corregimiento* of Lima, covering the city and its immediate vicinity, had been made into a subdelegacy in 1784, but Escobedo had decided that its *corregidor*, Pablo Patrón de Arnao, appointed in 1779, should remain in office as subdelegate.[5] Moreover, since by special privilege the Indians of Lima

[1] A.G.I., Aud. de Lima 1112, Escobedo to Sonora, no, 983, 20 Sept. 1787.
[2] Escobedo would have made Francisco Cuellar, governor of Tarma, the first intendant, but for strong suspicions that he had been involved in illegal trade— A.G.I., Aud. de Lima 1102, Escobedo to Gálvez, 5 April 1785.
[3] A.G.I., Aud. de Lima 1101, Escobedo to Gálvez, no. 495, 5 June 1785.
[4] A.G.M.R.E., Portilla to *cabildo* of Cuzco, 23 Jan. 1790.
[5] A.G.I., Aud. de Lima 620, Gardoqui to Bajamar, 13 Jan. 1792.

were exempt from the obligation to pay tribute, it was decided that the subdelegate should continue to receive the salary previously assigned to the *corregidor*. This amounted to 1572 pesos, of which almost half was paid by the exchequer and the remainder from Indian communal funds. The subdelegate's duties were limited to the management of minor judicial affairs and to aspects of public administration, due to the Indians' exemption from tribute and to the fact that the superintendent controlled military matters.[1] The only other *partido* carrying a fixed salary was Huarochirí, also in the intendancy of Lima, which was commanded by a military governor who received a salary of 4000 pesos.[2] The area had been given this special status after an Indian rising. Although it was pointed out in 1795 that it no longer contained either troops or militia for the governor to organize or hostile Indians for him to fight, no alteration was made to the existing arrangements.[3]

Those appointed as subdelegates were required to be of Spanish blood.[4] Since creoles and peninsular-born Spaniards were included in this definition, there was no legal barrier to the appointment of creoles.[5] It is clear, moreover, that in practice most subdelegates were creoles, although in many cases it is difficult to establish their origins, since it was rarely considered necessary to distinguish between creoles and Europeans. An applicant for appointment would often describe himself simply as '*español*'. Only in the intendancy of Cuzco was there a declared policy of appointing Europeans as subdelegates. The president-intendant Ruiz reported in 1806 that one of the aims of a recent plot, organized by José Manuel de Ubalde and Gabriel Aguilar, had been to have their fellow creole conspirators appointed as subdelegates.[6] The president thought it imperative that his subdelegates, especially those administering remote *partidos*, such as Quispicanches, Tinta,

[1] Consequently the marqués de Bajamar insisted on referring to the district as a *corregimiento*—A.G.I., Aud. de Lima 620, Bajamar to Gardoqui, 6 Feb. 1792.
[2] A.G.I., Aud. de Lima 1068, 'Razón de los salarios y cargos de Real Hacienda'.
[3] A.G.I., Indif. General 1525, Joaquin Bonet to viceroy, 29 Dec. 1795.
[4] *Ord. Ints.*, art. 9.
[5] Comradrán, op. cit., 83–5.
[6] A.G.I., Aud. de Cuzco 7, Ruiz to crown, no. 89, 29 May 1806.

Chumbivilcas and Aymaraes, should be 'Europeans entirely satisfactory to me for their ability, loyalty, zeal and activity'. He gave details of steps taken to ensure the appointment of subdelegates with these qualifications. There is, however, no evidence that other intendants shared Ruiz's preference for Europeans; on the contrary, due note was taken of Escobedo's advice that these posts should normally be filled by 'the natives of the country'.[1]

The selection of subdelegates was initially a matter for the individual intendants, and they were to remain in office as long as the intendants wished, although in each case their decisions required the approval of the *junta superior* and the superintendent in Lima.[2] While Escobedo filled the superintendency this procedure seemed to present few difficulties. But after the transfer of the superintendency to the viceroy the whole question of appointment and removal of subdelegates was complicated by the wider struggle between the viceroys and the intendants. Part of the general policy of restoring authority to the viceroys involved the gradual reduction of the intendants' control over their subdelegates. In the early months of 1788 four cases arose in which the *junta superior*, now headed by the viceroy, upheld the appeals for restoration made by subdelegates who had been dismissed from office by their intendants.[3] One of them, Gregorio Jalavera, was restored to the *partido* of Vilcashuamán, in the intendancy of Huamanga, despite the fact that he had undertaken a *repartimiento*, since the *junta* considered that a first offence of this nature was not sufficiently serious to justify dismissal.[4]

With the creation of such a precedent, the *junta superior* was flooded with appeals from subdelegates who considered themselves harshly treated by their intendants.[5] In the belief that some check needed to be imposed upon what it regarded as the capricious abuse of authority by intendants, the *junta*

[1] A.G.I., Aud. de Lima 1117, Escobedo to Croix, 1 July 1784.
[2] *Ord. Ints.*, art. 9.
[3] A.N.P., Superior Gobierno 20, *cuaderno* 547, report of *fiscal* Viderique, 21 April 1788.
[4] Ibid. It was added that even repetition of the offence would not automatically bring dismissal.
[5] A.G.I., Aud. de Lima 695, Gil to Porlier, no. 20, 30 June 1790.

ordered that no subdelegate could be removed from office without its approval. Moreover, for every new appointment an intendant would be required to present a list of three candidates to the viceroy, and it would be the latter's responsibility to make the final choice. Viceroy Gil believed that the adoption of this method provided a just measure of protection for subdelegates, by assuring them a reasonable tenure of office, but recognized that it also allowed a number who governed badly to remain in office, because of the difficulty which the intendants faced of proving cases against them.[1] He suggested in 1790 the introduction of a five-year term of office, which would reduce the dangers of the 'resentments and mistakes' made possible by too long a period of command in the same place. Subdelegates who governed well would benefit from moving to new *partidos* every five years, while less impressive officials could be made to retire at the end of their terms, to make way for the many applicants seeking appointment. Although profits were small, the subdelegacies were eagerly sought after, since few other forms of employment carrying similar status were available to the viceroyalty's inhabitants. Gil asked that the crown confirm the adoption of the new system of appointment, known as the *terna*, but with the reservation, that, if the viceroy so desired, he could ignore all three candidates suggested by an intendant, 'because he who commands a kingdom must have sufficient authority to appoint and remove officials without being obliged to make his reasons known to the public'. Gil's advice was closely followed. The royal order of 19 January 1792 approved the *terna* method and laid down a five-year term of office.[2] The viceroy was given authority to ignore the proposals of the intendants, but whenever he adopted this course of action was to provide the crown with a detailed account of his reasons.

Gil made extensive use of these reserve powers. In 1793 fifteen of the subdelegates appointed were men selected by the viceroy, not by the intendants.[3] Gil explained that in some cases none of the candidates proposed by the intendants had seemed suitable for office. In others, however, he had been

[1] Ibid.   [2] Lynch, op. cit., 75.
[3] A.G.I., Aud. de Lima 707, Gil to Acuña, no. 11, 5 Jan. 1793.

guided in part by the fact that the subdelegacies offered him the only opportunity to obey the numerous royal orders he received instructing him to provide individuals with suitable employment.[1] This explanation was not well received in Spain, and the viceroy was strongly criticized for having deviated from the intendants' nominations without providing adequate reasons or detailed information about the individuals whom he considered worthy of appointment.[2] Moreover, in some cases he had waited over two years before informing the crown of appointments he had made, so that by the time royal confirmation of these reached Peru the five-year term of office would become one of eight years. In the case of Joaquin de Aranzaval, subdelegate of Jauja, on the other hand, Gil had removed him before the end of his five-year term, by counting it from the date of issue of the *título*, rather than from the date of the actual assumption of authority. It was realized that such a policy, if extended, could be used to justify the dangerous principle of service by substitutes.

This comprehensive condemnation of viceregal policy reached Peru after the replacement of Gil by Osorno. The latter acknowledged its receipt, promising not to repeat the errors of his predecessor.[3] He pointed out, however, that it would be frequently necessary to ignore the nominations of the intendants, particularly in the case of the smaller intendancies. In his view suitable candidates were to be found only in Lima, Cuzco and Arequipa. Those residents of smaller cities and towns seeking employment were in most cases 'of the type known as men of fortune'. Some were merchants, seeking an opportunity to renew the *repartimientos*. Such men were nominated for subdelegacies by the intendants merely because of the enforced friendships made necessary by residence in small, isolated towns. Even in the larger settlements, however, it was difficult to obtain suitable candidates. Talented men, possessing the capacity and qualifications to serve the crown, were reluctant to accept appointment, because material rewards would be small: 'Since these subdelegacies and former *corregimientos* have

[1] A.G.I., Aud. de Lima 707, Gil to Acuña, no. 30, 20 July 1793.
[2] A.G.I., Aud. de Lima 648, Llaguno to viceroy, 30 Nov. 1795.
[3] A.G.I., Aud. de Lima 647, Osorno to Llaguno, no. 14, 26 Sept. 1796.

ceased to be valuable and profitable, important army officers and others of honourable birth no longer present themselves for service'. This lack of profitability was, Osorno suggested, the basic cause of the frequent disputes over whether occupancy should be counted from the date of the issue of the *título* or from that of the assumption of authority. Since subdelegates were unable to save for their retirement, they were reluctant to relinquish posts which provided some income, however inadequate. The viceroy's suggestion for the resolution of the particular problem of length of service was that the term of office should become one of six years, to allow one year of temporary occupation, while awaiting royal confirmation, and five years of proprietary tenure.

The crown adopted this suggestion in 1797, but offered no remedy for the problem of reconciling the intendants' demands to be allowed to select subdelegates with viceregal insistence on the right to reject their nominations.[1] The right to appoint subdelegates implied, too, the right to dismiss them. A serious clash developed in 1797 between Osorno and the intendant of Trujillo, Vicente Gil, because the viceroy refused to agree to the dismissal of the subdelegate of Piura, Joaquin de Rosillo Velarde, despite the production of evidence that he had imposed illegal taxes upon his *partido*'s inhabitants.[2] When the intendant threatened to use his right to communicate directly with the crown on the issue, Osorno accused him of insubordination, threatening imprisonment if he continued to complain.[3] In this and other cases the basic problem of ensuring good government at a local level became involved in the continuing struggle for authority between intendants and viceroys.

While explaining his reasons for ignoring the nominations made by the intendant of Tarma to the vacant subdelegacy of Cajatambo, viceroy Avilés complained in 1802 that the persons proposed by the intendants were usually those who paid most for the privilege.[4] Subdelegacies obtained by means of this 'public and scandalous commerce' usually cost between 4000

[1] A.G.I., Aud. de Lima 647, royal order, 21 June 1797.
[2] A.G.I., Aud. de Lima 763, Vicente Gil to Llaguno, 26 Jan. 1797.
[3] A.G.I., Aud. de Lima 763, Osorno to Gil, 17 March 1797.
[4] A.G.I., Aud. de Lima 623, Avilés to Minister of Grace and Justice, no. 37, 26 Oct. 1802.

and 6000 pesos, money which the subdelegates recovered by oppressing the inhabitants, especially the Indians, of their *partidos*. The general allegation was repeated in 1808 by the president of Cuzco, Francisco Muñoz de San Clemente.[1] He reported that on his journey to Peru from Buenos Aires he heard it said that in Peru subdelegacies were sold 'like pears in the marketplace', an allegation which seemed to be borne out when he received a number of offers for the vacant subdelegacy of Abancay. In the following year, 1809, it was alleged, admittedly by an unreliable informant, that the intendant of Arequipa, Bartolomé María de Salamanca, had sold a subdelegacy for between 4000 and 8000 pesos.[2] In all except the final case these allegations were couched in general terms, and were unsupported by specific examples. Nevertheless, Avilés was convinced that the problem was a real one, and that the powers of the viceroy to control it were inadequate. He sought the right to appoint and remove subdelegates at will, without the obligation to provide reasons for his decisions, since 'often they are difficult to prove, or it is not convenient that they be made public'.[3]

The viceroys insisted that unless the appointment of subdelegates was put into their hands the intendants would be dominated by local interests and social and economic pressures. The intendants, on the other hand, complained that the viceroys were ignorant of local needs, conditions and reputations, and that their interference made it impossible for the intendants to control the subdelegates. Demetrio O'Higgins, intendant of Huamanga, complained in 1803 that Avilés had ignored his nominations for the subdelegacies of Cangallo and Huanta, appointing instead Juan Alcensio Monesterio and Juan Miguel Escurra.[4] The latter, he continued, was notorious for his maladministration of justice and mistreatment of the Indians, and had made a *repartimiento* of mules. The intendant's attempts

[1] B.N.P., MS D10290, Abascal to intendant of Huancavelica, 28 June 1808, enclosing a recently received, but undated, letter from Muñoz.
[2] A.G.I., Aud. de Lima 627, Santiago Aguirre to crown, 10 April 1809. See below, 210–1.
[3] A.G.I., Aud. de Lima 623, Avilés to Minister of Grace and Justice, no. 37 26 Oct. 1802.
[4] A.G.I., Aud. de Lima 763, O'Higgins to Cavallero, 24 Oct. 1803.

to prevent Escurra from continuing this commercial activity, by banning the import of mules into his *partido*, were frustrated by the viceroy's decision that the ban must be raised, on the grounds that it would hamper legitimate trade. Under cover of what O'Higgins interpreted as viceregal protection, a further 2000 mules were forcibly distributed in the *partido*.[1] Both Escurra and Monesterio knew that they owed their appointment to Avilés; they also knew that the intendant was powerless to dismiss them. As a consequence they had no respect for his authority and ignored his orders, a situation which led O'Higgins to complain bitterly: 'the intendancies have become reduced to mere skeletons, destined solely to circulate the orders of others.... The superior government corresponds directly with these two subdelegates, ignoring the authority of the intendant of Huamanga.'

Many subdelegacies were filled by amicable agreement between the viceroys and the intendants. However, the system for appointment and control was defective, providing ample scope for disagreements on both points of detail and matters of principle. The basic struggle for authority between viceroys and intendants was complicated by indecision and vacillation in Spain, where ministers produced compromises which satisfied neither side. Viceroys, intendants, the central government and subdelegates themselves frequently proclaimed their concern to secure good local government. In practice, behind the constant disputes over methods of provision, length of service and other details, the corrupt local government which had characterized the old system of administration in Peru was allowed to continue under the new.

The most notorious abuses practised by the *corregidores* had been associated with the *repartimiento* system, forbidden in Peru first by the decree of Jáuregui in 1780, then by royal order, and subsequently by the Ordinance of Intendants.[2] In 1783 the crown had second thoughts about the complete ban on official trade with the Indians, largely as a result of complaints from the viceroy of the Río de la Plata that without stimulation they

[1] A.G.I., Aud. de Lima 764, O'Higgins to Cavallero, 3 Dec. 1804, enclosing a copy of the viceregal decree of 26 May 1804.
[2] *Ord. Ints.*, art. 9. See above, 13–16, 20–1.

would refuse to work.[1] For the Indian sector was important not only as a market for consumer goods but also as a source of labour. To procure labour it was necessary to advance credit and equipment to the Indians with sanctions as to their use. Under the old system officials in collusion with merchants forced goods on the Indians and in effect forced them to work in order to defray the cost. Thus the Indians had been turned into producers as well as consumers, but also into rebels when the abuse of the *repartimiento* system became intolerable. It was now ordered that arrangements be made to provide those Indians who needed them with mules, iron and tools, on credit and at cost price, at the expense of the exchequer.[2] The intendants, after consulting treasury officials, were to select distribution points and appoint trustworthy officials to undertake the operations, which were to be given 'the name of *socorros*, but never of *repartimientos*. . .'.

Escobedo welcomed this modification of the original ban, describing it as 'a resolution which could come only from the generous heart of our sovereign'.[3] His plan was to prepare a scheme whereby the *consulado* of Lima would buy and distribute merchandise, while local treasury ministers would collect the money in instalments to pay for the goods provided.[4] The quantities and prices of goods, as well as the places for distribution, would be decided, after consideration of reports on local needs provided by the subdelegates, by a joint committee of the *consulado* and the *junta superior*.[5]

The *consulado* agreed to the scheme in principle, but a week later Escobedo received a new royal order, issued in June 1784 as a result of the unenthusiastic response of the intendants of the viceroyalty of the Río de la Plata to the general idea of *socorros*.[6] This restricted the scope of any possible plan, insisting, for example, that goods could be provided only as a result of

---

[1] Lynch, op. cit., 197.
[2] A.G.I., Aud. de Buenos Aires 354, royal order, 5 Aug. 1783.
[3] A.G.I., Aud. de Lima 1098, Escobedo to Gálvez, no. 323, 20 Aug. 1784.
[4] A.G.I., Aud. de Lima 1099, Escobedo to Gálvez, no. 307, 16 July 1784.
[5] A.G.I., Aud. de Lima 1098, Escobedo to Gálvez, no. 323, 20 Aug. 1784, art. 28 of enclosed plan.
[6] A.G.I., Aud. de Lima 1097, Escobedo to Gálvez, no. 383, 20 Dec. 1784. See also Lynch, op. cit., 198.

voluntary requests from the Indians.¹ This and other safeguards made unfeasible the comprehensive system envisaged by Escobedo.² In his view *socorros* were essential for a number of reasons. Simply at an economic level, he argued, the abolition of the *repartimiento* had created shortages, especially of mules, which were encouraging the Indians to be idle. But, unless some way could be found to stimulate them to work and produce, the plans of the intendants to bring about an economic revival in Peru would be doomed to failure. Escobedo defended his scheme on social grounds, too, suggesting that, if it were abandoned, it would be replaced by the greater evil of the revival of the old *repartimiento* system. The scramble to obtain appointments as subdelegates convinced him that those who sought the posts intended to behave as the *corregidores* had done, an opinion borne out, he continued, by the subdelegates' failure to inform the intendants of the needs of their *partidos*, since they wanted, not an orderly, regulated distribution of goods, but the opportunities to trade without checks. A further consideration behind Escobedo's scheme was the vague idea of making a small profit which might be used to supplement the salaries of the subdelegates.

Escobedo's plans were turned down by the crown in 1785, on the grounds that the Indians should not be obliged to accept goods involuntarily.³ However, it had been abandoned already by Escobedo before this decision was known in Peru, due to disagreement with the *consulado* over the percentage of profit which it should be allowed to make on the operations.⁴ By 1786, then, it had been clearly established that the official distribution of goods to the Indians was unacceptable to the crown in principle and to the merchants of Lima in practice. As the old *repartimiento* system had been abolished by the Ordinance, commercial relations between Spaniards and Indians were to be governed only by free and private enterprise. Despite misgivings about the effectiveness of his orders, it was to this that Escobedo now gave his full support.⁵ Sub-

[1] B.M., Eg. MS 1815, ff. 109–12, royal order, 8 June 1784.
[2] A.G.I., Aud. de Lima 1097, Escobedo to Loreto, 16 Dec. 1784.
[3] A.G.I., Aud. de Lima 1107, Escobedo to Gálvez, no. 649, 1 April 1786, acknowledging royal orders of 23 July 1785 and 18 Sept. 1785.   [4] Ibid.
[5] A.G.I., Aud. de Lima 1110, Escobedo to Sonora, no. 689, 20 May 1786, enclosing decree of *junta superior* that only private enterprise was to be permitted.

delegates who sought permission to co-operate with merchants were firmly rebuked, despite the fact that, since the Indians generally had insufficient capital to pay the full cash price on goods they obtained, merchants were reluctant to provide them on credit unless assured of the support of '*la justicia*' to enforce the payment of instalments.[1] The subdelegate of Yauyos, for example, was refused permission to assist with the credit sale of 1500 mules, even though it was recognized that a serious shortage existed in his *partido*.[2]

Some subdelegates, it is clear, were prepared to abide by the decisions of the *junta superior* on this matter. They made genuine efforts to govern according to the letter of the Ordinance of Intendants, and a number acquired excellent records in public administration and local government. The subdelegate of Paruro, Francisco Bruno López, for example, was warmly praised by the president of Cuzco in 1802 for his honest administration of justice, fair collection of tribute, encouragement of religion and improvement of public administration in the villages under his jurisdiction.[3] Similarly José María Egaña, the *teniente de policía* of Lima for nearly twenty years, subsequently became a very successful subdelegate of Chota, in the province of Trujillo. The Indians' representatives asked in 1812 that he should be allowed to serve a second term, emphasizing that 'he undertakes trade in none of the villages'.[4] Many similar examples could be given. But it is significant that the Indians of Chota should consider it a mark of Egaña's distinction that he had not distributed merchandise to the villages. There is, in fact, abundant evidence that for the Indians of the viceroyalty as a whole the new system of administration brought few improvements. Many subdelegates, especially in the *sierra*, continued the *repartimientos* and other abuses, and the intendants, as a result of indifference, or impotence, or both, failed to check their activities.

[1] An alternative view was that trade would now flourish, since it was open to all merchants rather than to the handful of former monopolists—B.M., Add. MS 13981, ff. 23-4, 'Noticias del comercio del Perú ... por un buen patriota español...'.
[2] A.G.I., Aud. de Lima 1107, Escobedo to Juan Ignacio Rodríguez, 7 Jan. 1786.
[3] A.G.I., Aud. de Cuzco 7, Ruiz to Cavallero, no. 21, 7 April 1802.
[4] A.G.I., Aud, de Lima 804, the 'Alcaldes, procuradores y demas naturales de la provincia de Chota...' to crown.

Juan de la Guisla Larrea, the former *corregidor* of Cajamarca, was allowed by Escobedo to remain in office as subdelegate. In 1787 he was charged by the intendant of Trujillo with having arranged for the distribution of goods to Indians in his *partido*.[1] The intendant's decision to suspend him from office was upheld while Escobedo remained superintendent;[2] his replacement by Croix, a development welcomed by Guisla, led to the subdelegate's restoration.[3] It seems that the standards of local administration were equally low elsewhere in the province of Trujillo. Considerable evidence was produced in 1797 to show that the subdelegate of Piura was making illegal demands upon the Indians, forcing them, for example, to purchase licences before they were allowed to grow sugar.[4] In this case, too, the intendant's efforts to dismiss the offending official were frustrated by the viceroy.[5] Faced with viceregal obstruction, some intendants lost their reforming zeal. When it was again alleged in 1802 that the subdelegate of Cajamarca mistreated Indians in his *partido*, extorting money and making them provide unpaid labour, the judicial official who made the denunciation added that, although aware of the abuses, the intendant made no effort to prevent them.[6]

What occurred in the province of Trujillo occurred in other provinces, on perhaps an even greater scale. In Huancavelica the subdelegate of Angaraes used the announcement of the intendant's plan to tour the province as an excuse to collect contributions from the Indians towards his expenses, on the grounds that this had been the practice when the *corregidor* made a tour.[7] The inability of the *audiencia* of Cuzco to prevent the *repartimientos* undertaken by subdelegates in the province of

[1] A.N.P., Superior Gobierno 20, *cuaderno* 527, Saavedra to *junta superior*, 25 Nov. 1787.
[2] A.N.P., Superior Gobierno 20, *cuaderno* 527, decree of *junta*, 5 Dec. 1787.
[3] A.N.P., Superior Gobierno 20, *cuaderno* 527, decree of *junta*, 14 Jan. 1789. In his letter of 5 Jan. 1788 Guisla referred to his need that 'en el dia ... sea ocupado este sup'r empleo por un Gefe de la grandeza de V.E.'
[4] A.G.I., Aud. de Lima 802, *cabildo* of Piura to crown, 20 April 1797.
[5] See above, 86.
[6] A.N.P., Superior Gobierno 30, *cuaderno* 942, Manuel Fernando Soriano, *protector* of the Indians of Cajamarca, to José Pareja, *fiscal* and *protector general*, 8 Nov. 1802.
[7] B.N.P., MS c3170, Márquez to Gregorio Delgado, 26 Oct. 1785; Delgado to Márquez, 3 Nov. 1785.

Puno had been the chief reason for the province's transfer to the viceroyalty of Peru.[1] Abuses continued, however, after the transfer. In 1801, for example, it was alleged that Antonio Coello y Doncel, subdelegate of Azángaro, was using his tribute money to buy unminted gold from miners, and was making Indians work without pay.[2] After further investigation the intendant removed Coello from office, only to become involved in a dispute with the *audiencia* of Cuzco over the issue of whether jurisdiction lay in his hands or with the *audiencia*. The misdeeds of the subdelegate were forgotten, as the *audiencia* rebuked the intendant, fined his legal adviser and ordered the subdelegate's restoration.[3]

The general inspection of the province of Huamanga, completed by O'Higgins in 1802, revealed that the Indians still suffered at the hands of the subdelegates, who continued to forcibly distribute various commodities, especially mules.[4] To have them dismissed, the intendant was required to provide the viceroy with documented proof of their misdeeds, a difficult task, since the subdelegates often conducted their commercial operations through third parties. Similarly, even though the intendant might be aware of their faulty administration of justice, this, too, was often difficult to prove to the satisfaction of the viceroy, since subdelegates often failed to pass on official records of the cases which came before them.[5]

There is little doubt that many subdelegates did continue to distribute goods forcibly to the Indians, despite the prohibition contained in the Ordinance of Intendants. Such behaviour did not surprise many observers, however, for the basic flaw in royal policy was to attempt to abolish what had been the main source of income for the *corregidores*, without providing adequate salaries in its place. The honour of serving the crown and three per cent of the tribute were not sufficient rewards for the subdelegates, and many took steps to supplement their incomes by continuing to operate the *repartimientos*. Escobedo pointed out in 1784 that it would be difficult to

[1] See above, 49–52.
[2] A.G.I., Aud. de Cuzco 7, report of *audiencia*, no. 104, 10 May 1801.   [3] Ibid.
[4] A.G.I., Aud. de Lima 764, O'Higgins to Cavallero, 16 June 1802.
[5] The intendant's chief concern was his own prestige and authority rather than the welfare of the Indians.

obtain worthy subdelegates unless adequate salaries were provided.[1] His recommendation was that the *partidos* should be classified into three groups, with salary scales of 1500, 2000 and 3000 pesos.[2] A system of this type, he argued, would succeed in producing a professional class of subordinate administrators, composed largely of creoles. A subdelegate would serve his first post in one of the *partidos* in the lowest-paid group, but would be able to expect promotion to a higher grade every five years, with the ultimate prospect of appointment as a treasury official or even as an intendant. It would thus be possible to foster within each *partido* the professionalism and integrity which it was hoped the intendants could bring to the provincial capitals. In contrast, the existing arrangements for the remuneration of subdelegates made it clear that they would have the choice of starving or misgoverning, since, if they were to rely solely on their percentage of tribute, few could expect more than 1000 pesos a year.[3] The majority would get between 400 and 600 pesos, while a few could expect less than 100.

While this information was being slowly digested in Spain, a growing amount of evidence was reaching Escobedo to confirm his earlier forebodings. The subdelegate of Chancay, Luís Martínez de Mata, protested in 1786 that the 300 pesos he received for collecting the tribute was inadequate even for the expenses of making the required personal inspection of his *partido*.[4] In passing on the complaint to the Minister of the Indies, Escobedo stressed that the provision of adequate salaries for these officials was 'a matter of the greatest seriousness and importance in the new plan of intendancies'.[5] He assured Sonora of his efforts to prevent the repetition of 'the disorders and old abuses of the former *repartimientos*', but drew his attention to the fact that an inadequate legal income seemed to some subdelegates to justify the continuation of former practices.[6] Although confident that there were no such irregu-

[1] A.G.I., Aud. de Lima 1117, Escobedo to Gálvez, no. 306, 16 July 1784.
[2] A.G.I., Aud. de Lima 1117, Escobedo to Croix, 1 July 1784.
[3] A.G.I., Aud. de Lima 1117, Escobedo to Gálvez, no. 306, 16 July 1784.
[4] A.G.I., Aud. de Lima 974, Martínez de Mata to Croix, 10 Jan. 1786
[5] A.G.I., Aud. de Lima 974, Escobedo to Gálvez, no. 650, 1 April 1786.
[6] A.G.I., Aud. de Lima 974, Escobedo to Sonora, no. 995, 20 Oct. 1787.

INTENDANTS, SUBDELEGATES AND INDIANS 95

larities in his own province, Escobedo was alarmed that other intendants were finding it more difficult to control their subdelegates, a fact illustrated by the growing number of cases coming to the attention of the *junta superior*. The problem would remain, he repeated, until the subdelegates were provided with adequate incomes. The subdelegate of Ica, for example, received 200 pesos a year, a sum inadequate even to pay the salary of his clerk.[1]

These reports of Escobedo, together with further detailed reports sent in 1787 by both the superintendent and the viceroy, were examined in Spain in 1790.[2] The *contador general* informed the Council of the Indies of his admiration for Escobedo's original proposal to divide the *partidos* into three salaried groups, but drew attention to 'the major problem of a shortage of money, and the deficit of the Lima treasury which makes impossible the imposition of this new burden.'[3] Nevertheless, he recommended that a full investigation be made, and it was ordered on 14 December 1790 that copies of the file be sent to each viceroy.[4] Each was to collect evidence and obtain advice from various individuals and financial tribunals in his capital, in particular from the tribunal of accounts and the chief accountant of tributes, and then to provide the crown with the judgement of his *junta superior*.

Viceroy Gil welcomed the investigation and stressed the impossibility of obtaining good subdelegates 'without giving them enough money even to eat properly'.[5] He was clearly in favour of providing decent salaries. So, too, was the tribunal of accounts of Lima, which argued in 1793 that the financial problem could be overcome if the revenue of tribute itself were used for this purpose.[6] It explained that this would not be an innovation, since before 1779 parts of this revenue had been earmarked for specific ends, including not only the maintenance

[1] A.G.I., Aud. de Lima 974, Ramon Urrutia to Escobedo, 11 Oct. 1787.
[2] A.G.I., Aud. de Lima 974, Escobedo to Sonora, no. 1004, 5 Nov. 1787; Croix to Sonora, 16 Nov. 1787.
[3] A.G.I., Aud. de Lima 974, *contador general* to Council, 9 Dec. 1790. The estimated cost of a new salary structure, including those of the intendants and their legal advisers, was 138,000 pesos. Salaries paid to the *corregidores* had cost 83,000.
[4] A.G.I., Aud. de Lima 974, royal order, 14 Dec. 1790.
[5] A.G.I., Aud. de Lima 707, Gil to Acuña, no. 301, 20 July 1793.
[6] A.G.I., Indif. General 1525, report of tribunal of accounts, 12 Jan. 1793.

of churches and the salaries of priests but also the salaries of judicial officials. Moreover, in its flourishing state this branch of the exchequer could easily support an extra burden.[1]

On the instructions of the *junta superior* an official of the tribunal of accounts, Joaquin Bonet, prepared a detailed plan for the provision of salaries, which on its completion in 1795 was passed on to the viceroy.[2] Like Escobedo, Bonet proposed the creation of a three-tier system of subdelegacies, but with smaller salaries, of 1200, 1800 and 2400 pesos, for the respective groups. The plan provided details of the size, population, prosperity and economy of each *partido*, as well as information about its tribute revenue, the value of its former *repartimiento* and the average fees collected for judicial administration. In short Bonet's plan was a detailed document, based upon a thorough assessment of local needs and conditions. As such it was approved by the *junta superior* and submitted in March 1796 to the Minister of Finance, with the recommendation that it be applied in Peru.[3]

Bonet's proposals joined the mass of papers collected during this decade on the intendant system, and were incorporated in the New Ordinance of 1803, which finally gave formal recognition to the need to provide salaries for subdelegates. Article forty-three ordered the application in each viceroyalty of the three-tier scheme, re-affirming the abolition of the *repartimiento* system.[4] Articles forty-four and forty-five gave details of the system for promotion to higher grades of subdelegacies at the end of six-year terms of office.[5] If the New Ordinance had been applied in Peru it could conceivably have raised the standards of local government by correcting abuses which had survived the removal of the *corregidores*. The failure to apply it meant that twenty years work and pressure to put local government on a solid foundation had been wasted. After 1803 officials in both Peru and Spain seem to have resigned themselves to the inevitability of corruption and abuse in local administration, and to have conceded that they were powerless to prevent it.

[1] For details of increase in tribute revenue see below, 111–14.
[2] A.G.I., Indif. General 1525, Bonet to viceroy, 29 Dec. 1795.
[3] A.G.I., Aud. de Lima 1119, *junta superior* to Minister of Finance, 24 March 1796.
[4] *Nueva Ordenanza*, art. 44.   [5] Ibid., arts. 45, 46.

The Council of the Indies, for example, decided in 1807 that it would issue no further prohibition against the *repartimiento* system, even though complaints against its continuation by subdelegates were still reaching Spain, because it had already made its disapproval clear on a number of previous occasions.[1] It contented itself with the fact that prohibitions had been issued, but made no comment on the fact that they were ignored. There are, too, suggestions that intendants accepted the fact that they were powerless to control their subdelegates in this matter, or perhaps that it would be unreasonable of them even to try, in view of the fact that subdelegates were entitled to a decent standard of living. The priest of the parish of Guarocondo, in the *partido* of Abancay, complained bitterly in 1809 that he had been imprisoned, at the order of the president of Cuzco, merely for having opposed the illegal *repartimiento* of the subdelegate, Domingo de Pagasa.[2] The net result of his efforts to protect his parishioners was greater exploitation, since in the priest's absence a new subdelegate, José de Muros, was able to make even greater demands of them.

The report provided in 1812 by the intendant of Tarma, José González de Prada, on the deplorable state of judicial administration in his province was both an admission of his own inability to deal effectively with the problem and an indication that criticisms of the *corregidores* made thirty years earlier could still be applied to the subdelegates.[3] He reported: 'The administration of justice is confused because of the ignorance of the judges; it is slow because of their disinterest and carelessness, and because they are interested solely in their own illegal trade . . . ; it is corrupt because of bribery, venality, ambition and abuse'. González conceded that the organized framework of the *repartimiento* was less rigid than under the *corregidores*, and as a result the degree of compulsion involved was less. But the consequences of this, in his view, were even more pernicious. The *corregidores* had, at least, made the Indians work; the subdelegates contented themselves with making them pay for

[1] A.G.I., Aud. de Lima 1119, report of Council, 7 Feb. 1807.
[2] A.N.P., Superior Gobierno 33, *cuaderno* 1057, report of representative of Dr D'n Juan de Dios Niño de Guzman, undated, but marginal note indicates made in July 1809.
[3] A.G.I., Aud. de Lima 649, González to Ignacio de la Pezuela, 24 Sept. 1812.

goods without bothering about how they obtained the money. As a result, many communities which had been relatively prosperous were now stripped of their wealth and property. Their destitute inhabitants had fallen into idleness, to become 'an insupportable burden' on the state.

In 1811 the Cortes ignored financial logic and abolished the Indian tribute; in 1812 it also abolished the *mita* system and personal service.[1] Although ineffective in practice, these measures aroused hopes in some reformers that there was now the possibility of decisive action to get to grips with the problems of local administration in Peru.[2] The deputy to the Cortes for the province of Puno, Tadeo Garate, gave details in 1814 of the maladministration of justice by subdelegates and of their impositions upon the Indians, and asked that, to remedy this situation, reasonable salaries be provided for the subdelegates.[3] After the restoration of Ferdinand VII, Garate's request was referred to the *contador general* in Madrid. He replied that, although aware that problems existed, he lacked 'sufficient information' to deal with them.[4] The only remedy suggested was that the viceroys should undertake surveys of their provinces, prepare reports and provide the crown with plans for salaries.

In 1814 the standards of local administration in Peru were little better than those which had caused the Túpac Amaru rebellion in 1780. Indeed the support which thousands of Indians gave to the rising in Cuzco in 1814 gives some indication of their continuing discontent.[5] The problem of providing honest, progressive and efficient government at a local level was one which the crown was unable to solve. To a considerable degree responsibility lay with the crown, due to its failure to face up to the fact that local officials denied adequate, legal incomes would obtain money by illegal means. It lay, too, with some intendants, who either governed corruptly themselves or tolerated corruption in their subdelegates. But those intendants who attempted to control the activities of their subdelegates by

[1] For explanation of summoning of Cortes see below, 113–18.
[2] See below, 114. A.G.I., Aud. de Lima 764, decree of Cortes, 9 Nov. 1812, declared abolition of *mita* and personal service.
[3] A.G.I., Aud. de Lima 613, summary of Garate's report, 27 July 1814.
[4] A.G.I., Aud. de Lima 613, report of *contador general*, Aparici, 11 Nov. 1814.
[5] See below, 225–31.

removing offenders from office found their freedom of action increasingly restricted by viceroys, more concerned with controlling patronage than with supporting the intendants' efforts to improve administrative standards. In many cases attempts to discipline subdelegates turned into sterile trials of strength between intendant and viceroy, or intendant and *audiencia*.

The problem of the subdelegates, described by one historian as 'the Achilles heel' of the intendant system, showed above all that neither the crown nor the intendants had solved the problem of enforcing decisions detrimental to the private interests of those entrusted with their application at a local level.[1] The attempt merely caused administrative confusion and disputes in Peru, and underlined the weaknesses of the peninsular authorities. Meanwhile there was no appreciable improvement in the administration of justice and the treatment of the Indians. The ambitious hopes of Avilés, Escobedo, Gálvez and others that the intendant system would bring with it a dramatic reform of local government were unfulfilled.

[1] Navarro, *Intendencias en Indias*, 109.

CHAPTER V

Intendants and the Exchequer

THE OUTBREAK of the Túpac Amaru rebellion in 1780 drew attention to the social problems of government in Peru, and, by making clear to the Spanish crown that the maintenance of internal security would be dependent upon the drastic reform of local government, provided it with a powerful stimulus to introduce the intendant system to the colony as soon as possible. To improve the standard of local administration was one of the main tasks of the new intendants. It was not, however, their sole duty, nor, from a general imperial point of view, their most important function. For the fulfilment of their basic aims of extending royal authority and strengthening imperial security the Bourbon reformers needed money. The success of the whole programme of imperial reform depended on major expansion of crown revenue; this was the goal which motivated the imperial commercial reforms, in the expectation of generating economic growth, which in turn would provide increases in customs revenues. A vital preliminary, however, was the need to reform the outdated, inefficient system of exchequer administration within the empire, so that taxes which had been evaded and revenues which had been usurped by dishonest officials would in future be collected honestly and efficiently, and so that new wealth created by economic expansion could be promptly tapped by the crown. Those entrusted with the fulfilment of these aims were the intendants in their provinces and the superintendents in the viceregal capitals, a fact underlined by the Ordinance of Intendants itself. This was a predominantly financial instruction, indicating clearly the preoccupation of its authors with exchequer affairs.[1]

The application of the Ordinance in Peru was the climax of

[1] *Ord. Ints.*, arts. 72-219.

INTENDANTS AND THE EXCHEQUER 101

a process of investigation and reform of the Peruvian exchequer begun during the government of viceroy Amat.[1] As in other spheres of administration Peru was notorious for the corruption of its exchequer system, and the urgent need to overhaul and purify it was the chief reason for the decision, taken in 1776, to send a *visitador general* to the viceroyalty.[2] Areche's authority in financial affairs was strengthened in 1780 by the transfer to him from the viceroy of the superintendency of economic and financial matters, a key reform subsequently incorporated in the Ordinance of Intendants.[3] With this extra authority he had made considerable progress by the end of 1780 with the reform of the tribunal of accounts in Lima and the reorganization of the provincial exchequer machinery.[4] His work, however, had been disrupted by viceregal opposition and local riots against his innovations, and was finally brought to a halt by the effects of the Túpac Amaru rebellion; the latter committed the superior government to drastically increased military expenditure, while at the same time reducing its income, by interfering with industry, agriculture and trade, and making the collection of taxes impossible in many areas.[5] In the four years 1777-80 exchequer income was 12,717,289 pesos and total expenditure 12,790,577 pesos;[6] in 1782 income was 4,181,489 pesos, while expenditure reached 5,393,057 pesos.[7] Defence was the main item of expenditure in 1782. The preparation of the navy to meet an expected British attack cost 683,651 pesos, but this was overshadowed by the cost of troops, munitions and supplies needed for the suppression of the Indian

[1] See G. Céspedes del Castillo, 'Reorganización de la hacienda virreinal peruana en el siglo XVIII', *Anuario de Historia del Derecho Español*, xxiii (1953), 331.
[2] Céspedes, *Lima y Buenos Aires*, 145.
[3] Céspedes, 'Reorganización de la hacienda virreinal peruana', 334.
[4] Céspedes, *Lima y Buenos Aires*, 160.
[5] See above, 21-3, 29.
[6] Palacio, op. cit., 52. No reliable figures are available for 1779 alone; those for the four year period show the average annual income as 3,179,322 and average expenditure as 3,197,644. But the turnover was undoubtedly higher in the second half of this period—in 1777 income was only 1,724,135 pesos and expenditure 2,070,053 pesos (Céspedes, *Lima y Buenos Aires*, 145)—and income in 1779 was probably about 4,000,000 pesos. The most important point in comparing this with figures for 1782 is not so much the amount of revenue but rather the gulf in the latter year between income and expenditure.
[7] A.G.I., Aud. de Lima 1104, Escobedo to Gálvez, no. 409, 5 Feb. 1785.

rebellion. Escobedo estimated in 1785 that the total cost of these items was 2,582,979 pesos.[1] The deficit of 1,211,568 pesos for 1782 and smaller deficits for other years had to be met by borrowing, usually from the *consulado* or from the funds of the tobacco monopoly.[2] Total borrowing between 1779 and early 1784 amounted to the considerable sum of 2,781,919 pesos, which in itself imposed a further burden upon the stretched resources of the exchequer, since it carried annual interest charges of 81,604 pesos. Debts contracted before 1779 carried further interest charges of 58,305 pesos, giving a total of 139,909 pesos.[3]

Escobedo took office as *visitador* and superintendent in June 1782, at the height of the viceroyalty's political and financial crisis. He arrived in Lima to find that the treasury contained less than 130,000 pesos.[4] Heavy borrowing provided a temporary respite, but he realised that, in the long term, resort to this expedient made the exchequer's plight even more serious. Permanent improvement required eradication of corruption and dishonesty at the centre, greater vigilance and efficiency in the provinces, and a period of peaceful economic expansion to provide new wealth. Between 1782 and 1784 he occupied himself with the reorganization of the exchequer machinery in the provinces, preparing the way for the intendants. Such work he regarded not as a deviation from the main aims of the *visita* but as an integral part of the general programme of exchequer reform with which he had been entrusted. In his general report on all aspects of the *visita* to Peru, submitted to the crown in October 1785, he described the creation of the intendancies as his 'most important aim', and the completion of the task as the *visita*'s ultimate achievement.[5] He remained conscious of the weakness of the Peruvian exchequer, terribly vulnerable to the effects of European warfare, which cut off trade and made necessary increased expenditure on defence. He was cautiously

[1] Ibid., enclosure C.
[2] See G. Céspedes del Castillo, 'La renta del tabaco en el virreinato del Perú', *Revista Historica*, xxi (1954), 162.
[3] A.G.I., Aud. de Lima 1104, Escobedo to Gálvez, no. 409, 5 Feb. 1785, enclosure B.
[4] Ibid.
[5] A.G.I., Aud. de Lima 1102, Escobedo to Gálvez, no. 561, 20 Oct. 1785.

optimistic, however, about future prospects.[1] If extraordinary expenditure could be kept down he was confident that the exchequer would benefit from the intendants' efforts to stimulate economic activity and revenue collection in their provinces.

The Ordinance of Intendants made it clear that the control of exchequer affairs in the provinces was to be the responsibility of the intendants, who were granted the exercise of contentious jurisdiction, previously enjoyed by local treasury officials, in cases arising from exchequer matters.[2] The intendants were directly responsible to the superintendent in the viceregal capital, and he in his turn was responsible to the Minister of the Indies in Madrid.[3] In his capital the superintendent was to preside over a weekly *junta superior de real hacienda*, composed of the regent, *fiscal* and one *oidor* of the *audiencia*, the dean of the tribunal of accounts and the chief accountant of the treasury of Lima.[4] The function of this powerful committee would be to assist the superintendent in general economic and financial affairs, to co-ordinate for the whole viceroyalty the administration of justice in fiscal matters, and to supervise the financial aspects of military organization.[5] Within the provinces the subdelegates were to be judges of first instance in exchequer cases. Appeals from their decisions were to be made to the intendants, while appeals from the decisions of the intendants could go only to the *junta superior*.[6] In his provincial capital each intendant was to hold a weekly *junta de gobierno*, attended by the chief treasury ministers of the province, for the examination of the management and progress of each branch of the exchequer.[7] At the first meeting of each month the previous month's accounts were to be examined, but the *junta*'s role was to be purely advisory, with responsibility for final decisions resting with the intendant.[8] Further provision was made for the formation of a *junta provincial de real hacienda*, composed of the intendant, his legal adviser and the chief treasury officials, which was to meet only when the intendant sought to use provincial funds for extraordinary expenditure.[9]

[1] A.G.I., Aud. de Lima 1104, Escobedo to Gálvez, no. 409, 5 Feb. 1785.
[2] *Ord. Ints.*, art. 72.
[3] Ibid., art. 219.
[4] Ibid., art. 3.
[5] Ibid., art. 5.
[6] Ibid., arts. 73–4.
[7] Ibid., arts. 204–5.
[8] Ibid., art. 207.
[9] Ibid., art. 100.

Each province was to have a principal subtreasury, usually in its capital, subordinate to the general viceregal treasury in Lima, but superior to subordinate subtreasuries which, if necessary, might be created elsewhere in the province.[1] In applying this part of the Ordinance Escobedo adapted it slightly to meet the special needs of Peru, and by 1784 it had been established that each of the provincial capitals, except for Tarma and Huancavelica, should have a principal subtreasury.[2] The chief subtreasury for the province of Tarma was to remain in the important mining centre of Pasco, where, it was hoped, the change of personnel enforced by Escobedo would eradicate the proverbial inefficiency and corruption. A second subtreasury in the province, at Jauja, was closed with the agreement of the intendant.[3] The closure of superfluous subtreasuries was a process begun by Areche and continued by Escobedo. Areche had closed that of Piura in 1782, a decision confirmed by Escobedo, leaving the subtreasury of Trujillo as the only one for the province.[4] He confirmed, too, the closure of the subtreasury of Cailloma, in the province of Arequipa, but allowed the subordinate subtreasury of Arica to remain open for the collection of the port's *alcabala* revenue. An innovation of Areche's which Escobedo dismantled was the creation in some parts of the viceroyalty of *administraciones de rentas unidas*, from which treasury officials collected, in addition to their normal revenues, the customs and sales taxes previously collected from the *aduanas*, or customs houses. The experiment was not a success; indeed it caused confusion. In Cuzco, therefore, Escobedo re-established the subtreasury, and formed a new *administración de alcabalas* for the collection of sales taxes and the administration of state monopolies.[5] To complete the structure of exchequer machinery in the provinces he made special arrangements for the provinces of Huamanga and Huancavelica. Under the old system of administration the subtreasury of Huancavelica had dealt with the collection and accounting of revenue for the whole bishopric of Huamanga.

[1] Ibid., art. 91.
[2] A.G.I., Aud. de Lima 1102, Escobedo to Gálvez, no. 561, 20 Oct. 1785.
[3] A.G.I., Aud. de Lima 1104, Escobedo to Gálvez, no. 473, 5 May 1785.
[4] A.G.I., Aud. de Lima 1102, Escobedo to Gálvez, no. 561, 20 Oct. 1785.
[5] Ibid.

With the division of the diocese into two intendancies it was decided to replace the subtreasury with a *contaduría de azogues* to deal with the financial aspects of the mining and distribution of mercury, and to establish a new principal subtreasury in Huamanga to deal with exchequer affairs for both provinces.[1]

The rationalization of the location of subtreasuries was accompanied by zealous efforts to improve their efficiency and to eradicate corruption, a task which involved changes in both personnel and organization. The general subtreasury of Lima, Escobedo's particular responsibility, was reorganized into specialist departments, despite the opposition of its staff to the alteration of traditional practices.[2] Since the poverty of officials had been one of the causes of maladministration in the past, Escobedo increased salaries, providing officials of the Lima treasury with annual salaries of 4000 pesos, and the two chief officials of each principal subtreasury with salaries of 2000 pesos.[3] As well as its subtreasury each province had a separate office, usually known as the *administración de rentas unidas de alcabalas y tabacos*, to deal with the collection of *alcabala* and *almojarifazgo*, taxes on sales and trade, and with the revenue of the state monopolies of tobacco, powder, playing-cards and stamped paper.[4] Provision was made for the establishment of subordinate offices in the *partidos*, where necessary. Supervision of these offices was just as much the responsibility of the intendants as was control of the subtreasuries. The powers of contentious jurisdiction previously enjoyed by customs officials were transferred to them, and they were to handle all cases arising from contraband, whether by land or sea.[5] This provision made superfluous the *dirección de alcabalas*, which existed in Lima for the general administration of this branch of revenue, and which Escobedo now closed.[6]

The Ordinance ordered the establishment in the viceregal capital of a *contaduría de retazas*, to examine the assessments made by intendants and subdelegates for the collection of Indian tribute.[7] This provision, however, was directed towards the

[1] Ibid.   [2] Ibid.   [3] Ibid.
[4] Céspedes, 'Reorganización de la hacienda virreinal peruana', 355.
[5] *Ord. Ints.*, arts. 130–1, 212.
[6] A.G.I., Aud. de Lima 1105, Escobedo to Gálvez, no. 610, 20 Jan. 1786.
[7] *Ord. Ints.*, arts. 122–3.

needs of Buenos Aires, which, unlike Lima, had no existing machinery for the control of tribute collection.[1] Since Lima already had a *contaduría de tributos*, Escobedo decided to retain this office instead, and to extend its powers from the examination of assessments to the general inspection of the collection, accounting and administration of this important branch of revenue. One of the benefits of this arrangement would be its ability to provide the superintendent with prompt advice and information.

The provision of information and statistics for the exchequer as a whole was to be the responsibility of the tribunal of accounts in Lima, to which the monthly and annual accounts of the principal subtreasuries were to be sent for examination.[2] Having verified their accuracy, the tribunal was to co-ordinate the financial information from each province and draw up annual general accounts for the whole viceroyalty. So notorious was the tribunal's inefficiency and corruption before 1776 that the first specific task entrusted to Areche by the instructions which governed his *visita* was to examine and reform it.[3] He had made some progress by 1782, but much remained to be done when Escobedo took over the *visita*. Shortly after his arrival in Lima the new *visitador* asked the tribunal to provide him with a general statement of exchequer income and expenditure. This statement, based on figures for 1782, was not ready until January 1785.[4] Escobedo appointed extra officials to meet complaints of overwork made by the tribunal's staff, but throughout 1785 and 1786 efforts to improve its efficiency were obstructed.[5] The superintendent reported in 1786 that complex accounts were being handled by inexperienced junior officials, since only one of the three senior accountants attended the office.[6] He complained in the following year that officials were divided into factions by disputes over seniority and promotion and paid little attention to their work.[7] The intro-

[1] A.G.I., Aud. de Lima 1099, Escobedo to Gálvez, no. 369, 20 Nov. 1784.
[2] *Ord. Ints.*, arts. 104, 208, 214.
[3] A.G.I., Aud. de Lima 1102, Escobedo to Gálvez, no. 561, 20 Oct. 1785.
[4] A.G.I., Aud. de Lima 1104, Escobedo to Gálvez, no. 409, 5 Feb. 1785.
[5] A.G.I., Aud. de Lima 1103, Escobedo to Gálvez, no. 416, 20 Feb. 1785.
[6] A.G.I., Aud. de Lima 1105, Escobedo to Gálvez, no. 608, 20 Jan. 1786.
[7] A.G.I., Aud. de Lima 1111, Escobedo to Sonora, no. 958, 20 July 1787.

duction of a new system of accounting, based on double-entry book-keeping, which few of its staff could understand, threw the tribunal's operations into even greater confusion.[1] The new system of accounting was withdrawn in Peru in 1790, but the inefficiency continued. In short the efforts of Areche and Escobedo, and subsequently of successive viceroys, to reform the tribunal were unsuccessful. Indeed one of the reasons for the difficulty in obtaining a detailed picture of the overall progress of the Peruvian exchequer after 1784 is that the tribunal failed to provide annual general statements.[2]

The new exchequer machinery in the provinces came into operation in 1785, following the arrival of most intendants in the second half of the previous year. The immediate effect in many areas was a dramatic rise in revenue. In the province of Arequipa, for example, the income of the principal subtreasury was almost doubled between 1784 and 1788.[3] Its income increased as follows:

>   1783: 212,040 pesos
>   1784: 272,572   ,,
>   1785: 308,250   ,,
>   1786: 405,218   ,,
>   1787: 465,705   ,,
>   1788: 522,873   ,,

It should of course be noted that part of this increase was attributable to the collection of debts owed to the exchequer from the confused period before 1784. After the peak year of 1788 the income of the Arequipa subtreasury fell back, but over the next two decades it remained steady at the average figure of about 350,000 pesos a year.[4] This represented a considerable improvement over the situation which existed before the creation of the intendancy. A similar pattern of spectacular beginning followed by a levelling-off, representing

[1] A.G.I., Aud. de Lima 1106, Escobedo to Sonora, no. 753, 5 Sept. 1786. See also Croix, *Memoria*, 306–7.

[2] Annual general statements of the type envisaged in the Ordinance seem to have been produced only for 1787 (A.G.I., Aud. de Lima 1068) and 1812 (A.G.I., Aud. de Lima 1136).

[3] A.G.I., Aud. de Lima 1120, Álvarez to Gardoqui, no. 29, 20 March 1796.

[4] A.N.P., Superior Gobierno 25, *cuaderno* 1156, ministers of Arequipa subtreasury to intendant, 8 Aug. 1814.

an overall improvement in collection and of efficiency in administration, can be detected in other areas. The first year in office of the first intendant of Huamanga was marked by an increase there in revenue from 185,315 pesos to 223,864 pesos.[1] The accounts of the general treasury of Lima make it clear that even greater progress was made in the viceroyalty as a whole. Money remitted to it by the principal subtreasuries, after the payment of provincial expenses, totalled 646,542 pesos in 1784.[2] The figure rose to 961,292 pesos in the following year, and rose again to 1,085,304 pesos in 1786.[3]

Throughout the viceroyalty there was an immediate increase in the revenue of the *alcabala*, a sales tax, charged at six per cent on an article virtually every time it changed hands. Its increased yield reflected a revival of trade in some areas, improved methods of collection and a more effective control of contraband. *Alcabala* profits in Cuzco rose from 63,277 pesos in 1784 to 71,982 pesos in 1785.[4] Similar progress was made in Trujillo. Since the accounts for 1784 were in disorder, it was not possible to calculate the increase in *alcabala* revenue in 1785 for the whole province.[5] It was known, however, that in the city of Trujillo revenue increased by 4807 pesos in 1785, and by a further 10,966 pesos in 1786.[6] The increase in revenue for the whole province in 1786 was 14,819 pesos.[7] *Alcabala* revenue in Arequipa reached 88,569 pesos in 1785, an unexpectedly high total, which induced Escobedo to decide that the official in charge of collection should in future receive a fixed salary of 3000 pesos, in place of the former emolument of ten per cent of the money collected.[8] The precaution was a wise one, since in the following year, 1786, revenue rose again to 99,602 pesos.[9] The accounts of the Lima treasury show that the total amount of *alcabala* revenue remitted to it from the principal subtreasuries rose from 110,262 pesos in 1784 to

[1] A.G.I., Aud. de Lima 1112, Escobedo to Sonora, no. 1011, 20 Nov. 1787.
[2] A.G.I., Aud. de Lima 1150, accounts of treasury of Lima, 1784.
[3] A.G.I., Aud. de Lima 1151, 1152, accounts of treasury of Lima, 1785-6.
[4] A.G.I., Aud. de Cuzco 35, Mata to Sonora, no. 41, 23 Oct. 1786.
[5] A.G.I., Aud. de Lima 1105, Escobedo to Gálvez, no. 629, 20 Feb. 1786.
[6] Ibid.
[7] A.G.I., Aud. de Lima 1114, Escobedo to Sonora, no. 868, 22 Feb. 1787.
[8] A.G.I., Aud. de Lima 1101. Escobedo to Gálvez, no. 503, 5 June 1785.
[9] A.G.I., Aud. de Lima 1114, Escobedo to Sonora, no. 875, 28 Feb. 1787.

221,843 pesos in 1786, while, over the same period, revenue from the tax in the province of Lima rose from 463,933 pesos to 628,723 pesos.[1] Of course this revenue was vulnerable to fluctuations in the viceroyalty's supply of goods from Europe. If, in any year, fewer ships arrived, *alcabala* revenue was bound to fall. According to viceroy Avilés the effect of a suspension of trade caused by warfare in Europe was to reduce *alcabala* revenue alone by between 300,000 and 600,000 pesos.[2] Thus perhaps it would be unwise to attach too much significance to the fall in this revenue from 850,566 pesos in 1786 to 678,776 pesos in 1787, since even the lower figure was a considerable improvement over the 1784 figure of 574,195 pesos.[3] Moreover, revenue rose again to 728,953 pesos in 1788; between 1790 and 1794 it reached an average of 810,000 pesos.[4]

The role of the intendants was to improve efficiency and honesty in the collection of *alcabala* revenue. The wider question of the number of ships and the volume of goods reaching Peru from Spain was one which they could not control, although their efforts to stimulate economic activity in the provinces could influence it. The available figures show that there was a rapid rise in revenue after 1784, reflecting increased efficiency and better supervision at a provincial level. It is true that contraband trade, which meant evasion of duties, continued, but this, by its very nature, cannot be quantified.[5] The levelling-out in revenue after the first few years suggests that, having succeeded in improving the collection and administration of the *alcabala*, the intendants were unable, for a variety of reasons, to stimulate the steady increase in economic activity upon which further regular increases in revenue were dependent.[6]

This basic factor influenced the yield of other taxes, in

[1] A.G.I., Aud. de Lima 1150, 1151, 1152, accounts of the treasury of Lima 1784–6.   [2] Avilés, *Memoria*, 66–91.

[3] For 1787 figures see Croix, *Memoria*, appendix, 4–9, table 2.

[4] For 1788 figures ibid, appendix, 11–17, table 3. For summary of 1790–4, when total *alcabala* revenue was 4,047,030 pesos, see Gil, *Memoria*, appendix, 26–30, table ix.

[5] For a detailed account of the difficulties of preventing contraband in the province of Arequipa see J. R. Fisher (ed.) *Arequipa 1796–1811. La relación del gobierno del intendente Salamanca* (Lima, 1968), 54–63.

[6] See below, Chapter VI.

particular *cobos* and *diezmos*, levied on gold and silver mined in the viceroyalty. Here, too, the duties of the intendants were twofold, to increase the efficiency of collection by eliminating the illegal export of unminted silver, and to increase potential at source by stimulating the mining industry.[1] Results were encouraging in the years immediately after 1784. The money minted in Lima, at the only mint in the viceroyalty, increased from 3,909,829 pesos in 1784 to 4,246,575 pesos in 1787, 4,393,633 pesos in 1788, 5,205,851 in 1790 and 6,093,037 in 1794.[2] The revenue of *cobos* and *diezmos* rose accordingly, from 365,242 pesos in 1787 to 395,130 in 1788, and to an annual average of about 500,000 when the annual total minted reached 6,000,000 pesos.[3] Throughout the decade 1790 to 1799 annual output of the Lima mint was always over 5,000,000 pesos, but thereafter never again reached this figure. In 1812, when the output was 4,462,927 pesos, taxation revenue totalled 401,503 pesos.[4]

A further responsibility of the intendants was to eliminate the illegal production and sale of tobacco, to root out fraud in the administration of the monopoly, and to exercise contentious jurisdiction in any cases which arose.[5] The tobacco monopoly was a valuable and reliable source of revenue for the crown, and during the period of financial difficulty between 1780 and 1784 the deficits of the general exchequer had to a considerable degree been met from its funds.[6] The intervention of the intendants in its administration after 1784 caused a certain amount of confusion. In 1786, for example, its director complained that the intendants were exceeding their powers, interfering in the economic aspects of the monopoly and in such matters as the appointment of junior officials, which the

[1] *Ord. Ints.*, arts. 133–6.
[2] For complete table see Appendix 3.
[3] Croix, *Memoria*, appendix, 4–9, 11–17, tables 2–3; Avilés, *Memoria*, 71–4. As the name indicates the *diezmo* on silver was levied at a rate of 10 per cent; the tax on gold was levied at 3 per cent. In addition *derechos de fundición y ensaye*, or *de cobos*, were charged on both metals at a rate of 1½ per cent—see Céspedes, 'Reorganización de la hacienda virreinal peruana.'
[4] A.G.I., Aud. de Lima 1136, *estado general* of exchequer for 1812.
[5] *Ord. Ints.*, arts. 72–4, 76, 131.
[6] Céspedes, 'La renta del tabaco', 162. The total provided in these years was 1,403,554 pesos.

Ordinance had left in the hands of a central office in Lima.[1] He criticized specifically intendant Saavedra of Trujillo, whose province contained one of the two major factories in the viceroyalty for the manufacture of cheroots.[2] The decision to operate state-owned factories had been taken by Escobedo, but the new structure aroused public discontent, partly because the quality of the factory product was allegedly low, partly because in the past many poorer families in Lima had depended for their livelihood upon purchasing tobacco from the monopoly and producing cheroots on a domestic basis. Consequently viceroy Gil ordered in 1791 that the factory system be abandoned, and that the role of the monopoly be limited to the purchase, distribution and sale of tobacco.[3] Before this decision took effect the monopoly's profits had risen from 284,240 pesos in 1785 to 315,213 pesos in 1792, although they were liable to fluctuate from one year to another, according to the amount of revenue devoted to the purchase of new stocks.[4] Both turnover and profits began to fall as Gil's decision to close the factories took effect. Thereafter an annual profit of between 160,000 and 180,000 pesos could be expected, although in 1810 it soared to 284,967 pesos, only to fall disastrously to 16,548 pesos in 1814.[5]

It is clear that the revenue from a number of taxes increased sharply for several years after 1784, but thereafter remained steady, or even fell, as the viceroyalty's general economic situation suffered the effects of prolonged warfare in Europe and consequent damage to communications with the colony. An exception to this pattern was the revenue from the tribute, which not only rose remarkably after 1784 but continued to rise for as long as the tax was levied. Even without the intendants to supervise collection this revenue would probably have increased, since first Areche and then Escobedo had made encouraging progress with the preparation of more accurate, up-to-date tribute lists before news reached Peru of the decision to introduce the intendant system.[6] But the task was a long

[1] A.G.I., Aud. de Lima 1228, Miguel de Otermin to Escobedo, 23 Oct. 1786.
[2] Céspedes, 'La renta del tabaco', 139, 153–4. The other factory was in Lima.
[3] Ibid., 158–9.   [4] Ibid., 160–1.
[5] A.G.I., Aud. de Lima 1222, 1136, 1228, for annual accounts of monopoly.
[6] A.G.I., Aud. de Lima 1097, Escobedo to Gálvez, no. 297, 16 June 1784.

one: in many areas the lists in use in the middle of 1784 had been unrevised for many years and failed to reflect Indian population growth from about the middle of the eighteenth century. Those for the *partido* of Santa dated from 1674, those for Conchucos from 1727, those for Cuzco from 1734 and those for Cajamarca from 1736.[1] The situation left considerable room for improvement, either by the registration of Indians previously overlooked or, more commonly, by the collection for the exchequer of the tribute of unregistered Indians which had previously been collected and kept by *corregidores*. Escobedo was anxious that the reform and reorganization of the structure should proceed promptly and efficiently, and he supplemented the detailed instructions provided for the intendants by their Ordinance with a clear instruction of his own, explaining how reassessments should be made and how the revenue should be collected and accounted.[2]

The procedure followed for the preparation of new lists was intricate and precise, involving the appointment of inspectors and interpreters and the collection of local details from parish clergy and Indian representatives.[3] The intendant of Cuzco, Mata, feared in 1785 that to make reassessments in his province might antagonize the recently pacified Indians, but with Escobedo's encouragement he ordered that the work should continue, and by the end of the year new tribute lists were ready for the entire province.[4] The results were so striking that even Escobedo, who expected improvement, described them as 'unbelievable'.[5] The number of tributaries in 1784 had been 24,908, paying an annual total of 187,409 pesos;[6] the reassessments increased the number of tributaries to 37,729, despite the deaths of thousands of Indians in the recent rebellion, and

[1] Ibid.
[2] *Ord. Ints.*, arts. 116–28. A.G.I., Aud. de Lima 1099, Escobedo to Gálvez, no. 369, 20 Nov. 1784, enclosing a copy of the instruction sent to the intendants.
[3] A.N.P., Superior Gobierno 21, *cuaderno* 578, for a detailed account of *revisita de tributarios* in the *partido* of Camaná in 1789.
[4] A.G.I., Aud. de Cuzco 35, Mata to Gálvez, no. 7, 14 March 1785, and Mata to Sonora, no. 41, 31 Oct. 1786.
[5] A.G.I., Aud. de Lima 1117, Escobedo to Sonora, no. 837, 20 Jan. 1787.
[6] A.G.I., Aud. de Cuzco 35, *estado general* enclosed with Mata to Sonora, no. 41, 31 Oct. 1786. All figures quoted for tribute include a much less important tax, the *contribución de hospital*, collected with it.

revenue in 1786 was 281,346 pesos. Increases in other provinces, where the Indian population was smaller, were less spectacular, but proportionally of equal significance. In the *partido* of Moquegua, in the province of Arequipa, tribute revenue increased from 15,402 pesos in 1784 to 23,460 in 1785, while in the *partido* of Santa, part of the province of Lima, it more than doubled, from 544 pesos to 1167.[1] In the viceroyalty as a whole reassessments had been completed in sixteen *partidos* in time for the 1785 collection: their effect was to increase revenue in those areas from 208,421 pesos in 1784 to 250,220 pesos in 1785.[2]

The viceroyalty's tribute revenue rose steadily from 705,942 pesos in 1784 to 752,835 pesos in 1785, and to 914,502 pesos in 1790, as the process of making new assessments continued.[3] It continued to rise, as fresh reassessments were made every five years, and in 1798, after the transfer to Peru of the intendancy of Puno, totalled 1,179,555 pesos. Despite its social evils, the method in use for the remuneration of the subdelegates clearly provided a powerful incentive for the registration of as many Indians as possible. Some intendants believed that revenue would be even higher if they were given a freer hand in the appointment of the commissioners who made the reassessments. O'Higgins complained in 1803 that, although the Ordinance conferred this authority upon the intendants, in practice the appointments were made in Lima, with the result that those selected were often inexperienced and ignorant of the areas they were to visit.[4] The only province where the arrangements for tribute collection seem to have been particularly difficult was Huancavelica. By 1811 the province's accumulated debts for this tax amounted to 66,000 pesos, the subdelegate of one *partido* having paid nothing for two years.[5] The intendant, Lázaro de Rivera, attributed responsibility to the officials of the subtreasury of Huamanga, since, after the restoration to them in 1809 of the exercise of contentious jurisdiction, they were apparently incapable of ensuring that

[1] A.G.I., Aud. de Lima 1105, Escobedo to Gálvez, no. 629, 20 Feb. 1786.
[2] Ibid.   [3] See Appendix 4.
[4] *Ord. Ints.*, art. 106. A.G.I., Aud. de Lima 763, O'Higgins to Cavallero, 3 Nov. 1803.
[5] A.G.I., Aud. de Lima 1116, Lázaro de Rivera to José Canga Arguelles, no. 6, 16 July 1811.

subdelegates handed over the money which they had collected.[1] Despite this local difficulty, the tax as a whole continued to flourish. Tribute revenue in 1811 was 1,271,141 pesos, more than double the figure for 1780.[2] This improvement was basically the result of the efforts of the intendants and subdelegates, and it reflected Indian demographic expansion in the later colonial period.

At this point, with tribute revenue at the highest level ever recorded, the Cortes, meeting in Cádiz, ordered that in the interests of liberalism and equality tribute should be abolished and replaced by a personal tax on all inhabitants.[3] The decision horrified viceroy Abascal, since, at a time of grave political and financial crisis, it suddenly eliminated the most profitable and reliable branch of the exchequer's income.[4] The *contaduría de tributos* remained open to supervise the collection of outstanding debts, but in 1812 this source provided only 288,659 pesos, a comparatively trivial sum compared with the previous year's total.[5] Moreover, administrative costs swallowed up almost 165,000 pesos.[6] According to Abascal, the Indians of some areas, largely in the intendancy of Puno, insisted that they be allowed to contribute to the needs of the exchequer.[7] Their 'voluntary contribution' brought in a further 32,993 pesos in 1812.[8] Further debts, of about 300,000 pesos, were cleared up in the following three years, but this income was clearly no substitute for the loss of a tax which, before its abolition, had accounted for over twenty per cent of the exchequer's total receipts.[9] Its restoration was ordered in March 1815, but by then irreparable harm had been done to the Peruvian exchequer.[10]

Decisions of the central government which adversely affected

[1] Ibid.   [2] Appendix 4.   [3] Abascal, *Memoria*, i, 288–9.
[4] A.H.M.H., Colección Santamaría, MS 00216, *borrador* of Abascal to first secretary of state, 23 May 1812. See below, 121–2.
[5] A.G.I., Aud. de Lima 1136, *estado general* for 1812.   [6] Ibid.
[7] A.H.M.H., Colección Santamaría, MS 00217, *acta of junta general de tribunales*, 11 July 1812. It seems unlikely that the Indians benefitted; in view of the freedom of action enjoyed by subdelegates, it seems probable that they continued to collect the tax, without handing on the revenue to the exchequer.
[8] A.G.I., Aud. de Lima 1136, *estado general* for 1812.
[9] A.G.I., Aud. de Lima 1133, certificate of Juan Jph de Leuro, 3 Feb. 1815.
[10] Abascal, *Memoria*, i, 328.

the Peruvian exchequer were obviously limiting factors upon the ability of the intendants to improve the viceroyalty's financial structure. Similarly the maintenance of peace in Europe and communications with Spain was out of their hands. There were other factors, too, which seriously restricted their ability to bring about the financial reformation for which the founders of the new administrative structure had hoped. The restoration of the superintendency to the viceroy in 1787, for example, was clearly of great significance.[1] The viceroy was already overburdened with administrative and bureaucratic tasks, and was clearly unable to provide the intendants with the prompt, expert guidance which had characterized Escobedo's superintendency. On the contrary, Croix's exercise of this office was marked by an unsympathetic, even hostile attitude towards the intendants' activities in exchequer affairs. Despite the rise in *alcabala* revenue, he complained in 1789 that the arrangements for collection introduced by Escobedo were defective, and charged the intendants with the mismanagement of the judicial and supervisory powers granted by the Ordinance.[2] He suggested the restoration of a *dirección general de alcabalas* in Lima, which, under viceregal supervision, should be empowered to issue instructions to the intendants, and would examine *alcabala* accounts before they were submitted to the tribunal of accounts. To support his argument that the tax had been collected more efficiently before the closure of this office, Croix provided statistics to show that the revenue from ships arriving at Callao was twenty-five per cent higher in the years 1781 to 1784 than in the period 1785–8. He ignored, however, the fact that in the viceroyalty as a whole *alcabala* revenue had increased considerably. A fall in revenue at Callao probably meant that merchandise previously shipped there was now being supplied through other ports, such as Arica or, more probably, Buenos Aires. The more general criticism of the intendant system, submitted by Croix at the same time, acknowledged that after its extension to Peru revenues had increased, but insisted that the improved methods of bookkeeping and accounting which he believed to be responsible

[1] See above, 59–61.
[2] A.G.I., Aud. de Lima 1181, Croix to Valdés, 16 May 1789.

for the improvement could have been introduced without the new system of administration.[1]

Viceregal hostility towards the intendants represented the reaction of conservative forces, resentful of the sweeping changes in the distribution of authority and in traditional administrative and fiscal practices made necessary by the new structure of provincial government. This attitude was shared by treasury officials, conscious of the fact that the powers of contentious jurisdiction now granted to the intendants had previously been in their hands. Indeed a further demand made by Croix in 1789 was that this jurisdiction should be restored to treasury officials, since its exercise by the intendants was causing delay and inefficiency in the collection of debts.[2] After considerable discussion of this request in Spain, it was reaffirmed in 1796 that jurisdiction should remain with the intendants.[3] The authority of treasury officials was to be limited to preparing cases and bringing them to the intendants for decision, although it was suggested that it might be convenient for the intendants to delegate judicial authority to treasury officials serving in remote areas.

Escobedo had found it necessary to act firmly to support the authority of the first intendants in some provinces. The accountant of the subtreasury of Arequipa, Anselmo Camborda, was dismissed in 1786 for alleged incompetence and obstruction of the reforms of intendant Álvarez.[4] In the same year Álvarez imprisoned the administrator of the city's postal service for gambling with public funds, making it clear that this punishment was intended as a warning to other officials with financial responsibilities.[5] The accountant of the *contaduría de azogues* of Huancavelica, Juan Luque Marmol, was dismissed in 1785, in response to complaints from the intendant about his uncooperative behaviour, while in 1786 both senior officials of the subtreasury of Huamanga were removed from office.[6] The

---

[1] See above, 62-4.
[2] A.G.I., Aud. de Lima 974, report of Council of the Indies, 9 Dec. 1795.
[3] A.G.I., Aud. de Lima 609, *cédula*, 10 April 1796.
[4] A.G.I., Aud. de Lima 1108, Escobedo to Sonora, no. 804, 18 Dec. 1786.
[5] A.G.I., Aud. de Lima 646, Álvarez to Sonora, no. 21, 24 Aug. 1786.
[6] A.G.I., Aud. de Lima 1108, Escobedo to Gálvez, no. 10 (letters dealing with Huancavelica are numbered separately from general correspondence), 20 Feb. 1786.

accountant at Huamanga, Ignacio Leguanda, was removed partly because he showed little professional competence, but chiefly because he had taken the side of the bishop in the complex dispute between intendant and bishop.[1] The treasurer, Joaquin Cuenca, had, it seems, refrained from interfering, but he, too, was dismissed in the hope that a clean sweep of senior administrators would help to bring stability to Huamanga in the future.[2]

The hope was not fulfilled. Although elsewhere in the viceroyalty initial tension was followed by amicable co-operation between intendants and treasury officials, Huamanga continued to be disturbed by complicated administrative disputes. The city was small and isolated, with only 327 of its 8349 inhabitants classified as *'españoles'* in 1795.[3] It seems that the claustrophobic social structure of this small community was particularly conducive to the growth and persistence of factional disputes, reflecting administrative rivalries and personal animosities. The experiences of the first intendant have already been examined.[4] The second, Menéndez, had difficulty in exercising effective control over the officials encharged with the collection of sales taxes and customs duties.[5] It was, however, during the command of O'Higgins, who served in Huamanga from 1799 until 1812, that administrative confusion there reached its most serious levels. Mutual complaints were first made in 1801, after the intendant decided to deprive the accountant of the subtreasury, Juan de la Rosa, of a large garden attached to the house which he occupied.[6] This somewhat trivial matter was further complicated by O'Higgins's resentment at the accountant's efforts to draw his attention to debts owed by former subdelegates, and by a dispute between the treasury officials and members of the *cabildo*, dating from the period before O'Higgins took up his post.[7] The treasury officials insisted that they had the right to carry the royal

[1] See above, 40–1.
[2] A.G.I., Aud. de Lima 1109, Escobedo to Gálvez, no. 637, 5 March 1786.
[3] See Appendix 2. [4] See above, 37–43.
[5] A.N.P., Superior Gobierno 25, *cuaderno* 737, for complaints of Menéndez against the *administrador de rentas unidas*.
[6] A.H.M.H., Miscelánea, MS 1117, the tribunal of accounts to Avilés, 18 May 1803. [7] Ibid.

standard during public ceremonies, while members of the *cabildo*, led by the *regidor* Francisco de Chaves, claimed that the honour belonged to representatives of the *cabildo*.[1] The *cabildo*, however, was not a united body, since about half its members supported the argument of the treasury ministers because of their personal dislike for Chaves.[2] O'Higgins, on the other hand, became identified with this *regidor*'s cause.[3]

In this context relatively unimportant administrative details were given a disproportionate significance. It had long been established that during the absence of an intendant from his capital temporary command should go to his *teniente asesor*; if this official, too, were absent command should go to the senior treasury official.[4] During O'Higgins's absence in 1804 la Rosa showed extreme reluctance to recognize the authority of the *asesor*.[5] On the other hand, when both the intendant and the *asesor* were absent in 1806, the *cabildo* would recognize la Rosa's authority only in exchequer affairs, insisting that 'political' authority should be exercised by the senior *alcalde*.[6] The accountant's retirement in 1808, for reasons of age, provided some respite from these destructive squabbles. Tensions remained, however, and re-emerged in 1811. In 1809 the *Junta Central* had ordered that, because of repeated complaints that debts owed to the exchequer had increased, the exercise of contentious jurisdiction should be restored to treasury officials.[7] The intendants retained the authority to investigate complicated cases, but the use of legal sanctions was taken out of their hands. O'Higgins now complained that the effect of this decision was to make the Huamanga treasury officials completely contemptuous of his authority.[8] Moreover, they were so excited with the restoration of their former powers that they were devoting all their time to the collection of old debts, ignoring current business.

[1] A.H.M.H., Miscelánea, MS 1204, Francisco de Chaves to O'Higgins, 18 Feb. 1802. A.N.P., Cabildo 12, *acta cap.* of *cabildo* of Huamanga, 6 Feb. 1801.
[2] A.H.M.H., Miscelánea, MS 1201, *acuerdo* to O'Higgins, 23 Feb. 1802.
[3] A.H.M.H., Miscelánea, MS 1217, Juan de la Rosa to Avilés, 15 June 1805.
[4] A.G.I., Aud. de Buenos Aires 354, royal order, 5 Aug. 1783, declaration 6.
[5] A.H.M.H., Miscelánea, MS 1144, la Rosa to O'Higgins, 8 March 1805.
[6] A.H.M.H., Miscelánea, MS 1228, la Rosa to *cabildo*, 3 Jan. 1806.
[7] B.N.P., MS D5969, royal order, 12 April 1809.
[8] A.G.I., Aud. de Lima 1116, O'Higgins to Council of Regency, 11 May 1811.

The royal order of 1809 referred specifically to inadequate supervision of the exchequer in the viceroyalty of the Río de la Plata, making no reference to Peru.[1] It is clear, however, that the cumulative debt owed to the Peruvian exchequer was considerable. At the beginning of 1812 it exceeded 4,000,000 pesos, but by the end of that year had been reduced by ten per cent due to the efforts of treasury officials.[2] The available figures suggest that, although the intendants succeeded in increasing the yield of individual taxes, considerable difficulty was experienced with debt collection. It is difficult, however, to give a detailed picture of the progress of the Peruvian exchequer as a whole, since the tribunal of accounts failed to provide the annual general statements required by the Ordinance. Moreover, those accounts which are available seem in some cases to be distorted to reflect either credit or discredit upon those entrusted with financial responsibilities. One factor which makes comparison difficult is that some accounts distinguish between revenue due and that actually collected, while others fail to make the distinction.

The general condition of the viceregal exchequer improved considerably between 1782 and 1787. Income in 1782 had been 4,181,489 pesos and expenditure 5,393,057 pesos.[3] By 1787 revenue due had risen to 4,788,272 pesos and expenditure had been reduced to 3,805,164 pesos.[4] Even though the amount actually collected was only 3,871,984 pesos, the outstanding sum represented mainly 'good debts' and could be counted on the credit side. In the following year, 1788, the situation improved further. Revenue due was 4,664,896 pesos, the amount collected 4,114,658 pesos, and the expenditure of 4,638,938 pesos included the repayment of almost 500,000 pesos previously borrowed by the exchequer.[5] The efforts of the intendants in their provinces, especially their success in increasing the yield of tribute and the *alcabala*, had brought some improvement to the general fiscal situation. Their ability to influence expenditure was more limited, and this remained

---

[1] B.N.P., MS D5969, royal order, 12 April 1809.
[2] A.G.I., Aud. de Lima 1136, *estado general* for 1812.
[3] See above, 101–2. [4] Croix, *Memoria*, appendix, 4–9, table 2.
[5] Ibid., appendix, 11–17, table 3.

high. In 1787 military expenditure was 1,341,806 pesos, including 432,000 pesos sent in aid to Panamá, Valdivia and Chiloé; and in 1788 it rose even further to 1,897,731 pesos. In the quinquennium 1790-4 military and naval expenditure amounted to 7,500,000 pesos, including over 2,000,000 pesos sent to other parts of the empire.[1] In these years, according to figures supplied by viceroy Gil, the exchequer was able on average to count on a small annual surplus. He reported total revenue to be 23,000,000 pesos, an annual average of 4,600,000, and total expenditure slightly under 20,000,000 pesos. He made it clear, however, that this general situation dissatisfied him, and he declared that income would have been higher if the intendants had exercised closer control over treasury officials, and had made more effective use of their own powers to enforce the payment of debts.[2]

By 1799 income had risen slightly to just over 5,000,000 pesos, but so, too, had expenditure.[3] The increase in revenue was due to the addition to Peru of the intendancy of Puno, rather than improvement elsewhere in the viceroyalty. In this second half of the decade, in fact, the Peruvian economy and the exchequer suffered the effects of renewed Spanish involvement in war with Britain. In peacetime the exchequer could show a small surplus, but the arrival of news of European warfare always upset this fine balance, first by necessitating increased expenditure on the navy and on coastal defences, and subsequently by its stagnating effect on economic activity. Osorno pointed out that improved supervision of the exchequer could have only a limited value. The basic problems were economic and strategic. The viceroyalty was underpopulated, with little industry or commerce, and the existing economic life was very vulnerable to outside influences.[4]

The situation was summed up by viceroy Avilés in 1806. He explained: 'the slightest disturbance in Europe has the unfortunate effect of paralysing the commerce of these dominions, at the same time causing expenditure which stretches the

[1] Gil, *Memoria*, 7; appendix, 26-30, table 13.   [2] Ibid., 202.
[3] Donoso, op. cit., 466, report of Osorno, 26 June 1799.
[4] Ibid. B.M., Add. MS 13975, ff. 151-4, Osorno to Príncipe de la Paz, 26 July 1797, giving details of defence preparations on arrival of news of outbreak of war with England.

resources of the exchequer'.[1] Suspension of trade led to a drastic fall in *alcabala* revenue, while a shortage of mercury, necessary for the extraction of silver from silver ore, caused a fall in mining production and in the yield of the taxes on mining.[2] Moreover, in such difficult economic and financial conditions the viceroyalty was increasingly faced with demands from Spain for money to help it carry on with the very war which was causing such distress. Avilés arrived in Peru to find a treasury containing about 7,000,000 pesos, but in the years 1802–04 sent 8,500,000 pesos to Spain, and by the middle of 1804 it was empty.[3] Although suggesting that a more efficient collection of debts by the intendants would bring some improvement, Avilés acknowledged that they, like himself, were relatively powerless to influence these basic problems.[4]

The demands for remittances to Spain became more frequent and more desperate after the entry of Spain into the war against Napoleon in 1808.[5] Donations made it possible for Abascal to send 570,000 pesos in April 1809, but a 'voluntary loan', collected by order of the *Junta Central*, brought in only 21,500 pesos.[6] The viceroy was faced not only with demands from Spain but also with the heavy expense of trying to suppress revolution in other parts of the empire. In 1812, for example, 2,000,000 pesos were devoted to military expenditure within the viceroyalty, 820,000 pesos were sent to the royalist forces in Upper Peru, and a further 372,000 pesos were sent to Montevideo, Chile, Quito and Acapulco.[7] Moreover, Abascal had to face the year in the knowledge that tribute had been abolished by the Cortes. The effect of the decision was offset to some degree by heavy borrowing and by determined efforts to collect old debts.[8]

---

[1] Avilés, *Memoria*, 67.   [2] Ibid. See Appendix 5 for mercury production.
[3] Avilés, *Memoria*, 69.   [4] Ibid., 71.
[5] See A. Nieto Velez, *Contribución a la historia del fidelismo en el Perú, 1808–1810* (Lima, 1960), 115–19.
[6] A.G.I., Aud. de Lima 1172, report of *contador general*, 3 March 1812.
[7] A.G.I., Aud. de Lima 1136, *estado general* for 1812. A further 53,000 pesos were needed for salaries of refugees from areas held by insurgents—A.H.M.H.. Miscelánea, MS 1409, See also Abascal, *Memoria*, i, 312–14, 320–1.
[8] A.N.P., Superior Gobierno 34, *cuaderno* 1134, for details of individuals and institutions contributing 1,049,300 pesos. 87,000 pesos came from donations, 145,000 pesos were loaned free of interest and the remaining 772,000 carried interest charges of 6 per cent.

Although income due for the year was only 4,867,498 pesos, the total collected was 5,270,933 pesos.[1] Expenditure, however, rose to 5,352,582 pesos.

The revenue to be expected from donations was obviously limited and Abascal was increasingly forced to resort to other financial expedients to meet growing demands for money. When, however, he sought the advice of the *cabildo* of Lima on possible means of filling the gap caused by the abolition of the tribute, he was bluntly informed that to impose new taxes on the non-Indian minority would be to make them into new tributaries.[2] Increased taxes on luxury items and on trade in general were also ruled out by the *cabildo*, on the grounds that the taxes paid by merchants were already punitive.[3] The viceroy, however, had little alternative but to increase taxes. Thus in 1815 the rates of *alcabala* and other import taxes were increased by one per cent, taxes on silver were increased, the prices of items sold by state monopolies were doubled, and heavy taxes were imposed on coffee houses and places of amusement.[4] In the previous year Abascal had introduced a rudimentary system of paper money, by issuing five hundred 1000 peso bills, redeemable within a year, which could be used to make payments to the subtreasuries.[5] The *consulado* was asked to persuade its members to accept them voluntarily; if they refused compulsion would be used. Abascal's successor, Pezuela, faced the same problems, but in an even more acute form. He, too, found it necessary to adopt measures which inevitably had the cumulative effect of alienating moderate opinion. In 1819, for example, it was decided that to meet the needs of the exchequer a further 1,000,000 pesos should be raised by a forced loan, 400,000 from the merchants, the remainder from the ordinary citizens of the capital.[6]

As Spanish rule in Peru neared its end the viceregal exchequer

[1] A.G.I., Aud. de Lima 1136, *estado general* for 1812.
[2] A.H.M., Libro de Cabildo 42, ff. 79–81v, *acta cap.*, 29 Oct. 1811.
[3] See below, 198–9, for further discussion of *cabildo*'s view.
[4] A.N.P., Superior Gobierno 35, *cuaderno* 1191, report of *junta general extraordinaria*, 28 April 1815.
[5] A.N.P., Superior Gobierno 35, *cuaderno* 1162, viceroy to *consulado*, 19 June 1814.
[6] A.N.P., Superior Gobierno 37, *cuaderno* 1308, certificate of *contaduría* of *consulado*, 27 Nov. 1821.

lay in ruins. Indeed for a decade before 1821 it faced tremendous difficulties, as warfare and rebellion, first in neighbouring regions and then within Peru, disrupted economic activity and caused heavy military expenditure. Even before 1810 the structure was precariously balanced. In a normal year a small surplus could be expected, but from 1796 onward few years were normal, as the mother country was involved in almost continuous warfare. Thus an assessment of the success or failure of the intendants in their management of exchequer affairs must be set against this general background. For perhaps a decade after 1784 they succeeded in improving the exchequer's overall performance. Revenue rose in response to improved supervision and the eradication of fraud and corruption. Thereafter, with some exceptions, the revenue of individual taxes and of the exchequer as a whole ceased to increase significantly. To some degree this may have been a consequence of the failure of the intendants to use effectively their powers of contentious jurisdiction against debtors. Basically, however, this stagnation indicated that improved supervision of exchequer machinery at a local level could have only a limited effect on the general financial condition of the viceroyalty. A continuous improvement depended upon economic expansion of the type experienced in this period in the Río de la Plata, in New Spain and in Venezuela. The viceroyalty of Peru, however, did not share in Spanish America's general economic advance during the late eighteenth century. Consequently its financial structure remained as weak and fragile in 1810 as it had been in 1780.

CHAPTER VI

Intendants and the Economy

CONTEMPORARY ANALYSTS of the economic structure of the viceroyalty of Peru were prone to enumerate its great range of natural resources. Juan and Ulloa, for example, marvelled at the variety and wealth of mineral deposits, plants and wild life, so rich 'that it seems nature did her best to enrich the kingdom with all the things most worthy of esteem for the service of mankind'.[1] The coastal valleys were capable of producing sugar, rice, the vine, cotton, tobacco, a variety of cereals and many vegetables and plants.[2] In most parts of the *sierra* agriculture was restricted to the production of potatoes, maize, *coca* and other items consumed by the Indians. But the sterility of the soil was balanced to some degree by extensive grazing of sheep, *llamas*, *alpacas* and *vicuñas*, and especially by the abundance of mineral resources. Silver and gold were the only minerals mined in large quantities, but there existed, too, extensive deposits of tin, lead, copper, zinc, iron, mercury and other minerals. The provinces to the east of the *sierra* excited the imagination of contemporaries to an even greater extent than those possessing precious metals.[3] The eastern part of the province of Tarma and the missionary territories beyond contained vast resources of exotic plants and trees, yielding cinnamon, cloves, *cacao*, *cascarilla* (the bark from which quinine is produced), *calaguala*, *raicilla*, *cinchona* and balsam, all of which were in great demand in Europe. If the French or English colonies in America had possessed such potential wealth, suggested Juan and Ulloa, no effort would have been spared to

[1] Juan and Ulloa, op. cit., 415.
[2] B.M., Eg. MS 771, 'Idea succinta del comercio del Perú...', ff. 96–113, 131v–149v, for a description and alphabetical list of Peru's animal and vegetable resources.
[3] B.M., Add. MS 17591, 'Descripción del Perú', by Tadeo Haënke, ff. 27–9.

exploit it, but in Spanish hands it was neglected.[1] The problem existed 'because we subject ourselves to the production of gold and silver, ignoring everything else, only to see ourselves obliged to hand over our bullion to other nations in exchange for the very commodities we previously scorned'.

The consequence was that, although supplied with large quantities of bullion, Spain was relatively poor, while her European rivals, especially France and Britain, had grown rich upon the exploitation of agricultural resources and the growth of trade in sugar, coffee and other items. The English colonists in North America were held up as an example of people who had prospered from the rational exploitation of natural resources. Their products were sold at great profit, 'and with their paper money they have built cities of silver and gold'.[2]

The illusory nature of the wealth provided by gold and silver and the damage done to Spain by bullionist theories were common themes in the writings of commentators of the first half of the eighteenth century. Campillo urged the need to reform the empire's outdated commercial structure, designed primarily to ensure the shipment of bullion to Spain in exchange for small quantities of European merchandise, insisting that instead it should be developed as a market for Spanish manufactures and a source of raw materials for Spanish industry.[3] It was now realized that these aims could be achieved only by liberalizing trade, reducing duties, opening ports and extending permission to trade from small monopolist groups to a wider mercantile community.[4] These measures were a major feature of the Bourbon programme of imperial reform, and they culminated in the opening of all major ports in the empire to direct trade with Spain. They helped to bring prosperity in the last quarter of the century to areas previously neglected. Cuban and Mexican sugar, Venezuelan tobacco and hides from the Río de la Plata began to challenge silver as the props of the imperial economy.[5] Ministers in Spain were gratified by the results of the new emphasis upon agricultural resources, and hoped that

[1] Juan and Ulloa, op. cit., 457.   [2] Ibid., 458.
[3] See above, 2-3.   [4] See above, 3.
[5] For commercial expansion in the Río de la Plata see Lynch, op. cit., 42-5, 121-2.

general administrative reform within the empire would stimulate even further their exploitation. Among their many other duties the intendants were charged with the encouragement of agriculture and, in general, with the development and exploitation of the economic resources of their provinces.[1]

The Ordinance specifically ordered that efforts should be made to extend the cultivation of grain to feed the empire's inhabitants, and of cotton, hemp and flax to feed the peninsula's textile factories. In extending the new system of administration to Peru Escobedo endorsed this general aim, but devoted more time to drawing the attention of his intendants to the rich and varied resources of each of their *partidos*.[2] The intendants of Cuzco, Huancavelica and Huamanga were informed that, although economic activity in their provinces rested largely upon mining activity, considerable scope existed for the expansion of agriculture in the river valleys, where crops of maize, sugar and vegetables were already grown. These items, together with cloth, were exported from Cuzco to Upper Peru, and, in even greater quantities, from Arequipa, whose fertile valleys and plains produced sugar, oil, wine, vegetables, cereals and cochineal.[3] Further north the province of Trujillo was capable of increasing the production of many items, including sugar, rice, salt, oil, hams, cotton, wool, hides and tobacco, if only the costs of production could be lowered and new markets found.[4] Similarly the province of Tarma, as well as the eastern part of the province of Cuzco, possessed virtually untapped resources of a wide range of plants and shrubs, such as *coca*, *cacao* and *cascarilla*, as well as enormous reserves of high quality timber.[5] Wherever economic activity included the manufacture of cloth for local consumption the intendants were to make discreet efforts to prevent increased production, lest the market for Spanish textiles should be reduced.[6] This, however, was the

[1] *Ord. Ints.*, arts. 57–9.

[2] A.G.I., Aud. de Lima 1098, instructions from Escobedo to each intendant.

[3] A.G.I., Aud. de Lima 1098, instruction to Mata, arts. 15–23; to Márquez, arts. 15–19; to Manrique, arts. 15–25; to Menéndez, arts, 16–24.

[4] A.G.I., Aud. de Lima 1098, instruction to Saavedra, arts. 17–27.

[5] A.G.I., Aud. de Lima 1098, instruction to Gálvez, arts. 17–32.

[6] A.G.I., Aud. de Lima 1098, instruction to Mata, art. 18, referring to *partido* of Paruro, informs him 'En los obrajes y chorrillos de este part'o se trexe Ropa de la Tierra, y, aunque estos son utiles por el comercio y fomento actual q'e dan al

only qualification to the general instruction to take all possible measures to encourage economic growth and to stimulate the increased exploitation of natural resources.

The first intendants promptly set about the task of inspecting their provinces, collecting information about their needs, making maps and generally providing statistical information to be used as the basis for a rational direction of economic affairs.[1] There is evidence, too, of determined efforts to encourage the export of previously neglected resources. The intendant of Tarma, for example, sent to Spain not only a report on the *cascarilla* of his province but also samples of the bark, to demonstrate its quality.[2] Efforts of this kind were laudable but were unlikely to produce dramatic benefits, in view of the sheer size and complexity of the economic problems facing the viceroyalty. The intendants arrived in their provinces to find them in the grip of a serious economic depression. In Tarma, for example, trade was at a standstill in many areas, since the abolition of the *repartimiento* system had made merchants unwilling to provide the Indians with goods on credit, while many Indians, without a stimulus to work, had fallen into idleness.[3] Moreover, villages along the main trade routes, which had previously provided men and mules for the transport of merchandise, were now experiencing severe hardship.

In Cuzco, too, economic conditions were depressing.[4] The abolition of the *repartimiento* system was partly responsible, since, without this stimulus to produce, the Indians refused to work. Without their cheap labour the cost of growing maize and other crops exceeded their market value. The serious disruption of economic activity and the destruction of *obrajes* and estates during the Túpac Amaru rebellion were further causes of economic decline. Intendant Mata made efforts to encourage the export of cochineal, produced in the *partido* of Aymaraes, but

Pais, y R's Dros que producen, deven con prudencia y disimulo impedir se aumenten, por el perjuicio que causan a las fabricas nacionales de la Matriz'. Similar instructions were given to other intendants.

[1] See below, 158–69.
[2] A.G.I., Aud. de Lima 1108, Juan María Gálvez to Gálvez, 18 Sept. 1786. Escobedo to Sonora, no. 810, 18 Dec. 1786.
[3] A.G.I., Aud. de Lima 646, Juan María Gálvez to Sonora, no. 21, 17 Oct. 1786.
[4] A.G.I., Aud. de Cuzco 35, Mata to Sonora, no. 43, 13 Nov. 1786.

was pessimistic about the general prospects, since the heavy cost of transport to the coast made the province's products uncompetitive. The greatest threat to the province's economy, however, came from the growing flood of imports, especially of European textiles, partly through Lima but, above all, through Buenos Aires. The effect was not only to undermine the former lucrative export of cloth and agricultural items from Peru to Upper Peru but also to flood the market within Peru itself, draining it of its circulating media and making its remaining *obrajes* uneconomical.[1]

The activities of the port of Buenos Aires were also blamed to some extent for the decadence of agriculture in the province of Trujillo. The city's *cabildo* believed that one reason for the decline in sugar production was the illegal import of cheaper Brazilian sugar into the Spanish empire through Buenos Aires.[2] The accuracy of the claim was questionable.[3] Nevertheless, it is clear that economic distress in the province was widespread. The *haciendas* in the valleys of Chisno, Chicama and Viru, for example, which had produced much wheat and sugar in the seventeenth century, had been in decline ever since the serious earthquake of 1687, which caused a temporary halt in production.[4] Thereafter the landowners were unable to recapture their former markets. The Lima sugar market had been taken over by the *partidos* of Cajamarca and Huamachuco, while the growing import of cheap Chilean grain made wheat production uneconomical. The abolition of the *flota* system in 1740 was a further blow, since the ships bound for Panamá had always taken on supplies in Paita. The situation in 1784 was that, despite fertile land and good water supplies, the majority of the ninety-one *haciendas* in the three valleys had fallen into disuse, because their crops could be produced more cheaply elsewhere. Not only was there little prospect of finding an international market, but, mainly because of a serious shortage of labour, there was no apparent possibility of ousting Chilean grain from its dominant position within the viceroyalty. The total number of slaves on all the *haciendas* in the three valleys around Trujillo

[1] See below, 132–5.
[2] A.G.I., Aud. de Lima 1100, Escobedo to Gálvez no. 181, 16 Jan. 1784.
[3] Ibid.   [4] Ibid.

was only 1375, and continuing depression meant that, even when new slaves were available, landowners were unable to afford them.[1]

In Cuzco and Arequipa, and indeed in Lima, the separation of Upper Peru in 1776 and the opening of the port of Buenos Aires to transatlantic and inter-colonial trade were blamed for Peru's economic decline. These measures certainly had serious economic consequences for the viceroyalty, but they aggravated rather than caused a trend already underway before 1776.[2] The Peruvian economy had been depressed since at least the beginning of the eighteenth century, as the agricultural problems of Trujillo indicated. Even at the height of Lima's power and wealth her pre-eminence in South America was based, not upon a sound and diversified economic development in the viceroyalty as a whole, but upon a monopoly of the import and distribution of merchandise from Europe and of the export of bullion.[3] The monopoly was never watertight, and by the beginning of the eighteenth century the old fleet system to which it was linked had fallen into decay.[4] The abolition of the fleet system did not involve the removal of Lima's monopoly, but it did cause local problems, and the replacement of the fleets by *registros*, single licensed vessels, sailing around Cape Horn, increased the opportunities and pressure for direct trade between Spain and Buenos Aires, as well as with smaller Chilean ports.[5] Although the Lima monopoly survived in theory, it appeared increasingly artificial, an inevitable candidate for rationalization, as the Peruvian economy, and in particular its agriculture, declined in importance. Natural disasters such as the earthquake of 1687, a diminishing supply of slaves and local factors, such as the break up of efficient Jesuit estates after 1767, increasingly made agriculture less competitive.[6] The rate of imports from other areas, especially Chile, increased proportionately.[7] By 1776 the *haciendas* of Peru served only to supply a

[1] For efforts to increase the supply of slaves, see below, 148–9.
[2] Céspedes, *Lima y Buenos Aires*, 55–6.
[3] Ibid., 24.
[4] See A. C. Loosley, 'The Puerto Bello Fairs', *H.A.H.R.*, xii (1933), 314–35.
[5] Vargas, *Historia del Perú. Virreinato (Siglo XVIII) 1700–1790*, 195.
[6] Ibid., 338. Céspedes, *Lima y Buenos Aires*, 55–6.
[7] Céspedes, *Lima y Buenos Aires*, 58.

population of one million, of whom many thousands lived at subsistence level, with those commodities which were not imported, and to provide food supplies for the mining centres of Upper Peru. The *obrajes* of the *sierra* sent their coarse textiles to the same region. The whole economic structure rested upon the exchange of local products for the silver of Upper Peru, upon the export of silver through Lima and upon the maintenance of Lima's monopoly of trade with Europe.

The separation of the richest mining areas, for incorporation in the newly-created viceroyalty of the Río de la Plata, and the final removal of Lima's monopoly of overseas trade between 1776 and 1778 came as catastrophic blows to an already weakened structure.[1] Economic forces alone would have diverted the flow of Upper Peruvian silver away from Lima and towards Buenos Aires. The order of viceroy Cevallos, issued in Buenos Aires in July 1777, that unminted gold and silver might no longer be sent from Upper Peru to Lima merely hastened the process.[2] Traditionally goods imported from Lower Peru had been paid for with unminted bullion, which was then taken to Lima for coining, since the mint at Potosí was notoriously inefficient and incapable of handling all the gold and silver mined in Upper Peru. To confine the export of bulk bullion from the mining provinces to Buenos Aires was in effect to paralyse the trade between Upper and Lower Peru.[3] The embargo was not completely effective, and trade between the two Peru's survived to some degree. But it was only a shadow of its former self.

Reform and reorganization of the Potosí mint, undertaken by Escobedo as Areche's subdelegate, brought some improvement to this general situation, by increasing the supply of coinage, the export of which to Peru was not prohibited.[4] In the meantime, however, economic disruption in Lower Peru, to which the viceroyalty of Peru was now confined, was intensified by the effects of renewed Anglo-Spanish warfare, which impeded trade with Europe, by the Túpac Amaru rebellion, which

[1] Ibid., 56. [2] Ibid., 120–1.
[3] Ibid. For an eloquent appeal for the restoration of Upper Peru to the viceroyalty of Peru see B.M., Add. MS 17588, ff. 1–10.
[4] Escobedo served in Potosí until appointed to succeed Areche as *visitador*.

brought economic activity in the interior provinces to a virtual standstill, and by the abolition of the *repartimiento* system, which tended to remove the Indian sector from the market economy.[1] The material and psychological effects of these factors upon the merchant community of Lima made its members extremely reluctant to risk their capital, either in mining or in the development of other products.[2] It was in these circumstances that the intendants were faced with the task of encouraging the exploitation of Peru's neglected natural resources and, in general, of reviving her economic life.

Measures such as those taken by the intendant of Tarma to increase the export of *cascarilla* brought some improvement.[3] The value of exports other than bullion rose from 733,587 pesos in 1785 to 906,022 pesos in 1787.[4] Yet between 1784 and 1787 the general economic position of the viceroyalty seemed to deteriorate even further. The *consulado* of Lima complained bitterly in 1787 that a flood of imports had saturated the market, and that the viceroyalty's circulating capital was being extracted at such a rate that there was no hope of replacing it.[5] It blamed this upon the fact that 'free trade' was bringing an excessive amount of merchandise, and demanded that a two-year moratorium be imposed upon the import of European goods through the viceroyalty's own ports. Even greater hostility was revealed towards trade with Buenos Aires. The Lima merchants sought a complete ban on trade between Buenos Aires and the viceroyalty of Peru. When forwarding their representation to Spain Escobedo commented upon its contents.[6] He agreed that the Peruvian market was saturated. Between 1785 and 1787 goods worth 24,000,000 pesos had been landed at Callao, to be sold in a viceroyalty producing each year for export bullion and other goods worth less than 5,000,000 pesos. He agreed, too, that an excessive amount of bullion had been exported. The twenty-eight ships which sailed for Europe between 1784 and April 1787 carried 33,074,731 in coins, as well as a further 500,000 pesos in unminted bullion. Some of this was capital owed for

[1] See above, 29, 101–3. [2] Céspedes, *Limya y Buenos Aires*, 155.
[3] See above, 127. [4] Gil, *Memoria*, appendix, 12–13, table 5.
[5] A.G.I., Aud. de Lima 1111, *consulado* to Escobedo, 5 May 1787.
[6] A.G.I., Aud. de Lima 1111, Escobedo to Sonora, no. 973, 5 Sept. 1787.

goods imported in previous years, or money which had accumulated in Peru while war between Spain and Britain disrupted normal commercial activity. Nevertheless, he believed that bullion exports for current trade were in excess of current mining production, and agreed that the viceroyalty's plight was serious.

The basic problem, however, in Escobedo's views, was not that freer trade had led to excessive imports. The problem was an internal one, the fact that, despite vast resources, Peru remained almost entirely dependent upon the export of bullion to pay for its imports. Other exports consisted only of *cascarilla cacao*, largely produced in Guayaquil and re-exported through Callao, a small amount of copper from Chile and some *vicuña* wool. Apart from these items the only commodities exported on the twenty-eight ships which carried over 33,000,000 pesos in bullion between 1784 and April 1787 were wool (37,198 lbs), indigo (32,198 lbs) and a few hundred furs. In terms of percentage of value in Lima, figures tended to vary from one year to another, but over the quinquennium 1785-89 bullion exports accounted for over 88 per cent of total exports.[1] A mere temporary ban on imports would then do nothing to solve the basic economic problem.[2] Even a reduction in duties on sugar, wool and cotton would have little value, since high costs of production, caused by a shortage of labour, low internal consumption and high transport costs, would still prevent these commodities from competing effectively with the products of less remote parts of the empire.

Escobedo was more sympathetic to the *consulado*'s second demand, that there should be a ban upon the import into Peru of goods which passed through Buenos Aires. Whereas Croix felt it to be a matter of no importance that one part of the empire should suffer because of the prosperity of another area, as long as the empire as a whole benefited, Escobedo felt that some consideration should be given to Peru's problems.[3] Buenos Aires had not only taken over from Lima the supply of European

---

[1] Gil, *Memoria*, appendix, 12-13, table 5. In this period bullion exports totalled 27,861,700 pesos; other exports were worth 3,733,567 pesos.
[2] A.G.I., Aud. de Lima 1111, Escobedo to Sonora, no. 973, 5 Sept. 1787.
[3] Céspedes, *Lima y Buenos Aires*, 175, for Croix's opinion.

goods to Upper Peru but had even begun to compete effectively with Lima in the supply of goods to large areas of Lower Peru. For example a bale of linen, worth 250 pesos in Cádiz, could be supplied to Arequipa through Buenos Aires at an increased cost of 87 pesos, after payment of transport costs and customs and sales taxes. The same bale of linen supplied to Arequipa through Lima would increase in price by 111 pesos, mainly because of higher rates of taxation.[1] In general the supply of European goods to Arequipa and Cuzco was being taken over by Buenos Aires, while Lima declined in commercial importance. As trade decreased the prospects of reviving agriculture diminished, while lower mercantile profits reduced the amount of capital available for investment in mining.

The saturation of the market was followed after 1787 by a reduction in both the supply of goods and the export of bullion, with the result that hysterical fears that Peru was to be denuded of its coinage diminished.[2] However, as the turnover of trade was reduced so, too, was the export of agricultural goods, their value falling from 906,022 pesos in 1787 to 448,095 pesos in 1790.[3] Some observers challenged the view that 'free trade' had had detrimental effects. Writers in the *Mercurio Peruano* acknowledged that its introduction had reduced the fortunes and power of the former monopolist merchants, but claimed that it had succeeded in spreading prosperity to a wider segment of society.[4] It was further claimed in 1794, in the detailed analysis of the viceroyalty's trading pattern prepared by Ignacio de Leguanda, that 'free trade' had stimulated both imports and exports and had led to a reduction in contraband.[5] Leguanda recognized, however, that a general decline had occurred in the prosperity of Lima and of the viceroyalty as a whole.[6] This was caused, in his view, basically by the separation of Upper Peru, although he added that a further factor in

[1] A.G.I., Aud. de Lima 1111, Escobedo to Sonora, no. 973, 5 Sept. 1787.
[2] For an article rejecting the view that there was a currency crisis, see *Mercurio Peruano*, no. 27, 3 April 1791, 250–1.
[3] Gil, *Memoria*, appendix, 12–13, table 5.
[4] *Mercurio Peruano*, no. 1, 2 Jan. 1791; no. 26, 31 March 1791, 238–45; no. 27, 3 April 1791, 249–50.
[5] B.M., Eg. MS 771, ff. 34, 155v.
[6] Ibid., ff. 50–62.

Lima's decline was the creation of the intendant system, since it decentralized the administration of judicial affairs.[1]

The *consulado* continued to press for a restriction of imports from Europe to a level not greater than the annual production of the mines and of agricultural goods for export.[2] The annual import of goods worth about 4,750,000 pesos should, it suggested, be regarded as a maximum, and it decisively rejected the argument that unrestricted import would act as a stimulus to produce more for export. Its main grievance, however, was the continuing arrival in Upper and Lower Peru of goods imported through Buenos Aires. The detailed representation prepared in 1790 provided a variety of statistics to illustrate the fragility of the Peruvian economy. Much of the report merely repeated points made by Escobedo in 1787, but information about trade with other parts of the empire was a new feature. It was shown that, on average, trade with Chile, Chiloé, Santa Fe and Guatemala gave Peru an annual deficit of about 445,000 pesos.[3] Only trade with Upper Peru provided a balance in Peru's favour, since the mining area, although now supplied with textiles through Buenos Aires, remained dependent upon Peru for agricultural products. The province of Arequipa provided wine, *aguardiente*, oil, *pimientos* and sugar, worth an annual average of 1,300,475 pesos, receiving in return 911,215 pesos in minted bullion and other merchandise worth 389,260 pesos. Cuzco provided sugar, grain and some cloth worth an average annual total of 734,505 pesos, receiving in return merchandise worth 475,530 pesos and 258,975 pesos in bullion. The balance of trade in Peru's favour was 1,170,190 pesos, giving a net balance on inter-colonial trade of 725,190 pesos. The profits made by shipowners and by the owners of mule teams which carried goods from Arequipa to Upper Peru added a further 400,000 pesos to this balance.[4] The *consulado* claimed, however, that the import of European goods through Buenos Aires had not only reduced drastically the export of

[1] Ibid., f. 70. For Leguanda's opposition to Manrique, when the latter served as intendant of Huamanga, see above, 40–1.
[2] See R. Vargas, 'Informe del tribunal del consulado'.
[3] See articles in *Mercurio Peruano*, no. 24, 24 March 1791, and no. 25, 27 March 1791, which use the same arguments and statistics as the *consulado*.
[4] Ibid., no. 31, 17 April 1791, table 10.

textiles from Peru to Upper Peru but also had hit the market for Peruvian cloth within Peru's own boundaries.[1] The merchandise now sent to Arequipa and Cuzco in return for their agricultural products consisted mainly of European textiles, cheaper and of better quality than those produced by local *obrajes*. The general effect of this process was to damage all aspects of economic activity, by reducing the volume of capital available for investment. Moreover, the *consulado* was pessimistic about the prospects of increasing agricultural exports. It expected the demand for *cascarilla* to rise, but pointed out that wool and other items produced in the *sierra* were costly to transport to the coast, while sugar could be produced more cheaply elsewhere in the empire. The only practicable suggestion for improvement which it was able to make was that the rate of the *alcabala*, then at six per cent, should be halved.

The basic grievances of the *consulado*, that Lima had declined as Buenos Aires prospered, that Peruvian industry had been hit by European imports, were clearly based upon harsh reality. There is no doubt, however, that as a conservative group, seeking the restoration of lost privileges, the Lima merchants were determined to place the worst possible construction on the existing circumstances. In fact, there are signs that as economic life in general became more settled, after the hectic eighties, efforts to exploit natural resources began to have some effect, and the export trade became slightly less dependent upon bullion. In 1791 bullion accounted for all but 736,892 pesos of total exports worth 5,699,591 pesos, but, with the exception of cotton, the quantities of non-mineral exports (*cascarilla, vicuña*, skins and hides) increased considerably in comparison with the previous year.[2] In 1792 bullion exports reached 8,285,840 pesos and other exports were worth 955,111 pesos. Comparable figures for 1793 were 1,408,707 and 344,020, and for 1794 3,903,344 and 1,643,131.[3] Clearly the export trade tended to fluctuate wildly from one year to another, but the overall trend between 1790 and 1794 was one of improvement. In the quinquennium

[1] Vargas, 'Informe del tribunal del consulado'.
[2] For detailed analysis of trade in 1791 see *Mercurio Peruano*, no. 52, 3 July 1791, and no. 129, 29 March 1792; for summary see Gil, *Memoria*, appendix, 12–13, table 5.
[3] Gil, *Memoria*, appendix, 12–13, table 5.

1785–9 bullion exports had accounted for eighty-eight per cent of total exports (27,861,700 pesos in bullion, 3,624,657 pesos in 'frutos y efectos'), while in the quinquennium 1790–4 they fell to eight-five per cent of the total. In this second period the value of total exports fell by about 3,500,000 pesos, with bullion exports falling to 23,780,977 pesos. The value of other exports rose, however, to 4,127,250 pesos.[1] In view of the difficult circumstances in which the intendants and others charged with the stimulation of agriculture had to work, this improvement was creditable. Nevertheless, the viceregal economy remained almost wholly dependent upon the export of bullion and, even more significantly, vulnerable to the effects of a suspension of trade with Europe. The demise of the informative *Mercurio Peruano* in 1795, the replacement in the following year of viceroy Gil by Osorno, who was far less interested in economic affairs, and Osorno's failure to leave a *Memoria* make it more difficult to build up a detailed picture of economic life in the second half of the decade. It is clear, however, that after 1796 the effects of Spanish involvement in European warfare and in particular the cutting of imperial communications by the British navy brought to an end the brief period of economic recovery enjoyed by Peru from about 1790.[2] Thereafter economic life once again declined and, apart from sporadic fluctuations, remained depressed for the remainder of the colonial period.[3]

The internal factors retarding agriculture—shortage of capital and labour, and poor communications—also restricted the exploitation of mineral resources.[4] Despite the separation of Upper Peru, mining, especially silver mining, remained the basis of the entire economy. Although the crown sought to lay increasing emphasis upon the exploitation of animal and vegetable resources, this aim by no means involved any attempt deliberately to run down the mining industry. On the contrary, determined efforts were made to increase the production of the mines, since only a healthy mining industry would provide the

---

[1] Ibid.   [2] For effects on exchequer, see above, 120–1.
[3] See below, 151–4.
[4] B.M., Add MS 17588, ff. 7–8, raises the additional problem of the operation of the *mita* after the separation of Upper Peru.

capital for investment in other spheres and the purchasing power to stimulate trade. Moreover, increased production would increase crown revenues from the taxes of *cobos* and *diezmos*. It was to this aspect that the Ordinance drew the attention of the intendants, when charging them with the general control and development of mining within their provinces.[1]

There is evidence that in 1785 and 1786 some intendants made zealous efforts to fulfil this obligation. The intendant of Arequipa, Menéndez, enthusiastically reported in 1785 the discovery of new gold deposits in the *partido* of Tarapacá.[2] His successor, Álvarez, took the initiative in encouraging the working of newly-discovered rich silver deposits in the same area.[3] Most active among the new intendants was Gálvez of Tarma, whose province contained the extremely rich mining centre of Cerro de Pasco. Production of silver at Pasco in 1784 amounted to 68,208 marks, each mark yielding slightly over 8½ pesos when minted.[4] Production rose by 5247 marks in 1785, and then rose dramatically by a further 35,645 marks in 1786, to a total of 109,100 marks. The large increase was the result of a complex draining project, directed by the subdelegate of Pasco, Francisco Cuellar, with the intendant's full support. Production in 1786 was equivalent to over twenty-five per cent of the total amount of silver minted in the viceroyalty in the following year.[5] It yielded 107,416 pesos in taxation and, equally important, it acted as a stimulus to economic activity throughout the province.[6] Pasco was supplied with grain and flour from Tarma, Jauja and Huamalíes, with cloth from Conchucos, *coca* from Huánuco, sugar and cloth from Huaylas and salt from Cajatambo and Chancay.[7] Thus, as mining advanced the entire province benefited; if mining stagnated economic depression was felt in a wide area. Pasco continued to flourish, in fact. By 1789 production had risen to almost 122,000 marks, and

[1] *Ord. Ints.*, arts. 133–6.
[2] A.G.I., Aud. de Lima 1117, Menéndez to Gálvez, 4 June 1785.
[3] A.G.I., Aud. de Lima 646, Álvarez to Gálvez, no. 6, 28 Feb. 1786; Álvarez to Valdés, no. 11, 12 June 1789.
[4] A.G.I., Aud. de Lima 646, Gálvez to Sonora, no. 25, 3 Feb. 1787.
[5] At 8 pesos 5 reales a mark, production in 1786 was worth 940,987 pesos; total silver minted in 1787 was 3,581,281 pesos—see Appendix 3.
[6] A.G.I., Aud. de Lima 646, Gálvez to Sonora, no. 25, 3 Feb. 1787.
[7] A.G.I., Aud. de Lima 646, Gálvez to Sonora, no. 21, 17 Oct. 1786.

viceroy Osorno reported in 1799, when total production in the viceroyalty was worth just over 6,000,000 pesos, that the mining industry as a whole was almost entirely dependent upon two key centres, Pasco, and Chota in the province of Trujillo.[1]

Mining made steady progress between 1790 and 1799. Gil described the industry as in 'el mas brillante estado' in 1796, although he pointed out that there was considerable room for improvement in technical matters and complained of a shortage of labour.[2] Production fell by 800,000 pesos in 1797, rose to over 6,000,000 in 1799, but then fell by 1,300,000 pesos in 1800, remaining low thereafter.[3] The general decline after 1799 was a consequence of the cumulative effect of European warfare, which, by disrupting communication between Peru and Spain, cut off supplies of mercury and reduced the mercantile capital available for investment.[4] During this period the responsibility of the intendants for mining was considerably reduced. They remained committed to doing what they could to encourage the industry at a local level, but from the beginning of 1787 direct responsibility for its management throughout the viceroyalty rested with the newly-created mining tribunal in Lima.

Throughout 1786 preparations were made in Lima by Escobedo and in the provinces by his intendants for the application in Peru of the Mining Ordinance of New Spain.[5] The intendants arranged for the election of provincial committees by the miners in the main centres of the industry, and by the end of the year the local committees had elected representatives to the mining tribunal, which began to operate in Lima at the beginning of 1787.[6] Charged with control of the economic and judicial aspects of mining, as well as with its general administra-

[1] *Mercurio Peruano*, no. 3, 9 Jan. 1791, 17–21. See also Donoso, op. cit., 465, for report of Osorno of 26 June 1799.
[2] Gil, *Memoria*, 153–7. [3] See Appendix 3.
[4] For criticism of mercantile reluctance to advance capital see *Mercurio Peruano*, no. 3, 9 Jan. 1791, 21–2. The anonymous author attributed the prosperity of mining in New Spain to the readiness of merchants there to advance 50,000 or 100,000 pesos to individual merchants. Peruvian merchants, he complained, would never advance more than 10,000 or 12,000 pesos, and even then insisted on carefully supervising its expenditure.
[5] A.H.M.H., Libro de Cédulas 900, f. 74, royal order, 8 Dec. 1785. For development of the institution in New Spain see W. Howe, *The mining guild of New Spain and its tribunal general, 1770–1821* (Cambridge, Mass., 1949).
[6] A.G.I., Aud. de Lima 1106, Escobedo to Sonora, no. 708, 20 June 1786.

tion, the tribunal was financed by a levy of one *real* on every mark of silver produced in the viceroyalty, collected from August 1786.[1] Its funds were to be used in particular to provide development loans, to finance *bancos de rescates*, where the miners could exchange their bulk bullion for minted coins, and for the foundation of a chemical laboratory in the capital.[2] Attempts to modernize the inefficient methods and technical processes of mining at a local level, a task already tackled in some areas by the mining commission of José Coquet and Santiago Urquizu, began on a large scale in 1790, with the arrival in Peru from Potosí of the mining mission of Baron Nordenflicht, staffed largely by German experts.[3] Nordenflicht's principal task was to improve the antiquated methods used to extract the metal from silver ore, although he was subsequently entrusted with wider responsibilities, including the inspection of the Huancavelica mercury mine, the exploitation of newly-discovered silver deposits and management of the chemical laboratory in Lima.[4] He continued his work until 1810, when the mission was ordered to end.[5] By then mining production was considerably lower than it had been in 1790, due probably to general economic conditions rather than to the failure of Nordenflicht, or indeed of the mining tribunal, to fulfil their obligations.[6] But the tribunal was scathing in its criticism of the European experts, and complained bitterly in 1813 of

> not only the uselessness of the Commission to America but also of the most grave financial injury it has caused to many individual miners, as well as to the industry's general funds, a total loss

[1] Ibid.
[2] The provision of *bancos de rescates* in the mining centres was a valuable innovation, since previously the miners, unable to transport their bullion to the provincial subtreasuries, had been obliged to sell it at a discount to middle-men. Details of how such a bank was intended to operate are given in A.N.P., Superior Gobierno 33, *cuaderno* 1065, instructions of mining tribunal to administrator of bank of Huarochirí, 14 May 1792.
[3] Details of work of Coquet and Urquizu are in A.G.I., Aud. de Lima 1110, Escobedo to Gálvez, no. 644, 20 March 1786, and Escobedo to Sonora, no. 682, 5 May 1786. For Nordenflicht's work at Potosí see Lynch op. cit., 145.
[4] See A. Z. Helms, *Travels from Buenos Aires by Potosí to Lima* (London, 1807), for the experiences of one of Nordenflicht's chief assistants.
[5] B.N.P., MS D48, tribunal to crown, 31 March 1813, referring to royal order of 22 Sept. 1810.
[6] See Appendix 3.

estimated to reach 500,000 pesos. Their disgraceful experiments, their lack of skill and their ignorance have caused serious loss to all establishments entrusted to their control.[1]

Undoubtedly technical improvements, the provision of capital and other reforms were of great significance for the progress of mining, but even more important was the maintenance of a regular supply of the materials without which the industry could not function. Items such as tallow for candles, powder and salt were always in demand, but the key commodity was mercury, since it was by amalgamation with mercury that silver was extracted from the ore. Without mercury the whole industry would grind to a standstill, since a halt in the extraction process would inevitably be followed by a lack of capital to continue operations. Although the general organization of the industry became the duty of the mining tribunal, the provision of mercury remained the responsibility of successive intendants of Huancavelica. Indeed, it was the fact that the only significant source of mercury in the whole of Spanish America was the mine of *Santa Barbara* at Huancavelica which led Escobedo to create an intendancy there.[2] The first intendant, Márquez, was provided with a detailed account of the mine's history and problems, and was clearly instructed that its management and the maintenance of a regular supply of mercury to the viceroyalty were to be his main duties.[3]

Márquez inherited control of a mine which for many years before 1784 had been increasingly unable to meet the demands made upon it, due to a combination of bad management, administrative confusion, financial corruption and technical inefficiency, especially in the refining of the ore.[4] In 1760 Antonio de Ulloa, then governor of Huancavelica, compared the *Santa Barbara* mine to 'an old woman slowly losing her teeth'.[5] Areche's efforts to revive it by transferring control from a guild of miners to an individual contractor ended in administrative chaos and financial scandal, and from 1782 the mine was

[1] B.N.P., MS D48, tribunal to crown, 31 March 1813.
[2] A.G.I., Aud. de Lima 1100, Escobedo to Gálvez, no. 375, 20 Nov. 1784.
[3] Ibid.
[4] For a general history of the mine see A. P. Whitaker, *The Huancavelica mercury mine* (Cambridge, Mass., 1941).
[5] A.H.M.H., Colección Santamaría MS 00110, note of Ulloa, 18 May 1760.

operated directly on behalf of the exchequer.[1] By 1784 little progress had been made in reviving it. When, in October of that year, a ship arrived from Spain with 3000 *quintales* of mercury (a *quintal* was 100 lbs) Escobedo commented that the arrival was 'most fortunate... because of the shortage of mercury from Huancavelica, which remains in a state of decadence'.[2] Early in the following year he complained of requests to supply mercury to Potosí, in the viceroyalty of the Río de la Plata, since Huancavelica was unable to meet even the needs of the viceroyalty of Peru.[3] Annual demand in Peru was between 5000 and 6000 *quintales*. However, during the three years from 1 January 1782, when direct operation on behalf of the crown began, and 14 December 1784, when Márquez took office as intendant, total production was only 5592 *quintales*.[4] Moreover, the average cost of production in this period was over 116 pesos a *quintal*, while the commodity was sold to miners from the subtreasuries at a fixed price which at times was less than half the cost of production.[5] In peacetime supplies could be obtained from the rich Spanish mines at Almadén at a much lower cost, but reliance upon this source increased the danger that interruption of communication with Spain would lead to the paralysis of the mining industry. Mercury deposits were known to exist in a number of areas within Peru, but efforts to exploit them, although encouraged by Escobedo, were unsuccessful.[6] Huancavelica remained the sole domestic source of supply, and Escobedo was cautiously optimistic that the presence of an intendant would ensure a more honest and efficient exploitation of its resources.

Progress in 1785 was promising. Márquez reported in July of

[1] A.G.M.R.E., Areche to *corregidor* of Cuzco, 16 Sept. 1779. A.G.I., Aud. de Lima 1103, Escobedo to Gálvez, no. 411, 5 Feb. 1785. Palacio, op. cit., 52-4.
[2] A.G.I., Aud. de Lima 1097, Escobedo to Gálvez, no. 359, 5 Nov. 1784.
[3] A.G.I., Aud. de Lima 1103, Escobedo to Gálvez, no. 415, 5 Feb. 1785.
[4] A.G.I., Aud. de Lima 778, Gálvez to Gardoqui, no. 22, 28 July 1797, enclosing table of production 1782-95.
[5] Ibid., note 3 on the table, which gives details of price fluctuations: on 1 Nov. 1779 reduced from 79 pesos 3 reales a *quintal* to 55 pesos; on 1 Jan. 1783 old price restored, but reduced to 60 pesos on 1 June 1784; raised to 73 pesos on 26 Aug. 1788, remaining at that price thereafter.
[6] A.H.M.H., Miscelánea, MS 1020 deals with abortive attempts to produce mercury in the province of Tarma, 1791-9.

that year that weekly production was about 100 *quintales*.[1] Escobedo's satisfaction at this situation was offset, however, by growing suspicion that the improvement resulted not from the discovery of new deposits of ore but from the working of rich ore previously untouched, because it was contained in stone props, arches and buttresses, which literally held the mine together.[2] The suggestion that Márquez was being deceived by the mine's director, Francisco Marroquin, was first made by Juan Luque Marmol, who had been dismissed from his post of *contador de azogues* for alleged obstruction of the intendant's reforms.[3] Escobedo's initial reaction was to disbelieve Marmol, but as the rumours of negligence increased he made a number of diplomatic appeals to the intendant to be vigilant.[4] Márquez was indignant that his supervision of the mine should even be questioned, and he complained bitterly to Gálvez on a number of occasions in 1785 that the superintendent was too ready to listen to malicious rumours.[5] After a further warning from Escobedo of the need to watch Marroquin closely, Márquez informed the Minister of the Indies in February 1786 that he was completely satisfied with the director's conduct.[6] He pointed out with satisfaction that during the previous nine months 4316 *quintales* of mercury had been produced. Escobedo remained uneasy, suspicious that the intendant was being deceived, although confident of his integrity.[7] His forebodings were justified when on 25 September 1786, while the intendant was touring his province, the *Santa Barbara* mine collapsed.[8]

The intendant was able to disguise the extent of the damage for about nine months by refining low grade ores from hills around the main mine. His first reports to Lima suggested that the damage had been caused by an earthquake, which had even had beneficial results, since it revealed new deposits of ore.[9]

[1] A.G.I., Aud. de Lima 777, Márquez to Gálvez, no. 3, 8 July 1785.
[2] A.G.I., Aud. de Lima 1108, Escobedo to Gálvez, no. 10, 20 Feb. 1786.
[3] Ibid. [4] Ibid.
[5] A.G.I., Aud. de Lima 777, Márquez to Gálvez, nos. 3 and 4, 8 July 1785, and no. 6, 30 Sept. 1785.
[6] A.G.I., Aud. de Lima 777, Márquez to Gálvez, no. 7, 8 Feb. 1786.
[7] A.G.I., Aud. de Lima 1108, Esccobedo to Sonora, no. 14, 5 July 1786.
[8] A.G.I., Aud. de Lima 1115, Pedro de Lerena to Porlier, *reservada*, 9 May 1790.
[9] See Croix, *Memoria*, 369–87, for a full discussion of what the viceroy described as 'el mayor y mas grave cuidado que ha ocupado mi atención'.

However, as production dropped in 1787 to half that of the previous year the true extent of the damage became clear. In 1787 the intendant dismissed Marroquin and other officials; at the end of the following year the viceroy decided that Márquez, too, should be removed from office, and that a full investigation of the causes of the disaster and of current problems at Huancavelica should be undertaken by the *oidor* Pedro de Tagle.[1] Tagle remained in control there from March 1789 until August 1790, and his conclusion was that the mine had collapsed because of the mining of ore from pillars and buttresses.[2] The net result of the disaster and of the confusion which followed it was a fall in mercury production from almost 4800 *quintales* in 1786 to 2400, 2668, 1619 and 2016 *quintales* in 1787, 1788, 1789 and 1790 respectively.[3]

The second proprietary intendant of Huancavelica, Ruiz, took up his post in August 1790.[4] During the first three years of his government production fell even further. Indeed during the whole four years he served in Huancavelica the royal mine produced only 6644 *quintales*, at an average cost of 109 pesos a *quintal*.[5] But the situation began to improve remarkably from March 1793, when, faced with the increasing difficulty of obtaining high grade ore from the main mine, the intendant gave permission to private enterprise to work the abundant mercury deposits in the surrounding hills.[6] The benefits of the innovation were threefold. It led to a sudden increase in mercury production, which reached over 4000 *quintales* in 1794. Moreover, mercury produced by this system of *pallaqueo* was sold to the exchequer by individual miners for 73 pesos a *quintal*, whereas the cost of producing mercury from the *Santa Barbara* mine

[1] Ibid., 371–8.
[2] Ibid., 379. Legal proceedings against Márquez were complicated by suits between him and Marroquin, and dragged on for many years, held up by appeals and counter-appeals. The case was still unresolved when it was decided in 1796 to make Márquez an *oidor* of the *audiencia* of Santa Fe—A.G.I., Aud. de Lima 778, report of Council of the Indies, 4 March 1796.
[3] See Appendix 5.
[4] Ruiz's appointment was announced in 1788, but Croix suspended it while Tagle completed his investigations—B.N.P., MS c2933, Croix to Márquez, 16 March 1789.
[5] A.G.I., Aud. de Lima 778, table enclosed with Gálvez to Gardoqui, no. 22, 28 July 1797.
[6] Ibid., notes 1 and 4.

had never fallen below 108 pesos a *quintal* since 1784.[1] The final benefit was that public opinion in Huancavelica was satisfied. Indeed, when news arrived in 1794 of Ruiz's promotion to the presidency of Cuzco the representative of the *cabildo* of Huancavelica appealed that he be allowed to remain, because of the benefits which the new system of mining had brought to the town.[2] The miners, he reported, were even prepared to pay his salary.

However, the new intendant, Juan María Gálvez, who arrived from Tarma in September 1794, soon made it clear that he, too, was a firm believer in the *pallaqueo* system. During his first year of office 4361 *quintales* were produced by this method, mostly from the new, rich mine of *Nuestra Señora del Carmen* in the Cerro de Silla Casa, while only 414 *quintales* were produced from the royal mine, where mining was gradually brought to a halt.[3] But renewed hopes that production would rise sufficiently to meet the average annual demand of 6000 *quintales* again receded as, with the exhaustion of the more accessible of the new deposits, it fell steadily, totalling only 2204 *quintales* in 1802.[4] It rose above 3000 *quintales* in 1804 and 1805, but thereafter, except in 1811, remained below that figure. As long as he remained at Huancavelica Gálvez at least paid lip-service to the need to keep production at the highest possible level. His successor, Juan Vives, who arrived at Huancavelica in July 1807, pursued a declared policy of running down production and devoting resources to the exploitation of nearby silver deposits. Writing in January 1808 to Miguel Cayetano Soler, the Minister of Grace and Justice, Vives reported on the steps he had taken

as a result of the most secret royal order, dated 28 November 1800, which Your Excellency personally handed to me at Aranjuez on 9 January 1806, explaining the king's reasons for issuing it and his

---

[1] Ibid., average cost under Márquez was 108 pesos a *quintal*; under Tagle 131 pesos; under Ruiz 109 pesos.

[2] A.G.I., Aud. de Lima 777, Juan Gregorio de Eyzaguirre, *procurador síndico* of Huancavelica, to crown, 1 May 1794.

[3] A.G.I., Aud. de Lima 778, table enclosed with Gálvez to Gardoqui, no. 22, 28 July 1797.

[4] See Appendix 5.

desire that the production of mercury should be ended throughout his American dominions.[1]

The motive, according to Vives, was the conviction that self-sufficiency in this vital commodity would induce the empire's inhabitants to revolt, whereas dependence upon Spain for supplies would act as a restraining influence. The intendant was convinced that if he, like his predecessors, had been commissioned to stimulate mercury production he could double it within a year, since the hills around the town contained plentiful deposits. Their existence suggested that no useful purpose would be served by completely destroying the *Santa Barbara* mine, since the town's inhabitants would still have access to other deposits, but, he went on,

if the king still desires that its future working should be made completely impossible, this end could be achieved within six months, without people realising my intention, simply by throwing the mine open to the general public. In that short time they would destroy the remaining props and buttresses ... simply to get the rich ore which they contain, and would thus cause the mine's total destruction.

Viceroy Abascal denied knowledge of the royal order invoked by Vives to explain his conduct.[2] He added that, even if such an order had been issued, the intendant had been unwise to make known to the public his intention to reduce mercury production still further. Throughout 1808 the viceroy became increasingly aware of tension, suspicion and even disorder in Huancavelica, and it was clear that the town's inhabitants knew of the intendant's intentions.[3] In January 1808, for example, a group of residents, led by Gregorio Delgado, the *alférez real* of the *cabildo*, complained that Vives had repeatedly announced

that this royal mine and all those around it worked by individuals are no use to the state, and how he wished that there was not even a trace of mercury in them, since he had come to attend this town's funeral.[4]

[1] A.G.I., Aud. de Lima 778, Vives to Soler, no. 7, *reservadísima*, 18 Jan. 1808. The orders cited by Vives are in A.G.I., Aud de Lima 1335.
[2] A.G.I., Aud. de Lima 602, summary of Abascal's letter of 23 July 1808 in report of Council of the Indies, 8 Feb. 1812.   [3] Ibid.
[4] A.G.I., Aud. de Lima 778, representation of Gregorio Delgado, Bernardo Quevedo and Josef de Pedregal y Mollinedo, 30 Jan. 1808.

On Abascal's advice the *Junta Central* ordered in February 1809 that Vives be removed from office, that he hand over to the viceroy any secret orders in his possession, and that the viceroy should take all measures necessary for the maintenance of peace and order in Huancavelica until the arrival of a new intendant.[1]

The failure of successive intendants of Huancavelica to increase mercury production left Peru permanently short of this vital commodity, and without it silver mining could not continue indefinitely. In peacetime supplies could be sent from Almadén, but stocks were never large enough to withstand the effects of a prolonged isolation from Spain. After 1796 the maintenance of communication with the peninsula became increasingly difficult, and, although the decline in silver production after 1799 was caused basically by a number of general economic factors, there is no doubt that a shortage of mercury was a most significant contributory cause.[2] The problem was pointed out repeatedly by intendants, individual miners and the mining tribunal.[3] The crown's ministers sympathized, declaring that they would take all possible measures to increase supplies from Spain.[4] But they were unable or, if Vives's testimony is to be believed, unwilling to arrange for the provision of quantities sufficient for the maintenance of the mining industry during a long period of disruption of trade with the mother country.

Even in peacetime communication with Spain was a problem, since Peru's isolated position made it extremely difficult for her goods to compete effectively with the products of less remote parts of the empire. Peruvian sugar and tobacco, for example, could not compete in the European market with the products of Cuba and Venezuela, which, besides being produced more efficiently, could be transported to Spain more easily and at

---

[1] A.G.I., Aud. de Lima 602, royal order, 4 Feb. 1809. For Vives's defence and subsequent developments, see below, 207–10.

[2] Avilés, *Memoria*, 68.

[3] For example, B.N.P., MS D482, mining tribunal to crown, 22 Oct. 1812 and 31 March 1813.

[4] A.H.M.H., Libro 1141, f. 149, Soler to viceroy, 5 Dec. 1804, informing him that, on receipt of request from mining tribunal for 24,000 *quintales*, officials in Cádiz have been ordered to send whatever is available.

lower cost. Difficulties of communication within Peru were a further problem, limiting the likelihood of a more thorough exploitation of the natural resources of her interior provinces. The predominantly mountainous and rugged nature of the terrain, broken by many small rivers, made the transport of merchandise to the coast expensive. The repair of roads and bridges, the provision of inns and signposts, and the general task of promoting easier and safer travel within their provinces were among the many duties of the intendants.[1] There is evidence that, at a local level, impressive efforts to fulfil this obligation were made by some intendants, but in general they lacked the resources to initiate a comprehensive programme of improvement.

Parts of the main roads from Cuzco to Lima and Potosí were repaired in 1790 at the initiative of the regent-intendant Portilla.[2] In 1787 work began on the construction of a new bridge at Jequetepeque, in the *partido* of Lambayeque, which, when completed, made overland communication between Lima and Quito safer and easier.[3] The second intendant of Trujillo, Vicente Gil, arranged for the repair of roads and bridges around his capital, as well as for the provision of signposts.[4] Intendant O'Higgins of Huamanga conscripted Indian labour and imposed a tax on landowners for the construction of a new bridge over the river Huatatas, near his capital, while his uncle, Osorno, spent 343,600 pesos on the construction of a new road from Lima to Callao, opened in 1798.[5] The *Mercurio Peruano* emphasized the need to improve communications, to the extent of offering a gold medal for the best dissertation on how to solve the problem without burdening the Indians with excessive work or increasing taxation.[6] Seven months later, when only one entry, presenting no original ideas, had been received, it was decided to end the competition and withold the prize.[7]

[1] *Ord. Ints.*, arts. 60–4.
[2] A.G.I., Aud. de Cuzco 5, Portilla to Cernadas, 20 March 1790, and Corral to Porlier, no. 34, 10 July 1791.
[3] Croix, *Memoria*, 137.
[4] A.G.I., Aud. de Lima 1120, 'Relación de méritos...', 1819.
[5] A.G.I., Aud. de Lima 601, report of Council of the Indies, 14 May 1807. Donoso, op. cit., 380.
[6] *Mercurio Peruano*, no. 74, 18 Sept. 1791.
[7] Ibid., no. 137, 26 April 1792.

One original idea, put forward in 1799 by Tadeo Haënke, was that the rich natural resources to be found to the east of the Andes might be exported to Europe down the Amazon.[1] He was aware that such a scheme might cause problems with the Portuguese, but suggested that France might be induced to make the necessary arrangements on Spain's behalf.[2] Neither Haënke's impractical schemes nor the efforts of the intendants to improve roads and bridges made any appreciable difference to the problem of communication. The task was formidable, in view of the limited resources available and the almost insuperable natural barriers, and Abascal complained in 1816 that the inadequacy of the existing facilities remained one of the chief obstacles to Peru's economic development.[3]

A shortage of manpower likewise restricted the possibility of economic development. The small population of the viceroyalty, although increasing in the late eighteenth century, offered only a limited scope for expansion of the domestic market for Peru's products, while a shortage of labourers for the *haciendas* made efficient production impossible. As a labour force the Indians were highly immobile and were not easily tempted to the coast. Instead the large coastal *haciendas* relied traditionally upon negro slaves, but increasingly in the eighteenth century landowners complained that slaves were no longer brought to Peru; the few who arrived were very costly. The small number supplied by the Philippine Company in 1788, for example, were sold at 1250 pesos each.[4] The crown was not unresponsive to appeals from Peru, and, following the issue of *cédulas* in 1789 and 1791 which reduced import duties, it was decreed in 1796 that slaves could be imported into the viceroyalty duty free.[5] This concession proved inadequate to persuade Spanish merchants to take slaves to Peru, and as a result sympathetic consideration was given to the request of the conde de Premio Real, a *regidor* of Lima, made through his son, Antonio Lavalle, in 1798, for permission to transport 2000 slaves to Peru within three years.[6] His intention was to send ships from Cádiz to the west African

[1] B.M., Add. MS 17591, ff. 27–9.
[2] Ibid., f. 30v.   [3] Abascal, *Memoria*, i, 170.
[4] A.G.I., Indif. General 2827, Escobedo to Saavedra, 6 April 1798.
[5] A.H.M., Libro de Cédulas 29, ff. 288–9, Gardoqui to viceroy, 1 July 1796.
[6] A.G.I., Indif. General 2827, Lavalle to crown, 10 March 1798.

coast, and, having obtained slaves, to sail to Buenos Aires, taking them overland to Peru from there.

The proposal was referred to Escobedo, then a minister of the Council of the Indies, who gave it full support.[1] He argued that the provision of slaves was vital for the revival of agriculture in Peru, since, even if alternative labour were available, the impoverished landowners would be unable to pay wages. He was dubious, however, about Lavalle's further request that permission be given for the free import of eighty bales of cloth to clothe the slaves carried by each ship, since this need could be met by the use of coarse cloth produced in Peru. Moreover, a formal decision that foreign goods could be imported duty free could easily be abused. The main request, however, was granted. The licensee, or his agents, could send Spanish ships, or while the current war persisted ships of neutral or friendly nations, in search of slaves.[2] Their import into Peru could be paid for by the duty-free export of agricultural products. The scheme had moved ahead slowly by 1802, and in July of that year a French ship left Bordeaux to make contact with an agent in Mozambique and to collect from him 700 slaves for transport to Buenos Aires.[3] But there is no evidence that these slaves ever reached Peru, Viceroy Avilés informed his successor in 1806 that the shortage of slaves was a great problem and complained that no action had been taken by the crown to deal with it.[4] It appears likely that any slaves which did reach Buenos Aires were sold there, where they were in great demand for household duties.

When convinced that discriminatory concessions would benefit economic life in declining parts of the empire, without weakening the structure as a whole, the crown was prepared to grant them. Before it was prepared to act, however, it required convincing evidence that proposed concessions were essential. Inevitably the process of lengthy investigation and discussion which this cautious attitude entailed made the process slow, and when concessions did come they were often too late to be

[1] A.G.I., Indif. General 2827, Escobedo to Saavedra, 6 April 1798.
[2] A.G.I., Indif. General 2827, unsigned note in the *expediente*, dated 16 April 1798, reports that permission was granted on 13 April 1798.
[3] A.G.I., Indif. General 2827, unsigned, undated document, referring to 1802.
[4] Avilés, *Memoria*, 96.

effective. The pattern is illustrated by the crown's response to reports of agricultural decadence in the province of Trujillo.[1] Escobedo recommended in 1784 that this could be alleviated by the removal of duties on agricultural goods exported from the province, by the reduction of import duties, and by the reduction from five to three per cent of the rate of interest payable on *censos*.[2] The *contador general* in Spain, to whom the matter was referred, pointed out that to remove export duties and reduce those on imports would be a drastic measure, difficult to redress and setting a dangerous precedent, and he recommended that no action should be taken until more information could be obtained.[3] The second proposal, for the reduction of interest on *censos* was referred to the viceroy and the *junta superior* in Lima for their advice.

Reference to the viceroy was often merely a polite way of shelving an issue indefinitely. The appeal for the removal of duties was dealt with relatively quickly, and it was ordered in 1796 that privileges granted to a number of Caribbean ports in 1789 should be extended to Huanchaco and Pascamayo.[4] Agricultural goods exported through these ports were to be freed from export duties and from import duties on arrival at other ports in the empire. Moreover, goods for which they were exchanged could be freely imported into the province of Trujillo through the same two ports. This was a valuable concession, which facilitated the export of sugar and other crops to ports such as Valparaíso and Guayaquil.[5] Progress on the second request, however, was slower. No action had been taken by successive viceroys when in 1793 landowners around Trujillo again appealed for a reduction of interest rates.[6] The inten-

---

[1] See above, 128–9.

[2] A.G.I., Aud. de Lima 1100, Escobedo to Gálvez, no. 181, 16 Jan. 1784. Throughout the empire many estates were mortgaged to the Church, which preferred to invest indirectly rather than directly in land. These mortgages were called *censos*, and traditionally carried an annual interest charge of 5 per cent.

[3] A.G.I., Aud. de Lima 610, report of *contador general*, 12 Feb. 1785.

[4] A.N.P., Superior Gobierno 27, *cuaderno* 822, royal order, 17 Sept. 1796, and copy of royal decree, 28 Feb. 1789.

[5] A.N.P., Superior Gobierno 27, *cuaderno* 822, Vicente Gil to Osorno, no. 544, 13 May 1798.

[6] A.G.I., Aud. de Lima 609, preamble to *cédula* of 22 March 1816, referring to representation of landowners of 6 Aug. 1793.

dant supported their request, reporting that six of the twenty-five sugar plantations in the Chicama and Caña valleys had gone out of production entirely, while the remainder had less than half the slaves they needed. The religious communities to whom the landowners were indebted recognized that agriculture had declined, but attributed the fact to the failure of the landowners to treat their slaves properly and to their expensive, luxurious living, rather than to the burden of *censos*.[1] They added, moreover, that most interest payments were made in kind, and when the produce thus received was sold by the communities their net profit was often only three per cent. Complaints about the burden of *censos* came from other areas. The intendant of Huamanga reported in 1802 that the decadence of agriculture in his province was in part attributable to these interest payments.[2] The belated response from the peninsula was the decision in 1816 that in the provinces of Trujillo, Huancavelica and Huamanga the rate of interest should be lowered to three per cent, but only when payment was made in cash; payment in kind was to remain at the rate of five per cent.[3]

The crown's efforts to redress Peru's economic decline were too feeble to affect the general situation, which grew even worse after 1810, as war and revolution in neighbouring areas disrupted commercial activity. The consequence was a growing sense of grievance and a feeling in many areas that their interests were being ignored, and would be better served by a devolution of authority. In the interior provinces of Peru this attitude was expressed in terms of a growing hostility towards control from Lima rather than in specifically anti-Spanish agitation. Representatives of the merchants of Cuzco, for example, suggested in 1811 that one way to revive economic activity in the province, which they described as in 'a deplorable state', would be to create a separate *consulado* in Cuzco, which would be able to deal quickly with the province's commercial matters and remove the need faced by many merchants to travel frequently to Lima.[4] They wanted, too, the creation of a separate

[1] Ibid.
[2] A.G.I., Aud. de Lima 764, O'Higgins to Cevallos, 16 June 1802.
[3] A.G.I., Aud. de Lima 609, *cédula*, 22 March 1816.
[4] A.G.M.R.E., instructions of *diputación de comercio* to deputy to Council of Regency, 27 March 1811.

captaincy-general, centred in Cuzco, completely independent of the superior government in Lima. The merchants had grievances against Spain. They complained of the problems caused to mining by the creation of a crown monopoly of the production and sale of powder, as well as of the fact that the *alcabala* was collected relentlessly and efficiently, despite its depressing effect on trade. Nevertheless, their demands were for freedom from Lima rather than from the mother country. A similar mood was expressed by the representatives of the province's miners.[1] They, too, wanted the creation in Cuzco of a separate captaincy-general, with its authority extending to the provinces of Huancavelica and Arequipa, as well as to Upper Peru. They felt that the mining tribunal in Lima understood little of their local problems, and demanded complete independence from its control for the provincial mining committee. A similar demand was put forward on behalf of the neighbouring province of Huamanga. Its former deputy to the Cortes described the decadence of mining there in 1814, and appealed on behalf of the *cabildo* of the provincial capital that the levy on silver produced in the province should be administered by the local miners' committee rather than by the tribunal in Lima.[2]

Provincial resentment of Lima was matched in the viceregal capital by a growing conviction that Spain either did not appreciate the seriousness of Peru's economic problems or was unwilling to do anything effective to resolve them. Complaints against commercial restriction and demands for freedom to trade directly with foreigners were made with increasing force, particularly by the *cabildo* of Lima, from 1809.[3] In November 1810 the *cabildo* instructed its deputy in Spain to seek licences for six annual expeditions to Canton, Coromandel and Malabar, each carrying 500,000 pesos in silver and supplies of agricultural goods.[4] The aim was simply to seek trade and to provide income for landowners and merchants badly hit by the disruption of trade with the peninsula, caused by war with first Britain and

[1] A.G.M.R.E., instructions of *diputación territorial de minería* to deputy to Council of Regency, 1 April 1811.
[2] A.G.I., Aud. de Lima 981, Martín Josef de Muxica to crown, 4 Nov. 1814, putting forward instruction from *cabildo* of Huamanga of 2 Aug. 1813.
[3] See below, 198-9.
[4] A.H.M., Libro de Cabildo 42, ff. 33-4, *acta cap.*, 23 Nov. 1810.

then France. Direct trade with Asia, it was patronizingly pointed out, would be unlikely to cause harm to Spanish commercial interests, since it was clear to Peruvians that Spain was not only unable to meet their trading needs in 1810 but also appeared to be unlikely to be in a position to do so in the future, owing to the destruction of Spanish factories during the peninsular war.

The *cabildo* again showed its resentment and frustration in January 1811, when it praised the 'zeal, activity and integrity' of its *procurador general*, Ignacio de Orue, for his uncompromising attack upon plans to increase taxation in order to raise money for the sending of troops to Upper Peru.[1] Such plans, claimed Orue, showed a complete ignorance of the viceroyalty's economic difficulties and commerical depression, caused by 'the restrictions she suffers, the lack of liberty to export her goods, the limits imposed upon her merchant ships, the prohibition of direct trade with Asia, the monopolies and other shackles. . .'.[2] So serious was the economic situation, he continued, that even contraband trade had declined, due to a lack of confidence among the merchant community of their ability to raise money. Instead of imposing new taxes to send troops to Upper Peru Abascal should arrange an armistice with the insurgents in Buenos Aires, on condition that they agreed to stay within their own viceroyalty, so that at least some trade might be revived. Orue insisted that the insurgents should be given time to consider such an offer; only if they rejected it should troops be sent against them. Abascal, determined to crush insurgency wherever it appeared, was horrified at such a proposal.[3] His unease grew as the abolition of tribute presented even more serious financial problems, making increased taxation inevitable.[4] When asked for his suggestions about which taxes should be increased, Orue replied in an extremely negative way.[5] He was opposed to any increase whatsoever, since many citizens already found it difficult to pay their taxes at the existing

[1] A.H.M., Libro de Cabildo 42, f. 49, *acta cap.*, 22 Jan. 1811.
[2] A.H.M., Libro de Cabildo 42, f. 45v–49, Orue to viceroy, 19 Jan. 1811.
[3] A.H.M., Libro de Cabildo 42, f. 49v, decree of Abascal, 19 Jan. 1811, announcing 'Con lo que dixe de palabra y por escrito al S'or Procurador General en 20 del corriente, crei haber tranquilizado su zelo por el bien publico. . .'.
[4] See above, 121–2.
[5] A.H.M., Libro de Cabildo 42, ff. 79–81v, Orue to viceroy, 26 Oct. 1811.

rates. A merchant engaged in trade with Chile, for example, was already required to pay total duties of 38½ per cent on each round trip. The prospect of even further increases filled Orue with despair. He asked rhetorically 'What will become of you my beloved country?' The answer, 'Your citizens will find themselves without food, without the means to support their families or to educate their children... *Infeliz época!*', was endorsed unanimously by the *cabildo*.[1]

Undeterred, Abascal insisted upon his duty to act as he saw fit to defend royal authority.[2] But increasingly he felt that the opposition expressed by the *cabildo*'s spokesman and by other influential critics, such as the *fiscal*, Miguel de Eyzaguirre, was undermining his position.[3] When the *procurador* took advantage of the freedom of the press in 1812 to inform the public of his opposition to proposed heavier duties on trade, Abascal complained bitterly that such activities could have a disastrous effect upon public opinion, by encouraging general hostility to fiscal innovations.[4] If the demands made by Orue and others for freer trade were met, the viceroy pointed out, 'It would be tantamount to decreeing the separation of these Dominions from the Mother Country, since, once direct trade with foreigners was established on the wide basis which they demand, the fate of European Spain would matter little to them...'.

In seeing clearly the implications of the *cabildo*'s demands, Abascal was more perceptive than Peruvians themselves. It is true that their sense of economic grievance was balanced by other factors, particularly the fear that political unrest might upset the delicately-balanced social structure, which held back the majority of creoles from a determined commitment to the cause of independence. Nevertheless, it is clear that by 1812 the leaders of creole opinion had reached the conclusion that continued attachment to Spain would mean increasing economic hardship, and had begun to make economic and commercial demands which, if granted, would lead to the disintegration of the empire.

[1] A.H.M., Libro de Cabildo 42, f. 79, *acta cap.*, 29 Oct. 1811.
[2] A.H.M., Libro de Cabildo 42, ff. 82v–83, *acta cap*, 12 Nov. 1811, includes transcript of *oficio* from viceroy of same date.   [3] See below, 216–17, 219–21.
[4] A.H.M.H., Colección Santamaría, MS 00216, *borrador* of Abascal to first secretary of state, 23 May 1812.

For a few years after 1790 it seemed possible that the general process of imperial economic advance, combined with the local efforts of intendants and others to encourage exploitation of Peru's vast range of natural resources, would lift the viceroyalty from the economic depression which, particularly from 1776, had hit all aspects of economic life. But the process of revival was brought to a halt by the cumulative effects of Spanish involvement in European warfare, which, by disrupting trade, not only took away Peru's export market but also created a shortage of materials essential for the wellbeing of the mining industry. The crown made some efforts to stem the viceroyalty's economic decline, but there was little that either the crown or the intendants could do, without upsetting the very foundations of the reformed economic and commerical structure of the empire. Lima's relative prosperity in the past had rested upon her monopoly privileges and upon her sovereignty over Upper Peru. To close the port of Buenos Aires or to restore Upper Peru to the viceroyalty of Peru, as Lima's merchants demanded, would make neither economic nor political sense from the general imperial standpoint. Consequently, deprived of Lima's commercial monopoly and of the mineral wealth of Potosí, Peru rapidly emerged as a casualty of imperial rationalization and reform, since she was unable to compete economically with other parts of the empire. This was so even in peacetime, despite some economic improvement. When, in time of European war, disruption of communications with Spain was added to the perennial problems of low domestic demand, shortage of capital and labour, difficulty of internal communication and geographical isolation, continuing economic decline was inevitable. Inevitable, too, was the growing conviction of Lima's creole élite that freedom to trade with the world at large would bring some relief from economic problems.[1] The belief was not sufficiently strong to induce the creole leaders to fight for independence but when independence was brought to them from Chile and Colombia most were glad to accept it.

[1] For a brief discussion of the economic ideas of leading Peruvians see E. Romero, 'Apuntes sobre las ideas de orden económico durante la revolución por la independencia del Perú', *Mercurio Peruano*, xxi, 146 (1939), 35–41.

CHAPTER VII

Intendants and Public Administration

THE OVERHAUL of the imperial administrative structure undertaken in the reign of Charles III was intended to increase crown revenues, to eliminate fraud and corruption in government, and to make royal absolutism more effective. Improved judicial administration and the eradication of social abuses, it was hoped, would reduce Indian discontent, making the empire more secure against internal dissension, while military reorganization would make it safer against external aggression. Economic expansion would generate the wealth and the revenue yielded by taxation to pay for the programme of reform. However, to see administrative reform solely as a means of making absolutism more effective and taxation more profitable would be to ignore the equally important intention that it should bring genuine improvement in the happiness and well-being of the king's American subjects.

Like many contemporary monarchs, Charles III sought to improve the material conditions of his subjects. His approach to government was enlightened, and many efforts were made to ensure that it should become more rational, progressive and humane. The qualification was that reform should be dispensed by the monarch to the people. Royal absolutism should not only be continued but also improved, and, although the wishes and needs of the people would be considered, the crown's prime aim would always be the maintenance and increase of imperial authority. Ideas of democracy or representation were considered only after the political upheaval in Spain which followed the Napoleonic invasion. There remained, however, before 1808, within the framework of absolutism, considerable scope for bringing greater happiness and welfare to the empire's inhabitants.

One of the four main branches into which the duties of the intendants were divided was that of *policía,* or public administration.[1] Within this sphere they were to deal with 'whatever leads to the greater advantage of my subjects.'[2] Particular attention was drawn to the obligation of investigating economic conditions and needs in the provinces, the provision of maps, inns, signposts and other aids to travellers and merchants, the repair and construction of roads and bridges, and the elimination of highwaymen. Beggars were to be rounded up and put to useful work, while good order and morality were to be enforced by the provision of municipal by-laws. Agriculture was to be encouraged, if necessary by the redistribution of land, and the intendants were to ensure the maintenance of adequate supplies of inexpensive food to the towns. Public granaries were to be constructed if the intendants considered them to be needed. The indiscriminate construction of new churches was to be prevented by the need for those planning construction to submit plans and obtain prior permission for the work from the intendants, while great attention was to be paid to the maintenance and repair of houses, whether owned by Indians or Spaniards. The cleaning, paving and lighting of streets in towns and cities was considered of particular importance, and, in general, the intendants were to promote municipal improvements and the provision of amenities.

It is true that the successful application of these instructions could be expected to bring fiscal benefits. The improvement of communications, for example, would stimulate commercial expansion, which, in turn, would provide increased revenue for the *alcabala.* But the basic aim was the fulfilment of a paternalistic monarch's desire to improve the material conditions of life and labour among his subjects. The responsibilities of the intendants in this aspect of government were given even greater emphasis by Escobedo, whose aim in providing each intendant with a description of the size, problems and resources of each of his *partidos* was, in part, to give him the practical information needed for the promotion of sound public administration.[3] He realized, however, that it was imperative for each intendant to

[1] *Ord. Ints.*, arts. 53–70.   [2] Ibid., art. 53.
[3] A.G.I., Aud. de Lima 1098, instruction to Márquez, arts. 15–17.

obtain first-hand knowledge of the area he controlled: each was under the obligation to make extensive, personal tours of his intendancy.[1] These *visitas* would provide the intendants with detailed information on commerce, mining, agriculture, population, communications and similar topics, and reports submitted to Spain would give the central government the necessary information to enable it to build up a picture of the conditions and needs of the viceroyalty as a whole.[2] Escobedo realized that the provision of accurate maps would be a difficult task for the intendants, owing to a shortage of competent cartographers and engineers.[3] Nevertheless, they were to proceed with their *visitas*, paying particular attention to land ownership, and, in order to encourage its more efficient exploitation, redistributing land which had been usurped from either the crown or the Indian communities.[4] The intendants were to ensure, however, that this delicate responsibility was handled with caution, since it was known that not only creoles but also many Indian *caciques* held land to which they had no legitimate title.[5] It would clearly be dangerous to provoke their hostility by too ambitious a programme of redistribution.

The fear that detailed investigation into land ownership would disturb influential creoles in Cuzco and other towns was one of the reasons for Mata's reluctance to undertake a *visita* of his province.[6] Another was his conviction that his absence from his capital would provide disloyal creoles with greater opportunity to plot against the crown.[7] He was able, however, to gather considerable information about economic conditions in the *partidos* of his intendancy from the reports of the inspections made by his subdelegates for the purpose of overhauling the collection of tribute.[8] At the end of 1786 he sent to Spain detailed accounts of population distribution, communications and agricultural conditions, together with a map of each

---

[1] Ibid., art. 8. The same order was given to each intendant.
[2] *Ord. Ints.*, arts. 21–2.
[3] A.G.I., Aud. de Lima 1098, instruction to Menéndez, art. 15.
[4] *Ord. Ints.*, art. 57.
[5] A.G.I., Aud. de Lima 1098, instruction to Márquez, art. 19.
[6] A.G.I., Aud. de Cuzco 35, Mata to Gálvez, no. 7, 14 March 1785.
[7] Ibid. See above, 43–6.
[8] See above, 112–13.

partido.[1] Other intendants attempted to use their subdelegates in this way, too. The intendant of Huancavelica, for example, found it impossible to make a personal inspection of his whole province, since he considered his presence in the capital and supervision of the royal mine more important. However, he was able to use his subdelegates not only to make detailed reports on all foreigners living in the intendancy but also to provide economic and geographical information about their *partidos*.[2] In 1786 the subdelegate of Castrovirreina submitted statistical information about his *partido*, with details of its population, clergy, temperature, livestock and *haciendas*.[3] Attempts to repeat the process in other *partidos* were held up, however, by the reluctance of priests in remote parishes to provide the subdelegates with the information needed for their general reports.[4] Complaints to the bishop of Huamanga, whose diocese included the province of Huancavelica, succeeded only in provoking the retort that the provision of statistics was a task for the subdelegates, not for priests.[5] Reports on the *partidos* of Tayacaja and Angaraes were still unavailable in 1789, a deficiency which the second intendant, Ruiz, attempted to remedy in 1791.[6] During a seasonal lull in the smelting of mercury ore he made preparations for a personal inspection of the intendancy, beginning at Tayacaja.[7]

Even for intendants without the special responsibilities of the intendant of Huancavelica the obligation to make annual *visitas* was unrealistic, since few could hope to complete such an inspection in a single year. The reaction of some intendants was to avoid making *visitas*, or to pass on responsibility for them to the subdelegates; others, however, zealously sought to achieve

[1] A.G.I., Aud. de Cuzco 35, Mata to Sonora, no. 46, 24 Nov. 1786. For maps see Torres Lanzas, op. cit., nos. 89–100.
[2] B.N.P., MS c1462, Márquez to subdelegate of Angaraes, 22 Feb. 1785, requesting details of 'estado, manejo, hacienda e ideas' of foreigners, and MS c1463, decree of Márquez, 12 Dec. 1785.
[3] B.N.P., MS c1463, Francisco Gómez Carrasco to Márquez, 26 April 1786, enclosing *estado general*.
[4] B.N.P., MS c1463, Márquez to Croix, 3 Jan. 1788 and 11 Aug. 1788.
[5] B.N.P., MS c1463, bishop to Croix, 5 Oct. 1788.
[6] A second report on Castrovirreina was produced in 1788—B.N.P., MS c1463, Tagle to Croix, 16 Dec. 1788, enclosing *estado*.
[7] B.N.P., MS c3219, decree of Ruiz, 15 Jan. 1791.

a literal application of their Ordinance, realizing that improvements in public administration, as well as in other spheres of government, depended upon personal investigations. The first intendant of Tarma, Juan María Gálvez, provided in April 1785 a detailed report on his inspection of the *partido* of Jauja.[1] Despite an abundance of agricultural produce, the provision of foodstuffs to the district capital, Atun Jauja, was unsatisfactory. Other public services were non-existent. The intendant's solution was to form a *cabildo*, to persuade the town's inhabitants to accept municipal office, and to use it to promote public administration.[2] Work was begun on the construction of an aqueduct to ensure the provision of adequate supplies of water, while the wealthier inhabitants were persuaded by the intendant to build a new bridge over the nearby river to increase the prospects of trade with Cuzco and Huamanga.[3] The new *cabildo* co-operated, too, with the introduction of arrangements for the cleaning and paving of the streets, and for the whitewashing of houses in the town.

A year later Gálvez had completed his provincial inspection, although he held back his report for several months, until he had been able to find cartographers to draw the necessary maps.[4] He finally submitted his report to the crown in October 1786, enclosing with it a general map of the intendancy and more detailed maps of each *partido*.[5] Details of products, communications and population distribution were accompanied by information of the measures taken in each area to promote better public administration and to stimulate agriculture and mining. A *cabildo* was founded in Tarma to provide the town with the machinery for municipal improvement, and a tax was levied on *aguardiente* to make funds available for the new corporation. With the *cabildo*'s support a cemetery was opened, while in another sphere measures were taken to regulate the

---

[1] A.G.I., Aud. de Lima 763, Juan María Gálvez to José de Gálvez, no. 6, 18 April 1785.
[2] See below, 178–9.
[3] A.G.I., Aud. de Lima 763, Juan María Gálvez to José de Gálvez, no. 6, 18 April 1785.
[4] A.G.I., Aud. de Lima 1117, Juan María Gálvez to José de Gálvez, no. 13, 19 April 1786.
[5] A.G.I., Aud. de Lima 646, Gálvez to Sonora, no. 21, 17 Oct. 1786.

provision of meat to the town. In Huánuco work began on the construction of a public fountain, and in Conchucos particular attention was paid to ensuring that the owners of *obrajes* did not maltreat their Indian workers. The information provided by the intendant was precise, detailed and relevant to the demands of the Ordinance of Intendants. Indeed, such was his zeal for rapid reform and his conviction that the new system of government could revive Peru, that he soon became frustrated with what he interpreted as the lack of urgency felt in Madrid. He complained strongly in February 1788 that twenty-five of the thirty reports he had submitted to the crown since taking office, including those dealing with his *visita*, remained unacknowledged and unanswered.[1] In his subsequent posts at Huancavelica and Lima Gálvez showed little interest in making *visitas* comparable to that which he completed in Tarma, possibly because of the lukewarm response to these early efforts.[2] However, his successor in Tarma, Francisco Suárez de Castilla Valcárcel, spent much of the time between his arrival in the intendancy in 1793 and his death in 1795 making a comprehensive provincial inspection similar to that undertaken by Gálvez. He began the work at the mining centre of Cerro de Pasco, but was obliged to leave abruptly to deal with an invasion of hostile Indians in the eastern part of the *partido* of Jauja.[3] On his return to Pasco, which was an extremely unruly place, he found that in his absence there had been considerable disturbance, involving robberies, murders and arson, stirred up by the lawless element to be found in most mining towns.[4]

The most extensive and detailed provincial inspection undertaken by any of the Peruvian intendants was that made between 1786 and 1794 by Álvarez, intendant of Arequipa.[5] Álvarez took up his post in November 1785 and spent his first year in office making meticulous preparations for the inspection. After only a few months in Arequipa he was aware that there would

[1] A.G.I., Aud. de Lima 1120, Gálvez to Valdés, no. 1, 18 Feb. 1788.
[2] For his later career see biographical appendix.
[3] B.N.P., MS C1341, Suárez to Gil, no. 379, 24 Dec. 1793.
[4] B.N.P., MS C1341, Suárez to Gil, no. 384, 24 Jan. 1794.
[5] See Fr. V. M. Barriga, *Memorias para la historia de Arequipa. Relaciones de la visita del intendente de Arequipa don Antonio Álvarez y Jiménez* (3 vols., Arequipa, 1941–8). The original reports are in A.G.I., Aud. de Lima 805 and 806.

be many abuses to be remedied in connexion with land ownership and judicial administration at a local level. In order to deal thoroughly with these and other problems he sought permission to take with him on his tour various advisers and assistants, including a surveyor, a secretary, a legal adviser and two clerks.[1] However, his request for financial assistance to pay their salaries was rejected by Escobedo and Croix, who attempted to moderate the intendant's zeal for an immediate literal application of the Ordinance.[2] Permanent reform, they argued, could not be achieved overnight, but only by 'hard work and perseverance, combined with prudence'.[3] Álvarez was advised to continue with the proposed inspection and to remedy problems which presented few difficulties, but to consult with the authorities in Lima on more complicated matters.

Undeterred by this unenthusiastic reaction to his proposals, Álvarez began his *visita* in December 1786, at the town of Chiguata in the *partido* of Arequipa.[4] During the first month expenses totalled 398 pesos and had to be paid from the intendant's salary of 6000 pesos a year.[5] Requests for financial assistance were again rejected.[6] This basic difficulty underlined the problems of applying the general requirements of the Ordinance at a local level. It was not only impossible for an intendant to make a thorough *visita* without the assistance of a cosmographer, clerks, a surveyor and other officials but also physically impossible for him to make every year an effective inspection of a vast province poorly endowed with roads.[7] Even those who made the inspection over a longer period had no effective authority to reform many abuses. For example, Álvarez's hopes of being able to reclaim crown lands held without title by influential inhabitants of Arequipa were dashed

[1] A.G.I., Aud. de Lima 646, Álvarez to Sonora, no. 12, 23 May 1786, and Álvarez to Escobedo, 8 May 1786.
[2] A.G.I., Aud. de Lima 646, Alvarez to Sonora, no. 23, 29 Aug. 1786.
[3] A.G.I., Aud. de Lima 646, Croix to Escobedo, 10 June 1786, sent to Álvarez by Escobedo on 11 July 1786 as the official reply to his request for financial assistance.
[4] Barriga, op. cit., i, 6.
[5] A.G.I., Aud. de Lima 806, Álvarez to Escobedo, 29 Jan. 1787.
[6] A.G.I., Aud. de Lima 612, Machado to Gardoqui, 10 Feb. 1792. A.H.M.H., Libro de Cédulas 900, f. 220, Gardoqui to Gil, 11 May 1792.
[7] *Ord. Ints.*, art. 22.

by orders from Lima that he should ignore the matter, since the prospects of hostility and interminable legal disputes were too daunting.[1]

In Madrid, too, ministerial support for the literal observance of the Ordinance waned quickly after the deaths of José de Galvez and Charles III.[2] In 1791 Álvarez sent to Spain detailed reports on his *visita* to the *partido* of Condesuyos.[3] In the following year he sent further reports on the *partidos* of Moquegua and Arica, giving details of his work in each of the spheres of government defined by the Ordinance.[4] Rather than praise his diligence, the Council of the Indies criticized the intendant for sending to Spain 'almanacs of the current year', which appeared to have little relevance to the improvement of public administration.[5] Such reports, he was informed, were of little value to officials in Madrid, who were unable to judge their accuracy. In the future he should communicate on matters of public administration only with the viceroy and the *audiencia* in Lima.[6]

The subsequent waning of enthusiasm within Peru for the comprehensive type of *visita* undertaken by Juan María Gálvez and Álvarez was a natural result of this official indifference. Álvarez's successor, Salamanca, succeeded in making *visitas* only to the *partidos* of Tarapacá, Cailloma and Condesuyos during his fifteen years in office.[7] He acknowledged that greater activity in this aspect of government would have had beneficial results, but pleaded that pressure of work restricted the time which could be devoted to it. Within their smaller areas some subdelegates continued to make *visitas*, similar in aim and method to those undertaken on a larger scale by intendants. For example, the subdelegate of Chota, José María Egaña, made a successful *visita* to his *partido*, arranging for the rebuilding of villages, improved water supplies and better communications.[8] But the majority of the second and subsequent generations of

[1] A.G.I., Aud. de Lima 806, Álvarez to Escobedo, 29 Jan. 1787.
[2] See above, 60.
[3] A.G.I., Aud. de Lima 805, Álvarez to Porlier, no. 17, 2 Jan. 1791.
[4] A.G.I., Aud. de Lima 805, Álvarez to Bajamar, no. 23, 1 June 1792.
[5] A.G.I., Aud. de Lima 805, *mesa* to Bajamar, 10 March 1793.
[6] A.G.I., Aud. de Lima 805, *cédula*, 12 March 1793.
[7] Salamanca, *Relación*, 29–31.
[8] A.G.I., Aud. de Lima 804, the 'alcaldes, procuradores y demas naturales de a provincia de Chota' to crown, 1812.

intendants and subdelegates lacked the pioneering spirit of some of their predecessors, and showed little awareness of the need for extensive personal inspections of their provinces.

The exception was Bernardo O'Higgins. His predecessor in Huamanga, Menéndez, seems to have been relatively inactive during his fourteen years in office, not only in the sphere of public administration but also in all other aspects of government.[1] O'Higgins explained that Menéndez's negligence was due partly to his advanced age and delicate constitution, but above all to his desire for a quiet life, free from the problems which radical efforts to reform government would have caused.[2] Thus, it was left to O'Higgins to undertake the first general inspection since the founding of the intendancy.[3] His investigation revealed widespread economic depression, caused to some degree by alcoholism among the Indians, who were unwilling to do any more work than the minimum necessary to provide for subsistence and payment of the tribute. It also uncovered much abuse of authority by the parish clergy, who were active in extorting excessive dues from their parishioners, but idle and immoral in all other aspects of their work. A second *visita* was made in 1804 to check on the effectiveness of remedial measures taken in 1801.[4] O'Higgins found that some progress had been achieved in the promotion of public works, but appealed for an engineer to be sent to the province, since a number of major projects were being delayed by the lack of a competent specialist to direct them. He reported some improvement in the general standards of government, but complained that it was extremely difficult to exercise effective control over his subdelegates, mainly because of the viceregal reluctance to support his authority. Moreover, he added, the balance of power between viceroy and intendants defined by the Ordinance had now shifted considerably in favour of the viceroy, with the result that urgent reforms were often delayed by the need to obtain permission for them from Lima.

O'Higgins's reports were sent to the Council of the Indies in

[1] A.G.I., Aud. de Lima 764, O'Higgins to Cevallos, 16 June 1802.
[2] Ibid.   [3] Ibid.
[4] A.G.I., Aud. de Lima 608, O'Higgins to Soler, 3 Oct. 1804—published as appendix to Juan and Ulloa, op. cit., 471–526.

1804 and 1805, for consideration of his recommendations, including the proposal to reduce the rate of interest on *censos*.[1] The Council did not deal with them until 1816. Its main conclusion was that in future intendants should not submit general reports covering many points of administrative detail, since they merely confused officials in Madrid.[2] Instead they should provide ministers with separate reports on individual points of administration. With the exception of O'Higgins, later intendants showed little interest in general *visitas*. The Regency attempted to revive the idea in 1811, ordering that intendants should submit copies of reports of *visitas* made by their predecessors, and reminding them of their obligation to make maps.[3] The intendants produced a variety of excuses to explain their inactivity in this sphere. Manuel Quimper, intendant of Puno, reported that his predecessor had begun a *visita*, but had been forced to end it, owing to an accident.[4] Lázaro de Rivera, intendant of Huancavelica, ordered a thorough search of the provincial archive, but was unable to produce more than a number of 'papeles sueltos', which indicated that Ruiz and Gálvez had made inspections of some *partidos*.[5]

Despite the activity of the first generation of intendants in promoting public administration, viceroy Gil complained in 1790 that little progress had been made in this aspect of government.[6] He was concerned, since he believed that this was the one field in which the intendants should have been particularly active. Judicial and exchequer affairs, he reported, were in practice dealt with by subdelegates and exchequer officials, while military affairs required little attention. However, a close examination of Gil's criticisms suggests that they reflected general viceregal hostility towards the new system of administration, rather than an honest appraisal of its achievements.[7] One of his complaints was that the intendants had

[1] A.G.I., Aud. de Lima 608, royal orders, 29 Dec. 1804 and 13 March 1805. See above, 151.   [2] A.G.I., Aud. de Lima 602, report of Council, 27 Jan. 1816.
[3] A.H.M.H., Miscelánea, MS 0006, Abascal to intendant of Puno, 4 Sept. 1811, forwarding royal order of 20 March 1811.
[4] Ibid., marginal note signed by Quimper.
[5] B.N.P., MS D10959, decree of intendant, 20 Dec. 1811; report of secretary to Rivera, 8 Jan. 1812.
[6] A.G.I., Aud. de Lima 647, Gil to Porlier, no. 7, 30 April 1790.
[7] See above, 65–6.

failed to provide maps of their provinces. It is true that some had failed to fulfil this obligation, possibly because of the difficulty in finding cartographers to draw them. But, given the general geographical ignorance before 1784, progress thereafter had been impressive. In 1786 Mata provided a map of each of the *partidos* of the province of Cuzco, while Juan María Gálvez's report of his *visita* was accompanied by a map of the intendancy of Tarma and a more detailed map of each *partido*.[1] Álvarez, too, provided a variety of maps and plans dealing with the province of Arequipa. Six plans of the capital and smaller towns in the *partido* of Arequipa were sent to Spain in 1786, to be followed in 1789 by a detailed map of the whole intendancy.[2] A map of the coastline of the *partidos* of Moquegua, Arica and Tarapacá was completed in 1791, and six further maps and plans of the *partico* of Arica had been prepared by 1793.[3] The intendant of Trujillo, Saavedra, sent a map of the *partido* of Cajamarca to Spain in 1787.[4] Thereafter intendants of Trujillo did little to provide further maps, with the exception of plans of the Hualgayoc mining centre, but the deficiency was remedied to some degree by the work of the bishop of Trujillo, Baltasar Jaime Martínez Compañon.[5] O'Higgins provided a plan of the city of Huamanga in 1803, and two years later sent a general map of the intendancy to Spain, together with plans of two bridges near his capital.[6] It seems that the intendants of Huancavelica did fail to prepare maps, although plans of the royal mine were sent to Spain.[7]

Gil's criticism was unjustified. However, his special interest in

[1] B.M., Add. MS 15740, ff. 39–43, map of province of Tarma and one each for *partidos* of Tarma, Jauja, Cajatambo and Huamalíes. The maps of the *partidos* are published in H. Ruiz, *Relación histórica del viage* . . ., edited by J. Jaramillo (2 vols., Madrid, 1952), ii, plates IX, XII, XVI and XVIII, together with a map of Huánuco produced for Juan María Gálvez (plate XV).

[2] Torres Lanzas, op. cit., nos. 87–8, 101–4. For a general map of the province and a plan of its capital see B.M., Add. MS 15740, ff. 46–7.

[3] Torres Lanzas, op. cit., nos. 122, 132–7.

[4] Ibid., no. 85.

[5] Torres Lanzas, op. cit., 148–9. See J. Domínguez Bordona (ed.), *Trujillo del Perú a fines del siglo XVIII. Dibujos y acuarelas que mandó hacer el obispo d. Baltasar Jaime Martínez Compañon* (Madrid, 1936).

[6] Torres Lanzas, op. cit., nos. 152, 158–9.

[7] A.G.I., Aud. de Lima 778, Vives to Soler, no. 6, 18 Jan. 1808, enclosing plan of mine.

public administration had the effect of urging the intendants to even greater efforts in this aspect of government as a whole. The viceroy personally encouraged them to examine their provinces in detail and to obtain the precise statistical information needed for economic improvement.[1] During his term of office a nautical academy was installed in the viceregal palace, and one of its staff, captain Andrés Baleato, was commissioned by Gil to make maps.[2] Those he produced included a general map of the viceroyalty, an excellent map of the intendancy of Trujillo and a map of the western *montaña*.[3] The fact that Baleato was commissioned to prepare a map of this potentially rich region to the east of the Andes rather than of more familiar territory nearer Lima was indicative of Gil's desire to exploit untapped resources. In fact, the maps of the province of Lima prepared before Gil took office were of poor quality, but he considered it necessary to concentrate upon areas which offered the best prospects for economic development.[4]

Those intendants who made *visitas* included in their reports details of the size and distribution of the population in each area. This valuable work was co-ordinated and brought to a peak by Gil, who arranged for a census of the whole viceroyalty, completed in 1792.[5] The census showed a total population of 1,076,122, of whom 608,000 were Indians, although it was believed that the actual number of Indians was even greater.[6] Gil's census was used as a basis for part of the work of Bonet, who, in the preparation of his plan to provide the subdelegates with salaries, collected information of the size, climate and economy of each *partido*, as well as on its population and racial composition.[7] His figures for Indian population were based upon the most recent investigations made by subdelegates, and the increase in their numbers was largely responsible for the estimated increase in total population to 1,115,207.[8]

[1] See above, 65.   [2] Donoso, op. cit., 338.
[3] B.M., Add. MS 17672, map D (Trujillo), Add. MS 15740, f. 33 (viceroyalty); Gil, *Memoria*, 394, facing (*montaña*).
[4] For maps of Lima see Torres Lanzas, op. cit., nos. 109–12, B.M. Add. MS 15740, ff. 37–8, and Ruiz, op. cit., i, plates VI, VIII, XVII.
[5] Gil, *Memoria*, appendix, 6–9, table 3.
[6] B.M., Add. Ms 17580, f. 52, note of Ignacio Leguanda.
[7] See above, 96.   [8] See Appendix 2.

168   INTENDANTS AND PUBLIC ADMINISTRATION

Gil's interest in public administration, particularly in economic affairs, was reflected, too, by the publication in Lima between 1791 and 1795 of the *Mercurio Peruano*. This bi-weekly periodical was produced by the *Sociedad de Amantes del País*, a small group consisting not only of intellectuals such as Hipólito Unanue but also of administrators, churchmen and merchants, both creole and Spanish.[1] It provided excellent articles on general economic affairs, on agriculture, mining and communications, as well as on literary and historical themes. One of the first numbers contained a detailed analysis of the population of Lima, prepared on Gil's instructions by the city's *teniente de policía*.[2] There also appeared frequent articles describing the history, geography, population and economies of a number of *partidos*, including Tinta in the province of Cuzco, Arica in the province of Arequipa, Piura, Chachapoyas and Trujillo in the province of Trujillo, and all the *partidos* of the province of Tarma.[3] Most of them were clearly based upon reports made by intendants.[4]

There is ample evidence that the intendants paid considerable attention to the fulfilment of other tasks in the sphere of public administration, notably the improvement of the towns and cities of their provinces. Intendant Gálvez found his capital, Tarma, dirty and shabby, with municipal activity almost non-existent. The remedy in Tarma, as in smaller towns such as Jauja and Huaylas and in the city of León de Huánuco, was to found new *cabildos* or to revive those which were inactive.[5] The municipal authorities were then encouraged to join with the intendant in the promotion of public administration. One of Gálvez's most notable achievements in this context was the provision of a cemetery outside Tarma, since the former practice of burying dead beneath the town's churches was rightly considered a significant cause of frequent epidemics.[6] Gálvez was attracted by the prospects of exploiting the resources of the *montaña*, which bordered his intendancy to the east, as well as of

[1] For names of members and patrons see *Mercurio Peruano*, no. 210, 6 Jan. 1793.
[2] Ibid., no. 10, 3 Feb. 1791.
[3] Ibid., nos. 139, 162, 165–6, 188, 191, 193, 247–54, 258–9, 263.
[4] Articles on the province of Tarma in nos. 162, 258 and 259 are virtually identical to Gálvez's report on his *visita*.
[5] See below, 178–9.   [6] *Mercurio Peruano*, no. 8, 27 Jan. 1791.

converting its Indians, and gave active support to efforts to explore and settle the area.[1] In 1788 he personally commanded an expedition to the fertile Vitoc valley, an area which Spanish settlers had been forced to evacuate in face of Indian attacks after the rebellion in 1742 of Juan Santos.[2] This new expedition founded the towns of Colla and Pucara, and by 1792 more than eighty families had settled in the area, founding forty *haciendas*, which had begun to produce cotton, *coca*, coffee, wheat and *cacao*.[3]

Municipal improvement and rebuilding was an urgent task for the intendants of Arequipa, since much of the city was destroyed in the serious earthquake of May 1784, As soon as he took office at the end of 1785 Álvarez directed work on clearing the remaining rubble from the streets and making buildings secure.[4] Ambitious plans for the construction of a new centre to house all the exchequer offices and the *cabildo*, on the site of the ruined municipal offices and the prison, were held up by the *junta superior*'s reluctance to sanction the necessary expenditure.[5] Permission for the project was finally refused in 1792, much to Álvarez's disgust.[6] However, his successor, Salamanca, was able to complete the more modest task of rebuilding the old municipal offices.[7] In accordance with the obligation to prevent a proliferation of churches and convents, both intendants ensured that permission to rebuild was given only in exceptional cases, and always with the condition that the new buildings must be architecturally attractive.[8] Like his colleague in Tarma, Álvarez considered it necessary for the public health of his capital to provide a new cemetery. Work on this project was completed by Salamanca, who also provided the city with two new hospitals, partly at his own expense, and with a new public fountain.[9]

In Cuzco plans for the maintenance of roads and buildings

---

[1] A.G.I., Aud. de Lima 763, Juan María Gálvez to José de Gálvez, no. 6, 18 April 1786.
[2] See above, 14.   [3] *Mercurio Peruano*, no. 107, 12 Jan. 1792.
[4] A.G.I., Aud. de Lima 1117, Álvarez to Gálvez, no. 3, 31 Dec. 1785.
[5] A.G.I., Aud. de Lima 1115, Álvarez to Lerena, no. 19, 25 Feb. 1792, noting that plans were first submitted on 29 May 1786.
[6] Ibid.   [7] Salamanca, *Relación*, 13–14.   [8] Ibid., 40–1.
[9] Ibid., 13–14, and B.M., Eg. MS 1813, ff. 317–19, for reports from *cabildo*.

and for street-cleaning were pushed ahead with the active support of the new *audiencia*, while in Trujillo Saavedra introduced improved arrangements for street-cleaning, and carried out important repairs to the main Lima-Quito road.[1] His successor, Vicente Gil, undertook further work on the paving and lighting of his capital's streets, established night patrols for the maintenance of good order and arranged for an improved water supply.[2] In addition he organized the repair of roads and bridges around the city, and provided signposts for the benefit of travellers.

In the viceregal capital Escobedo set a good example for the other intendants in his handling of the problems of public administration. His first task was to revive the city's *cabildo* and to bring some order to the chaotic municipal finances.[3] With the *propios* and *arbitrios* overhauled, he made plans to use the revenue from them for the promotion of public administration, dividing the city into forty districts, each in charge of an official known as an *alcalde de barrio*.[4] This ambitious scheme brought some immediate results, including a comprehensive naming of Lima's streets and the numbering of houses in each street, but little progress was made with the wider problems of cleaning and lighting, largely because the *alcaldes* lacked any real sanctions for the enforcement of their authority.[5] Escobedo's solution was to create at the beginning of 1787 a *tenencia de policia*, headed by José María Egaña.[6] Under the *teniente*'s direction, rapid progress was made with paving and lighting, the removal of refuse heaps and the improvement of Lima's water supply.[7] He remained in office after Escobedo's departure, making regular reports to Croix on measures taken for the maintenance of public order and the control of fires and disease.[8] When Gil was viceroy, Egaña assisted him with plans for the provision of a rudimentary refuse collection service, and continued with the endless task of paving the city's streets.[9]

[1] A.G.I., Aud. de Cuzco 6, Corral to Minister of Grace and Justice, no. 11, 3 Nov. 1791. See above, 147.
[2] A.G.I., Aud. de Lima 1120, 'relación de los méritos y servicios' of Gil, 1819.
[3] See below, 177–8, 181–2, 184–6.
[4] A.G.I., Aud. de Lima 1113, Escobedo to Sonora, no. 834, 20 Jan. 1787.
[5] Ibid.   [6] Ibid.   [7] See below, 186.
[8] Croix, *Memoria*, 132–3.   [9] Gil, *Memoria*, 102–3.

Gil arranged, too, for major repairs to some of Lima's important buildings, including the cathedral, the royal chapel, the *aduana* and the viceregal palace.[1] Later viceroys continued to make improvements to the capital, although perhaps all tended to exaggerate the significance of their individual contributions. Avilés completed the removal of the city's open sewers and drains, while Abascal provided, at a cost of 100,000 pesos, the new cemetery outside the city walls, which had been planned since the time of Croix.[2] He also played an important part in the foundation of the medical college of San Fernando, opened in 1809. Abascal's zeal to improve the roads around Lima was impressive, but it provoked protests against the use of Indian communal funds for the work.[3]

Municipal improvement was a task which intendants and viceroys tackled with energy and enthusiasm. Their concern for the physical and material well-being of the inhabitants of Peru's towns and cities was matched by a paternalistic preoccupation with their moral welfare. Álvarez's *auto de buen gobierno* for Arequipa not only made provision for a variety of local amenities, including a fire service, but also forbade indecency, adultery, vagrancy and gambling.[4] O'Higgin's *auto* for Huamanga, issued in 1800, forbade blasphemy, indecent songs and dances, transvestitism, adultery, gambling and drunkenness, and also imposed a ten o'clock curfew.[5] He arranged, too, for the formation of a fire brigade and the lighting of every doorway, while householders were ordered to have the fronts of their houses swept every eight hours. Quimper's *bando de buen gobierno* for Puno, issued in 1806, covered a similar range.[6] Vagrants and those breaking the curfew would be punished with a month's public work, stray dogs would be shot and their owners prosecuted, those selling inferior fruit or meat would be punished, and all inhabitants were to beware of drunkenness, gambling and blasphemy. Vagrants, drunks, receivers of stolen property and dishonest traders discovered in Huancavelica were

[1] Ibid., 169–76.
[2] Avilés, *Memoria*, 30. Vargas, *Historia del Perú. Virreinato Siglo XVIII*, 107–13.
[3] A.G.I., Aud. de Lima 1172, report of *contador general*, 23 March 1811.
[4] Barriga, op. cit., i, 2–6, report of Álvarez, 1 March 1792.
[5] A.G.I., Aud. de Lima 764, *auto* of O'Higgins, 2 Jan. 1800.
[6] B.N.P., MS D127, *bando* of Quimper, 30 Dec. 1806.

liable, under the regulations announced by intendant Rivera in 1811, to fines or forced work in the mines.[1] Night patrols would check that *pulperías* closed at ten, while anybody found bearing arms without licence would be liable to summary justice. Similar regulations were issued by other intendants, and by the viceroys for the city of Lima. Viceroy Pezuela's *reglamento* of 1818, for example, forbade blasphemy, indecent language and transvestitism, and attempted to enforce religious observance.[2]

The aim of such codes was not interference with legitimate personal liberty but the fulfilment of the duty of a paternalistic monarch to create an orderly society, and to promote the moral and spiritual welfare of his subjects. In some aspects of public administration the intendants achieved little. Efforts to stimulate a revival of agriculture, for example, were unsuccessful.[3] More specifically, attempts to encourage the cultivation of new crops, such as hemp and flax, had little effect, partly because of a general conservatism among farmers and a shortage of capital to bring new land into production, and partly due to the realization that, since it was forbidden to manufacture hemp, cotton and linen products within Peru, the benefit from the growth of new crops would go, not to local interests, but to industrialists in Spain.[4]

In other aspects of public administration the intendants were able to stimulate striking progress. Despite a waning of interest in Madrid in a precise application of the Ordinance, a development which provoked a similar reaction among some officials in Peru, most intendants pushed ahead with the collection of economic information, the preparation of maps, the provision of local amenities, the regulation of food supplies and general municipal improvement. There is no doubt that in this local context the viceroyalty of Peru was better governed in 1814 than in 1784. But to some extent the overall effect of this success was to weaken rather than reinforce the bonds of empire. For many Peruvians improved municipal administration was small compensation for economic stagnation. After 1808 they were

[1] B.N.P., MS D10128, decree of Rivera, 29 May 1811.
[2] A.N.P., Superior Gobierno 36, *cuaderno* 1283, *reglamento de buen gobierno*, 31 Jan. 1818.
[3] See above, Chapter VI.
[4] *Ord Ints.*, arts. 57–8; Salamanca, *Relación*, 38–9.

INTENDANTS AND PUBLIC ADMINISTRATION

increasingly articulate in expressing their grievances, using as their mouthpieces their municipal corporations. When the intendants took office in 1784 the *cabildos* were decadent and lethargic, but thereafter became increasingly active and vigorous, directly as a result of the intendants' success in attempting to stimulate them to join in the process of improving public administration.[1]

[1] See below, Chapter VIII, and Lynch, op. cit., 287–8.

CHAPTER VIII

Intendants and *Cabildos*

ON THE EVE of the introduction of the intendant system the *cabildos* of Peru shared the inertia of other administrative bodies and corporations in the viceroyalty. The conditions of municipal life and government were as bad as, if not worse than, those which prevailed in the newly formed viceroyalty of the Río de la Plata.[1] After the golden age of municipal activity in the sixteenth century, local government had lost its enterprise, imagination and vitality, as the crown tightened its control and extended the practice of the sale of office.[2] Features of decline in the seventeenth and eighteenth centuries were less frequent *cabildo* meetings, reluctance to purchase municipal office, peculation and maladministration of inadequate municipal funds, absence of municipal building and expansion, and an inability to deal decisively with urgent matters of public administration.[3]

The number of *regidores* permitted for each *cabildo* varied according to the status of the settlement. In a *ciudad*, such as Lima, the legal maximum was twelve.[4] These posts were normally filled by creoles, and the *cabildos* were, in fact, the only important organizations capable of representing exclusively creole interests. These was no prohibition against *peninsulares* holding *cabildo* office, but the crown recognized the need of creole involvement. In 1781 the Council of the Indies confirmed the viceroy's decision to accept the lower of two bids for the

[1] Lynch, op. cit., 201–11.
[2] J. P. Moore, *The cabildo in Peru under the Hapsburgs* (Durham, N.C., 1954), 265. J. H. Parry, *The sale of public office in the Spanish Indies under the Hapsburgs* (Berkeley and Los Angeles, 1953), 70.
[3] Moore, op. cit., 265–83. See also Moore, *The cabildo in Peru under the Bourbons* (Durham, N.C., 1966), 82–4.
[4] For a detailed account of the functions and activities of *cabildos* see C. Bayle, S.J., *Los cabildos seculares en la América española* (Madrid, 1952).

INTENDANTS AND *CABILDOS* 175

office of *alcalde provincial* in the town of Cañete.[1] The higher bid came from a man born in Spain, but his offer was rejected on the grounds that he was socially inferior to his rival, the conde de Monteblanco, a descendant of a distinguished family of *conquistadores*. In such a case personal rivalry could increase the sums which applicants were prepared to pay, but on the whole enthusiasm to obtain municipal office was rare. The reason was not that the inhabitants of Peru could not afford to purchase posts. It was simply that, by the second half of the eighteenth century, the close control exercised over *cabildo* activities by royal officials had taken away the independence and freedom of action which they had enjoyed in earlier centuries, and consequently made the prospect of office unattractive. Outside of Lima the *cabildos* were dominated by the *corregidores*, who presided over their meetings, while the *cabildo* of Lima was firmly under viceregal control.[2] A special commissioner appointed by Areche in 1781 to undertake reform of municipal finances paid particular attention to the election of *alcaldes* and other officials in Lima for 1782. His conclusion was that the process of election was a sham since the *cabildo* was obliged to confirm decisions previously taken by the viceroy.[3] The pretence of free choice was preserved, but, in the words of the clerk of the *cabildo*, the process was 'a mere ceremony'. The names of those to be elected were public knowledge several days before the formal election. On 1 January, the traditional date for elections, the capitulars assembled to confirm unanimously, by acclamation, the viceroy's choices.[4]

The significance of this viceregal interference went beyond the fact that the *cabildo* was denied the right to choose freely its officers. The consequence was that the corporation had become a 'skeleton', stripped of its lustre and splendour, and unable to fill its vacancies, since citizens were not prepared to pay for membership of a body which was known publicly to be

[1] A.G.I., Aud. de Lima 598, report of Council, 23 Oct. 1781.
[2] There is also some evidence of ecclesiastical interference. In Huamanga, according to Croix, the *alcaldes ordinarios* elected for 1784 were chosen by the bishop—A.G.I., Aud. de Lima 599, Croix to Gálvez, no. 306, 16 Nov. 1785.
[3] A.N.P., Cabildo 7, *cuaderno* 13, Mata (later appointed intendant of Cuzco) to Areche, 25 Jan. 1782.
[4] A.H.M., Libro de Cabildo 37, f. 1, *acta cap.*, 1 Jan. 1782.

dominated by the viceroy.¹ Even those who held titles as *regidores* were reluctant to attend the regular *cabildo* meetings throughout the year, and in 1782 the viceroy was forced to request the appointment of temporary *regidores*, so that the corporation's work could continue.² Existing members were threatened with fines if their attendance failed to improve.³

For the *cabildos* the establishment of the intendant system did not involve increased interference with elections; on the contrary it led to determined efforts by Escobedo to ensure that the *cabildos*, particularly that of Lima, should regain a freedom of choice which had been denied them for many years.⁴ The grant to each intendant of the power to confirm the election of *alcaldes ordinarios* and to preside over meetings of the *cabildo* of his provincial capital involved merely a transfer of powers previously enjoyed by the viceroy and the *corregidor* respectively.⁵ In any case, there was a partial restoration of this authority to the viceroy in 1787, with the repeal of article eight of the Ordinance. Thereafter the confirmation of elections was in the hands of the viceroys or presidents of the *audiencias* in major cities.⁶ In towns more than fifteen leagues distant from the seat of a viceroy or a president, the intendants retained the right of confirmation, but were warned of the necessity of reporting promptly to the viceroy. In 1783, while preparing for the establishment of the new system of administration, Escobedo feared that the removal of the heavy hands of the *corregidores* in the provinces might make it difficult to prevent intrigue and faction appearing in some *cabildos*.⁷ Moreover, he was apprehensive lest the *cabildo* of Lima should make use of the actual ceremony of the installation of the intendants to follow the example of the *cabildo* of Buenos Aires, which had ostentatiously insisted on demonstrating its privileges.⁸

¹ A.N.P., Cabildo 7, *cuaderno* 13, Mata to Areche, 25 Jan. 1782.
² A.N.P., Cabildo 7, *cuaderno* 7, Jáuregui to *cabildo*, 6 Nov. 1782.
³ A.H.M., Libro de Cabildo 37, ff. 32v–33v, *acta cap.*, 11 Nov. 1782.
⁴ A.H.M., Libro de Cabildo 38, f. 27v, *acta cap.*, 1 Jan. 1785, which includes summary of *oficio* of Escobedo of 16 Dec. 1784.   ⁵ *Ord. Ints.*, arts. 8, 15.
⁶ A.H.M., Libro de Cédulas 29, ff. 61–3, Croix to *cabildo*, 18 May 1788. A.G.I., Aud. de Lima 598, royal order, 22 Nov. 1787.
⁷ A.G.I., Aud. de Lima 1117, Escobedo to Gálvez, no. 71, 16 June 1783.
⁸ A.G.I., Aud. de Lima 1117, Escobedo to Gálvez, no. 218, 16 Feb. 1784. It is not clear what form this demonstration took, although it was obviously related to the details of the public ceremony.

Escobedo was anxious to avoid friction over points of protocol. He saw the establishment of the intendancies as an opportunity to revitalize municipal life and government, and was determined that this important aim should not be frustrated by petty disputes. Thus for the benefit of both *cabildos* and intendants he issued an instruction regulating their joint ceremonies and providing a code of behaviour.[1] This emphasized the obligation of *regidores* and intendants to be regular in their attendance at meetings. To safeguard the authority of the intendants, *cabildos* were forbidden to make secret reports to other tribunals or superiors, unless they had good grounds for complaint.

One of the main tasks faced by Escobedo, as intendant of Lima, was to revive the *cabildo* over which he presided. In April 1784, before formally assuming the presidency, he began this process of reform by dismissing the *regidor* Antonio Álvarez de Ron, on the grounds of his notorious corruption and intrigue, and for having led the opposition to the attempts of Areche to reform the administration of the *proprios*.[2] The next step was to fill the vacancies among the *regidores*, since by July 1784 the *cabildo* had only three.[3] It was clear that the corporation could not fulfil its duties without members, but citizens had been unwilling to purchase the vacant offices. The solution proposed by Escobedo and eagerly accepted by Croix was that ten distinguished citizens should be persuaded to accept municipal office without charge and for life.[4] Those selected, all members of Lima's creole aristocracy, took office on the very day on which the *cabildo* formally received Escobedo. Their appointment for life was confirmed by the crown in the following year.[5] Escobedo's belief that this policy would make the office of *regidor* more attractive and ensure profitable sales when death led to vacancies was fully borne out in later years. In fact, the *cabildo* was to complain in 1797 that, owing to frequent attempts

[1] See above, 36.
[2] A.H.M., Libro de Cabildo 37, ff. 13–18, *acta cap.*, 4 May 1782. Includes correspondence between *cabildo* and Areche over the suspension of Mata's commission.
[3] A.G.I., Aud. de Lima 1117, Escobedo to Croix, 1 July 1784.
[4] A.H.M., Libro de Cabildo 38, f. 1, *acta cap.*, 13 July 1784, which includes Escobedo to Croix, 8 July 1784. A.G.I., Aud. de Lima 619, Escobedo to Gálvez, no. 321, 20 Aug. 1784.
[5] A.H.M., Libro de Cédulas 25, ff. 9v–10, royal order, 21 May 1785.

to purchase *varas* or to revive old titles, as well as to viceregal carelessness in approving such requests, *cabildo* membership had risen to a total of twenty *regidores*, eight above the official maximum.[1]

The shortcomings of the *cabildo* of Lima in 1784 mirrored those of the other *cabildos* of the viceroyalty. Most of the new intendants found it necessary to bring them up to strength before they could use them as instruments for the improvement of municipal affairs and public administration. Juan María Gálvez found his capital of Tarma without a *cabildo*.[2] He immediately appointed *regidores* and arranged for the election of *alcaldes* and the provision of municipal funds. The new corporation, which met twice a week, proceded to deal with street-cleaning, the regulation of food supplies and the general organization of town life. The intendant's provincial *visita* revealed much about the needs and conditions of municipal life outside his capital. In the city of León de Huánuco the few *regidores* did little work, and the *sala* of the *cabildo* was opened only for the annual election of an *alcalde ordinario*.[3] The streets were dirty, the roads ill-kept, and no attempt was made to undertake public works. Some of the lands intended to provide city funds had been usurped, others were let at very low rents and the remainder were unworked. The first step taken to remedy this state of affairs was to encourage citizens to fill the *cabildo* vacancies and to restore the practice of twice-weekly meetings. Gálvez then arranged for an inspection of municipal finances, appointing a commissioner to administer the *propios*, and was able to bring about a prompt increase in their annual yield from 300 to 600 pesos.[4] Before leaving Huánuco he arranged, too, for the construction of a public fountain and for a tree-lined public walk in the city centre.

In Huaras, capital of the *partido* of Huaylas, the intendant founded a *cabildo* of four *regidores* and two *alcaldes*.[5] He formed a *cabildo* in the town of Atun Jauja, capital of the *partido* of Jauja, hoping to use the corporation as an agent to encourage the

[1] A.H.M., Libro de Cédulas 26, ff. 269v–70, *cabildo* to viceroy, 23 Nov. 1797.
[2] A.G.I., Aud. de Lima 646, Gálvez to Sonora, no. 21, 17 Oct. 1786.
[3] Ibid.
[4] *Mercurio Peruano*, no. 260, 30 June 1793, 140–2.
[5] Croix, *Memoria*, 176.

inhabitants to exploit the area's rich mineral resources.[1] In each case steps were taken to ensure a regular supply of municipal funds. In Jauja, for example, the *cabildo* was to let out the management of bullfights to a contractor. Aided by public contributions, it co-operated with Gálvez in the improvement of public administration, one of the first projects being the construction of an aqueduct to improve the town's water supply. To illustrate his claim to have succeeded in stimulating a new interest in public affairs in Jauja Gálvez reported that the saleable office of *alguacil mayor*, previously unwanted because of the tight control exercised over the incumbent by the *corregidor*, was now sought after by applicants eager to participate in useful work. He added that all the streets were cleaned regularly, some had been paved, and a number of houses had been repaired and whitewashed.

Clearly an improvement in municipal administration depended to some degree upon the provision of adequate municipal funds. Throughout the viceroyalty the arrival of the intendants led to the inspection and reform of the *propios* and *arbitrios*. In one case, that of Trujillo, considerable progress had been made before 1784. There Escobedo was able to increase the yield of the *arbitrios* of *mojonazgo* and *sisa*, charged on *aguardiente* and wine, by transferring their collection from a private contractor to the exchequer officials.[2] The contractor had paid the *cabildo* 1000 pesos a year; under the new arrangement the yield in the first five months, July to November 1783, was 1175 pesos 3 reales, and at the beginning of 1784 the *cabildo*, which had been resentful of Escobedo's interference, thanked him for the benefits of the reform.[3] As *visitador*, Escobedo had full authority to inspect and reorganize municipal finances throughout the viceroyalty, but, on learning of the decision to introduce the intendant system, resolved to leave this work outside the province of Lima to the individual intendants, although they would be subject to the supervision of the *junta superior*; these arrangements, he hoped, would avoid confusion and clashes of jurisdiction.[4]

[1] A.G.I., Aud. de Lima 763, Juan María Gálvez to José de Gálvez, no. 6, 18 April 1785.
[2] A.G.I., Aud. de Lima 1100, Escobedo to Gálvez, no. 180, 16 Jan. 1784.
[3] Ibid.
[4] A.G.I., Aud. de Lima 1097, Escobedo to Gálvez, no. 350, 20 Sept. 1784.

The Ordinance of Intendants contained precise instructions on the procedure for establishing a machinery of control over municipal revenues and over the communal funds of Indian villages.[1] Having obtained information from the *cabildos* on the collection and expenditure of municipal funds, the intendants were to issue provisional *reglamentos* for their future administration. These were to be submitted for approval to the *junta superior* in Lima. In each city and town funds were to be controlled by a *junta municipal*, composed of the senior *alcalde ordinario*, two *regidores* and the *procurador general*, the latter without a vote. It was made clear that the *cabildo* as a body was not to interfere with the work of the *junta*.[2] Each *junta*, acting under the supervision of the intendant, was to elect a *mayordomo*, who would be responsible for the security of the existing funds and prepare the annual accounts for the *contaduría general* in Lima. Further articles described the procedure for the transfer of surplus funds to the provincial subtreasuries and the accounting to be carried out by exchequer officials.[3] Owing to the heavy burden of work on the Lima treasury officials, Escobedo decided that in the province of Lima these duties should be performed by the *contador general de propios*.[4]

Areche's attempts to investigate and reform the administration of municipal finances in Lima had ended in failure in 1782, mainly because of the *cabildo*'s reluctance to co-operate with his special commissioner.[5] In 1784, however, Escobedo found that the corporation was anxious to assist with the task of ensuring the good administration of the *propios*.[6] This new attitude reflected the general enthusiasm associated with the appointment of the new *regidores*. A report prepared by the *cabildo*, based on statistics for 1783, showed that the annual yield from *propios* and *arbitrios* in Lima was 36,379 pesos, while fixed costs, such as salaries, interest on debts and costs of *fiestas*, amounted to 20,591 pesos, leaving only 15,786 pesos for extraordinary expenses and public works.[7] A *reglamento* issued by

[1] *Ord. Ints.*, arts. 23–44. [2] Ibid., art. 30.
[3] Ibid., arts. 39–40.
[4] A.G.I., Aud. de Lima 1104, Escobedo to Gálvez, no. 486, 20 May 1785.
[5] A.H.M., Libro de Cabildo 37, ff. 13–16, *acta cap.*, 4 May 1782.
[6] A.G.I., Aud. de Lima 1087, Escobedo to Gálvez, no. 387, 20 Dec. 1784.
[7] A.G.I., Aud. de Lima 1104, Escobedo to Gálvez, no. 487, 20 May 1785.

Escobedo in February 1785 initiated the programme of reform by reducing fixed costs by over 3000 pesos, to 17,387 pesos.[1]

Some intendants found it more difficult to obtain the detailed financial information needed for the preparation of the *reglamentos*.[2] The *contador general de propios* explained that this had been the reason for delay when, in 1787, he provided the general statement of municipal finances for the viceroyalty demanded by article forty-seven of the Ordinance of Intendants.[3] This showed that in the principal towns and cities of Peru the total income from *propios* and *arbitrios* was 54,491 pesos. Fixed expenditure, after initial regulation by the intendants, amounted to 31,266 pesos, leaving only 23,326 pesos for public works and administration. It was clear that throughout the viceroyalty there was an urgent need to increase the yield of the *propios* and to find new *arbitrios*. Some towns had virtually no funds for public works. In Huancavelica, for example, the annual income of 1199 pesos 6½ reales was barely adequate to pay the salaries of municipal employees, while in Arequipa 5107 pesos 4½ reales were consumed by fixed expenses, leaving a balance of only 535 pesos for public works. This sum was completely inadequate to meet the expenditure made necessary by the earthquake which destroyed many public buildings in 1784.[4] One method adopted by Álvarez to increase income was to raise the tax on maize used for making *chicha* from a half to one real on each *fanega*.[5]

In Lima Escobedo was anxious to find a new source of revenue to pay for public administration, without imposing further taxes on the general public. The solution was to collect an *arbitrio* known as *bodegaje* from shipowners carrying Chilean grain to Callao.[6] It was estimated that at the rate of one real on each *fanega* this would bring in over 28,000 pesos a year, to be used for the cleaning and lighting of the city's streets. In

[1] A.H.M., Libro de Cédulas 30, ff. 96v–103, *reglamento de propios y arbitrios*.

[2] A.G.M.R.E., Mata to *junta de propios* of Cuzco, 17 Sept. 1786, complaining of its lack of co-operation in municipal reform.

[3] A.G.I., Aud. de Lima 1112, 'Estado general que manifiesta las rentas de propios y arbitrios', 3 June 1787. See Moore, *Cabildo under the Bourbons*, 164–5.

[4] See above, 169.

[5] A.G.I., Aud. de Lima 1111, Álvarez to Sonora, no. 31, 13 March 1787. A.G.I., Aud. de Lima 763, Álvarez to Escobedo, 29 May 1786.

[6] A.G.I., Aud. de Lima 1101, Escobedo to Gálvez, no. 514, 5 July 1785.

fact, owing to complaints from shipowners, the tax was transferred from them to the merchants who carried the grain from the port to Lima.[1] Since they had previously been making a large profit, they were ordered to pay at the rate of one real on each *fanega*, but were forbidden to increase the prices charged to the capital's bakers. Although initial difficulties were experienced in enforcing payment, *bodegaje* was quickly established as a reliable source of income, with an average annual yield of about 25,000 pesos.[2]

Escobedo was also responsible for the regulation of the municipal funds of Ica, within the province of Lima. Since total revenue there reached only 284 pesos a year, it was considered essential to find new *arbitrios*.[3] The *cabildo* suggested that, since the *partido* produced 20,000 *arrobas* of chilli a year, a tax of 1½ or 2 reales should be added to the price of 14 reales an *arroba*. Escobedo and the *junta superior* accepted the scheme in principle, but limited the tax to one real, and partly offset the gain with the decision that, as the subdelegate of Ica lacked office accommodation and received only a small income, the rent of his house, 200 pesos a year, should be paid from the income of the *propios*. The *cabildo* seems to have had no objection to this arrangement, but a *cédula* of 1788 ordered that the subdelegate should meet his own domestic expenses.[4]

A further means of improving the financial condition of the municipalities was to eradicate waste, particularly in ceremonial functions, which often took precedence over constructive administration. This was especially true in Lima, where the *cabildo* was accustomed to spending large sums on the receptions of new viceroys. Despite a rebuke from the crown for having spent 30,000 pesos on the reception of Jáuregui, the *cabildo* spent 46,119 pesos on the ceremonies connected with the arrival of Croix in April 1784.[5] On reaching Callao, the viceroy was visited, at the *cabildo*'s expense, by all the public dignitaries of

[1] A.H.M., Libro de Cédulas 25, ff. 51v–3v, *auto* of *junta superior*, 9 Aug. 1786.
[2] A.N.P., Cabildo 9, Egaña to Croix, 30 April 1788. A.H.M.H., Miscelánea, MS 1394, *estado* of *propios*, 13 Feb. 1810.
[3] A.G.I., Aud. de Lima 1113, Escobedo to Sonora, no. 841, 5 Feb. 1787.
[4] A.H.M., Libro de Cédulas 26, ff. 90v–2, *cédula*, 14 April 1788.
[5] A.G.I., Aud. de Lima 1104, Escobedo to Gálvez, no. 488, 20 May 1785. Aud. de Cuzco 5, Mata to Gálvez, 6 April 1782.

the capital. Further expensive items included the adornment of the viceregal palace, a public reception in Lima and a bullfight in the viceroy's honour. These ceremonies not only used up existing reserves of capital but also made it necessary for the *cabildo* to borrow considerable sums. It was clear to Escobedo that, if public administration in the capital was to be improved, money could not be wasted in this way. The *cabildo* was reluctant to accept reform, because some of its members used the occasion to make profits, while others were always anxious to impress a new viceroy. However, with the co-operation of Croix, who shared his desire for a more productive use of resources, Escobedo prepared new regulations, ordering that the costs of future receptions should not exceed 12,000 pesos.[1] Although the *cabildo* frequently sought permission to exceed this figure, the most expensive reception in subsequent years, that of Avilés in 1801, cost only 15,000 pesos.[2]

The pattern which emerges is that in Lima and in other cities and towns the establishment of the intendancies was marked by attempts to revive the *cabildos* and to improve municipal finances, in order to make funds and energies available for the improvement of public administration. An exception to this general pattern was the case of Cuzco, where Mata was too obsessed with alleged creole plots against the crown to attempt to stimulate the only corporation in the city composed largely of creoles. In 1785, for example, he reported the need to remove from office the *regidor* Buenaventura Guevara, whom he claimed to be one of a closely interwoven net of conspirators.[3] Moreover, there is evidence that in Cuzco *cabildo* initiative in matters of public administration was stifled by the creation of the *audiencia*, which itself supervised such matters as public order and hygiene.[4]

Elsewhere the arrival of the intendants was marked by a genuine revival of municipal activity. The *cabildo* of Trujillo expressed its gratitude in 1785 for the moderation of Saavedra, and praised his good management of public administration.[5]

[1] A.H.M., Libro de Cédulas 30, ff. 132–6.
[2] A.H.M., Libro de Cabildo 40, f. 17v, *acta cap.*, 9 Oct. 1801.
[3] A.G.I., Aud. de Cuzco 35, Mata to Gálvez, no. 21, 15 Oct. 1785.
[4] A.G.I., Aud. de Cuzco 6, Corral to crown, 30 Nov. 1791.
[5] A.G.I., Aud. de Lima 1117, *cabildo* to crown, 27 Nov. 1785.

The *cabildo* of Huancavelica testified in 1788 to the great improvement in the town since Márquez's arrival.[1] When the intendant took office the town was dirty, with an inadequate water supply and poor roads, but he promptly arranged for the repair of the old fountain, for the construction of a new one, and for the improvement of roads and drainage, while with the *cabildo*'s co-operation he built a new bridge to facilitate the supply of food to the town. The *cabildo* emphasized that Márquez was an honest official, and expressed its satisfaction with his 'temperate behaviour towards the citizens'.

Comparable reports came from Arequipa, where in 1787 and 1788 the *cabildo* praised Álvarez's activities.[2] It was particularly impressed with his work to increase the yield of the *propios*, to provide schools, repair the prison, hospital and bridges, and generally to repair the ravages of the recent earthquake. But beneath the surface relations between Álvarez and some of the *regidores* were less harmonious. The intendant reported in 1790 that three of the *regidores* had protested to the viceroy that municipal officials, such as the schoolteacher, the surgeon, the *asesor* of the *cabildo*, and others whose salaries were paid from the revenue of the *propios*, should be appointed by the *cabildo* rather than by the intendant.[3] The power to appoint to these posts rested with the intendant as a result of the *reglamento* of *propios* and *arbitrios*, drawn up by him in 1787 and approved then by the *cabildo*.[4] Álvarez pointed out that in exercising this authority he was in no way usurping rights previously enjoyed by the *cabildo*, since few of the posts had existed before he had created them. The complaint made against the intendant's authority cannot be defined as a representation of the *cabildo*, since it was made by only three *regidores*. Indeed, the incident is evidence, not of a protest against the usurpation of *cabildo* rights, but of the improvement of municipal affairs by the intendant, which in turn led members of the *cabildo* to seek to assume a greater responsibility for the management of their own affairs.

Escobedo hoped that an improvement in the affairs of Lima

[1] A.G.I., Aud. de Lima 802, *cabildo* to crown, 11 April 1788.
[2] A.G.I., Aud. de Lima 763, *cabildo* to crown, 9 May 1787 and 28 Oct. 1788.
[3] A.G.I., Aud. de Lima 763, Álvarez to Porlier, 20 June 1790.
[4] A.G.I., Aud. de Lima 1111, Álvarez to Sonora, no. 31, 13 March 1787.

would follow the revitalization of the *cabildo* and the improvement of municipal finances. Throughout 1784 and 1785 orders and regulations were issued to deal with public administration, especially with the cleaning and lighting of the streets, the regulation of food supplies and prices, the control of guilds and the restoration of the city walls.[1] But in December 1785 Escobedo felt it necessary to complain strongly to the *cabildo* that little real progress had been made in the past eighteen months.[2] He recalled that in August 1784 the *cabildo* had been entrusted with the task of controlling the cleaning of the streets, which were dirty and insanitary, mainly because of the many open drains and sewers which ran along them. As a result of his pressure the city was divided in December 1784 into four *cuadras*, each supervised by a *regidor*, and in April 1785 each *cuadra* was divided into ten *barrios*, each administered by an *alcalde de barrio*. Escobedo was optimistic about the likely results of this scheme, especially after the decision to use *bodegaje* to finance the work. But the *alcaldes* made little progress, mainly because they had no effective means of imposing their authority over the citizens. In June 1785 Escobedo accused the corporation of a lack of interest in the enforcement of its decisions, and also expressed concern at the failure of some *regidores* to attend meetings.[3] In December he again insisted that the city's public administration was in a deplorable state, and accused the *cabildo* of being in large measure responsible, since, although prepared to discuss ideas and approve plans, it lacked the interest and determination to ensure that they were enforced.

In its reply the *cabildo* acknowledged the superintendent's good intentions, but suggested that his impression of the progress made was too pessimistic.[4] It admitted that the *alcaldes de barrio* had experienced difficulty in enforcing their orders, but pointed out that success had been achieved in other matters, such as the provision of cheap supplies of food to the city. It explained also that the failure of some *regidores* to attend meetings was due in some cases to illness and in others to the need to attend to

[1] A.G.I., Aud. de Lima 802, *cabildo* of Lima to Escobedo, 31 March 1786.
[2] A.G.I., Aud. de Lima 802, Escobedo to *cabildo*, 14 Dec. 1785.
[3] A.H.M., Libro de Cédulas 28, ff. 425-6, Escobedo to *cabildo*, 15 June 1785.
[4] A.G.I., Aud. de Lima 802, *cabildo* to Escobedo, 31 March 1786.

haciendas outside the city, but assured Escobedo that there were always sufficient in attendance to deal with necessary business. Despite these assurances, it appears that the task of stimulating the *cabildo* to take an active part in the improvement of Lima was greater than Escobedo first imagined. The creole élite was eager to accept privileges and posts of honour, but less ready to assume responsibilities. However, Escobedo persevered and under his constant pressure considerable advancement was achieved. After the receipt of royal approval for the establishment of the *alcaldes de barrio*, he proceeded to draw up a new *reglamento* for the *policía* of Lima, establishing constables, paid from the profits of the public lottery, for the assistance of the *alcaldes*.[1] Moreover, in a radical attempt to provide central direction, he decided to appoint one of the most distinguished *alcaldes de barrio*, José María Egaña, to a new post of *teniente de policía*, with the honours of *regidor* and a salary of 3000 pesos a year.[2] The results of this innovation were quickly evident. By April 1787 not only were the streets of Lima free from refuse, but considerable progress had been made with paving and lighting.[3]

The relationship of Escobedo with the *cabildo* in 1787 was mixed. There are signs that the corporation resented the new efficiency and centralization of authority brought about by the creation of the *tenencia de policía*. Moreover, conscious of its prestige and privileges, it objected strongly to the innovation whereby Escobedo's legal adviser, Manuel del Valle, presided over its meetings in the superintendent's absence.[4] For his part Escobedo saw himself as the protector of the *cabildo*'s freedom to elect its *alcaldes ordinarios* without interference, when he fruitlessly protested against plans to restore the right to confirm the elections to the viceroy.[5] He claimed that the four *alcaldes* elected since July 1784 were the first in memory to have obtained their posts, not as a result of pressure or bribery, but by free vote of the *regidores*. The evidence available in the

[1] A.G.I., Aud. de Lima 1113, Escobedo to Sonora, no. 834, 20 Jan. 1787.
[2] Ibid.
[3] A.G.I., Aud. de Lima 1111, Escobedo to Sonora, no. 918, 20 April 1787.
[4] A.G.I., Aud. de Lima 1113, Escobedo to Sonora, no. 828, 5 Jan. 1787. A.H.M., Libro de Cédulas 29, f. 184, cédula, 16 March 1788.
[5] A.G.I., Aud. de Lima 1113, Escobedo to Sonora, no. 829, 5 Jan. 1787.

minute-books of the *cabildo* bears out this assertion. Moreover, it is clear that, even after the restoration of the power to confirm elections to the viceroy in 1787, the *cabildo* continued to elect freely. The records show that in the twenty-four years between 1787 and 1810 the *alcaldes* were elected by secret vote on nineteen occasions, while in only five years were they appointed by acclamation.[1] On twelve occasions voting was unanimous; on the other twelve a split in voting was recorded.

At first sight unanimity and acclamation might suggest the possibility of outside pressure. However, the vehement protests made by the *cabildo* on the two occasions when the viceroy did try to interfere with its right to elect freely indicate that it had become accustomed after 1784 to elect its *alcaldes* and other officials without viceregal interference. When Avilés ordered in 1805 that the incumbent of the post of *procurador general* should be elected for a further year, the *cabildo* resisted and persuaded the viceroy that it should not be dictated to over elections.[2] At the end of 1809, having elected its *alcaldes* for the coming year, the *cabildo* was surprised to learn that Abascal had allowed those chosen to persuade him that they were too busy to serve, and had ordered fresh elections.[3] After considerable discussion the *cabildo* decided to conform, swayed by the need to prevent the public learning of any disagreement with the viceroy. However, in view of the need to defend the 'privileges and rights of the *cabildo*', it insisted on sending to the viceroy 'a respectful but firm representation'. Abascal was informed that his right to confirm elections was a mere formality and that in no circumstances could he alter the *cabildo*'s decisions or resist its wishes.[4] In reply the viceroy promised that, in the future, he would not allow those elected to renounce their posts without first consulting the *cabildo*.[5]

One of the many complaints made against the intendants by

---

[1] A.H.M., Libros de Cabildo 38 (ff. 60, 64, 87, 191v, 270, 315v), 39 (ff. 22v, 44v, 73v, 86, 117, 135, 172, 192), 40 (ff. 23v, 61v, 115v–16, 184–6), 41 (ff. 31v–32, 84v–5, 135, 181–2, 221–4v).
[2] A.H.M., Libro de Cabildo 40, ff. 185–6, *acta cap.*, 2 Jan. 1805.
[3] A.H.M., Libro de Cabildo 41, ff. 221–3, *acta cap.*, 19 Dec. 1809.
[4] A.H.M., Libro de Cabildo 41, ff. 223–4v, *cabildo* to viceroy, 22 Dec. 1809.
[5] Ibid. The *cabildo* notes his assurance 'que nunca mas volveria a mesclarse en admision de excusas, y que todo lo que ocurriese lo remitiria al Exmo Cabildo'.

Croix in 1789 was that they oppressed the *cabildos* and ignored their decisions and privileges, with the result that the citizens of the viceroyalty refused to take an active interest in public affairs.[1] The available evidence contradicts this assertion. The *cabildos* had been lethargic and inactive, with little real independence before 1784, and they co-operated in the reform and revitalization stimulated by the intendants. Municipal life was far healthier in 1789 than it had been in 1784. Complaints which the *cabildos* eventually made about the authority exercised by the intendants were provoked, not by oppression, but by increased awareness of the scope and possibilities of local government instilled by the intendants. When *cabildos* came to demand 'the restoration of rights', what they were really seeking was the power to control that which the intendants had created.

This development is illustrated by the attitude of the *cabildo* of Lima to the *tenencia de policía*. According to Croix, the *cabildo* welcomed the practical benefits of the organization, but would have been happier if it had been granted the right to appoint the *teniente*, perhaps arranging for the *regidores*, in turn, to fill the office.[2] Moreover, it seems that the *cabildo* came to resent the increasing authority and efficiency of Egaña, and made a number of complaints to the viceroy about encroachment upon its privileges.[3] The complaints ceased only when the *tenencia* was abolished in 1802 and its valuable source of income, *bodegaje*, was transferred to the *cabildo*'s direct control.[4] In 1791 the *cabildo* made a request similar to that made earlier by some members of the *cabildo* of Arequipa. Through its representative in Madrid it demanded the restoration of its traditional right annually to re-elect or dismiss municipal employees, such as the *asesor*, the steward, the archivist and the porters.[5] Escobedo had made such appointments permanent, but the *cabildo* now sought a declaration that it could freely appoint and remove the officials. The Council of the Indies rejected the application.[6]

The evidence indicates a continuing co-operation between intendants and *cabildos* after the first years of the operation of

[1] A.G.I., Indif. General 1714, Croix to Valdés, 16 May 1789. See above, 62–4.
[2] Croix, *Memoria*, 134.
[3] Moore, *Cabildo under the Bourbons*, 160–1.   [4] See below, 191.
[5] A.G.I., Aud. de Lima 599, representation of *apoderado*, 12 Dec. 1791.
[6] A.G.I., Aud. de Lima 599, report of Council, 29 April 1793.

the new system of provincial administration, paralleled by a growing desire in the towns and cities for more freedom in the expenditure of municipal funds, and generally for more freedom from centralized control. Arequipa is an example. In 1793 the *cabildo*, supported by the intendant, protested against a *cédula* of 1789, which ordered that in the intendant's absence from his capital command should devolve upon the senior military officer.[1] The protest bore fruit, with the Council of the Indies deciding that the officer's authority should be limited to military affairs, while matters political and financial would be controlled by the *teniente asesor*, aided by the *alcaldes*.[2]

In 1795, after ten years of distinguished service in Arequipa, Álvarez was informed of the decision to relieve him.[3] On receiving the news the *cabildo* issued a eulogy of the intendant, bemoaning the imminent loss of the 'declared protector', who had always treated it well.[4] It soon recovered from the loss and tried to exploit the situation to claim the privileges which some of its members had sought in 1790. In July 1796, through its representative in Madrid, it demanded the right freely to appoint to the posts of *asesor de juzgados*, schoolteacher, Latin master and surgeon.[5] The *reglamento* of *propios* and *arbitrios* drawn up by Álvarez had reserved the right of appointment to the intendant. The *cabildo* pointed out that it had not challenged this arrangement while Álvarez remained in office, out of respect for his outstanding personal qualities. However, to avoid disputes with the new intendant, who doubtless would wish to continue the policy of his predecessor, it wanted the 'restoration' of the right freely to elect not only to the posts already mentioned but also 'to all the others of the Republic'. Since public employees were paid from the income of the *propios*, 'which is the patrimony of the people', they should be acceptable to the people and to the *cabildos* which represented the citizens. The *cabildo* argued further that the existing system offered more chance for securing employment by 'illicit means'. It claimed, too, that these appointed ignored its authority,

[1] A.G.I., Aud. de Lima 599, *cabildo* to crown, 5 Feb. 1793.
[2] A.G.I., Aud. de Lima 599, report of Council, 30 June 1795.
[3] A.G.I., Aud. de Lima 630, *título* of Salamanca, 11 June 1795.
[4] A.G.I., Aud. de Lima 1120, *cabildo* to Álvarez, 19 Dec. 1795.
[5] A.G.I., Aud. de Lima 980, *apoderado* to crown, 6 July 1796.

becoming partisans of the intendant, to whom they owed their positions. The *cabildo* concluded with the assertion that the right to appoint to municipal posts was an integral part of 'the economic jurisdiction' which it enjoyed. Although it had temporarily renounced this in favour of Álvarez, it now wished to have it restored. The political ideas put forward by the *cabildo* are most important. It sought to justify its claim to control appointments on the grounds that since the people paid taxes they must have the right to control expenditure, an attitude which could have far-reaching consequences. It is clear that, stimulated by the efficiency and improvement in municipal affairs brought about by Álvarez, the *cabildo* sought to acquire powers which previously it had not enjoyed.

In other areas the *cabildos* were playing a leading part in provincial affairs. In 1784 the *cabildo* of Trujillo, in an attempt to help arrest the province's economic decline, had sought a ban on the import into the Spanish empire of Brazilian sugar, and requested that measures be taken to arrange for an adequate supply of slaves.[1] The removal of duties in 1796 on trade through Huanchaco and Pascamayo was due in part to its pressure.[2] The other *cabildos* in the province paid particular attention to the conduct of subdelegates. In 1797, for example, the *cabildo* of Piura complained that the subdelegate of the *partido* was making the Indians buy licences for the production of *aguardiente*.[3] In 1805 the subdelegate of Chachapoyas was dismissed as a result of complaints, including the charges of embezzling royal revenues and oppressing the Indians, made against him by the town's *cabildo*.[4]

Meanwhile it had become clear that the *cabildo* of Lima not only sought a greater control of affairs within the city but also saw itself as the mouthpiece for creole grievances in the viceroyalty as a whole. In January 1793, as José Baquíjano y Carrillo, the distinguished creole writer and reformer, prepared to travel to Madrid as the *cabildo*'s deputy-general, he was instructed not only to seek increased rights for the *cabildo* and

---

[1] A.G.I., Aud. de Lima 1100, Escobedo to Gálvez, no. 181, 16 Jan. 1784.
[2] See above, 105.
[3] A.G.I., Aud. de Lima 802, *cabildo* of Piura to crown, 20 April 1787.
[4] A.G.I., Aud. de Lima 608, *cabildo* of Chachapoyas to crown, 31 March 1805.

better creole representation in the *consulado* of Lima but also to insist that at least one third of the *oidores* of the two *audiencias* in Peru should be creoles, and that there should no longer be a bar against a creole serving as an *oidor* in the country of his birth.[1]

In Madrid Baquíjano and his successor, Tadeo Bravo de Rivero, pressed hard for increases in the *cabildo*'s privileges.[2] Success came in 1802 when the *cabildo* was granted the same 'style, honours and distinctions' as were enjoyed by the *cabildo* of Mexico.[3] Some of the privileges concerned nothing more than protocol, such as the right of *regidores* to cover their seats with velvet during public ceremonies, or to be addressed as 'excellency'. Of much greater importance was the abolition of the *contaduría general de propios*, established by Escobedo, and the restoration to the *cabildo* of full responsibility for the collection, accounting and expenditure of the revenue from *propios* and *arbitrios*. The *tenencia de policía* was also to be abolished, its employees dismissed, and its functions and income taken over by the *cabildo*. These decisions swept away two of the most important municipal reforms associated with the creation of the intendant system, and brought large sums of money under the *cabildo*'s direct control. In 1802 the revenue from the *propios* reached 36,827 pesos, while *bodegaje* and *sisa*, which had provided funds for the *tenencia*, brought in a further 32,529 pesos.[4]

It is not difficult to find the reason for the crown's decision to accede to the *cabildo*'s requests for these concessions. The royal decree of 23 May 1802, which was issued before the *cédula*, stated that the *cabildo* could use its funds as it saw fit, and could freely make donations to the crown through its representative in Madrid.[5] On 12 May the representative in Madrid of the Philippine Company had informed the Minister of Grace and Justice that arrangements were complete whereby the company would make available in Madrid the sum of 100,000 *pesos fuertes* (132,812 pesos), which the *cabildo* of Lima wished to

---

[1] J. de la Riva Agüero, 'Don José Baquíjano y Carrillo', *Boletín del Museo Bolivariano*, no. 12 (Aug. 1929), 471.
[2] A.G.I., Aud. de Lima 600, contains full details of *cabildo*'s requests, 1794–1804.
[3] A.G.I., Aud. de Lima 801, *cédula*, 15 Sept. 1802.
[4] Avilés, *Memoria*, 28. *Sisa* was a tax on the sale of cattle.
[5] A.G.I., Aud. de Lima 622, royal decree, 23 May 1802. Moore, *Cabildo under the Bourbons*, 183–6.

donate to the crown. All that was lacking was permission for the *cabildo* to spend the revenue of the *propios* and *arbitrios* as it wished, and even to borrow on their security, on occasions 'like the present when it wishes to make a similar demonstration of its loyalty'. The decree of 23 May granted these powers, and on 28 May 100,000 *pesos fuertes* were paid into the Madrid treasury by the treasurer of the Philippine Company.[1] On receiving confirmation of this, the *cabildo* of Lima took immediate steps to raise a loan of 150,000 pesos, with which to pay its debt to the company, and to meet the expenses of its own representative.[2] Clearly the whole affair was a straightforward financial arrangement, whereby the *cabildo* paid the impoverished crown a handsome sum in return for a substantially increased control over municipal affairs.

The formula worked again in 1805, after the conditional offer of another large donation to the crown.[3] The *cabildo*'s wishes were met on further matters of protocol, it was granted full jurisdiction over places of entertainment and guilds, previously exercised by the *audiencia*, and its two *asesores* were granted the honours of *oidores*. A loophole in its control of municipal finances was plugged by the decision that a number of religious organizations in Lima should lose their right to receive fixed annual payments from the revenue of *sisa*.[4] Profuse thanks were again extended by the corporation to its deputy in Madrid. When it was learned that the total bill for the new privileges totalled 149,122 pesos rather than the 85,000 pesos offered, two *regidores* voted that the *cabildo* should refuse to make the donation, but the majority decided to take the necessary steps to borrow a further 150,000 pesos at six per cent interest.[5] However, on being informed in 1808 that Bravo had offered the crown a further 25,000 pesos, this time without authorization, the *cabildo* ordered him to refrain from commit-

[1] A.H.M., Libro de Cédulas 27, f. 88, certificate of chief accountant of Philippine Company, Madrid, 28 May 1802.
[2] A.H.M., Libro de Cabildo 40, ff. 62v–4v, *acta cap.*, 19 Dec. 1802.
[3] A.H.M., Libro de Cabildo 40, ff. 190v–1, *acta cap.*, 22 Jan. 1805. A.G.I., Aud. de Lima 624, 'Expediente sobre el donativo de 60,000 p's f's hecho al rey por la ciudad de Lima. . .'.
[4] A.H.M., Libro de Cabildo 41, f. 56, *acta cap.*, 3 June 1806, which includes letter of Bravo of 17 Dec. 1805.
[5] A.H.M., Libro de Cabildo 41, ff. 77–8v, *acta cap.*, 24 Oct. 1806.

ting it to further expenditure, since its funds were virtually exhausted.[1]

The aspirations of other *cabildos* were less ambitious than those of the *cabildo* of Lima, but, on a smaller scale, there is evidence of a continuing demand for greater freedom in the management of local affairs. The *cabildo* of Huamanga, although by no means a united body, showed increasing determination to resist what it regarded as outside interference.[2] In 1803 viceroy Avilés decided that the cause of a prolonged dispute between the *cabildo* and the treasury ministers of Huamanga was the obstinacy and malevolence of one of the *regidores*, Francisco de Chaves.[3] He should be punished, Avilés ordered, by being called before a meeting of the full *cabildo*, at which a viceregal decree, suspending him from office for six months, would be read. But fellow *regidores*, sympathetic to Chaves's cause, were able to frustrate this order simply by refusing to attend *cabildo* meetings.[4] Moreover, in a further show of defiance, they elected Chaves to the office of *síndico procurador* at the beginning of 1804.[5] Avilés declared the election null and void, but the *cabildo* resisted his order that it should hold a fresh election.[6] O'Higgins, who attributed the corporation's excessive independence to the fact that Avilés had failed to uphold the authority of the intendant in a number of earlier disputes, attempted to find a compromise by personally appointing a new *síndico procurador*.[7] This, Avilés ruled, had no legal validity, and again, in July 1804, he angrily ordered that the *cabildo* obey his orders that Chaves be suspended from his office of *regidor* and that a new *síndico procurador* be elected.[8]

[1] A.H.M., Libro de Cabildo 41, f. 141v, *acta cap.*, 2 Feb. 1808.

[2] There were frequent disputes in Huamanga over *cabildo* elections. In 1801, for example, four members bitterly opposed the selections made by the other capitulars, and began protracted legal wrangling, accusing the intendant of siding with their opponents—A.H.M.H., Miscelánea, MS 1198, *apoderado* of Domingo Espinoza, Joaquin de Espinoza, José García del Hoyo and Domingo de la Riva Cosio to *acuerdo*, 4 May 1801.

[3] A.H.M.H., Miscelánea, MS 1183, decree of Avilés, 26 Nov. 1803. See above, 117–18.

[4] A.H.M.H., Miscelánea, MS 1217, Juan de la Rosa to Avilés, 15 June 1804.

[5] A.H.M.H., Miscelánea, MS 1181, decree of Avilés, 26 March 1804.

[6] Ibid.

[7] A.H.M.H., Miscelánea, MS 1208, O'Higgins to viceroy, 16 May 1804.

[8] A.H.M.H., Miscelánea, MS 1208, decree of Avilés, 14 July 1804.

The available documents provide no information on the final outcome of this case. Presumably, having demonstrated its attitude, the *cabildo* finally obeyed the viceroy's commands. But it continued to insist on upholding what it regarded as its rights. Early in 1805, for example, when O'Higgins was on leave of absence from Huamanga, his *teniente asesor*, temporarily in command of the provincial capital, attempted to obtain some legal documents from Miguel Ruiz de la Vega, the *alcalde de primer voto*.[1] However, he was rudely informed by Ruiz that he would deal only with the intendant, and was rebuked for what the *alcalde* interpreted as an unwarranted zeal to exercise authority. O'Higgins, in turn, rebuked Ruiz for his hostile attitude.[2] In the following year, when both the intendant and his legal adviser were absent, authority in Huamanga was exercised by the senior treasury minister, but the *cabildo* refused to co-operate with him.[3] It finally agreed to recognize his authority over exchequer affairs, but only after he agreed that 'political' matters should be controlled by the senior *alcalde*.[4] In March 1809 three *regidores* complained to the peninsular authorities that O'Higgins was preventing the *cabildo* from taking any initiative in matters of public administration, and had accused them of sedition merely for insisting on its right to take independent action to deal with a landslide.[5] They claimed, too, that the intendant had stolen public funds, adding that he should never have been given his office, since at the time of his appointment his uncle, Osorno, had been viceroy of Peru. Apparently unaware of the traditional problems of government in Huamanga, the Council of the Indies took these complaints at face value, and recommended that O'Higgins be removed from office.[6] The decision was reversed only when it was pointed out that no previous complaints had been made against the intendant, and that, on the contrary, he had been noted for his careful application of the Ordinance of Intendants.[7]

[1] A.H.M.H., Miscelánea, MS 1138, decree of *alcalde*, 23 March 1805.
[2] A.H.M.H., Miscelánea, MS 1138, decree of O'Higgins, 23 March 1805.
[3] A.H.M.H., Miscelánea, MS 1228, de la Rosa to *cabildo*, 3 Jan. 1806.
[4] A.H.M.H., Miscelánea, MS 1229, *acta cap.*, 4 Jan. 1806.
[5] A.G.I., Aud. de Lima 601, report of Council of the Indies, 30 March 1811. Contains summary of representation of *regidores* of 16 March 1809.
[6] Ibid.   [7] See below, 212.

In 1804 the *cabildo* of Arequipa warmly praised the activities of intendant Salamanca in matters of public administration.[1] But there are signs that all was not well there. When the *cabildo*'s representative appealed in 1806 for permission for the *regidores* to wear rich uniforms, he claimed that the aim was to make the office of *regidor* more attractive, since only five of the twelve places were occupied.[2] He added, without going into detail, that a further way for the crown to improve the situation would be to ensure that the *cabildo*'s rights and privileges were protected. This was, in fact, an oblique complaint against the intendant, and it is clear that in other towns and cities, too, a considerable amount of ill-will existed beneath the apparent admiration of the *cabildos* for the intendants. Although their ideas were historically inaccurate, many *cabildos* believed that rights and privileges had been taken away from them in 1784. The intendants, as the most prominent representatives in the provinces of royal authority, were easily identifiable scapegoats for any problems. As long as the absolutist structure of Spanish government remained intact, the intendants were free from serious pressure, but as cracks appeared the *cabildos* began to press their claims.

The news of the bewildering events in Spain in 1808 reached Peru in the second half of the year and early in 1809.[3] The Peruvian reaction to the crisis of the Spanish monarchy was, in general, one of loyalty. In Arequipa, for example, the news of the abdication of Ferdinand VII and of the formation of the *Junta Central* provoked fervent protests of despair and loyalty from the *cabildo*.[4] It wrote that all in the city considered themselves to be true Spaniards, and were ready to sacrifice their lives and estates in defence of the sovereign and the nation. Seven months later the six *regidores* who had signed this declaration with the intendant appealed for his dismissal.[5] For fourteen years, they claimed, they had suffered in silence, afraid to protest due to their belief that Salamanca was a favourite of Godoy, while the intendant had eroded their rights and 'turned

[1] B.M., Eg. MS 1813, ff. 317–19, *cabildo* to crown, 2 Oct. 1804.
[2] A.G.I., Aud. de Lima 600, summary of *apoderado* to crown, 4 June 1806.
[3] See below, 202.
[4] A.G.I., Aud. de Lima 802, *cabildo* to Ferdinand VII, 16 Jan. 1809.
[5] A.G.I., Aud. de Lima 627, representation of *cabildo*, 24 July 1809.

the city into the black palace of despotism'. They had finally been forced to protest, because of the danger of a public rising against Salamanca, and even against the *cabildo* for its failure to protect the citizens. The peninsular authorities, anxious to eradicate maladministration in the empire, were ready to accept somewhat uncritically the complaints made by *cabildos*, which were seeking to exploit Spanish administrative confusion to assert and increase their strength. After reading the *cabildo*'s complaint, and an even more suspect complaint from an individual citizen, the Council of Regency ordered that Salamanca be dismissed, and appointed in his place Josef Gabriel Moscoso, a native of Arequipa.[1]

Not only in Arequipa and Huamanga but also in other towns and cities *cabildo* intransigence was making itself felt after 1808. In Ica the *alcaldes ordinarios* openly defied the authority of the subdelegate in 1810, refusing to allow his nominee to exercise authority in the town in his absence.[2] Instead, they insisted, administration must be controlled by the *cabildo*. In Tarma, where no *cabildo* had existed when Juan María Gálvez took up office, a complex struggle for authority developed. At the end of 1808, having heard rumours that two men whom he regarded as unfitted for municipal office were likely to be elected *alcaldes* for the coming year, the intendant, Ramón Urrutia y las Casas, convoked a special meeting of the *cabildo*, at which he ordered that the two should be excluded from the list of candidates.[3] He argued that the power to take this step was a logical extension of the duty to confirm elections conferred by article eight of the Ordinance. After initial protests, the *cabildo* agreed to proceed with the elections on the appointed day, excluding the barred individuals. However, as the *alcalde de primer voto* for 1808 explained, it did so only to avoid the arrest of its members by the intendant.[4] Strongly-worded protests were sent to the viceroy, accusing Urrutia of 'despotism' and 'dictatorship'.[5] Despite the intendant's appeal for viceregal support, in view of the delicate political atmosphere created by turmoil in Spain,

[1] Fisher, op. cit., xii–xvi. See below, 210–11.
[2] A.N.P., Superior Gobierno 33, *cuaderno* 1094, Pedro Valdelomar to Abascal, 15 July 1810.
[3] A.N.P., Cabildo 15, Urrutia to Abascal, 2 Feb. 1809.
[4] A.N.P., Cabildo 15, Ramón Gavas to Abascal, 22 Feb. 1809.   [5] Ibid.

Abascal proceeded to censure him for abuse of authority, and ordered him to avoid similar excesses in the future.[1]

The election of *alcaldes* for 1810 took place without Urrutia's intervention. However, the intendant declared the election null and void, since a faction in the *cabildo* had ensured victory for its candidates by bringing forward the date of the election without informing some *regidores*, thus depriving them of their votes.[2] Those elected by these means were Manuel de la Secada, one of those barred by Urrutia a year earlier, and Antonio Barrena, who was reported to be under the control of Alonso Caviedes, the second man barred by the intendant. On this occasion Abascal gave full support to Urrutia's action, in view of widespread complaints from Tarma about unrest caused by the election and by the abuse of power by the new *alcaldes*.[3] He ordered that they be deposed and replaced by the two senior *regidores*, until new elections could be held at the beginning of 1811. But the matter did not end there, since a group of *regidores*, led by the most senior, who was Secada's uncle, ignored the viceroy's order, on the technical grounds that, since the *alcaldes* had appealed to the *audiencia* for reversal of the intendant's nullification of the elections, no further action could be taken while the matter was *sub judice*. This attempt 'to obstruct the authority of the Superior Government' forced Abascal to take 'the steps necessary to enforce the respect and obedience on which the security of the State depends'.[4] Unfortunately the available documents do not specify what these measures were. They seem, however, to have been effective, at least in the short term, since the new intendant, José González de Prada, who took up office in June 1811, informed Abascal in July of that year that the *cabildo* was docile and co-operative.[5]

In some parts of the viceroyalty the *cabildos* remained tranquil in 1808.[6] But even the most lethargic were stirred into activity

---

[1] A.N.P., Cabildo 15, decree of Abascal, 29 May 1809.
[2] A.N.P., Cabildo 15, undated representation of Juan Tomás Benavides, *regidor* and *procurador general* of Tarma.
[3] A.N.P., Cabildo 15, Abascal to regent of *audiencia* of Lima, 12 March 1811.
[4] Ibid.   [5] A.G.I., Aud. de Cuzco 3, González to Abascal, 24 July 1811.
[6] The *cabildo* of Lima, for example, requested that Abascal be allowed to exceed the normal viceregal term of office of five years, due to the need for firm government—A.H.M., Libro de Cabildo 41, ff. 167v–169, *acta cap.*, 5 Aug. 1808.

in the following year by the decision of the *Junta Central* that they should assist in the election of a deputy to be sent to Spain to represent Peru.[1] Each *cabildo* was to elect three men, of whom one, chosen by lot, would have his name sent to the viceroy. From the list of those chosen by the *cabildos* in this way, the viceroy was to select three, and the final choice would again be determined by lot. By October 1809 this process was complete, and José de Silva y Olave, the rector of San Marcos, had been chosen as Peru's deputy to the *Junta Central*.[2] The *cabildo* of Lima then supplied him with a set of instructions.[3] An examination of these is essential to any attempt to understand the attitudes of Peruvians towards Spanish authority on the eve of independence.

The *cabildo* began by praising the decision to summon deputies as a recognition that the Spanish possessions were not mere colonies, but formed an integral part of the monarchy. Silva was first instructed to insist upon the maintenance of the *cabildo*'s rights and privileges, but the rest of the instructions dealt, not with the corporation's private affairs, but with what it defined as 'the general interest of the kingdom and the capital'. They give a clear picture of Peruvian grievances, and show that the *cabildo* of Lima saw itself as responsible for the interests of the whole viceroyalty. It disapproved of the intendant system, claiming that the intendants were too powerful and that their subdelegates abused their authority. It insisted that the intendants had oppressed the *cabildos*, and asserted that, in general, the new system of government had brought no benefit to Peru. Silva was to seek the restoration of a modified system of government by *corregidores*, including the *repartimiento* system, which, it was argued, had been abolished without consideration for the interests of those who had supplied goods to the *corregidores*. Other financial and economic reforms introduced by Escobedo were also attacked. An end to all monopolies was demanded, since the existing system led to high prices for commodities such as mercury, tobacco, playing-cards, bitumen, sulphur and

---

[1] A.H.M., Libro de Cabildo 41, ff. 201–3, *acta cap.*, 16 June 1809. Includes royal order of 22 Jan. 1809. See Moore, *Cabildo under the Bourbons*, 200, 202–4.
[2] A.H.M.H., Miscelánea, MS 0001, *acta* of *acuerdo*, 19 Sept. 1809.
[3] A.G.I., Aud. de Lima 802, *cabildo* to Silva, 11 Oct. 1809.

powder. The monopoly of *papel sellado* was attacked as a burden on the litigant, while the collection of the *alcabala* in the provincial *aduanas* was interpreted as evidence of a heartless desire to increase the revenue of the exchequer at the cost of the 'oppression, anger and tears' of the Peruvians. A general appeal was made for freer trade, and a specific attack was directed against a new tax recently imposed on grain imported from Chile.[1]

A large part of the instructions was devoted to the demand that Americans should be given at least a half share in the government of the empire. This, declared the *cabildo*, was a request for the grant of what was theirs by right. It went on to complain that a creole seeking office was obliged either to travel to Spain or to act through a representative in Madrid, procedures which were both cumbersome and expensive. The laws passed to ensure equality of opportunity for creoles with *peninsulares* were ignored, and the few Peruvians who had succeeded in obtaining high office had been forced to serve in other parts of the empire. The general result, the *cabildo* concluded, was that, despite their fitness for office, the vast majority of Peruvians had been unable to obtain honourable positions, and instead were destined to be no more than 'farmers, clerics or lawyers'.

The attitude of the *cabildo* to Spanish rule in Peru is clear. It was highly critical of that rule, especially in its later Bourbon form, and looked for sweeping changes. The wealthy class which it represented had no desire to plot instant revolution. The creole élite were more interested in their economic interests and resented the restriction of their rights to property and labour implicit in the intendant system. Most would have been satisfied with a greater degree of self-government, a prospect which seemed possible during the liberal ascendancy in the peninsula between 1811 and 1814.[2] When the actions of the restored Ferdinand destroyed their hopes of reform they had already missed the opportunity to overthrow Spanish authority by their failure to support the revolt which came to a head in Cuzco in

[1] For further discussion of *cabildo*'s attitude to commercial affairs see above, 152–4.
[2] See below, 213–18.

1814, and they were incapable of organizing successful resistance to the powerful forces built up by Abascal.[1] Social factors, too, held back the leaders of creole society from an open commitment to the insurgent cause. Nevertheless, once it became clear that the demands made by the *cabildo* of Lima in 1809 could not be met within the framework of Spanish authority, logic inevitably pointed the way to independence.

In the years after 1808 a prominent part in viceregal affairs was played by the *cabildos* of Peru, incomparably stronger and more self confident than they had been before 1784. The idea that the intendants oppressed them is a myth. They reformed municipal finances and enlisted the support of new and revived *cabildos* for their programmes of municipal improvement, stimulating bodies which had been decadent and completely under the control of the viceroy and the *corregidores*. An unforseen result of this encouragement of municipal activity was that the *cabildos* soon sought to increase their powers, particularly over the expenditure of municipal funds and appointment to municipal office.[2] Moreover, as the structure of Spanish authority weakened, the *cabildos*, led by the intendants to seek wider powers and responsibilities, turned their attention from municipal and provincial affairs to national interests.

[1] See below, 225–31.   [2] See Lynch, op. cit., 287–8.

CHAPTER IX

Administration on the Eve of Revolution

DESPITE THE increasing financial and economic problems faced by Peru in the first decade of the nineteenth century, the viceroyalty's inhabitants remained docile and quiescent, nursing their grievances but, on the whole, failing to express them articulately. But even the most ardent supporters of absolutism were forced to re-examine their positions, to formulate their grievances and to consider where their true loyalties lay, when, beginning in March 1808, the political and administrative structure of the mother country began to fall apart. Between 1808 and 1814 a series of traumatic and bewildering events in the peninsula had repercussions in Peru which made the maintenance of the traditional stability of government virtually impossible. In Spain the abdication of Charles IV was followed, in quick succession, first by the accession and then by the abdication of Ferdinand VII.[1] While Napoleon's brother assumed the Spanish crown, to rule in Madrid as Joseph I, a national rising against the French rapidly spread through the country. In September 1808 the delegates of provincial committees formed to direct the struggle came together to create the *Junta Central*, which claimed to govern in the name of Ferdinand. As the French extended their control the Junta handed over its authority at the end of 1809 to a smaller Council of Regency. This new body in its turn arranged for the summoning of a Cortes, with a considerable number of deputies from the empire. The Cortes produced the famous liberal constitution of 1812, which made provision for the extensive overhaul of many aspects of government throughout the empire, and in particular for the regular election of deputies to an ordinary Cortes. The new body met from March 1813, first

[1] See R. Carr, *Spain 1808–1939* (Oxford, 1966), 79–119.

at Cádiz, like its predecessor, and then in Madrid. It continued to operate until, with his restoration in March 1814, Ferdinand VII declared its work null and void, and attempted to restore traditional absolutism.

News of the upheaval in the peninsula in 1808 had filtered through to Peru by the second half of the year, and information about the formation of the *Junta Central* arrived in January 1809.[1] Although the information received was, in the words of Abascal, 'confused, misleading and equivocal', it proved sufficient to evoke declarations of loyalty and support for Ferdinand's cause from many individuals and organizations within the viceroyalty.[2] In 1808 oaths of allegiance to him were formally sworn in Lima and other cities and towns, and the arrival of the news of the declaration of war against the French by the *junta* of Asturias led to a formal declaration of war in Lima on 5 November 1808.[3] This was followed in March 1809 by the swearing of allegiance to the *Junta Central*.[4] Similar recognition was subsequently accorded to the Council of Regency, the Cortes and, ultimately, the restored Ferdinand.[5]

The general Peruvian reaction to the crisis of the Spanish monarchy was one of loyalty, of determination to declare allegiance to the successive bodies in the peninsula upholding Spanish independence and the Bourbon monarchy against the French usurpers. This was the initial response of most major parts of the empire. Although there were attempted risings in Upper Peru and Quito in 1809, the viceregal capitals proclaimed their support for the *Junta Central*.[6] But when this body itself collapsed, creoles in many cities refused to recognize the authority of the Council of Regency, claiming instead the right to form their own *juntas* to govern in the absence of Ferdinand. This movement spread rapidly from Caracas to Buenos Aires and other cities.[7] But Lima failed to follow their example, and the viceroyalty of Peru as a whole emerged as the bulwark of Spanish authority in South America. Clearly the many peninsular and creole administrators, officials and merchants in the

[1] Nieto, op. cit., 14, 23–5, 51–2.   [2] Abascal, *Memoria*, i, 425.
[3] Nieto, op. cit., 91.   [4] Ibid., 54.   [5] Riva Agüero, op. cit., 474–7.
[6] See F. Díaz Venteo, *Campañas militares del virrey Abascal* (Sevilla, 1948), 45–79, 82–4.   [7] Ibid., 127–8.

ADMINISTRATION ON THE EVE OF REVOLUTION 203

capital felt that their interests would best be served by the maintenance of Spanish authority. Many creoles were dependent upon the crown for employment, while others had family and economic ties in the peninsula. It is true that many had grievances against Spain, but the spectre of the revival of widespread Indian rebellion made for conservatism.[1] Moreover, the leaders of creole opinion, men such as Baquíjano, Manuel de Villalta y Concha, Diego Cisneros and Cipriano Calatayud were elderly men who had neither the ability nor the desire to organize revolution. The wealthy merchants and landowners, many of them titled, who formed the backbone of the *cabildo* of Lima, had become highly critical of the defects of the imperial structure, but neither they nor the groups which they represented thought in terms of rebellion. Instead, they hoped that the reforms promised by the Spanish liberals would meet their wishes.[2]

The interior provinces of the viceroyalty had less respect for royal authority and were more susceptible to the influence of propaganda sent by insurgents in Upper Peru. Increasing frustration at the ineffectiveness of promised reforms led to a rising in Cuzco in 1814, which spread rapidly over half the viceroyalty.[3] But support for the movement from thousands of Indians and *mestizos*, protesting against continuing social injustice, effectively alienated creole opinion, and the rising was promptly crushed by Abascal's creole militia.[4] When the dismantling of the constitution by the restored Ferdinand destroyed the hopes of creoles in Lima for reform within the imperial structure, they found themselves impotent to challenge the powerful forces built up by the viceroy.

Without creole support Abascal would have found it impossible to react as he did to insurgency in Chile, the viceroyalties of the Río de la Plata and New Granada and, ultimately, within his own viceroyalty. In 1809 regular forces in the viceroyalty were limited to one regiment of less than 1500 men, based in Lima and with detachments in Cuzco, Tarma and Chiloé.[5] The militia organization increased the nominal manpower to

[1] Riva Agüero, op. cit., 474–7.
[2] See below, 213–16.
[3] See below, 225–30.
[4] See below, 230–1.
[5] Gil, *Memoria*, 309–19. Appendix, 32–3, table 15.

over 40,000, but the strength of these forces was perhaps rather illusory, since many companies were undermanned, badly armed, untrained and indisciplined.[1] Intendant Quimper of Puno pointed out in 1810 that it was extremely difficult to raise the 550 men which the president of Cuzco, as commander-in-chief of militia, had ordered him to send to Upper Peru.[2] Some companies were without officers, while others were commanded by inexperienced or aged men. But, despite these defects, it was upon the creole militia that Abascal was forced to rely. The viceroy's firm and uncompromising attitude towards revolutionaries and malcontents was perhaps the most decisive factor in the maintenance of Spanish authority.[3] Unlike the weak bureaucrats who meekly surrendered to pressure in other parts of the empire, he was constantly on his guard, determined to uphold the absolutist system of government in which he had such faith, disapproving not only of the vacillation of his colleagues elsewhere in Spanish America but also of the conciliatory policies of the successive groups which held authority in the peninsula. The emancipation movement was greatly assisted, he declared in his *Memoria*, by 'the attitudes and dangerous policies of those who occupied the government in the absence of the sovereign'.[4]

Even before 1809 Abascal was attempting to strengthen the defences of his viceroyalty. In August 1808, for example, he warned the governor of Mainas that the transfer of the Portuguese court to Brazil might lead to attacks from Portugal's English ally.[5] When, in the following year, he received news of the risings of May and June in Chuquisaca and La Paz, a force was rapidly despatched, under the command of José Manuel de Goyeneche, to suppress them.[6] Most of Goyeneche's troops were raised in Cuzco, by mobilizing the militia and conscripting Indians, while a further 650 came from Arequipa.[7] These initial risings were easily quelled, but fighting broke out again in 1810. The military problem mounted as the revolutionary

[1] Donoso, op. cit., 466–7, report of Osorno, 16 June 1799.
[2] B.N.P., MS D210, Quimper to president of Cuzco, 3 Aug. 1810.
[3] Nieto, op. cit., 9–11.   [4] Abascal, *Memoria*, ii, 553–4.
[5] A.G.M.R.E., Abascal to governor of Mainas, 12 Aug. 1808.
[6] A.G.I., Aud. de Lima 625, Abascal to secretary of state, no. 27, 23 Aug. 1809.
[7] Ibid. Salamanca, *Relación*, 112.

ADMINISTRATION ON THE EVE OF REVOLUTION 205

junta in Buenos Aires sent troops to Upper Peru.[1] Abascal's reaction was to decree the re-annexation of Upper Peru to his viceroyalty on 13 July 1810.[2] Fresh forces were rapidly organized for a second offensive against the insurgents.[3] In September news reached Lima of a rising in Quito, and in the same month Abascal imprisoned a number of *porteños*, resident in Lima, who were suspected of communicating with the *junta* of Buenos Aires. In addition to sending money and troops to both Quito and Upper Peru, he was able to send 300,000 pesos to the beleagured royalists in Montevideo in 1811.[4]

The outbreak of revolutionary activity on all sides put a tremendous strain upon the slender resources of the Peruvian exchequer. While warfare hampered economic activity and caused a decline in ordinary revenue, it also increased expenses.[5] Moreover, a growing number of officials and administrators from areas seized by insurgents fled to Peru, and the burden of providing them with salaries led to a further deterioration of the financial situation.[6] José González de Prada, the temporary intendant of Cochabamba until ousted by insurgents, returned to Peru in 1811 to take up a new post as intendant of Tarma.[7] Having served for almost twenty years, between 1783 and 1801, as senior treasury minister in Salta and Cochabamba, González felt competent to assess the causes of revolution in the viceroyalty of the Río de la Plata. The chief factor, in his view, was the mistaken belief of the creoles that unfair preferment was given to *peninsulares* in appointment to office.[8] He recognized that, in fact, European Spaniards held most of the important offices, but pointed out that they were better qualified than creoles. The instigators of the risings comprised a vociferous and persuasive minority group, for the most part lawyers and members of the lower clergy, who wanted independence in order to

[1] Díaz, op. cit., 128–9.
[2] J. T. Medina, *La imprenta en Lima 1584–1824* (4 vols, Santiago de Chile, 1904–5), iii, 407–8, *bando* of Abascal, 13 July 1810.
[3] Nieto, op. cit., 137–41. A.H.M.H., Miscelánea, MS 0003, Abascal to Quimper, 27 Aug. 1810.
[4] Nieto, op. cit., 140.   [5] See above, 121–2.
[6] A.H.M.H., Miscelánea, MS 1409, gives list of refugees in 1811, for whom the annual salary bill was 53,002 pesos 5½ reales.
[7] See below, 243.
[8] A.G.I., Aud. de Lima 764, González to Larrumbide, 27 July 1811.

attain 'a destiny for which they were not born and of which they are unworthy.'

Abascal shared González's view that creoles were unjustified in claiming that *peninsulares* had enjoyed a monopoly of remunerative offices.[1] He realized, however, that many creoles felt aggrieved, and recognized the need to make some gestures to ensure their future allegiance. After the death of the president of Cuzco, Francisco Muñoz, in June 1809, he nominated Goyeneche, a native of Arequipa, as temporary president, overruling the strong opposition of Cuzco's Spanish establishment, led by Manuel Pardo, the regent of the *audiencia*.[2] After the success of the first expedition to Upper Peru, Abascal was anxious that suitable honours should be bestowed upon Goyeneche and his principal officers, so that the crown's gratitude to creoles might be made clear.[3] Using his own powers, he nominated another native of Arequipa, Domingo Tristán, temporary intendant of La Paz, partly in recognition of his military qualities, partly to satisfy creole opinion.[4] He regretted the appointment when Tristán failed to defend the city against new rebel forces in the following year.[5]

The concessions which Abascal was prepared to make to creole opinion were few. He saw his main task as to remain firm, and to offer a military challenge to rebellion wherever it appeared. The successful fulfilment of this aim made the maintenance of strong government and administrative stability within the viceroyalty of Peru absolutely essential. But Abascal found it increasingly difficult to maintain this stability, mainly because the *Junta Central* and later the Regency and the Cortes favoured more radical measures to meet creole demands. One of the most serious manifestations of this indulgence was the process of dismissing intendants who had served for more than five years in one post, or against whom complaints had been made. Only Vicente Gil, the intendant of Trujillo, remained undisturbed between 1809 and 1811. After the death of Muñoz in 1809 Cuzco was governed by successive temporary presi-

[1] A.G.I., Aud. de Lima 625, Abascal to Minister of State, 21 June 1811.
[2] A.G.I., Aud. de Cuzco 7, Pardo to Ramón de Hernuda, 10 July 1809.
[3] A.G.I., Aud. de Lima 625, Abascal to Minister of State, 21 June 1811.
[4] A.G.I., Aud. de Lima 804, Abascal to Cortes, 13 Dec. 1813.
[5] Ibid.

dents, while the intendant of Puno, Quimper, was suspended from office and O'Higgins was almost dismissed from his post in Huamanga. The intendants of four other provinces, Tarma, Lima, Arequipa and Huancavelica, were removed from office. Even more indicative of confusion in the peninsula was the fact that Gálvez of Lima and Vives of Huancavelica were restored to office in 1811 and 1812.

Vives left Huancavelica in April 1809, on receipt of the order of the *Junta Central* that Abascal remove him from office.[1] The decision was taken as a result of complaints made against the intendant by inhabitants of Huancavelica and after consideration of a detailed report, submitted by Abascal on 23 July 1808, which suggested that, in view of the widespread hostility which Vives's policies had caused, it might be discreet to dismiss him.[2] It seems clear, however, that those who led the opposition within Huancavelica were not guided solely by altruistic motives. In fact, as Abascal gradually realized, the whole episode originated more from a clash of personalities and a struggle for authority within the town than from justifiable discontent with the intendant's mining policy.[3] After he had submitted his unfavourable assessment of Vives, Abascal received a wide-ranging list of more serious accusations from Gregorio Delgado, *alférez real* of Huancavelica and a leading critic of the intendant.[4] According to Delgado, the intendant's despotic conduct had brought the province to the brink of an insurrection. Moreover, it was widely claimed that Vives had obtained his post through the influence of Godoy, to whom he was recommended by Napoleon. Although Vives claimed to be a native of Pamplona, Delgado insisted that he had been born in France, near Bayonne, and reported that he frequently received bulky packages from Spain, arousing suspicion that he remained in league with the French. The fact of his French birth alone, Delgado went on, was sufficient reason to dismiss

[1] See above, 144–6.
[2] A.G.I., Aud. de Lima 602, report of Council of the Indies, 8 Feb. 1812.
[3] Ibid., summary of Abascal's letter of 23 Aug. 1809.
[4] A.N.P., Superior Gobierno 33, *cuaderno* 1065, 'Cuaderno del testimonio de las actuaciones reservadas en el expediente del D'n Gregorio Delgado, Alférez Real de Huancavelica contra... Vives'. A copy of part of the accusations is enclosed with Abascal to Josef Maria Vallarino, 28 Jan. 1809.

the intendant; another was the fact that he had married the illegitimate daughter of a French silversmith, José Lions, who owned a shop in Huancavelica.

Abascal did not accept these allegations at their face value. Instead he insisted that Delgado pay a deposit of 8000 pesos to support his charges, and circulated confidential copies to leading officials and administrators in Huamanga and Huancavelica, seeking their views on the veracity of the accusations.[1] Those consulted included treasury officials, *regidores*, sub-delegates and a militia commandant. Only one, the commandant of the militia infantry in Huamanga, supported Delgado's charges; the others were unanimous in praising the intendant, in their view a generous official, who was concerned only with the welfare of his province and of the state.[2] They agreed that there was some opposition to him in Huancavelica, but attributed it to the machinations of a minority.[3] When Abascal received these reports between January and March 1809, as well as a growing amount of evidence from the intendant of Delgado's belligerence, his opinion of Vives began to improve.[4] It was at this point that he received the royal order, issued in February, informing him of the intendant's dismissal. The order was enforced and Vives left the province in April, but immediately began to collect evidence to vindicate himself and to prove the falsity of the accusations made against him.[5] He claimed in May to have discovered that the true author of the charges was Santiago Corbalán, his temporary *teniente assesor*, whom he had previously suspended from office.[6] Corbalán, a friend of Delgado, was the intendant's 'secret

[1] Ibid.
[2] Ibid.
[3] Ibid. Vallarino reported that all but a few malcontents saw Vives as a 'buen magistrado' (reply of 17 Feb. 1809); Juan Zorilla marvelled at the 'arrogancia del denunciante' (26 Jan. 1809); Joaquin del Camino attributed the complaints to a 'cierto partido' (28 Jan. 1809); Bartolomé de Zubiri said he had heard 'algunos rumores pequeños de incomodidad de ciertas personas' (16 March 1809).
[4] A.G.I., Aud. de Lima 602, summary of Abascal's letter of 23 Aug. 1809 in report of Council, 8 Feb. 1812.
[5] A.N.P., Superior Gobierno 33, *cuaderno* 1065, Juan Estevan Terruas (temporary intendant of Huancavelica) to Abascal, 2 July 1809, forwarding testimonials for Vives. Superior Gobierno 32, *cuaderno* 1047, Vives to *consulado* of Lima.
[6] A.N.P., Superior Gobierno 32, *cuaderno* 1044, *apoderado* of Vives to Abascal, undated but clearly sent in May 1809.

ADMINISTRATION ON THE EVE OF REVOLUTION 209

enemy', who had plotted his downfall in the hope that command of the province would then be put in his own hands.

As investigations into Corbalán's conduct began, fresh accusations against Vives were received in July. A letter from Huancavelica, signed by 'Josef Man'l Guasabar Luque', reported that Vives's wife had burned papers incriminating the intendant in plots against the crown, and that she had forged a document extolling his virtues.[1] Further charges included rape and adultery, committed frequently. Abascal passed on these charges to Huancavelica's temporary intendant, with instructions to find out the truth about them and the *bona fides* of the accuser.[2] But it proved impossible to find anybody of that name, while all witnesses called insisted that the charges were false.[3]

In view of these changing circumstances, Abascal recommended that a suitable post be found for Vives, although continuing to hold the view that he lacked 'the reflection, prudence and judgement' required of an intendant.[4] Vives then returned to Spain to present his case personally. Even before he arrived the Council of the Indies had recommended that Lázaro de Rivera, appointed by the *Junta Central* in February 1809 to replace Vives, should be dismissed.[5] The matter was raised first by an individual member of the Council, who insisted that Rivera was unlikely to govern well, since in his earlier office as governor of Paraguay he had obstructed the efforts of the viceroy of Buenos Aires, then Avilés, to improve standards of administration and to eradicate social abuses.[6] Moreover, while in Paraguay he had become friendly with Santiago Liniers, who subsequently became viceroy of the Río de la Plata largely as a result of creole pressure.[7] The two maintained their friendship, since their wives were sisters, and it was feared that Rivera, like Liniers, might be politically unreliable. The full Council endorsed these views and

[1] A.N.P., Superior Gobierno 33, *cuaderno* 1065, Josef Man'l Guasabar Luque to Abascal, 2 July 1809.
[2] Ibid., Abascal to Francisco Xavier de Mendizabal, 5 Aug. 1809.
[3] Ibid., Mendizabal to Abascal, 2 Oct. 1809.
[4] A.G.I., Aud. de Lima 602, summary of Abascal's letter of 23 Aug. 1809 in report of Council, 8 Feb. 1812.
[5] A.G.I., Aud. de Lima 601, report of Council, 19 Feb. 1810.
[6] A.G.I., Aud. de Lima 601, report of Francisco Requeña, 14 Feb. 1810.
[7] Ibid. See Lynch, op. cit., 110–15.

recommended that Rivera should be removed from office.[1] When it was decided at the beginning of 1812 that Vives had been unjustly removed, the Council recommended that both problems could be solved by dismissing Rivera and restoring Vives.[2] Its advice was taken, and Vives returned to Peru to take up his former post in 1813.[3] But he was forced to abandon his province in the following year as the Cuzco rebels advanced, and when he reached Lima Abascal ordered that he again return to Spain.[4]

A precedent for the restoration of a dismissed intendant had already been set in the case of intendant Gálvez of Lima. His dismissal was ordered by the *Junta Central* on 12 April 1809.[5] No reason was given for the decision, but the *contador general*, to whom Gálvez's appeal for restoration was directed after his return to Spain, believed it was a result of the intendant's insistence that he was not allowed to perform any useful function.[6] However, this official criticized the decision and recommended that Gálvez be restored, partly because he had been removed unjustly, partly because he believed that the viceroys ought to be made to share their powers. The Council of the Indies agreed and, as a result of its report of 4 February 1811, Gálvez was restored to office.[7] But his return to Lima did little to enhance administrative stability; instead it led to a series of even more acrimonious disputes with the viceroy.[8]

A further case referred to the Council was that of Salamanca, intendant of Arequipa, whose removal from office was ordered by the Council of Regency in April 1810.[9] The decision was taken in view of a decree issued by the *Junta Central* a year earlier, ordering the relief of intendants who had served for more than five years in the same province, but more specifically on account of complaints made against Salamanca by Santiago

---

[1] A.G.I., Aud. de Lima 601, report of Council, 19 Feb. 1810.
[2] A.G.I., Aud. de Lima 602, report of Council, 8 Feb. 1812.
[3] A.G.I., Aud. de Lima 799, Romanillos to Vives, 24 Feb. 1812.
[4] See biographical appendix.
[5] A.G.I., Aud. de Lima 601, royal order, 12 April 1809.
[6] A.G.I., Aud. de Lima 610, report of Santelices, 18 Jan. 1811.
[7] A.G.I., Aud. de Lima 601, report of Council, 4 Feb. 1811.
[8] See above, 75-6.
[9] A.G.I., Aud. de Lima 627, royal order, 7 April 1810.

ADMINISTRATION ON THE EVE OF REVOLUTION 211

Aguirre.[1] Aguirre, an obscure *peninsular* resident of the province of Arequipa, made a variety of accusations in 1809, charging Salamanca with the sale of subdelegacies, oppression of the *cabildo* and participation in illegal trade with foreign merchants.[2] In fact, as Salamanca later pointed out, Aguirre himself had been imprisoned for contraband activities.[3] But, apparently without checking the accuracy of the charges or the character of Aguirre, the Regency proceeded to dismiss the intendant. The Council of the Indies upheld the decision, since a representation made by the *cabildo* of Arequipa seemed to confirm some of Aguirre's allegations.[4] The Council expressed the hope that the arrival of the newly-appointed intendant, Josef Gabriel Moscoso, himself a native of Arequipa, would restore harmony to the city. Moscoso was to prove a loyal but a short-lived intendant, since he was executed early in 1815 by the Cuzco rebels for refusing to support their cause.[5]

A fourth intendant to lose his post was Ramón Urrutia, in office in Tarma since 1796, who was removed as a result of the new five-year rule.[6] The transfer of authority to his successor, González de Prada, took place in 1811 without any evident animosity or difficulty. In Puno and Huamanga, however, there was confusion and instability, comparable to that in the intendancies of Arequipa and Huancavelica, although both intendants, Quimper and O'Higgins, were ultimately allowed to remain in office. Complaints against Quimper were first received by Abascal in February 1807, only four months after his nomination by the viceroy for the vacant intendancy of Puno.[7] Those making the protests included the militia commander, the postal official and the *alférez real* of the provincial capital. They alleged that the intendant had dismissed treasury

[1] A.G.I., Aud. de Lima 627, Varea to dean of Council of the Indies, 14 July 1811. He pointed out that the decree of 28 April 1809 which imposed the five-year term was repealed on 15 Aug. 1810.
[2] A.G.I., Aud. de Lima 627, Aguirre to Abascal, 10 April 1809.
[3] A.G.I., Aud. de Lima 627, Salamanca to Abascal, 9 Nov. 1810. Fisher, op. cit., xiv–xvi.
[4] A.G.I., Aud. de Lima 601, report of Council, 19 Feb. 1811. See above, 195–6.
[5] See biographical appendix.
[6] A.G.I., Aud. de Lima 1120, royal order, 2 Oct. 1809.
[7] A.G.I., Aud. de Lima 1120, Abascal to crown, no. 76, 23 April 1807, enclosing copy of representation from Puno of 16 Feb. 1807.

officials to create vacancies for relatives, and had forced other administrators to pay for permission to remain in office. The crown's reaction was to order Abascal to make an immediate investigation, suspending Quimper if necessary.[1] In fact, he remained in office until January 1810, when he was relieved by Diego Antonio Nieto, wno had been granted title to the office in 1806, but the new intendant died after only a few months in Puno.[2] Quimper returned as temporary intendant in June 1810.[3] Abascal made the nomination because Quimper had distinguished himself during the campaign of 1809, helping to restore royalist authority in La Paz, and in recognition the Council of Regency confirmed his appointment in 1811.[4] He remained in Puno until 1814, when he was transferred to Huamanga to replace O'Higgins, who had left for Spain in 1812, having been granted leave of absence on medical grounds.[5]

O'Higgins was one of the most experienced intendants in Peru, but he, too, was almost dismissed during the period of administrative confusion which followed the abdication of Ferdinand VII. Complaints having been made against him by members of the *cabildo* of Huamanga in 1809, the Council of the Indies recommended in 1811 that O'Higgins be dismissed.[6] Its advice was overruled only after the Minister of Finance pointed out that no previous complaints had been made against the intendant; on the contrary, he had been noted for his careful application of the Ordinance of Intendants.[7] O'Higgins remained in office until he left Peru voluntarily in 1812, but most of his fellow intendants were less fortunate. In every intendancy except Trujillo there was either a change of command or other evidence of instability in the crucial years of 1809–12.[8] The liberals in Spain who were responsible for the dismissals were

[1] A.G.I., Aud. de Lima 1120, royal order, 10 Feb. 1808.
[2] See below, 246.
[3] B.N.P., MS D210, Quimper to intendant of La Paz, 13 June 1810.
[4] A.G.I., Aud. de Lima 1121, Abascal to Minister of Finance, no. 426, 8 May 1810. Decree of Regency, 5 Feb. 1811.
[5] A.G.I., Aud. de Lima 1121, Quimper to crown, 22 Nov. 1820.
[6] A.G.I., Aud. de Lima 601, report of Council, 30 March 1811.
[7] A.G.I., Aud. de Lima 601, Varea to Larrumbide, 23 July 1811.
[8] Even in Trujillo there was a change of command, although Gil retained his title, since he was in Spain on leave between 1806 and 1810.

anxious to improve standards of government. It appears, however, that they paid less attention to the need for administrative stability; and the general structure of authority, already beginning to crack in some areas before 1808, suffered from the fact that the complaints made against intendants by individuals and by *cabildos* were taken at face value.

The *cabildos* were ready to exploit administrative confusion to assert and increase their own strength. In fulfilling this aim they were greatly assisted by the eagerness with which first the *Junta Central* and later the Council of Regency recognized the need for the various parts of the empire to send representatives to Spain and, more specifically, recognized the authority of the *cabildos* to control the election of these representatives. In 1809 each *cabildo* in the viceroyalty played a part in the selection of a single deputy to join the *Junta Central* as the representative of Peru.[1] When, early in the following year, the Council of Regency decided to summon a Cortes, it took the radical step of decreeing that the *cabildo* of the capital of each *partido* should elect a deputy to represent it in the forthcoming assembly.[2] Even more disturbing for Abascal were the words and sentiments of the Regency's letter, addressed to 'the Spanish Americans', which accompanied the decree.[3] They were informed that, since they had now been granted the right to elect representatives for the Cortes, 'your destinies no longer depend upon viceroys, governors and ministers; they are now in your own hands'. The Regency readily admitted that the absolutist structure of government had been deficient, but reassured creoles that their deputies in the Cortes would be able to 'remedy all the abuses, extortions and evils caused in those lands by the arbitrariness and inadequacy of the agents of the former government'. Although intended to confirm creole support for Spain, by holding out the prospect of a rosy future, the tone and assumptions of this letter, which was published and distributed widely, inevitably led to a decline in the prestige and authority of officials and administrators,

[1] See above, 198.
[2] A.G.I., Indif. General 1523, decree of Regency, 14 Feb. 1810.
[3] Ibid., 'El Consejo de Regencia de España e Indias a los Americanos Españoles', 14 Feb. 1810.

including Abascal himself, who had been appointed before the abdication of Ferdinand VII.[1] By definition they were the arbitrary and inadequate 'agents of the former government'.

The *cabildos* eagerly accepted their new responsibility, proceeding promptly to elect their deputies. The precise procedure adopted varied from one place to another, as did the intervention of administrators. In Cuzco the president of the *audiencia* presented a list of names to the *cabildo*, leaving it to select three men, of whom one was chosen by lot as the city's deputy.[2] In Lima, on the other hand, the *cabildo* seems to have acted without any guidance or control, electing three men by secret vote and making the final choice by lot.[3] The deputy chosen in this fashion, Francisco Salazar y Carrillo, was given for his guidance a copy of the instructions which the *cabildo* had provided in the previous year for Peru's deputy to the *Junta Central*.[4]

Deputies were elected not only in Lima and Cuzco but also in Guayaquil, Chachapoyas, Trujillo, Tarma, Arequipa, Puno, Huamanga and Huánuco, although only seven of them succeeded in reaching Cádiz in time for the promulgation of the constitution in March 1812.[5] In some areas the *cabildos* eagerly elected deputies, only to find themselves faced with the problem of providing them with funds. In Huamanga, for example, Miguel Ruiz de la Vega was elected deputy in August 1810, but was held up for eleven months by financial difficulties.[6] The *cabildo* eventually raised over 5000 pesos to meet his expenses, but on reaching Lima he was further delayed by illness.[7] When he recovered in April 1812 Ruiz decided to remain in Peru, having learnt that the current session of the Cortes was about to end. This decision served merely to precipitate a complex dispute over whether or not he should repay the money advanced by the *cabildo*.[8]

---

[1] See below, 216–17.
[2] A.G.I., Aud. de Cuzco 8, report of Cernadas, 10 Feb. 1812.
[3] A.H.M., Libro de Cabildo 42, ff. 17v–18, *acta cap.*, 27 Aug. 1810.
[4] A.H.M., Libro de Cabildo 42, ff. 20v–1, *acta cap.*, 14 Sept. 1810. See above, 198–9.
[5] Vargas, *Historia del Perú. Emancipación (1809–1825)* (Buenos Aires, 1958), 113.
[6] A.N.P., Cabildo 16, Ruiz to Abascal, 6 June 1812.
[7] A.N.P., Cabildo 16, *apoderado* of *cabildo* to Abascal, undated.
[8] A.N.P., Cabildo 16, viceregal decree, 25 Nov. 1812, ordered that because of Ruiz's death in Lima his executor should repay 5610 pesos to the *cabildo* of Huamanga.

Few deputies encountered as many difficulties as Ruiz, but none had reached Spain when the Cortes began to meet in September 1810. In their absence the seventy-five peninsular deputies were joined by thirty substitutes, chosen from Americans and Filipinos resident in Cádiz, who were to represent the empire until the elected deputies arrived.[1] These creoles were immediately united over the question of representation, demanding that it should be related to population, since the empire, with an estimated population of 15,000,000 compared with the peninsula's 10,500,000, seemed to be under-represented. The Peruvian deputies supported the demand, but cautiously, lest the election of deputies became a matter for the Indian and *mestizo* masses.[2] They sought to ensure that Indians could neither elect nor be elected. Vicente Morales Duárez, the *limeño* lawyer and intimate friend of Baquíjano and other liberals, emphazised the creole fear of the masses, pointing out 'the grave disadvantages which equality of this sort would have, notably in Peru'.[3]

The rest of the demands put to the Cortes by the American deputies were more palatable to creole opinion in Peru. On 16 December 1810, under the leadership of Morales, they put forward eleven propositions, seeking equality of representation, freedom to cultivate all crops, the removal of the prohibition on industry in the empire, free trade within the empire and with friendly nations, the abolition of monopolies, the free mining of mercury, the restoration of the Jesuits, and equality of access to public office, with at least half the public posts in each kingdom reserved for its natives.[4] These demands reflected all the traditional creole grievances, resembling closely those put forward by the *cabildo* of Lima in 1809.[5] Two of the Peruvian deputies sent a copy of the programme to the *cabildo* of Lima, requesting that the corporation arrange for its circulation.[6]

---

[1] See J. F. King, 'The Colored Castes and the American Representation in the Cortes of Cadiz', *H.A.H.R.*, xxxiii (1953), 35–44.
[2] Ibid., 46. [3] Ibid., 44.
[4] A.G.I., Aud. de Cuzco 3, 'Proposiciones que hacen al Congreso Nacional los Diputados de América y Asia', 16 Dec. 1810.
[5] See above, 198–9.
[6] A.G.I., Aud. de Cuzco 3, Vicente Morales and Ramón Feliu to *cabildo*, 26 Dec. 1810.

As soon as the documents arrived it decided not only to send copies to other provinces and to take advantage of press freedom to make them available to the public as a whole but also to send copies to the rebel *junta* in Buenos Aires.[1] The propositions were published in the *Gaceta de Gobierno* of 30 April 1811 and, although Abascal summoned an *alcalde* to explain their publication, he realized that he had no real alternative to allowing the periodical to be circulated.[2]

This issue of the *Gaceta* began by publishing a message from the *cabildo* of Lima to the *junta* of Buenos Aires, which clearly indicated that the *cabildo* was critical of past administration, expected drastic reforms and saw itself as Peru's mouthpiece in negotiations with the rebels.[3] The *porteños* were informed that they should return to allegiance to Spain, since, thanks to the Cortes, 'three hundred miserable years of ignominy, violence and degradation' had been swept away. In future Americans were to be treated as free men, with the right to sell their products in 'all the markets of the world'. A similar optimistic view was communicated to the *cabildo* of Cuzco, which was informed that, with the removal of former restrictions, Peru would be able finally to enjoy the prosperity for which she was destined by the quality of her products and the wealth of her resources.[4]

Abascal found himself in a serious dilemma when faced with the publication of such material. He believed it to be inflammatory, and liable to cause instability and perhaps even defiance of the authority of officials who had been in office before 1808; but he felt unable to suppress it, since it merely echoed the language and sentiments used in decrees of the Regency. A firm believer in absolutism and strong government, Abascal found himself representing a regime whose policy, in his view, could serve only to weaken Spanish authority. His forebodings seemed to be confirmed when intendants complained in June

[1] A.H.M., Libro de Cabildo 42, f. 59, *acta cap.*, 26 April 1811, and f. 64, *acta cap.*, 31 May 1811.
[2] A.G.I., Aud. de Cuzco 3, Abascal to Minister of State, no. 76, 8 June 1811, enclosing copy of relevant number of *Gaceta*.
[3] *Gaceta de Gobierno*, 30 April 1811, 'Oficio del Excmo Ay'o a la Excma Junta Gubernativa de Buenos Aires', 28 April 1811.
[4] B.N.P., MS D331, *cabildo* of Lima to *cabildo* of Cuzco, 28 April 1811.

ADMINISTRATION ON THE EVE OF REVOLUTION 217

and July 1811 that the deputies in Cádiz were writing directly to the *cabildos*, informing them that Spain was in a desperate position, almost completely overrun by the French.[1] They believed that such reports, even if true, should be suppressed, since they would inevitably weaken the creole determination to support the mother country. In response to these promptings Abascal finally protested to the government in August 1811, sharply criticizing not only the activities of the deputies to the Cortes but also the policies of the Regency itself.[2] He recognized that its members meant well, but insisted that they were clearly ignorant of the precarious state of Spanish authority in the empire. He criticized, in particular, the contents of the Regency's letter of 14 February 1810 to the empire's inhabitants; this, he believed, had endangered security by encouraging disrespect for and disobedience towards 'the legitimate authority'. In the future, he insisted, ministers in Spain must observe the advice of the viceroys or the empire would certainly be lost. More specifically, he demanded that the circulation of inflammatory messages should be stopped and that ministers alone should be allowed to communicate directly with the *cabildos* and other organizations. All correspondence from other groups and individuals should pass through the hands of the superior government in the viceregal capital.

The Regency ignored Abascal's rebuke; instead on the 18 March 1812 it approved and ordered the distribution and application of the constitution which was formally promulgated by the Cortes on the following day.[3] The commission which prepared the draft constitution had declared that the chief feature of the new order must be the stability which would derive from the strength of the principles on which the constitution was based.[4] The product of its work was in many ways an imposing document, but the effect of its application in the viceroyalty of Peru, which was completely devoid of experience of representative government, was to cause further

[1] A.G.I., Aud. de Cuzco 3, Rivera to Abascal, 21 June 1811, and González to Abascal, 24 July 1811.
[2] A.G.I., Aud. de Cuzco 3, Abascal to secretary of state, no. 80, 23 Aug. 1811.
[3] *Constitución política de la monarquía española* (Cádiz, 1812), 121–30, decree of Regency, 18 March 1812.
[4] Ibid., 116.

political instability, alienating absolutists on the one hand and, on the other, arousing in the hearts of critics and liberals hopes of reform which the restored Ferdinand proved unable to fulfil.

Copies of the constitution reached Lima in September 1812. Despite his misgivings, Abascal took immediate steps to arrange for their distribution and for the application of the relevant proposals.[1] The sections which caused most concern were those dealing with the abolition of the old hereditary *cabildos* and their replacement by elected bodies, and the election of deputies to the ordinary Cortes, which was due to assemble in September 1813.[2] Representation was to be on the basis of one deputy for every 70,000 inhabitants, and new elections were to be held every two years.[3] A special committee, composed of the viceroy, the archbishop, the intendant of Lima, the senior *alcalde* and two *regidores* of the *cabildo* of Lima, was appointed to work out how many deputies each province should elect.[4] It established that the viceroyalty's total representation should be twenty-two.[5] A further task for the same committee was to arrange for the election in Lima of a constitutional *cabildo*, which was to replace the old corporation at the end of 1812.[6] On 9 December meetings of citizens were held in the city's seven parishes, and each elected delegates to go forward to a meeting of electors. Four days later these twenty-five electors, most of them priests and lawyers, met under the presidency of Abascal to elect two *alcaldes*, sixteen *regidores* and two *síndicos procuradores*.[7] The new *cabildo* took office on 15 December and proceeded immediately to the routine task of electing to minor municipal posts.[8] The whole process took place without any disturbance or apparent discord. The new corporation itself reported that its installation took place 'in great tranquillity, with the general support of the public and the authorities'.[9]

[1] A.G.I., Aud. de Lima 799, Abascal to secretary of state, 13 Oct. 1812.
[2] *Constitución*, arts. 34–103, 309–23.   [3] Ibid., arts. 27–33.
[4] A.G.I., Indif. General 1524, *cédula*, 23 May 1812.
[5] A.G.I., Indif. General 1524, Abascal to Minister of Grace and Justice, no. 388, 28 Feb. 1813.
[6] A.N.P., Superior Gobierno 34, *cuaderno* 1138, *bando* of Abascal, Dec. 1812.
[7] A.H.M., Libro de Cabildo 43, ff. 1–3, *acta cap.*, 13 Dec. 1812.
[8] A.H.M., Libro de Cabildo 43, ff. 3–4v.
[9] A.H.M., Libro de Cabildo 43, f. 8, *acta cap.*, 5 Jan. 1813.

But beneath this calm exterior serious cracks were beginning to form in the general structure of authority in the city.

Abascal was extremely dissatisfied with the composition of the new *cabildo*, since only four of its *regidores* were Europeans, and even these, he reported, had been elected only as a result of the pressure which he had been able to exert as president of the electoral committee.[1] He considered the majority of its members to be troublemakers and political malcontents, and ascribed their predominance to the fact that the parochial meetings held to choose electors had been dominated by agitators, acting under the guidance of Miguel de Eyzaguirre, the creole *fiscal del crimen* of the *audiencia* of Lima. The constitution granted suffrage to heads of families resident in the respective parishes, but according to the viceroy the *fiscal* had used his authority to grant votes to sons of creole families, while denying them to all *peninsulares* unable to produce the passports given to them when they sailed to America. When protests had been made at electoral meetings against the granting of votes to men partial to Eyzaguirre's faction, the objectors had been shouted down by the mob, and Eyzaguirre announced that 'the sovereign people' had vested the right to vote in the men in question. Consequently, Abascal concluded, decent citizens and Europeans were intimidated into abandoning meetings, and in their absence extremists selected creole electors. Inevitably 'it followed that a *cabildo* chosen by such men should conform with their ideas'.[2]

Hostility between the viceroy and the *fiscal* had deep roots, but it was not until 1812 that it became serious. In May Eyzaguirre protested against restrictions on imperial trade in general and especially against Abascal's prohibition on the import of European goods from Chile.[3] He sided with the *cabildo* in its opposition to proposed new taxes and, in his capacity as protector general of the Indians, criticized the viceroy for plans to impose taxes on them.[4] Abascal made his first serious counter-charges in October, when he reported the

[1] A.G.I., Aud. de Lima 977, Abascal to crown, no. 340, 27 Feb. 1813.
[2] Ibid.
[3] A.G.I., Aud. de Lima 793, report of Eyzaguirre, 9 May 1812.
[4] A.G.I., Aud. de Lima 978, report of Eyzaguirre, 8 Aug. 1812. See above, 153-4.

receipt of an anonymous letter, which accused the *fiscal* of supporting the rebel cause in Chile.[1] He found the idea credible, not only because of Eyzaguirre's increasing intransigence but also because he was a native of Santiago de Chile and his brother, Agustín, was one of the leaders of the independence party which had emerged there. Making a retrospective examination of the *fiscal*'s conduct from 1807 to 1812, Abascal enclosed documents to illustrate the growth of his hostility to Spanish rule in Peru.[2] According to the viceroy this process had begun in 1807, with strong protests about the treatment of Indians by subdelegates. When Indian risings broke out in the intendancy of Tarma in 1812 the *fiscal* showed a marked reluctance to prosecute either rebellious Indians or creoles discovered posting inflammatory lampoons. Completing his indictment with details of Eyzaguirre's attack on his commercial policy and with a copy of a compromising letter sent by the *fiscal* to his brother in Santiago, Abascal concluded that 'Eyzaguirre appears to favour the cause of his compatriots', and demanded his dismissal.

With the restoration of Ferdinand VII and the absolutist reaction in Spain, Eyzaguirre was ordered to relinquish his post and go to the peninsula.[3] But throughout 1813 and 1814 he remained in office, providing, at the very core of the structure of government, a powerful lever for the preservation of creole interests and the expression of hostility against the absolutist trend of Abascal's policies. The election of deputies to the Cortes provided a further opportunity for the exertion of this influence. The procedure to be followed was clearly laid down in the constitution: after the allocation of a quota of deputies to each province, the heads of families in all parishes were to hold electoral meetings for the selection of delegates to attend secondary meetings in the capital of each *partido*.[4] These delegates were to elect representatives to attend meetings in

[1] A.G.I., Aud. de Lima 977, Abascal to Minister of Grace and Justice, no. 297, 13 Oct. 1812.
[2] Ibid., enclosures 1, 2, 13, 14, 15.
[3] A.G.I., Aud. de Lima 978, Abascal to secretary of state, no. 75, 24 Oct. 1815. In fact, Eyzaguirre was able to delay his journey until April 1818—Pezuela to secretary of state, no. 150, 4 July 1818.
[4] *Constitución*, arts. 35–103.

each provincial capital, where they would elect the appropriate number of deputies.

The process of electing the two deputies allocated to the province of Lima began in January 1813 with parochial meetings, and by the end of March electors representing each *partido* had gathered in the capital to make the final selection.[1] Eyzaguirre attended as the elector for the city and *partido* of Lima, but was excluded from the committee by the viceroy on the grounds that ministers of justice were not allowed to serve as electors. The fiscal acknowledged that such an order had been issued, but argued that since it had not reached Peru until March 1813 it could not be used to prevent him fulfilling a task which he had accepted in good faith.[2] Abascal refused to relent, and the remaining members of the committee proceeded to elect deputies. But neither Eyzaguirre nor the city's constitutional *cabildo* were satisfied. The *fiscal* accused Abascal of using his powers arbitrarily, while the *cabildo* complained that the *partido* of Lima had been unjustly denied representation.[3] Moreover, after learning of Abascal's claim that the electoral meetings in the city had been disorderly, the *cabildo* informed him that this suggestion was unjust and libellous.[4] It requested that its letter making this point should be published and circulated in Lima, to quieten malicious rumours and to protect the reputations of those who had been chosen as electors.

Abascal became increasingly resentful of such criticism, even though it was couched in respectful terms. In May 1813 he reported that the *cabildo* had no respect for his authority and he complained bitterly of 'the criminal abuse with which malcontents seek to make use of the sacred axioms of the constitution to further their own sinister aims . . . '.[5] Eyzaguirre retaliated in July, attacking the viceroy for the 'complete arbitrariness' which he displayed in resisting the *fiscal*'s attempts to check military expenditure which, allegedly, had been undertaken without proper authority.[6] In September, as the

[1] A.G.I., Indif. General 1524, Abascal to secretary of Cortes, 14 April 1813.
[2] A.G.I., Aud. de Lima 799, Eyzaguirre to 'V.A.', 3 April 1813.
[3] Ibid. A.H.M., Libro de Cabildo 43, f. 23v, *acta cap.*, 2 April 1813.
[4] A.H.M., Libro de Cabildo 43, f. 26v, *cabildo* to Abascal, 23 April 1813.
[5] A.G.I., Aud. de Lima 745, Abascal to secretary of state, no. 27, 31 May 1813.
[6] A.G.I., Aud. de Lima 973, Eyzaguirre to 'Ser'o Senor', 22 July 1813.

time approached for new municipal elections, the *cabildo* again refuted suggestions of disorder in those held in the previous year, admitting only to 'a small disturbance', which, it claimed, was totally unrepresentative of the general pattern.[1] Indeed the *cabildo*'s insistence that it had been chosen by an orderly process seems to have represented a genuine conviction, underlined by the fact that when a real element of popular agitation appeared to be entering the electoral process the members were anxious to co-operate with the viceroy in repressing it. The elections held in 1813 passed off without incident, but a year later, in November 1814, Gaspar Vargas y Aliaga, a member of one of Lima's leading families, protested on behalf of the residents of his parish—Sagrario de la Santa Iglesia Catedral—that the parochial meeting held to choose electors for the committee which would elect new *regidores* and other officials had been disorderly.[2] It had been controlled by a clique, which, by canvassing, enrolling and bringing to the meeting those entitled to vote, had been able to have its candidates elected. The persons elected, reported Vargas disapprovingly, were mostly '*mulatos* and *mestizos*, tailors, silversmiths, painters and others without any known occupation'. When the *cabildo* considered the complaint, the *alcalde* who had presided at the meeting confirmed that Vargas's analysis was accurate and added that very few 'honourable citizens' had been present. The details were passed on to the viceroy, and the *cabildo* fully supported his decision that a new electoral meeting should be held in the parish.[3]

Even the constitutional *cabildo* of Lima remained cautious and conservative in its basic attitudes towards social affairs, maintaining the traditional aloofness of the creole upper class. There is little evidence that its members held the revolutionary aims which Abascal attributed to them. Nevertheless, it is clear that the whole process of applying the constitution in the capital caused confusion and instability, and increased the viceroy's

[1] A.H.M., Libro de Cabildo 43, f. 65v, *acta cap.*, 10 Sept. 1813. After a year in office half the *cabildo* was to stand down and new elections were to be held.

[2] A.H.M., Libro de Cabildo 43, f. 153v, *acta cap.*, 8 Nov. 1814. Details of 1813 elections on ff. 86–7.

[3] A.H.M., Libro de Cabildo 43, f. 155, *acta cap.*, 11 Nov. 1814. The new electoral meeting took place without incident—ff. 158–9v, *acta cap.*, 2 Dec. 1814.

difficulties in maintaining his authority, while presenting his critics with a safe platform from which to attack him. In other parts of the viceroyalty, too, difficulties arose over the election of deputies to the Cortes, with the newly-elected constitutional *cabildos* playing prominent roles in criticizing intendants and other officials. Indeed, one of Abascal's reasons for his determination to take a firm line with Lima's new *cabildo* in 1813 was the fact that he had received reports from Cuzco, Puno and Arequipa which showed that the *cabildos* there were interfering with the work of the intendants, criticizing and opposing policies with which they disagreed.[1]

Cabildos were just as likely to criticise each other. After the election in July 1813 of three deputies to represent the province of Tarma in the Cortes, the *cabildo* of Tarma complained that 'intrigue' and 'seduction' had been used to further the chances of one candidate, Juan de Mateo Arnao.[2] It argued that two of the electors supporting him, representing the *partidos* of Conchucos and Huánuco, should have been disqualified from voting, since one was of French nationality and the other had a criminal record. Other *cabildos* in the province responded by defending the reputations of the deputies and of their supporters. The cabildo of Jauja described them as 'worthy men, notorious for their honour and integrity'.[3] It was supported by the *cabildo* of Sicaya, which argued that the members of the *cabildo* of Tarma were 'enemies of the peace'.[4] This accusation was repeated by the *cabildo* of Huánuco, which insisted that the *cabildo* of Tarma was sympathetic to the rebel cause, and sought to have the election nullified simply because its own candidates had been unsuccessful.[5]

Elections seem to have taken place without incident in Huancavelica and Huamanga. In Trujillo, however, where they were held in June 1813, they led to a number of allegations of improper conduct.[6] The details are vague, but some citizens

---

[1] A.G.I., Aud. de Lima 745, Abascal to secretary of state, no. 27, 31 May 1813.
[2] A.G.I., Aud. de Lima 799, *cabildo* to crown, 14 July 1813. Indif. General 1524, *cabildo* to crown, 28 Aug. 1813.
[3] A.G.I., Indif. General 1524, report of *cabildo*, 17 Aug. 1813.
[4] A.G.I., Indif. General 1524, report of *cabildo*, 24 Aug. 1813.
[5] A.G.I., Aud. de Lima 799, report of *cabildo*, 21 Aug. 1813.
[6] A.G.I., Aud. de Lima 764, *acta* of election.

complained in July and September that intendant Gil, the president of the electoral committee, had been guilty of 'despotism and intrigues', and had been able to bully it into selecting candidates whom he favoured.[1] In Puno three deputies were elected in May 1813, but when they reached Callao in April of the following year Abascal refused to allow them to continue their journey, since the session of the Cortes for which they had been elected was due to end.[2] When new elections were held to choose deputies for the proposed second session the *cabildo* of Puno protested bitterly that they had been conducted improperly.[3] It claimed that even before the process of holding elections in the *partidos* was complete the names of those to be elected as deputies were known. A further reason for its demand that the elections should be nullified was that Quimper, the intendant of Puno, was chosen by the electoral committee as one of the province's deputies.

One of the men elected in 1813 to represent the province of Arequipa was Domingo Tristán.[4] Abascal had appointed him as temporary intendant of La Paz in 1809, but rapidly lost confidence in his trustworthiness when he allowed rebel forces to recapture the city.[5] On that occasion Tristán had escaped punishment only because Goyeneche, a friend of the family, had intervened on his behalf. But Abascal retained a low opinion of him and on learning of his election described him as 'perhaps the most immoral, corrupt and wicked' of Arequipa's citizens, attributing his election to the pressure of 'the seditious, the bold and the intriguers.'[6] In Arequipa as in Lima, the viceroy asserted, many decent citizens stayed away from the parochial electoral meetings to avoid the insults and the violence of unruly mobs of extremists. He made no move, however, to nullify the elections held there or to prevent Tristán leaving Peru, mainly

[1] A.G.I., Aud. de Lima 799, representation of Miguel Tinoco, Juan Alejo Palacios and José María Nuñez, 14 Sept. 1813.
[2] A.G.I., Aud. de Lima 799, Remigio, bishop of La Paz, Juan Francisco de Reyes and Isidro José de Gálvez to 'V.M.', 1 Aug. 1814.
[3] A.G.I., Aud. de Cuzco 2, Concha to Minister of Grace and Justice, no. 15, 25 July 1814, enclosing report of *cabildo* of Puno of 2 July 1814.
[4] A.G.I., Aud. de Lima 804, Abascal to Cortes, 13 Dec. 1813.
[5] See above, 206.
[6] A.G.I., Aud. de Lima 804, Abascal to Cortes, 13 Dec. 1813.

because he considered that he would be less dangerous in Spain than within the viceroyalty.[1]

Abascal's distaste for Arequipa's deputy was perhaps influenced to some degree by reports from Spain about the conduct of Mariano Rivero, who had been sent to Cádiz by the *cabildo* of Arequipa, under the rules issued by the Regency in 1810, to represent the city in the Cortes.[2] On reaching Spain Rivero pressed for the redress of Arequipa's traditional grievances, demanding, for example, that the province should be transferred from the jurisdiction of the *audiencia* of Lima to that of the *audiencia* of Cuzco.[3] Of more concern to Abascal was Rivero's claim, presented to the Cortes in March 1813, that the viceroy's despotic rule was preventing the reform of government in Peru.[4] Abascal retaliated, producing in November a fully documented accusation of sedition against the whole Rivero family.[5] Manuel Rivero, the father of the deputy, was arrested on a charge of plotting rebellion, while Antonio Rivero, the brother of Mariano, was dismissed from his post as subdelegate of Ancón, on charges of communicating with rebels in Upper Peru and of allowing the circulation of propaganda.

It is clear that from 1809 a variety of factors—chaos in Spain, the removal of intendants, revolution in adjacent areas, elections and the application of the constitution—brought increasing instability to the viceroyalty of Peru. Abascal's firmness counterbalanced the process to some degree, but weak and confused administration appeared in many areas. It reached its most critical level in the city and province of Cuzco, and was a significant cause of the serious rising which broke out there in 1814. In an analysis of the background to the rebellion, prepared in 1816, Manuel Pardo, the regent of the *audiencia* of Cuzco, reported that a marked decline in respect towards the established authorities set in after news of the formation of *juntas* in Spain reached the city.[6] Creoles in Cuzco,

[1] Ibid.   [2] See above, 213.
[3] A.G.I., Aud. de Lima 802, representation of Rivero, 10 Oct. 1812.
[4] A.G.I., Aud. de Lima 745, Abascal to Cortes, 30 Nov. 1813.
[5] Ibid., enclosures 1–4.
[6] A.G.I., Aud. de Cuzco 8, Pardo to Minister of Grace and Justice. Published in M. de Odriozola (ed.), *Documentos históricos del Perú* (10 vols., Lima, 1863–79), iii, 31–46.

Pardo reported, wanted to form their own *junta*. Instability in the city was aggravated by the fact that, after the death of Muñoz in June 1809, Cuzco was governed by a succession of temporary presidents. The first of these, Goyeneche, was nominated by Abascal despite the opposition of Pardo, but with Goyeneche's departure for Upper Peru control reverted first to the regent and then to the senior *oidor*, Pedro Antonio de Cernadas.[1] The conservative *audiencia*, representing Europeans and office-holders, remained firmly in control of the city's administration, while there rapidly grew up an opposition party of liberals, or *constitucionales*, formed of creoles and *mestizos* who sought the rapid application of the political and administrative reforms which were being promised from Spain.[2]

The creole *oidor*, Manuel de Vidaurre, differed from his colleagues in the *audiencia* by sympathizing with and encouraging the reformers. He complained in December 1812 that the corruption and conservatism of former presidents, especially Cernadas, had caused disrespect for royal authority, since under their control 'office was acquired by prostitution and influence; administrators were guided by venality and faction ... the poor and the helpless groaned, but the rich and influential encountered no opposition to their wicked policies'.[3] These charges were vague, couched in terms similar to those used by the Regency itself, and Pardo felt that Vidaurre was guilty of no more than imprudence, a tendency which he attributed simply to excessive drinking.[4] But when rebellion broke out in Cuzco Vidaurre was the only member of the *audiencia* to escape imprisonment. Although he declined the rebels' request that he accept command of the city, he was allowed to travel freely to Lima.[5] There he was given a hostile reception by Abascal, who suspected him of collaborating with the rebels.[6]

[1] See above, 206.
[2] Vargas, *Historia del Perú. Emancipación*, 46. A.G.I., Aud. de Cuzco 8, Cernadas to Regency, 26 April 1811.
[3] A.G.I., Aud. de Cuzco 7, report of Vidaurre, 10 Dec. 1812.
[4] A.G.I., Aud. de Cuzco 4, Pardo to Council of State, 25 March 1813.
[5] A.G.I., Aud. de Cuzco 8, Vidaurre to Minister of Grace and Justice, 7 Dec. 1814.
[6] A.G.I., Aud. de Cuzco 8, Pardo to Minister of the Indies, 18 May 1815.

Vidaurre's insistence on the need for urgent reform of government was not heeded by his colleagues, and it was their reluctance to accept the radical provisions of the constitution which turned latent creole discontent into open hostility. Pardo himself acknowledged that it was the arrival in the city on 9 December 1812 of copies of the constitution which led to real trouble.[1] On 14 December Rafael Ramírez de Arellano, a lawyer, issued a manifesto, signed by thirty inhabitants, which complained that no steps had been taken to arrange for the election of a constitutional *cabildo*.[2] The existing *cabildo*, criticized by Ramírez as an ineffective and inactive body, was due to be replaced on 1 January 1813.[3] He gave a warning that continued failure to arrange for elections would have serious consequences, since 'the people' saw the old corporation as 'a skeleton stripped of all its powers', and would ignore it after 31 December.

At this time the temporary president was the Indian brigadier, Mateo Pumacahua, noted for his firm allegiance to the Spanish cause ever since he had helped to defeat Túpac Amaru.[4] Behind him, directing policy, stood the *audiencia*. Their reaction to Ramírez's activity was twofold, but in each case dilatory. Ramírez and some of his supporters were arrested at the beginning of February 1813, and arrangements were finally made for the election of a *cabildo*.[5] At one of the parochial electoral meetings, held in February, Manual Borja, a lawyer arrested with Ramírez, was chosen as a delegate to the committee which was to elect the constitutional *cabildo*. Under pressure from a demonstrating mob and faced with the danger of a riot, Pumacahua agreed to release both Ramírez and Borja.[6] The decision encouraged the belief of the creole leaders that the *audiencia* and the president would give way to pressure. After his release Ramírez was elected *síndico procurador* of the constitutional *cabildo*, and his supporters formed a majority in the corporation.[7]

[1] A.G.I., Aud. de Cuzco 8, Pardo to Minister of Grace and Justice, 13 July 1816.
[2] Ibid., enclosure 1.   [3] *Constitución*, art. 314.
[4] See L. A. Eguiguren, *La revolución de 1814* (Lima, 1914), 29–31.
[5] A.G.I., Aud. de Cuzco 8, Pardo to Minister of Grace and Justice, 13 July 1816.
[6] Ibid., enclosure 3, Pumacahua to Abascal, 26 April 1813.
[7] Ibid.

As the year progressed instability increased, partly as a result of the weakness of the temporary presidents, Pumacahua and his successor, Martín Concha, partly because of continual disputes between the *audiencia* and the new *cabildo*. In August 1813, for example, the *audiencia* complained that the *cabildo*, directed by Ramírez, was interfering in administrative affairs which did not concern it, especially by attempting to scrutinize the appointments of subdelegates.[1] The *cabildo* subsequently complained that, despite promises of reform made by the Cortes, subdelegates were still being appointed on the basis of influence and corruption, and that the *audiencia* made no effort to ensure that they governed well.[2] But the *audiencia* believed that documents presented to the *cabildo* by Ramírez when he protested at the appointment of Ramón Castedo as a subdelegate were libellous and inflammatory.[3] It argued that since his attitudes and behaviour were causing the spread of dangerous ideas the government should order him to leave Cuzco.

Tension grew when a number of arrests were made in October 1813, after the alleged discovery of a plot, organized by Vicente Angulo, Gabriel Bejar and Juan Carbajal, to attack the barracks.[4] The temporary president, Concha, increased security precautions on hearing of a plan to free the prisoners, and on the night of 5 November guards fired into a demonstrating crowd, causing two deaths. The *cabildo* immediately reacted by condemning the decision to open fire, criticizing the clumsy handling of a delicate situation and protesting that neither the president nor the *audiencia* had attempted to consult it. The *audiencia* again took exception to what it regarded as unwarranted interference in matters of government, and accused leading members of the corporation—Ramírez, the *alcalde* Martin Valer, Francisco Galdos and Augustín Ampuero—of being 'revolutionaries'.[5]

On receiving the *audiencia*'s report Abascal ordered a full judicial investigation into the conduct of Ramírez, Valer and Ampuero.[6] They were arrested at the beginning of 1814, and

[1] A.G.I., Aud. de Cuzco 8, *audiencia* to Regency, 10 Aug. 1813.
[2] A.G.I., Aud. de Lima 804, report of *cabildo*, 3 March 1814.
[3] A.G.I., Aud. de Cuzco 8, *audiencia* to Regency, 10 Aug. 1813.
[4] A.G.I., Aud. de Cuzco 8, *audiencia* to Abascal, 11 Dec. 1813.   [5] Ibid.
[6] A.G.I., Aud. de Cuzco 8, Pardo to Minister of Grace and Justice, 13 July 1816.

for a time were held in Lima.[1] On return to Cuzco they joined their fellow-creoles imprisoned in 1813, although the conditions under which they were held were clearly lax and inadequate from the point of view of security, since they were allowed to leave the prison on parole during daylight.[2] The legal action against them continued, in the traditionally slow and meandering fashion, until it came to an abrupt end on the night of 2 August 1814, when, with the aid of their guards, the prisoners escaped and, with their supporters, immediately imprisoned most of the Europeans and officials in Cuzco.[3] Pardo argued in 1816 that order could have been re-established if the civil and ecclesiastical *cabildos* and the bishop had organized resistance to the rebellion.[4] Instead, they co-operated with the escaped prisoners, approved the nomination of José Angulo as military commander and nominated a triumvirate, led by Pumacahua, to govern the city.[5] All those connected with these developments, Pardo asserted, hated the *peninsulares* and were opposed to the maintenance of Spanish authority; but it seems that, although a minority aimed at independence, many supported the rebellion simply in the hope of obtaining better government within the framework of Spanish rule.

The rebellion was at first bloodless. Its leaders demanded the genuine application of the constitution and attempted to obtain the approval of Abascal and other officials for what they claimed was a mere change of administrative personnel in Cuzco. Angulo informed the intendant of Puno 'in reality there has been no change in government, merely the removal of officials who abused their authority'.[6] His letters to Abascal expressed the same theme and proclaimed loyalty to Ferdinand VII.[7] They complained, however, not only of corruption under the former administrators in Cuzco but also of the heavy demands made upon the province by the obligation to supply men, money and supplies to the royalist forces in Upper Peru.

---

[1] A.H.M., Libro de Cabildo 43, f. 102, *acta cap.*, 11 Feb. 1814, records a request from the prisoners that the *cabildo* report to Spain on their behalf.
[2] A.G.I., Aud. de Cuzco 8, Pardo to Minister of Grace and Justice, 13 July 1816.
[3] Abascal, *Memoria*, ii, 197–8.
[4] A.G.I., Aud. de Cuzco 8, Pardo to Minister of Grace and Justice, 13 July 1816.
[5] Ibid.   [6] Odriozola, op. cit., iii, 244–6, Angulo to Quimper, 11 Aug. 1814.
[7] Ibid., iii, 246–52, Angulo to Abascal, 13 Aug. 1814.

Abascal's reaction to these overtures was an uncompromising demand that Angulo should restore the deposed authorities or be treated as an enemy.[1] Angulo responded by taking up a more extreme position, announcing that he would resist force and demanding that the viceroy should make peace with the rebels in Upper Peru in order to end 'the devastating war which has afflicted these unfortunate lands for five years'.[2] Declaring his neutrality towards the rebels in Upper Peru, he sent his forces, which included thousands of Indians loyal to Pumacahua, into the neighbouring provinces of Huamanga, Puno, Huancavelica, La Paz and Arequipa.[3]

The rebels advanced quickly, meeting resistance only in Arequipa, but Abascal's determination to stand firm ended any possibility that the rising might remain a bloodless reform movement. Faced with the prospect of fighting royalist troops, moderate reformers withdrew their support, a process which made the movement more extreme, while the enthusiastic support of the Indian masses revived fears of social upheaval. Manuel Hurtado de Mendoza's manifesto to the inhabitants of Castrovirreina and Yauyos called upon Indians and creoles to unite in driving the Europeans from America.[4] But many creoles chose to stand firm with the *peninsulares*. Pardo reported that the rebels' wealthier supporters were the first to withdraw, as they began to feel the burden of the 'voluntary donations' required to sustain the movement.[5] An anonymous observer pointed out that all property owners, creole and European, rapidly realized that 'the revolution and the war is directed against all who have property to lose'.[6]

A disciplined force, 1200 strong, sent from Upper Peru by the royalist commander, experienced little difficulty in driving back the rebel masses.[7] Pumacahua's forces had been ostenta-

[1] Ibid., iii, 253–4, Abascal to Angulo, 2 Sept. 1814.
[2] Ibid., iii, 256–8, Angulo to Abascal, 17 Sept. 1814, and 260, Angulo to archbishop of Lima, 28 Nov. 1814.   [3] Eguiguren, *La revolución de 1814*, 47–77.
[4] A.H.M.H., Colección Santamaría, MS 00237, manifesto of Hurtado, 30 Dec. 1814.
[5] A.G.I., Aud. de Cuzco 8, Pardo to Minister of Grace and Justice, 13 July 1816.
[6] Odriozola, op. cit., iii, 77.
[7] See 'Memoria militar del general Pezuela, 1813–15', *Revista Historica*, xxi (1954), 256–61. Odriozola, op. cit., iii, 49–82, 'Diario de la expedición del mariscal del campo Ramírez sobre las provincias de La Paz, Puno, Arequipa y el Cuzco'.

tiously welcomed in the towns and cities of neighbouring provinces, but as the royalists advanced they, too, were greeted with similar displays of loyalty and affection. It rapidly became clear that, although numerous, the rebels were disorganized and inexperienced. Royalist forces commanded by general Juan Ramírez inflicted a decisive defeat on Pumacahua's army of 'more than 20,000' in the middle of March 1815.[1] As news of Ramírez's approach reached Cuzco there was a royalist reaction in the city and by the end of the month the leading rebels had all been executed.

The threat of social revolution led to a rapid withdrawal of creole support for the rebellion. Yet this began as a reform movement, backed by creoles, who were frustrated at the fact that, despite the promises of the Regency and the Cortes, standards of government and economic conditions had deteriorated. The heavy demands made upon the province to support the war in Upper Peru provided an additional source of grievance, while the conservative *audiencia*'s reluctance to apply the constitution made it an easily identifiable scapegoat. In the absence of a permanent president—executive authority changed hands five times between 1809 and 1814—it was able to control government in the province. Administrative instability was a feature not only of Cuzco but also of the viceroyalty as a whole. In nearly every province intendants were dismissed abruptly, while public attacks by the Regency on administrators appointed before 1808 seriously embarrassed many officials. The election of deputies in 1810 gave the *cabildos* in particular and creole opinion in general even greater opportunities for self-assertion, a problem intensified by the application of the 1812 constitution. This widened existing cracks in the structure of government and in the general framework of authority, manifested in some areas by disputes over elections, and aroused hopes of reform which, in the short term, could not be fulfilled. Realization that conditions had changed only for the worse brought rebellion in Cuzco in 1814; in other areas, notably Lima, social conservatism and lingering optimism combined to maintain creole loyalty. But the restoration of Ferdinand VII in 1814 and the withdrawal of the constitution

[1] 'Memoria militar del general Pezuela', 260.

put an end to hopes of radical reform within the framework of Spanish control.[1] Pardo pointed out in 1816 that, although the royalists had defeated Pumacahua, they had not succeeded in winning creole sympathy.[2] Creoles continued to fight for Spain, but the majority, he insisted, were eagerly awaiting the opportunity to throw off Spanish rule. They hated Spaniards and coveted their wealth and offices. Pardo concluded with the pessimistic observation: 'they have declared war in their hearts...'

[1] See below, 233-4.
[2] A.G.I., Aud. de Cuzco 8, Pardo to Minister of Grace and Justice, 13 July 1816.

CHAPTER X

Conclusion

THE LEADERS of creole opinion in Peru stood aloof from the Cuzco rising, distrusting it as a popular movement which threatened to subvert the existing social order. They, too, sought political, economic and commercial concessions from Spain, but they hoped to achieve them through the more pacific channels of debate and pressure in the Cortes. While the rebellion was at its height, however, news began to reach the viceroyalty of the withdrawal of the constitution and the renewal of absolutism by Ferdinand VII. The latter re-entered Madrid on 2 May 1814; two days later, as Abascal informed the *cabildo* of Lima in September, he decreed the withdrawal of the constitution.[1] News arrived in October of the abolition of elected regional committees.[2] Since no specific order had been received relating to the composition of the *cabildos*, municipal elections were held normally at the end of 1814.[3] But on 27 December the *cabildo* of Lima received not only a letter from the province's deputies, informing it of the closure of the Cortes, but also news from its own representative in Spain of the abolition of the constitutional *cabildos*.[4] The royal decree of 30 July, ordering their immediate dissolution and the restoration of the former oligarchic corporations, was passed on by the viceroy on 28 December.[5] The elected *cabildo* of Lima meekly submitted and the *regidores* who held office before the application of the constitution returned to their posts on 31 December.[6] An electoral meeting held in the city

[1] A.H.M., Libro de Cabildo 43, f. 147v, *acta cap.*, 7 Sept. 1814.
[2] A.H.M., Libro de Cabildo 43, f. 150, *acta cap.*, 25 Oct. 1814, recording royal order of 24 May 1814.   [3] See above, 355–6.
[4] A.H.M., Libro de Cabildo 43, f. 166, *acta cap.*, 27 Dec. 1814.
[5] A.H.M., Libro de Cabildo 43, ff. 166v–7, *acta cap.*, 30 Dec. 1814.
[6] A.H.M., Libro de Cabildo 43, f. 167, *auto* of constitutional *cabildo*, 30 Dec. 1814. Libro de Cabildo 44, f. 1, *acta cap.*, 31 Dec. 1814.

on 18 December had already chosen José Antonio Errea and Francisco Moreyra as *alcaldes* for the coming year.[1] With the deposition of the constitutional *cabildo* these elections were automatically nullified and the restored *cabildo*'s first task was to elect new *alcaldes*. By acclamation it unanimously chose Errea and Moreyra, a decision which clearly demonstrated its solidarity with the creole cause and its determination to continue to press for the redress of creole grievances.[2]

The process of dismantling the reforms introduced during the liberal ascendancy in the peninsula continued in 1815. In March Abascal published the *cédula* of 6 September 1814, restoring censorship of the press and stage.[3] Many creoles who had been induced to believe that a new era of prosperity and contentment was at hand were now faced with a simple choice: to accept the complete restoration of the old political, economic and commercial structure, or to commit themselves to the cause of independence. For the time being the question remained academic, since the strength of the royalist forces, especially after the defeat of the Cuzco rebellion, was too formidable to challenge. But, as economic difficulties increased, many creoles, although not prepared to join the insurgents, lost faith in Spain, and would refuse to fight for her when the real crisis came. As rebel forces gradually converged on Peru from north and south, the choice which faced the creoles became less remote. Spanish authority survived as long as royalist forces remained stronger than those of the insurgents. But in the absence of a new initiative from Ferdinand VII and in default of further reinforcements the passage of time brought an inevitable decline in royalist supremacy.

The negative, unimaginative response of the Spanish crown to the Cuzco rebellion of 1814 contrasted sharply with its reaction to the Túpac Amaru rising of 1780. Charles III and his ministers had agreed that the Indian rising should be vigorously repressed, but they used it as the springboard to introduce their reform programme in Peru, traditionally the centre of conservatism and corrupt government. Túpac

[1] A.H.M., Libro de Cabildo 43, ff. 164-5, *acta* of elections, 18 Dec. 1814.
[2] A.H.M., Libro de Cabildo 44, f. 1, *acta cap.*, 31 Dec. 1814.
[3] A.N.P., Superior Gobierno 35, *cuaderno* 1197, *bando* of Abascal, 11 March 1815.

CONCLUSION

Amaru's principal demands—the abolition of the *repartimiento* system, the removal of the *corregidores* and the creation of an *audiencia* in Cuzco—were met soon after his execution. The introduction of the intendant system in Peru, a task successfully completed by Escobedo in 1784, was not merely an attempt to alleviate Indian discontent but the keystone of the general programme of administrative, judicial and financial reform in the viceroyalty, begun by Areche and continued by Escobedo. It was hoped that the new regime would increase the yield of taxation, raise Peru from her economic decline, improve the standards of justice and of public administration, and in general make imperial authority more effective.

With the formal completion of the *visita general*, Escobedo remained in Lima as provincial intendant and superintendent. The many disputes between Escobedo and viceroy Croix revealed increasing viceregal hostility towards the new system of government, but the restoration of the superintendency to the viceroy in 1787 was a consequence of a shift in general policy in Madrid rather than of conflict between viceroy and superintendent. Yet after Escobedo's departure Croix's hostility towards the intendants became even more marked. His demands for the total abolition of the new system were ultimately rejected, but the review of administration carried out in the 1790s brought some modifications, among them the transfer to Peru of the intendancy of Puno. The *New Ordinance*, approved by the Council of the Indies in 1803, remedied many defects in the Ordinance of 1782, but for obscure reasons it was withdrawn. One of the proposed modifications, the appointment of intendants to the viceregal capitals, was, in fact, introduced. In Lima, however, the change brought continual disputes between intendant and viceroy rather than improved administration. The viceroys, with the exception of Croix, were prepared to accept the intendant system as a permanent reform, but all were ready to criticize individual intendants. At the same time intendants kept a close watch upon viceroys, and it is clear that government at the centre became less corrupt than in the days of Amat.

At a local level government was never completely reformed. The intendants found it impossible to exercise effective supervision over their subdelegates, partly because of the failure of the viceroys to give them adequate support, while the crown's refusal to provide the subdelegates with adequate salaries made the continuation of old abuses inevitable. The now illegal *repartimiento* system remained in force, a symbol of the crown's inability to enforce legislation detrimental to the interests of those entrusted with its local application. The massive Indian participation in the 1814 rebellion was a clear indication of their continuing discontent over the abuses suffered at the hands of their creole masters.

In financial affairs the improvement brought about by administrative reform was satisfactory for more than a decade after 1784. The complex exchequer machine, headed by the intendants in their provinces and by the superintendent in Lima, cut down fraud and corruption in the collection of revenue. But the benefits to be gained from improved management alone were limited, and the exchequer system stagnated in the 1790s, reflecting the general economic stagnation of the viceroyalty. In economic affairs progress in the decade after 1784 had given grounds for optimism. The efforts of the intendants to stimulate the exploitation of natural resources, together with the effects of general imperial economic development, brought a temporary revival to economic life and led to the increased export of agricultural goods. But the Spanish entry into European warfare brought an end to this revival, since the commercial disruption caused by British maritime predominance not only cut off Peru from her European market but also created a severe shortage of mercury, essential for the mining industry. The crown and the intendants made some efforts to halt economic decline; but, short of removing some of the vital components of imperial reform, there was little that they could do, for the basic factor in Peru's economic depression was the loss of the monopolistic privileges upon which her former prosperity had been built. The creation of the viceroyalty of the Río de la Plata and the opening of Buenos Aires to European trade not only removed the provinces of the Plate and Upper Peru from Lima's economic control but also undermined economic activity within Lower Peru, as the import of European textiles through Buenos Aires hit domestic industry. Moreover, geographical isolation, poor communications and a

CONCLUSION 237

shortage of labour made it impossible for Peruvian agriculture to compete with that of other parts of the empire in the European market.

The improvements in public administration which the intendants succeeded in stimulating were overshadowed by the basic economic problems. However, despite a waning interest in Madrid, many intendants made impressive efforts to inspect their provinces, collect economic information, have maps made and improve local amenities. Attention to municipal affairs, including the reform of local finances, development of public works and general municipal improvement, was particularly strong. For the fulfilment of this work the intendants enlisted the support of the *cabildos*, reviving decadent corporations in some areas, founding new ones in others. An unforseen consequence was that the *cabildos*, representing creole opinion, soon sought to extend their powers over the expenditure of municipal funds and to control the efficient systems of municipal administration created by the intendants. As the structure of Spanish authority weakened from 1808, following political and military chaos in the peninsula, the *cabildos* widened their aims and led creole demands for comprehensive economic, political and commercial reforms.

The reforming zeal of the liberals who came to power in Spain in the absence of Ferdinand VII made the continuation of sound government impossible in Peru. While encouraging the *cabildos* in their demands for wider responsibilities, the *Junta Central* and the Regency dismissed many of the intendants governing in Peru, sometimes on the strength of unreliable evidence. The promises of reform and the condemnation of past abuses instilled a renewed optimism in the viceroyalty, but the application of the constitution brought also further administrative instability. This became most serious in Cuzco, where the conservative *audiencia*, controlling government, resisted the aspirations of creoles seeking rapid reforms. The rebellion of 1814 spread rapidly, but its popular character alienated moderate opinion, and, after its initial success, it was easily crushed by royalist forces. By 1815 order had been restored, but the foundations of Spanish authority were weakening. A prolonged period of warfare in neighbouring areas had already brought further deterioration in economic and financial conditions. Moderate creoles had made clear between 1809 and 1814 that they wanted basic solutions to Peru's economic problems—the instructions which the *cabildo* of Lima provided for its deputy to the *Junta Central* in 1809 give a detailed analysis of creole grievances. The era of liberal ascendancy in Spain raised some hopes that serious efforts would be made to redress these grievances; the restoration of Ferdinand suggested that they would be ignored. The return to absolutism meant that Spain would lose the allegiance of many moderate creoles, and, as a consequence, that her retention of Peru could only be temporary.

APPENDIX 1

Intendants of the Viceroyalty of Peru[1]

LIMA
Jorge Escobedo y Alarcón	1784–7
Juan María Gálvez	1805–9, 1812–20

AREQUIPA
José Menéndez Escalada	1784–5
Antonio Álvarez y Jiménez	1785–96
Bartolomé María de Salamanca	1796–1811
Josef Gabriel Moscoso	1811–15
Juan Bautista de Lavalle y Zugasti	1816–25

CUZCO
Benito de la Mata Linares	1784–8
Josef de la Portilla	1788–91
Carlos de Corral y Aguirre	1791–2
Manuel Ruiz Urries de Castilla	1794–1803
Francisco Muñoz de San Clemente	1806–9

HUMANGA
Nicolás Manrique de Lara	1784–5
José Menéndez Escalada	1785–99
Demetrio O'Higgins	1799–1812
Manuel Quimper Benites del Pino	1816–1819
Francisco José de Recavarren	1819–20

HUANCAVELICA
Fernando Márquez de la Plata	1784–9
Manuel Ruiz Urries de Castilla	1790–4

[1] The list includes all intendants who took office in 1784, whether or not their nominations were confirmed by the crown; thereafter temporary intendants are omitted.

Juan María Gálvez	1794–1804
Juan Vives y Echeverría	1807–9, 1813–14
Lázaro de Rivera y Espinosa	1810–13
Juan Montenegro y Ubalde	1818–20

PUNO

Tomás de Samper	1797–1801
Josef González y Montoya	1801–6
Manuel Quimper Benites del Pino	1806–10, 1810–14
Diego Antonio Nieto	1810
Tadeo Garate	1817–24

TARMA

Juan María Gálvez	1784–93
Francisco Suárez de Castilla Valcárcel	1793–5
Ramón Urrutia y las Casas	1796–1810
José González de Prada	1811–20

TRUJILLO

Fernando de Saavedra	1784–91
Vicente Gil de Taboada	1791–1820

BIOGRAPHICAL NOTES ON THE INTENDANTS

Antonio Álvarez y Jiménez

A native of Spain. Went to Lima as a young man but returned to Spain to follow a military career.[1] Appointed *teniente* in 1765; went to the Plate with Cevallos's expedition and, on his return to Spain, served at Gibraltar.[2] In 1784, when holding rank of captain, appointed intendant of Arequipa, and arrived in his province at end of 1785.[3] One of the outstanding intendants of Peru, Álvarez was particularly active in the sphere of public administration, and made a famous provincial *visita*. Replaced in 1796 and promoted to colonel. Made brigadier in 1798. Governor of Chiloé 1804–12. Most of his sons pursued military careers in new republics.

[1] Mendiburu, op. cit., i, 401.
[2] A.G.I., Aud. de Lima 764, 1120, for details of military career.
[3] A.G.I., Aud. de Lima 630, *título*, 2 Feb. 1784. Unless otherwise indicated details of appointment and issue of *títulos* for all intendants are from this *legajo*.

Carlos de Corral y Aguirre

Born in Spain, first went to America in 1783 as *teniente coronel* of the regiment of Soria, sent to Panama when news reached Spain of the outbreak of the Túpac Amaru rising. Following promotion to colonel, returned to Spain in 1787. Became brigadier in 1789 and appointed president-intendant of Cuzco at end of year (*título* 20 Jan. 1790). Arrived in Cuzco in February 1791.[1] Died in office in December 1792.[2]

Jorge Escobedo y Alarcón

Native of Jaén, Spain. Appointed *oidor* of *audiencia* of Charcas in 1776; served as Areche's subdelegate in Potosí following start of *visita* to Peru. Appointed to succeed Areche, 13 Sept. 1781. Put his faith in the intendant system as the solution to Peru's administrative, financial, economic and social problems, and from 1782 worked to adapt the Ordinance of Intendants of Buenos Aires to Peruvian needs and conditions. With the formal installation of the new system in July 1784, remained in Lima as intendant of the army, intendant of Lima and superintendent-subdelegate, continuing to serve these posts after the termination of the *visita* in 1785.

For the next three years fully occupied with problems arising from the creation of the new administrative structure. Set a good example for his fellow-intendants with his attempts to supervize closely the activities of subdelegates and to tackle the problems of municipal life and public administration in his capital. Sporadic disputes with viceroy over minor matters. In 1787 metropolitan government used one of these as pretext for application in Peru of general policy of restoring superintendencies of financial affairs to viceroys. Transfer of his powers to Croix ordered on 1 Aug. 1787. Escobedo returned to Spain to take up post as minister of Council of the Indies. There used his influence to defend the intendant system during the 1790s and in particular to reject the complaints of viceroy Croix. A member of the committee which drew up the *New Ordinance* of 1803.[3]

Juan María Gálvez

Born Ecija, Andalusia, of gentry stock. Went to Peru in 1781, as secretary of viceroy Jáuregui. Appointed first intendant of Tarma, taking up post in October 1784. Noted for programmes of municipal

---

[1] A.G.I., Aud. de Cuzco 2, Corral to Lerena, no. 3, 11 March 1791.
[2] Mendiburu, op. cit., iv, 224.
[3] See above, 69–71.

improvement and public administration. Transferred to Huancavelica in 1793 (*título* 22 Oct.), taking up post in Sept. 1794. Served there for ten years, making a moderate success of control of mercury mining. Appointed intendant of Lima in 1803 (*título* 2 Dec.), but unable to take up his post until 1805, due to viceregal obstruction.[1] His authority in this new post was limited to exercise of appellate jurisdiction and correspondence consisted of little more than complaints against the viceroy. Dismissed in 1809 but, following return to Spain, was reappointed. Returned to Lima in 1812, serving until his death in 1820.[2] Married Josefa de la Riva Agüero, daughter of José de la Riva Agüero, the superintendent of the *Casa de Moneda* of Lima.[3]

Tadeo Garate
A native of La Paz, studied and qualified as a lawyer in Cuzco. Served there as episcopal secretary, 1801-6. Appointed subdelegate of Chucuito in 1807. Elected as deputy to the *Cortes* by the *cabildo* of Puno in 1811. In Spain joined a conservative group, which welcomed the restoration of Ferdinand VII and his absolutist policies. Rewarded by appointment as intendant of Puno (*título* 13 July 1814). Returned to Peru in September 1816, and served in Puno 1817-24. Retired to Spain in 1825.[4]

Vicente Gil de Taboada
Born 1772 in Santiago, Galicia, son of conde Gil de Taboada. Travelled to Peru with his uncle, Francisco, on latter's appointment as viceroy. Nominated by his uncle to the intendancy of Trujillo in 1791, and appointment confirmed in the following year (*título* 28 March 1792). Served in this one post until 1820, although he returned to Spain on licensed leave 1806-10. Leave initially granted for two years but extended due to his capture by the English in Buenos Aires in 1806. In his absence the intendancy was served by Felipe del Risco, a nephew of Avilés. Returned to his post in 1810. Left Peru after declaration of independence in 1821, becoming, on return to Spain, intendant of first Seville and then Orense.[5]

José González de Prada
Born 1751 in Entrepeñas, Spain, into a long-established gentry family. After education in Madrid went to America in 1783, serving

[1] See above, 71-2.
[2] A.G.I., Aud. de Lima 1121, Pezuela to crown, no. 474, 28 March 1820.
[3] Mendiburu, op. cit., v, 323.   [4] Ibid., v, 399.
[5] Ibid., vi, 48-9. Details of services in A.G.I., Aud. de Lima 1120.

as senior treasury minister in Salta (1783–8) and Cochabamba (1788–1801). Became an accountant in the tribunal of accounts in Lima in 1801.[1] Appointed intendant of Tarma in 1809, but before taking up this post in 1811 served as temporary intendant of Cochabamba, until forced to flee by outbreak of revolution. Served in Tarma until 1820, until forced to flee to Lima due to advance of insurgents from north.[2] Appointed to succeed Gálvez as intendant of Lima (*título* 24 Oct. 1820), but independence declared in Lima before this took effect. He remained in Lima, unmolested by the independent government. After Ayacucho retired to Cochabamba, where he died in 1829.

Josef González y Montoya

A Spanish naval officer, appointed intendant of Puno in 1799 (*título* 23 July). Reached his capital in December 1801, serving until 1806. Reputed to have governed well, founding the *cabildo* of Puno, promoting public works, organizing the militia and ending the obligation of Indians in his province to provide *mita* service at Potosí.[3]

Juan Bautista de Lavalle y Zugasti

Born in Lima in 1779, fifth son of José Antonio de Lavalle y Cortés, a prominent member of the city's mercantile community; granted the title conde de Premio Real in 1782.[4] Followed his father into trade. Elected *alcalde* of Lima in 1814 and appointed *regidor* in 1816. Appointed intendant of Arequipa in 1815 (*título* 10 Sept.), serving there 1816–25. Given rank of brigadier and appointed president of Cuzco in 1823, but news of appointment reached Peru after Ayacucho. With independence continued in Peruvian public life until his death in 1851.[5]

Nicolás Manrique de Lara y Carrillo de Albornoz

Born in Lima in 1739, into one of the most distinguished of the city's creole families. Served as *alcalde* of Lima 1769–70, and in 1779 succeeded his father, Francisco, in the important office of *contador mayor* of the tribunal of accounts in Lima.[6] His nomination as intendant of Huamanga in 1784 was popular, since he was the only

---

[1] A.G.I., Aud. de Lima 1120, list of merits and services, 30 May 1814.
[2] Ibid. Mendiburu, op. cit., vi, 115–17.
[3] Ibid., vi, 113–14.
[4] Bromley, 'Alcaldes de la ciudad de Lima en el siglo XVIII', 346.
[5] Mendiburu, op. cit., vi, 421.
[6] Bromley, 'Alcaldes de la ciudad de Lima en el siglo XVIII', 338.

creole among those nominated. The appointment was not confirmed, however, and the short time he remained in Huamanga was most notable for complex disputes with the bishop. On his return to Lima he took up his old post in the tribunal of accounts, serving there until his retirement in 1798. From his father he inherited the title marqués de Lara, first granted in 1739 to his uncle, a member of the Council of Castile.[1] Died in 1815.

Fernando Márquez de la Plata
Born Seville in 1740, son of an *oidor* of the *audiencia* of Seville. Went to America with the expedition of Cevallos, as *auditor de guerra*, and went on to serve as *fiscal del crimen* in the *audiencia* of Charcas. After assisting in defence of La Paz against Indian rebels went to Lima, as *alcalde del crimen*.[2] Appointed first intendant of Huancavelica (*título* 21 Nov. 1783), but was relieved due to suspicion that the collapse of the *Santa Barbara* mine was due to his mismanagement. Returned to his former post in the *audiencia* of Lima, remaining there until appointment in 1796 as regent of the *audiencia* of Quito.[3] Transferred to regency of Santiago de Chile in 1801, serving there until his appointment to the Council of the Indies in 1806.[4] Granted a licence in 1785 to marry María Calvo Encalada y Recavarren Pardo, member of prominent Chilean family.[5]

Benito de la Mata Linares
Born in Madrid, the son of a member of the Council of Castile. Appointed *oidor* of the *audiencia* of Santiago de Chile in 1776 and in 1778 became *asesor de tabacos* for Chile. Transferred to Lima to serve as *oidor* there, and in 1781 appointed *juez conservador* of *propios* and *arbitrios*.[6] Although not formally installed as intendant of Cuzco until 1784 he took command of the city and province in 1783, arranging the trial and execution of Túpac Amaru and other members of his family. The role he played in the repression of the Indian rising has earned him the hostility of Peruvian historians—Mendiburu describes him as 'un hombre execrable'.[7] A rigid governor, preoccupied with problems of security, Mata aroused considerable hostility among creole opinion. Viceroy Croix recommended his

[1] A.N.P., Superior Gobierno 33, *cuaderno* 1085.
[2] A.G.I., Aud. de Lima 707, representation of Márquez, 22 Oct. 1793.
[3] A.H.M.H., Libro de Cédulas 1063a, f. 166, *cédula*, 12 July 1796.
[4] See C. Deustua Pimentel, 'El informe secreto del virrey Gil de Taboada sobre la audiencia de Lima', *Revista Histórica* (Lima), xxi (1954), 274–87.
[5] A.H.M.H., Libro de Cédulas 1063a, f. 37, *cédula*, 13 Nov. 1785.
[6] A.G.I., Aud. de Cuzco 5, Mata to Gálvez, 6 April 1782.
[7] Mendiburu, op. cit., vii, 365.

removal in 1786, for this reason. Travelled to Buenos Aires in 1788 to serve as regent of the *audiencia*, to which post he had been appointed in the previous year.[1]

José Menéndez Escalada
A native of Spain, nominated first intendant of Arequipa, in compensation for the abolition of his former post of *director general de alcabalas* during the exchequer reorganization undertaken by Areche and Escobedo.[2] Served for a year in Arequipa, but this appointment was not confirmed; instead sent to Huamanga to replace Manrique (*título* 19 June 1785). Remained there until 1799. Under him disputes with episcopal authorities abated and he gave some aid to missionary activity in the *montaña*. He seems, however, to have been a rather inactive and undistinguished intendant—his successor, O'Higgins, sharply criticized his neglect of public administration.[3]

José Montenegro y Ubalde
Born in Moquegua, near Arequipa, in 1766. Educated in Spain and followed a military career there, reaching rank of colonel. Appointed intendant of Huancavelica in 1815 (*título* 26 Sept.). Returned to Peru in 1818 to take up post and served in Huancavelica until 1820, when retreated in face of insurgents. Captured by patriots but rejoined royalists when they took Lima in 1823. Promoted to brigadier and given title of intendant of Huamanga, but was unable to take up post and, after Ayacucho, returned to Spain.[4]

Josef Gabriel Moscoso
Born in Arequipa, the son of colonel Juan Moscoso of Cochabamba and nephew of Juan Manuel de Moscoso, the famous bishop of Cuzco. Another uncle, Angel Mariano Moscoso, became bishop of Tucumán.[5] After fighting against Túpac Amaru's forces went to Spain to begin military career. In 1810, with rank of *teniente coronel*, appointed intendant of Arequipa (*título* 15 Oct.). Took up post in 1811. A strong supporter of Abascal's firm rule he offered armed resistance to the *cuzqueño* rebels in 1814, but failed to stop their advance. Captured and taken to Cuzco, he was executed there by the rebels on 29 January 1815.

Francisco Muñoz de San Clemente
Born in Spain and followed conventional military career. By 1804 lieutenant in Manila and sub-inspector of troops in Philippines.

[1] A.G.I., Aud. de Cuzco 3, royal decree, 12 Feb. 1787.
[2] A.G.I., Aud. de Lima 1118, Escobedo to Gálvez, no. 46, 16 March 1783.
[3] See above, 164.   [4] Mendiburu, op. cit., vii, 420.   [5] Ibid., viii, 37.

Appointed president of Cuzco (*título* 24 May 1804) and finally reached the city in September 1806.[1] Handed over authority to regent of *audiencia*, Manuel Pardo, on becoming ill in May 1809. Died the following month. Thereafter Cuzco was governed by a series of temporary presidents.

Diego Antonio Nieto

Appointment intendant of Puno in 1806 (*título* 15 Dec.). Finally arrived in January 1810 but died later in the year.

Demetrio O'Higgins

Born in Ireland in 1768. Followed family tradition of serving Spanish crown, entering the Irish regiment in 1782. Travelled to Peru in 1796, after the appointment of his uncle, Ambrosio, marques de Osorno, as viceroy. Thereafter his success was assured. He was appointed captain of the viceregal cavalry in 1797 and subsequently commander of a special cavalry squadron formed to repel possible English invasion.[2] Nominated by his uncle to fill the vacant intendancy of Huamanga in 1799, an appointed confirmed by the crown in 1802 (*título* 6 Jan.). A zealous intendant, he made two lengthy provincial *visitas*. Appointed to the intendancy of Tarma in 1805, due to mistaken belief in Spain that Urrutia had died, but remained in Huamanga when it was discovered that Urrutia was alive and well. Survived purge of 1809–10. In 1812 granted licence to return to Spain for two years, but in fact did not return to Peru. Died in Spain in 1816. Married a native of Lima, Mariana Echeverría Santiago de Ulloa, who after his death married José Bernardo de Tagle, marqués de Torre Tagle.[3]

Josef de la Portilla

A native of Spain. Prominent member of viceregal secretariat in Lima between 1781 and 1788, serving as *asesor general* and *auditor general* and, after Juan María Gálvez's appointment to Tarma, as viceregal secretary.[4] In 1787, after creation of *audiencia* of Cuzco, appointed regent and intendant of the province. Took up both posts in 1788 and served in this dual capacity until 1791. With the arrival in that year of a separate president-intendant, Portilla remained as regent. Temporary president 1792–3, after death of Corral, and 1803, in absence of Ruiz.

[1] A.G.I., Aud. de Cuzco 2, Muñoz to principe de la Paz, 11 Sept. 1806.
[2] A.G.I., Aud. de Lima 1121, for details of military career.
[3] Mendiburu, op. cit., viii, 190–1.
[4] Ibid., ix, 203.

Manuel Quimper Benites del Pino

Born in Lima but educated in Spain and began naval career there. In 1805 left post as treasury minister in Vera Cruz after receiving decree that he was to succeed O'Higgins as intendant of Huamanga.[1] However, the appointment was based on the mistaken belief that O'Higgins would be replacing Urrutia as intendant of Tarma. When it transpired that the latter was well, O'Higgins remained in Huamanga and Quimper found himself without a post. Nominated by Abascal as temporary intendant of Puno in 1806.[2] Relinquished this office in 1810, after the arrival of Nieto, but restored later in the year, due to Nieto's death and in recognition of his services with royalist army in Upper Peru. Appointment confirmed in 1811 (*título* 10 March). Fled in 1814 as *cuzqueño* rebels advanced. In same year appointed intendant of Huamanga (*título* 28 Aug.). Served there 1816–19. In 1817 Pezuela complained to crown about Quimper's maladministration suggesting, too, that his flight in 1814 raised doubts about his loyalty to Spain, and, as a result, it was ordered that he be dismissed and sent to Spain.[3] Reached the peninsula in 1820, but returned to Peru in following year to take legal action against those who had complained to viceroy about his activities in Huamanga. Remained in Peru after independence and served in republican navy until 1827. Died in 1844, aged 104.[4]

Francisco José de Recavarren

Born in Chile. Military career in Spain until appointed intendant of Cochabamba in 1809.[5] Remained in Cochabamba in 1814 while the town was occupied by rebels, and was subsequently suspended from office on suspicion of collaboration. Absolved of charges, however, and restored to office in 1815.[6] Appointed intendant of Huamanga in 1818 (*título* 2 Dec.) Took up new post in 1819, but died in office the following year.[7]

Lázaro de Rivera y Espinosa

A native of Spain. Military career. Appointed governor of Mojos in 1784 and promoted to office of intendant of Paraguay in 1796.[8]

[1] A.G.I., Aud. de Lima 1121, royal decree, 6 April 1805.
[2] A.G.I., Aud. de Lima 1121, Abascal to Minister of Grace and Justice, no. 22, 6 Oct. 1806.
[3] A.G.I., Aud. de Lima 1121, royal order, 28 Aug. 1818.
[4] Mendiburu, op. cit., xi, 266–7.
[5] A.G.I., Aud. de Lima 601, report of Council of the Indies, 19 Feb. 1810.
[6] A.G.I., Aud. de Lima 1121, Abascal to crown, 14 Dec. 1815.
[7] Mendiburu, op. cit., ix, 321.   [8] Lynch, op. cit., 297–8.

Reputedly a good administrator, but noted for disputes with superiors. Appointed intendant of Huancavelica in 1809, serving there 1810–13, but removed from office after the Council of the Indies looked into his background. The investigation revealed information about his intransigent opposition to the breaking up of the community system of the Guaraní Indians.[1] Further reason for dismissal was suspicion that his relationship with Santiago Liniers— Liniers was married to the sister of Rivera's wife—raised doubts about his loyalty to Spain.

Manuel Ruiz Urries de Castilla

A native of Spain. Serving as *corregidor* of Paruro when Túpac Amaru rising began and commanded one of the royalist columns which attacked rebels at Tungasuca.[2] In 1783 nominated by viceroy as military commander of Cuzco and the appointment was confirmed by the crown in 1787.[3] Appointed intendant of Huancavelica in 1788 (*título* 21 Oct.), but Croix suspended the appointment while Pedro de Tagle investigated the causes of the mining disaster of 1786. Finally took up post in 1790, serving there for four years. A successful intendant, popular with the inhabitants, mainly due to his decision to allow free working of mercury deposits in hills around *Santa Barbara* mine. Promoted to presidency of Cuzco in 1793 (*título* 18 July), serving there 1794–1803. When informed in 1802 of decision to relieve him, complained bitterly of royal ingratitude. Appointed president of Quito, taking up post in 1808. Imprisoned by insurgents in 1812 and died in prison.

Fernando de Saavedra

A native of Spain, who arrived at Peru in 1777 as accountant to Areche's *visita general*. Continued in this post when Escobedo took over the *visita* and was rewarded for his diligence and ability with appointment as first intendant of Trujillo in 1784. Noted for his activity in the realm of public administration. Died in office in 1791.

Bartolomé María de Salamanca

Born 1762 at Villa de Lora, near Seville, the second son of Fernando Rodríguez de Salamanca, conde de Fuente Elsalsa. Entered Spanish navy at age of 17. Had reached rank of *capitán de fragata* in 1794, when he lost an arm on active service.[4] Appointed

[1] A.G.I., Aud. de Lima 602, report of Council of the Indies, 8 Feb. 1812.
[2] A.H.M.H., Libro de Cédulas 900, f. 95, Valdés to viceroy, 20 Sept. 1787.
[3] A.G.I., Aud. de Cuzco 3, royal order, 26 Feb. 1787.
[4] B.N.P., MS D11619, family history, Sevilla 21 June 1803.

intendant of Arequipa in 1795 (*título* 11 June) in recognition of his merits and as compensation for his inability to continue with naval career due to disablement. Took up post in 1796. Like his predecessor, noted for activity in sphere of public administration. Although still only relatively young in 1810—then 48—his dismissal was ordered, following receipt in Spain of complaints against him from the *cabildo* of Arequipa and an obscure Spanish resident, Santiago Aguirre.[1] Exonerated in 1812 but was not restored to office. Instead given rank of *intendente de exército* and viceroy ordered to find him suitable employment. Fulfilled a variety of tasks; appointed temporary intendant of Lima in 1820.[2] Married a native of Arequipa, Petronila Ofelan in 1821. Remained in Lima until forced to abandon post by advance of insurgents. Left for Spain, but forced by illness to break journey at Rio de Janeiro and died there in 1824.

Tomás de Samper
A native of Spain. Military career. Appointed intendant of Puno in 1795. Took up post in 1797, serving until 1801, when he returned to Spain to take up army post in Madrid.[3] Travelled via Buenos Aires, attending to family and business affairs of his wife in La Paz and Oruro on the way.

Francisco Suárez de Castilla Valcárcel
Born in Spain in 1744. His uncle, marqués de San Juan de Piedras Albas, served as president of Council of the Indies. Began military career as cadet in 1754, reaching rank of colonel by 1775.[4] In 1789, when serving as colonel of militia regiment of Obona, appointed intendant of Tarma (*título* 27 April). Took up post in 1793 but served only a short time, dying in office in June 1795.

Ramón Urrutia y las Casas
Born in Viscaya in 1742. Appointed *corregidor* of Oruro, Upper Peru, in 1777. Took up post in 1779 and, after defending the city against Indian rebels, was forced to flee in 1781. Served with royalist troops fighting insurgents in 1782, and was granted rank of infantry captain in the following year. In 1784 appointed subdelegate of Ica by Escobedo.[5] Subsequently appointed subdelegate

---

[1] See above, 210-11.
[2] B.N.P., MS D11619, Pezuela to Salamanca, 17 Aug. 1820.
[3] A.N.P., Superior Gobierno 27, *cuaderno* 845, Samper to Osorno, no. 429, 31 Jan. 1801.
[4] A.G.I., Aud. de Lima 1120, representation of Suárez, 16 March 1789.
[5] A.G.I., Aud. de Lima 1120, *relación de méritos*, 1784.

of Piura and, although suspended from this post for suspected maladministration, appointed intendant of Tarma in 1796 (*título* 19 Jan.).[1] Served there until receipt of royal order of 2 Oct. 1809—an unspectacular but competent official. Died in Lima in 1812.

Juan Vives y Echeverría

Born at Larragueta, Navarre, in 1769, pursuing orthodox military career from 1780.[2] Appointed intendant of Huancavelica in 1805 (*título* 18 Dec.) and took up post in July 1807. A controversial intendant and unpopular with many in Huancavelica, since he paid a lot of attention to silver mining at Castrovirreina, but neglected the mining of mercury. This policy, claimed Vives, had been ordered by the Spanish government.[3] Removed from office in 1809, as a result of the complaints made against him, but, on his return to Spain, successfully agitated for restoration. Returned to Huancavelica in 1813 but was forced to flee in 1814, in face of the advance of the *cuzqueño* rebels. When he reached Lima Abascal sent him back to Spain. Appointed intendant of Huamanga in 1818 (*título* 11 Sept.), but died before he could take up the post.[4]

[1] A.G.I., Aud. de Lima 763, Gil to Llaguno, 26 Jan. 1797.
[2] A.G.I., Aud. de Lima 778, *relación de méritos*, 16 June 1804.
[3] Despite viceregal scepticism, Vives's claim was in fact, true. Details are in A.G.I., Aud. de Lima, 1335.   [4] Mendiburu, op. cit., xi, 352.

APPENDIX 2

Population of the Viceroyalty of Peru in 1795[1]

Province	Partido	Spaniards	Indians	Mestizos	Free Negroes	Slaves	Total
Lima	City	19,986	4,332	4,807	10,023	13,497	52,645
	Cercado	189	5,412	72	208	4,402	10,283
	Canta	77	10,873	1,723	—	—	12,673
	Chancay	992	7,534	1,081	758	3,604	13,969
	Cañete	499	6,962	737	992	3,363	12,553
	Huarochirí	245	13,939	592	19	84	14,879
	Ica	2,255	7,210	3,405	4,305	4,004	21,179
	Yauyos	25	12,591	93	1,451	—	14,160
	Santa	289	761	1,237	108	827	3,222
		24,557	69,614	13,747	17,864	29,781	155,563
Tarma	Tarma	1,713	18,972	14,300	77	—	35,062
	Cajatambo	929	11,824	4,686	629	—	18,068
	Conchucos	1,426	16,810	13,983	—	—	32,219
	Huaylas	3,682	22,093	15,971	138	116	42,000
	Huamalíes	611	9,363	4,623	—	43	14,640
	Huánuco	6,099	5,998	3,075	—	39	15,211
	Panataguas	—	1,463	—	—	—	1,463
	Jauja	1,829	23,976	21,922	—	58	47,785
		16,289	110,499	78,560	844	256	206,448

[1] A.G.I., Indif. General 1525, *estado* with Bonet to Gil, 29 Dec. 1795.

Province	Partido	Spaniards	Indians	Mestizos	Free Negroes	Slaves	Total
Huamanga	Huamanga	327	2,464	4,651	867	40	8,349
	Andahuaylas	3,020	15,586	4,000	—	—	22,606
	Huanta	93	18,923	10,080	9	—	29,105
	Lucanas	889	14,657	2,076	60	—	17,682
	Parinacochas	1,085	11,317	6,451	—	—	18,853
	Vilcashuamán	93	10,127	2,363	7	—	12,590
		5,507	73,074	29,621	943	40	109,185
Huancavelica	Angaraes	841	16,817	1,040	—	16	18,714
	Castrovirreina	124	9,225	771	—	25	10,145
	Tayacaja	1,415	12,042	2,724	—	—	16,181
		2,380	38,084	4,535	—	41	45,040
Cuzco	Cuzco	16,826	7,114	53	646	203	24,842
	Aymaraes	4,498	14,992	—	—	—	19,490
	Abancay	1,970	17,143	4,739	50	81	23,983
	Chumbivilcas	4,498	10,421	—	—	—	14,919
	Chilques y Maques	2,352	15,268	2,733	117	—	20,470
	Cotabambas	205	16,503	1,382	—	—	18,090
	Calca y Lares	360	9,216	320	—	—	9,896
	Tinta	351	24,396	5,420	152	—	30,319
	Paucartambo	780	8,106	957	7	—	9,850
	Quispicanches	63	19,717	4,306	21	—	24,107
	Urubamba	917	8,714	3,194	—	—	12,825
		32,820	151,590	23,104	993	284	208,791

Arequipa	Arequipa	22,712	5,099	4,908	2,487	1,225	36,431
	Arica	1,593	12,815	1,977	585	1,294	18,264
	Cailloma	240	16,554	1,417	335	29	18,575
	Condesuyos	3,684	11,150	4,358	34	44	19,270
	Camaná	5,128	1,220	1,021	1,747	887	10,093
	Moquegua	5,620	16,635	2,916	887	1,526	27,584
	Tarapacá	520	5,468	1,200	528	253	7,969
		39,587	68,941	17,797	6,603	5,258	138,186
Trujillo	Trujillo	1,638	4,582	1,549	2,557	1,582	11,908
	Cajamarca	5,653	27,314	13,188	336	171	46,662
	Chota	2,349	18,751	9,111	1,539	157	31,907
	Cajamarquilla	1,001	6,835	7,678	194	8	15,716
	Chachapoyas	1,431	12,021	10,954	486	13	24,905
	Huamachuco	2,337	27,336	18,367	250	79	48,369
	Piura	2,953	22,503	10,654	5,203	884	42,197
	Lambayeque	2,388	17,471	5,448	3,192	1,831	30,330
		19,750	136,813	76,949	13,757	4,725	251,994
Total for all provinces:		140,890	648,615	244,313	41,004	40,385	1,115,207

APPENDIX 3

Product of the *Casa de Moneda* of Lima, 1776-1820[1]

Year	Gold minted[2]	Silver minted	Total
1776	244,486	4,190,360	4,434,846
1777	456,684	4,245,245	4,701,929
1778	811,258	4,091,725	4,902,983
1779	1,042,964	3,636,230	4,679,194
1780	713,582	3,837,545	4,551,127
1781	524,730	4,180,517	4,704,947
1782	569,991	3,249,489	3,819,840
1783	527,582	3,223,272	3,750,854
1784	391,680	3,518,149	3,909,829
1785	433,024	3,120,739	3,553,763
1786	437,504	3,610,456	4,047,960
1787	665,294	3,581,281	4,246,575
1788	662,874	3,770,759	4,433,633
1789	767,040	3,580,757	4,347,797
1790	623,489	4,582,362	5,205,851
1791	755,990	4,363,082	5,119,072
1792	694,938	4,910,644	5,605,581
1793	646,961	5,294,745	5,941,707
1794			6,093,037
1795			5,949,030
1796	629,798	5,269,580	5,899,378
1797	583,724	4,516,206	5,099,930

[1] This table has been compiled from information contained in documents and manuscript books in the Casa de Moneda section of A.H.M.H. Those used, with relevant years in brackets, were:

Libros Generales 410 (1776-7), 411 (1778-9), 412 (1780-1), 413 (1782-3), 414 (1784-5), 415 (1786-7), 416 (1788-9), 417 (1790-1), 420 (1796-7).

Documentos 16-051 (1792-3), 18-044 (1794), 18-061 (1795), 19-007 (1797-8), 19-030 (1799), 19-051 (1800), 19-069 (1801), 20-006 (1802), 20-049 (1803), 21-001 (1804), 21-024 (1805), 21-039 (1806), 21-057 (1807), 22-019 (1808), 22-042 (1809), 22-067 (1810), 23-002 (1811), 23-021 (1812), 23-044 (1813), 24-001 (1814), 24-026 (1815), 25-003 (1816), 25-025 (1817), 27-001 (1818), 27-032 (1819), 28-006 (1820).

[2] Figures in pesos.

PRODUCT OF THE *CASA DE MONEDA*

Year	Gold minted	Silver minted	Total
1798	535,810	4,758,094	5,293,904
1799	496,486	5,512,345	6,008,831
1800	378,596	4,399,409	4,778,005
1801	328,051	4,523,932	4,851,983
1802	337,612	4,143,811	4,481,423
1803	350,200	3,990,593	4,340,793
1804	352,709	4,340,907	4,693,666
1805	399,932	4,383,793	4,783,725
1806	218,046	4,348,668	4,566,714
1807	385,898	3,774,532	4,160,430
1808	367,136	4,144,298	4,511,434
1809	340,624	4,338,102	4,678,726
1810	343,687	4,493,376	4,837,063
1811	339,627	4,509,526	4,849,153
1812	575,430	3,887,497	4,462,927
1813	683,500	4,090,674	4,774,174
1814	761,245	3,629,283	4,390,528
1815	502,528	3,745,791	4,248,319
1816	772,639	3,867,515	4,640,154
1817	778,889	3,389,081	4,167,970
1818	472,086	3,386,908	3,858,994
1819	517,607	3,271,208	3,788,815
1820	502,131	4,001,609	4,503,740

APPENDIX 4

Tribute Revenue, 1780-1811[1]

Razón de lo que ha producido los Ramos de tributos y Hospital desde el año de 1780 al de 1811, en que se extinguieron.

Años	Tributos[2]	Hospital	Total
1780	613,442	17,701	631,143
1781	645,855	18,769	664,824
1782	702,971	19,117	722,088
1783	716,459	20,933	739,392
1784	685,830	20,112	705,942
1785	732,241	20,594	752,835
1786	835,611	23,248	858,860
1787	856,680	24,679	881,360
1788	871,137	25,194	896,331
1789	906,113	26,554	932,667
1790	887,749	26,752	914,502
1791	891,640	26,129	917,769
1792	900,835	26,610	927,445
1793	903,798	26,581	930,379
1794	912,280	26,977	939,257
1795	921,283	27,243	948,626
1796	926,819	27,385	954,137
1797	935,966	27,670	963,635
1798	1,148,188	31,357	1,179,555
1799	1,158,665	33,056	1,191,720
1800	1,169,230	34,158	1,203,388
1801	1,178,954	34,460	1,213,414
1802	1,190,604	34,901	1,225,505
1803	1,196,916	36,443	1,233,358
1804	1,209,397	36,877	1,246,274
1805	1,206,789	36,943	1,243,732
1806	1,207,868	36,923	1,244,790
1807	1,211,219	37,079	1,248,298
1808	1,207,175	36,988	1,244,163
1809	1,210,419	37,082	1,247,501
1810	1,216,060	37,191	1,253,251
1811	1,239,347	37,795	1,277,141
	31,597,621	933,473	32,531,094

[1] A.G.I., Aud. de Lima 1133, certificate of Juan J'ph de Leuro, 11 Feb. 1813.
[2] Figures in pesos.

APPENDIX 5

Production of Mercury at Huancavelica, 1759-1812[1]

Year	Production[2]	Year	Production
1759	6,190.75	1786	4,798.59
1760	6,721. 2	1787	2,400
1761	6,147.39	1788	2,668.25
1762	5,322.11	1789	1,619.80
1763	5,801.55	1790	2,016. 4
1764	5,511. 7	1791	1,795.69
1765	6,352.99	1792	2,054.14
1766	6,385.40	1793	1,301.50
1767	5,717. 6	1794	4,172.92
1768	6,847.18	1795	4,725.47
1769	6,463.53	1796	4,182.14
1770	4,533.50	1797	3,927.32
1771	5,057.21	1798	3,422.58
1772	4,719.27	1799	3,355.92½
1773	4,262.75	1800	3,232.83
1774	4,833.66	1801	2,556.65
1775	5,014.21	1802	2,204.55
1776	3,741.73	1803	2,622.46
1777	4,263.97	1804	3,289.12
1778	2,848.36	1805	3,323
1779	4,477.75	1806	2,672
1780	5,803.50	1807	2,621
1781	3,062.50	1808	2,453
1782	1,782.55	1809	2,281
1783	2,463.31	1810	2,548
1784	1,612.89	1811	3,263
1785	4,493.37	1812	2,718

[1] A.G.I., Aud. de Lima 777, certificate of *contaduría general de azogues*, 5 July 1785, for production 1759–85.
Aud. de Lima 1117, certificate enclosed with Gálvez to Soler, no. 3, 8 July 1805, for production 1786–1805.
Mendiburu, op. cit., vi, 456, for production 1805–12.
[2] Figures in *quintales* and *libras*.

GLOSSARY OF SPANISH TERMS

Aduana: customs house
Aguardiente: spirit, consumed in large quantities in mining camps
Alcabala: sales tax
Alcalde del crimen: a judge of the *sala del crimen*, a subdivision of the *audiencia*, entrusted with criminal jurisdiction
Alcaldes ordinarios: municipal magistrates with executive and judicial authority, usually elected annually by the town councillors. Major urban centres had two *alcaldes*, the senior of them being the *alcalde de primer voto* and the junior the *alcalde de segundo voto*
Alférez real: standard bearer
Alguacil mayor: chief constable
Apoderado: proxy, attorney
Arancel: tariff, list of rates
Arroba: weight of about 25 pounds
Asesor: legal adviser appointed to act in judicial matters for an official with judicial responsibilities, such as an intendant or a viceroy
Audiencia: highest court of justice within a kingdom, with administrative, legislative and consultative authority
Auto: judicial decree, edict
Ayuntamiento: municipal council, *cabildo*
Azogue: quicksilver or mercury
Banco de rescate: a bank where bulk bullion could be exchanged for coin. Some sold mercury in small quantities
Bando: decree, proclamation
Barrio: municipal district
Cabildo: municipal council
Cabildo ecclesiástico: cathedral chapter
Cacao: chocolate-nut
Cacique: Indian chief or headman
Caja real: provincial exchequer office
Calaguala: medicinal fern
Cañaveral: sugar plantation
Casa de Moneda: mint
Cascarilla: bark from which quinine is produced
Cédula: a royal order issued through the Council of the Indies

Cercado: subdivision of a province, comprising the capital and its immediate vicinity

Cobos: a levy of 1½ per cent charged on gold and silver at the mint

Cocal: grove of *coca*, the narcotic leaves of which formed part of the staple diet of the Andean Indians

Consulado: merchant guild

Contador: accountant and auditor, one of the two senior officials in each provincial subtreasury. The other was the *tesorero*, or treasurer

Contador mayor: senior accountant in the viceregal capital

Corregidor: district officer with administrative and judicial authority

Corregimiento: area governed by a *corregidor*

Cura: parish priest

Diezmo: duty of 10 per cent on silver

Encomendero: person entrusted with right to tribute of a group of Indians and with responsibility for their physical and spiritual welfare

Estado: table of statistics

Estado general: statistical summary of annual performance of viceregal exchequer

Expediente: file of documents

Extracto: summary

Fanega: grain measure, about 1·5 bushels

Fiador: bondsman, guarantor

Fiscal: crown attorney prosecuting in an *audiencia*. The *fiscal del crimen* dealt with criminal suits, the *fiscal de lo civil* with civil

Hacendado: owner of *hacienda*

Hacienda: large landed estate

Informe: report

Junta: committee

Mestizo: offspring of union between Indian and white

Mita: forced labour recruitment of Indians on rotation basis

Montaña: unsettled forested area to east of Andes

Mulato: offspring of union between Negro and white

Obraje: textile workshop producing coarse cloth, usually for Indian consumption

Oficial real: treasury officer

Pallaqueo: name given to free working of mercury deposits in area around royal mine of *Santa Barbara* at Huancavelica

Papel sellado: stamped paper

Partido: subdivision of an intendancy, administered by a subdelegate

Peninsular: peninsular-born Spaniard

Peso: Spanish unit of currency, usually worth between 4s and 5s
Policía: public administration
Procurador general: municipal official elected to represent the *cabildo* before official bodies. Sometimes called *procurador síndico general*
Propios y arbitrios: municipal property and revenues
Provisión: decree or sentence
Pulpería: grocer's shop
Quintal: hundred-weight, 100 pounds
Real: one-eighth of a *peso*
Real acuerdo: executive session of an *audiencia* presided over by the viceroy
Registro: register ship
Reglamento: ordinance, by-law
Repartimiento: forced sale of goods to Indians
Revisita: inspection of Indian villages for preparation of lists of tributaries
Sala del crimen: branch of the *audiencia* exercising criminal jurisdiction
Sierra: highland area
Sisa: local tax on trade
Socorros: name given by Escobedo to his proposed scheme for a modified *repartimiento* system
Teniente: deputy
Teniente de policía: full-time official in charge of public administration in Lima
Título: title
Tribunal de la acordada: royal court with powers of summary justice outside municipal boundaries
Visita general: general inspection of a kingdom or province on behalf of the crown
Visitador general: official in charge of *visita general*
Zambo: offspring of union between Indian and Negro

BIBLIOGRAPHY

I. BIBLIOGRAPHICAL AIDS AND GUIDES TO ARCHIVES

BERMÚDEZ PLATA, CRISTÓBAL, *El Archivo General de Indias de Sevilla, sede del Americanismo* (Madrid, 1951).
BROMLEY, JUAN, 'Los libros de cédulas y provisiones del archivo histórico de la municipalidad de Lima. Indice de sus documentos', *Revista Histórica*, xix (1952), 61–202.
BUTLER, R. L., *Guide to the Hispanic American Historical Review, 1918–1945* (Durham, N.C., 1950).
BURRUS, E. J., 'An introduction to bibliographical tools in Spanish archives and manuscript collections relating to Hispanic America', *H.A.H.R.*, xxxv (1955), 443–83.
CASTELO DE ZAVALA, MARÍA, 'El Archivo Nacional del Perú', *Revista de Historia de America*, xx (1945), 371–86.
GAYANGOS, PASCUAL DE, *Catalogue of the manuscripts in the Spanish language in the British Museum* (4 vols., London, The Trustees, 1875–93).
GIBSON, CHARLES, *Guide to the Hispanic American Historical Review, 1946–1955* (Durham, N.C., 1958).
GÓMEZ MOLLEDA, D., *Bibliografía histórica española, 1950–1954* (Madrid, 1955).
GONZÁLEZ Y GONZÁLEZ, PEDRO, *Planos de ciudades iberoamericanas y filipinas existentes en el Archivo de Indias* (2 vols., Madrid, 1951).
Guia de los archivos de Madrid. Dirección General de Archivos y Bibliotecas (Madrid, 1952).
Guia de las bibliotecas de Madrid. Dirección General de Archivos y Bibliotecas (Madrid, 1953).
Handbook of Latin American Studies (Harvard University Press, 1936–50; University of Florida Press, 1951–).
HUMPHREYS, R. A., *Latin American history. A guide to the literature in English* (Oxford, 1958).
Indice de notarios de Lima y Callao cuyos protocolos se hallan en el Archivo Nacional del Perú (Lima, 1928).
Indice histórico español. Universidad de Barcelona. Centro de Estudios Históricos Internacionales (Barcelona, 1953–).
JONES, C. K., *A bibliography of Latin American bibliographies* (2nd edn, Washington, 1942).
LOHMANN VILLENA, GUILLERMO, 'Las relaciones de los virreyes del Perú', *Anuario de Estudios Americanos*, xvi (1959), 315–532.

—, 'La sección manuscritos de la Biblioteca del Ministerio de Relaciones del Perú', *Handbook of Latin American Studies 1940* (Cambridge, Mass., 1941), 518–20.

MÁRQUEZ ABANTO, ALBERTO, 'Indice general de la Revista del Archivo Nacional 1920–1946', *Revista del Archivo Nacional*, xix (1955), 94–141.

MEDINA, J. T., *La imprenta en Lima, 1584–1824* (4 vols., Santiago de Chile, 1904–5).

MOREYRA, MANUEL, 'Indice general de la Revista Historica', *Revista Historica*, xix (1952), 341–84.

PAZ, JULIÁN, *Catálogo de manuscritos de América existentes en la Biblioteca Nacional* (Madrid, 1933).

PEÑA CAMARA, JOSÉ MARÍA DE LA, *Archivo General de Indias de Sevilla. Guia del visitante* (Madrid, 1958; Sevilla 1959).

PORRAS BARRENECHEA, RAUL, *Fuentes históricas peruanas* (Lima, 1963).

ROMERO, EMILIO, *Indice de los 'Documentos' de Odriozola (1863–1877)* (Lima, 1946).

SÁNCHEZ ALONSO, BENITO, *Fuentes de la historia española e hispanoamericana* (3rd edn, 3 vols., Madrid, 1952).

SCHWAB, FEDERICO, *Catálogo de la sección colonial del Archivo Histórico* (Lima, 1944).

—, 'El Archivo Histórico del Ministerio de Hacienda y Comercio del Perú', *Revista de Historia de América*, xxi (1946), 29–44.

—, *Reales cédulas, reales ordenes, decretos, autos y bandos que se guardan en el Archivo Histórico* (Lima, 1947).

SILVA SANTISTEBAN, FERNANDO, 'Algunos archivos históricos y repositorios de Lima', *Fénix*, xii (1956–7), 145–82.

TORRE REVELLO, JOSÉ, *Los archivos españoles* (Buenos Aires, 1927).

—, *El Archivo General de Indias de Sevilla* (Buenos Aires, 1929).

TORRES LANZAS, PEDRO, *Relación de los mapas, planos, etc. del virreinato del Perú existentes en el Archivo General de Indias* (Barcelona, 1906).

VALCÁRCEL, CARLOS DANIEL, *Documentos de la audiencia del Cuzco en el A.G.I.* (Lima, 1957).

—, *Guia de indices* (Lima, 1966).

VARGAS UGARTE, RUBEN, S.J., *Manuscritos peruanos en las bibliotecas del extranjero* (Lima, 1935).

—, *Manuscritos peruanos en el Archivo de Indias* (Lima, 1938).

—, *Manuscritos peruanos en las bibliotecas de América* (Buenos Aires 1945).

—, *Manuscritos peruanos en las bibliotecas de Europa y América* (Buenos Aires, 1957).

—, *Historia del Perú. Fuentes* (Lima, 1945).

—, 'El archivo arzobispal de Lima', *Handbook of Latin American Studies 1936*, 443–8.

—, *Impresos peruanos (1763–1805)* (Lima, 1956).

—, *Impresos peruanos (1800–1807)* (Lima, 1957).

BIBLIOGRAPHY

II. PRIMARY SOURCES

1. ARCHIVES

Archivo General de Indias, Seville
  Audiencia de Buenos Aires: Legajo 354.
  Audiencia de Cuzco: Legajos 1–8, 13, 23, 35, 36.
  Audiencia de Lima: Legajos 598–604, 606–10, 612, 613, 618–25, 627, 630–7, 639, 640, 645–50, 695, 698, 707, 745, 763, 764, 777, 778, 788, 792–4, 798–802, 804–6, 810, 944, 955, 973, 974, 977–81, 1008, 1009, 1068, 1069, 1072, 1087, 1091–1122, 1124, 1125, 1131, 1133, 1136, 1150–3, 1158, 1171, 1172, 1181, 1216, 1222, 1228, 1335, 1579.
  Estado: Legajos 73–5.
  Indiferente General: Legajos 1523–25, 1713, 1714, 2827.
  Ultramar: Legajo 834.
Archivo General del Ministerio de Relaciones Exteriores, Lima
  Sección Colonial: various uncatalogued manuscripts.
Archivo Histórico del Ministerio de Hacienda y Comercio, Lima
  Sección Colonial: Legajo 51. Libros 900, 1063a, 1141.
  Casa de Moneda: Libros Generales 410–17, 420.
          MSS. 14–063, 16–051, 18–044, 18–061, 19–007, 19–030, 19–051, 19–069, 20–006, 20–049, 21–001, 21–024, 21–039, 21–057, 22–019, 22–042, 22–067, 23–002, 23–021, 23–044, 24–001, 24–026, 25–003, 25–025, 27–001, 27–032, 28–006.
  Miscelánea: MSS. 0001, 0003, 0006, 1020, 1117, 1138, 1144, 1181, 1183, 1198, 1201, 1204, 1208, 1217, 1228, 1229, 1394, 1409.
  Colección Santamaría: MSS. 00110, 00126, 00153–55, 00216, 00217, 00237.
Archivo Histórico Municipal, Lima
  Libros de Cabildo 36–44.
  Libros de Cédulas y Provisiones Reales 24–31.
Archivo Nacional del Perú, Lima
  Cabildo: Legajos 7–9, 12, 15, 16.
  Real Hacienda: Documentos sobre Túpac Amaru: Legajos 1, 2.
  Superior Gobierno: Legajos 18, 20, 21, 23, 25, 27, 30, 32–7.
Biblioteca Nacional del Perú, Lima
  MSS. C1288, C1341, C1462, C1463, C2933, C3024, C3170, C3219, C3558, C4014, C4129, C4555, D48, D127, D210, D331, D482, D5969, D10128, D10290, D10959, D11619.
British Museum, London
  Additional MSS. 13975, 13976, 13981, 13983, 15740, 17580, 17588, 17591, 17592, 17672, 20986.
  Egerton MSS. 771, 1810, 1812, 1813, 1815.

2. PRINTED DOCUMENTS AND CONTEMPORARY WORKS

ANGELIS, PEDRO DE, *Colección de obras y documentos relativos a la historia antigua y moderna de las provincias del Río de la Plata* (2nd edn, 5 vols., Buenos Aires, 1910), iv.

ANTÚÑEZ Y ACEVEDO, R., *Memorias históricas sobre la legislación y gobierno de los Españoles con sus colonias en las Indias occidentales* (Madrid, 1797).
BARRIGA, FR. VICTOR M., *Memorias para la historia de Arequipa. Relaciones de la visita del intendente de Arequipa, don Antonio Álvarez y Jiménez* (3 vols., Arequipa, 1941-8).
BUENO, COSME, *Geografía del Perú virreinal, siglo XVIII*, ed. C. D. Valcárcel (Lima, 1951).
CAMPILLO Y COSSIO, JOSÉ, *Nuevo sistema de gobierno económico para la América* (Madrid, 1789).
CASTILLO DE BODADILLA, G., *Política para corregidores* (2 vols., Madrid, 1775).
'Cédulas reales recibidas de 1768 a 1823', *Revista del Archivo Histórico del Cuzco*, iv (1953), 300-9.
Constitución política de la monarquía española (Cadiz, 1812).
DEUSTUA PIMENTEL, CARLOS, ed., 'El informe secreto del virrey Gil de Taboada sobre la audiencia de Lima', *Revista Histórica*, xxi (1954), 274-87.
—, 'El virreinato del Perú entre 1777 y 1786. Estudio de un informe', *Mercurio Peruano*, xxxv (1954), 106-22.
—, 'Un testimonio sobre la conciencia del Perú en el siglo XVIII', *La causa de la emancipación del Peru* (Lima, 1960), 239-335.
'Documentos del siglo XVIII', *Revista del Archivo Histórico del Cuzco*, iv (1953), 283-99.
Documentos referentes a la guerra de la independencia y emancipación política de la República Argentina. Archivo General de la Nación (3 vols., Buenos Aires, 1914-26), i.
DOMÍNGUEZ BORDONA, JESUS, ed., *Trujillo del Perú a fines del siglo XVIII. Dibujos y acuarelas que mandó hacer el obispo D. Baltasar Jaime Martínez Compañon* (Madrid, 1936).
DUNBAR TEMPLE, E., 'Un informe del obispo don Baltasar Jaime Martínez de Compañon en el juicio de residencia del virrey Amat'. *Documenta, año 2*, i (1949-50), 652-5.
EGUIGUREN, L. A., ed., *Guerra separatista. Rebeliones de Indios en Sur América. La sublevación de Túpac Amaru. Crónica de Melchor de Paz* (2 vols., Lima, 1952).
'El virrey caballero de Croix al bailio fray Antonio Valdés, sobre inconveniencia de aplicación de las ordenanzas de intendentes, año 1790', *Revista de la Biblioteca Nacional*, viii (Buenos Aires, 1943), 105-41.
'El virrey del Peru, Manuel de Amat, informa al rey del estado de las audiencias del virreinato, y en especial de la de Lima, compuestas por magistrados ignorantes y venales...', *Revista de la Biblioteca Nacional*, vii (Buenos Aires, 1942), 345-50.
FERRER DEL RIO, A., *Obras originales del conde de Floridablanca, y escritos referentes a su persona* (Madrid, 1912).
FISHER, J. R., ed., *Arequipa 1796-1811. La relación del gobierno del intendente Salamanca* (Lima, 1968).
FUENTES, MANUEL A., ed., *Memorias de los virreyes que han gobernado el Perú* (6 vols., Lima, 1859), v, vi.

GARCIA RAMOS, D., 'Don José Morales y Montero del Aguila', *Fénix*, v (1947), 283-347.
HELMER, MARIE, 'Documents pour l'histoire économique de l'Amérique du Sud. Commerce et industrie au Pérou a la fin du XVIIIme siècle', *Revista de Indias*, x (1950), 519-26.
HELMS, A. Z., *Travels from Buenos Aires by Potosí to Lima* (London, 1807).
JUAN Y SANTACILLA, JORGE, and ANTONIO DE ULLOA, *Noticias secretas de América* (2nd edn, Buenos Aires, 1953).
—, *Relación histórica del viage a la América meridional* (5 vols., Madrid, 1748).
LOAYZA, FRANCISCO A., ed., *Preliminares del incendio. Documentos del año de 1776 a 1780, en su mayoria ineditos, anteriores y sobre la revolución libertadora que engendro y dio vida José Gabriel Túpac Amaru en 1780* (Lima, 1947).
LORENTE, SEBASTIAN, ed., *Relaciones de los virreyes y audiencias que han gobernado el Perú* (3 vols., Lima and Madrid, 1867-72), iii.
MÁRQUEZ ABANTO, FELIPE, ed., 'Preocupaciones y gastos ocasionados al gobierno español, con motivo de la sublevación de Túpac Amaru. Gestiones a favor de la corona, por el visitador don José Antonio de Areche', *Revista del Archivo Nacional del Perú*, xxi (1957), 473-96.
'Memoria militar del general Pezuela', *Revista Histórica*, xxi (1955), 177-273.
Mercurio Peruano de historia, literatura y noticias publicas que da a la luz la Sociedad Académica de Amantes de Lima (12 vols., Lima, 1791-5).
Novíssima recopilación de las leyes de España (Madrid, 1805).
ODRIOZOLA, MANUEL DE, ed., *Documentos históricos del Perú* (10 vols., Lima, 1863-79), i-iii.
Oración fúnebre de Túpac Amaru (Buenos Aires, 1816).
Ordenanza general formada de orden de S.M. para el gobierno e instrucción de intendentes, subdelegados y demás empleados en Indias (Madrid, 1803).
PORRAS BARRENECHEA, RAUL, ed., 'La visita del colegio de San Carlos por don Manuel Pardo, 1815-1817, y su clausura de orden del virrey Pezuela, 1817', *Revista Histórica*, xvii (1948), 180-308.
'Prólogo de la memoria del virrey Amat', *Revista Chilena de Historia y Geografía*, 117 (1951), 42-64.
Récopilación de leyes de los reinos de las Indias (Madrid, 1791).
RODRÍGUEZ CASADO, VICENTE, and J. A. CALDERÓN QUIJANO, eds., *Memoria de gobierno del virrey Abascal* (2 vols., Sevilla, 1944).
RODRÍGUEZ CASADO, VICENTE, and F. PÉREZ EMBID, eds., *Memoria de gobierno del virrey Amat* (Sevilla, 1947).
RODRÍGUEZ CASADO, VICENTE, and G. LOHMANN VILLENA, eds., *Memoria de gobierno del virrey Pezuela* (Sevilla, 1947).
ROMERO, C. A., ed., *Memoria del virrey del Perú, marqués de Avilés* (Lima, 1901).
RUIZ, HIPÓLITO, *Relación histórica del viage...*, ed. J. Jaramillo, (2 vols., Madrid, 1952), ii.
SKINNER, J., *The present state of Peru* (London, 1805).
TÚPAC AMARU, INCA JUAN BAUTISTA, *Las memorias de Túpac Amaru* (Lima, 1964).
UGARTE Y UGARTE, E. L., 'La declaración de los derechos del hombre en Arequipa', *Fénix*, xi (1955-7), 76-93.

ULLOA, ANTONIO DE, *Noticias americanas entretenimiento físico-histórico sobre la América meridional y la septentrional oriental* (Madrid, 1772).

'Ultimos dias virreinales', *Revista del Archivo Historico del Cuzco*, v (1954), 370-95.

UNANUE, JOSÉ HIPÓLITO, *Guia política, ecclesiastica y militar del virreinato del Perú para 1793 (-1797)* (4 vols.. Lima, 1793-7).

—, *Obras científicas y literarias* (3 vols., Barcelona, 1914).

VARGAS UGARTE, RUBEN, S.J., ed., 'Informe del tribunal del consulado de Lima, 1790', *Revista Histórica*, xxii (1955-6), 266-310.

Ventajas de la constitución española (Mexico, 1821).

ZAMORA Y CORONADO, JOSÉ MARÍA, *Biblioteca de legislación ultramarina* (6 vols., Madrid, 1844-6).

III. SECONDARY WORKS

AITON, ARTHUR SCOTT, 'Spanish colonial reorganisation under the Family Compact', *H.A.H.R.*, xii (1932), 269-80.

ALAYZA Y PAZ SOLDAN, LUÍS, 'Influencia de la carta de Cádiz de 1812 en la emancipación y organización del Perú', *Revista del Instituto Sanmartiniano del Perú*, ix (1945), 41-100.

—, *Unanue geógrafo, médico y estadista* (Lima, 1954).

ALBI, F., *El corregidor en el municipio español bajo la monarquia absoluta* (Madrid, 1943).

ÁLCAZAR Y MOLINA, CAYETANO, *El conde de Floridablanca* (Madrid, 1934).

—, *Los virreinatos en el siglo XVIII* (Barcelona, 1945).

ÁLVAREZ REQUEJO, F., *El conde de Campomanes. Su obra histórica* (Oviedo, 1954).

ARTOLA, MIGUEL, 'Campillo y las reformas de Carlos III', *Revista de Indias*, xii (1952), 685-714.

BALLESTEROS, PÍO, 'La función política de las reales chancillerías coloniales', *Revista de Estudios Políticos*, xv (Madrid, 1946) 47-109.

BASADRE, JORGE, 'El régimen de la mita', *Letras*, iii (Lima, 1937), 325-64.

BAYLE, CONSTANTINO, S.J., *Los cabildos seculares en la América española* (Madrid, 1952).

BERNARD, M. G., 'Liste des sécrétaires d'état espagnols de l'avenèment des Bourbons jusqu'en 1808', *Revista de Archivos, Bibliotecas y Museos*, lxii (1956), 387-94.

BÉTHENCOURT MASSIEU, ANTONIO, *Patiño en la política de Felipe V* (Valladolid, 1954).

BLART, LOUIS, *Les rapports de la France et de l'Espagne après le Pacte de Famille, jusqu'à la fin du ministère du duc de Choiseul* (Paris, 1915).

BROMLEY, JUAN, 'Alcaldes de la ciudad de Lima en el siglo XVII', *Revista Histórica*, xxiii (1957-8), 5-63.

—, 'Alcaldes de la ciudad de Lima en el siglo XVIII', *Revista Histórica*, xxv (*1960-1*), 295-371.

—, 'Los alcaldes de Lima de 1801-1821', *Revista Histórica*, xxix (1966), 124-36).

—, 'Recibimientos de virreyes en Lima', *Revista Histórica*, xx (1953), 5–108.

—, 'Esquema del desarrollo histórico del municipio de Lima', *Boletín Municipal*, 1612A (15 Aug. 1955), 45–55.

BURGIN, MIRON, *The economic aspects of Argentine federalism 1820–1852* (Cambridge, Mass., 1946).

BURZIO, HUMBERTO F., *La ceca de Lima, 1565–1824* (Madrid, 1958).

CAMPRUBI ALCÁZAR, CARLOS, *El banco de la emancipación* (Lima, 1960).

CARR, RAYMOND, *Spain, 1808–1939* (Oxford, 1966).

CASTAÑEDA, CARLOS E., 'The corregidor in Spanish colonial administration', *H.A.H.R.*, ix (1929), 446–70.

CASTAÑEDA DOIG, G., 'El Mercurio Peruano y la Revolución Francesa' *La causa de la emancipación del Perú* (Lima, 1960), 218–37.

CÉSPEDES DEL CASTILLO, GUILLERMO, *Lima y Buenos Aires* (Sevilla, 1947).

—, 'La renta del tabaco en el virreinato del Perú', *Revista Histórica*, xxi (1954), 138–63.

—, 'La visita como institución indiana', *Anuario de Estudios Americanos*, iii (1946), 984–1025.

—, 'Reorganización de la hacienda virreinal peruana en el siglo XVIII', *Anuario de Historia del Derecho Español*, xxiii (1953), 329–69.

CHOY, EMILIO, 'Sobre la revolución de Túpac Amaru', *Revista del Museo Nacional*, xxiii (1954), 260–82.

CHRISTELOW, A., 'Economic background of the Anglo-Spanish war of 1762', *Journal of Modern History*, xviii (1946), 22–36.

—, 'French interest in the Spanish empire during the ministry of the duc de Choiseul, 1759–1771', *H.A.H.R.*, xxi (1941), 515–37.

—, 'Great Britain and the trades from Cádiz and Lisbon to Spanish America and Brazil', *H.A.H.R.*, xxvii (1947), 2–29.

COMRADRÁN RUIZ, JORGE, 'Los subdelegados de real hacienda y guerra de Mendoza, 1784–1810', *Revista del Instituto de Historia del Derecho*, x (1959), 82–111.

CORNEJO BOURONCLE, JORGE, 'El sentido libertario de la revolución de Túpac Amaru', *Revista del Archivo Histórico del Cuzco*, v (1954), 396–411.

—, *Túpac Amaru. La revolución precursora de la emancipación continental* (Cuzco, 1949).

COXE, WILLIAM, *Memoirs of the kings of Spain of the House of Bourbon* (2nd edn, London, 1815).

CRUCES POZO, JOSÉ, 'Cualidades militares del virrey Amat', *Anuario de Estudios Americanos*, ix (1952), 327–45.

DANVILA Y COLLADO, MANUEL, *El reinado de Carlos III* (6 vols., Madrid, 1890–6).

DESDEVISES DU DEZERT, G., 'Les institutions de l'Espagne au XVIIIe siècle', *Revue Hispanique*, lxx (1927), 1–556.

DEUSTUA PIMENTEL, CARLOS, 'La implantación de las intendencias y el pensamiento del virrey Gil de Taboada frente a la institución', *La causa de la emancipación del Perú* (Lima, 1960), 89–98.

—, *Las intendencias en el Perú, 1790–1796* (Sevilla, 1965).

DÍAZ-TRECHUELO, MARÍA DE LOURDES, 'La intendencia en Filipinas', *Historia Mexicana*, xvi (1966-7), 498-515.
DÍAZ VENTEO, FERNANDO, *Campañas militares del virrey Abascal* (Sevilla, 1948).
DONOSO, RICARDO, 'Autenticidad de las noticias secretas de América', *Revista de Historia de America*, xliv (1957), 279-303.
—, '*El marqués de Osorno, don Ambrosio O'Higgins* (Santiago, 1941).
DURAND FLORES, LUIS, 'El juicio de residencia en el Perú republicano', *Anuario de Estudios Americanos*, x (1953), 339-456.
EGUIGUREN, L. A., *Guerra separatista del Perú. La rebelión de León de Huánuco* (Lima, 1912).
—, *Apellidos y fisonomía moral de Pumaccahua* (Lima, 1959).
—, *La revolución de 1814* (Lima, 1914).
—, *La sedición de Huamanga en 1812. Ayacucho y la independencia* (2nd edn, Lima, 1935).
—, *Tentativa de segunda rebelión de Huánuco. Octubre de 1812–enero de 1813* (Lima, 1912).
FEBRES VILLARROEL, OSCAR, 'La crisis agrícola del Perú en el ultimo tercio del siglo XVIII', *Revista Histórica*, xxvii (1964), 102-99.
FISHER, LILLIAN ESTELLE, *The intendant system in Spanish America* (Berkeley, Calif., 1929).
—, *The last Inca revolt 1780-1783* (Norman, 1966).
—, 'Teodoro de Croix', *H.A.H.R.*, ix (1929), 488-504.
—, *Viceregal administration in the Spanish American colonies* (Berkeley, Calif., 1926).
GANDIA, ENRIQUE DE, 'Orígenes de las rivalidades entre los virreinatos del Perú y del Río de la Plata', *Revista del Centro de Estudios Históricos Militares del Perú*, xi (1957-8), 167-220.
GATES, E. J., 'Don José Antonio de Areche: his own defense', *H.A.H.R.*, vii (1928), 14-42.
HAMILTON, EARL J., 'Monetary problems in Spain and Spanish America 1751-1800', *Journal of Economic History*, iv (1944), 21-48.
—, 'Money and economic recovery in Spain under the first Bourbon, 1701-46', *Journal of Modern History*, xv (1943), 192-206.
—, *War and prices in Spain, 1651-1800* (Cambridge, Mass., 1947).
HARING, CLARENCE H., *The Spanish empire in America* (New York, 1952).
—, *Trade and navigation between Spain and the Indies in the time of the Hapsburgs* (Cambridge, Mass., 1918).
HERR, RICHARD, *The eighteenth century revolution in Spain* (Princeton, 1958).
HOWE, WALTER, *The mining guild of New Spain and its tribunal general, 1770-1821* (Cambridge, Mass., 1949).
HUMPHREYS, R. A., *Liberation in South America, 1806-1827. The career of James Paroissien* (London, 1952).
HUSSEY, R. D., *The Caracas Company, 1728-1784* (Cambridge, Mass., 1934).
KAMEN, HENRY, 'El establecimiento de los intendentes en la administración española', *Hispania*, xxiv (1964), 368-95.

KING, JAMES F., 'The colored castes and the American representation in the Cortes of Cádiz', *H.A.H.R.*, xxxiii (1953), 33–64.
KIRKPATRICK, F. A., 'Municipal administration in the Spanish dominions in America', Royal Historical Society, *Transactions*, 3rd series, ix (1915), 95–109.
KONETZKE, RICHARD, 'La condición legal de los criollos y las causas de la independencia', *Estudios Americanos*, v, vol. ii (1950), 31–54.
KREBS WILCKENS, RICARDO, 'Campomanes y la política colonial española en el siglo XVIII', *Boletin de la Academia Chilena de Historia*, liii (1955), 37–72.
KUBLER, GEORGE, 'The Quechua in the colonial world', *Handbook of South American Indians*, ed. J. H. Steward (7 vols., New York, 1963), ii, 331–410.
La causa de la emancipación del Perú. Testimonios de la época precursora, Instituto Riva Agüero (Lima, 1960).
LEWIN, BOLESLAO, *La rebelión de Túpac Amaru, y los origenes de la emancipación americana* (Buenos Aires, 1957).
LOHMANN VILLENA, G., 'La memoria de gobierno de don Manuel de Amat y Junyent', *Revista Chilena de Historia y Geografía*, cxxvii (1959), 67–91.
—, *Las minas de Huancavelica en los siglos XVI y XVII* (Sevilla, 1949).
LOOSLEY, A. C., 'The Puerto Bello fairs', *H.A.H.R.*, xii (1953), 314–35.
LORENTE, SEBASTIAN, *Historia del Perú bajo los Borbones, 1700–1821* (Lima, 1871).
LYNCH, JOHN, *Spanish colonial administration, 1782–1810* (London, 1958).
MARILUZ URQUIJO, JOSÉ M., *Ensayos sobre los juicios de residencia indianos* (Sevilla, 1952).
MARKHAM, SIR CLEMENTS R., *A history of Peru* (Chicago, 1892).
MATICORENA ESTRADA, MIGUEL, 'José Baquíjano y Carrillo, reformista peruano del siglo XVIII', *Anuario de Estudios Americanos*, xv (1958), 53–60.
—, 'Nuevas noticias y documentos de don José Baquíjano y Carrillo, conde de Vistaflorida', *La Causa de la Emancipación del Perú* (Lima, 1960), 145–207.
MEANS, P. A., *Fall of the Inca empire and the Spanish rule in Peru, 1530–1780* (New York and London, 1932).
—, 'The rebellion of Tupac Amaru II', *H.A.H.R.*, ii (1919), 1–25.
MECHAM, J. LLOYD, *Church and state in Latin America* (Chapel Hill, 1934).
MENDIBURU, MANUEL DE, *Diccionario histórico-biográfico del Perú. Parte I, que corresponde a la época de la dominación española* (2nd edn, 11 vols., Lima, 1931–5).
MOORE, JOHN PRESTON, *The cabildo in Peru under the Bourbons* (Durham, N.C., 1966).
—, *The cabildo in Peru under the Hapsburgs. A study of the origins and powers of the town council in the viceroyalty of Peru, 1530–1700* (Durham, N.C., 1954).
MUÑOZ PÉREZ, JOSÉ, 'El comercio de Indias bajo las Austrias y la critica del proyectismo del siglo XVIII', *Anuario de Estudios Americanos*, xiii (1956), 1–83.
—, 'La idea de América en Campomanes', *Anuario de Estudios Americanos*, x (1953), 209–64.

—, 'La publicación del reglamento de comercio libre de Indias de 1778', *Anuario de Estudios Americanos*, iv (1947), 615–64.
NAVARRO GARCÍA, LUÍS, *Intendencias en Indias* (Sevilla, 1956).
—, *Don José de Gálvez y la comandancia general de las Provincias Internas del norte de Nueva Espana* (Sevilla, 1964).
NIETO VELEZ, ARMANDO, 'Contribución a la historia del fidelismo en el Perú, 1808–1810', *Boletín del Instituto Riva-Agüero*, iv (1958–60), 9–146.
NOVOA, EMILIO, *Las sociedades económicas de amigos del pais. Su influencia en la emancipación colonial americana* (Madrid, 1955).
OTS CAPEDQUÍ, JOSÉ MARÍA, *Manual de historia de derecho español en las Indias* (Buenos Aires, 1945).
—, *El siglo XVIII español en América. El gobierno político del Nuevo Reino de Granada* (Mexico, 1945).
PACHECO VELEZ, CESAR, 'Las conspiraciones del conde de la Vega del Ren', *Revista Histórica*, xxi (1954), 355–425.
PALACIO ATARD, VICENTE, *Areche y Guirior. Observaciones sobre el fracaso de una visita al Perú* (Sevilla, 1946).
—, 'El asiento de la mina de Huancavelica en 1779', *Revista de Indias*, v (1944), 611–30.
—, 'El equilibrio de América en la diplomacia del siglo XVIII,' *Estudios Americanos* (1948–9), 461–79.
—, 'La incorporación a la corona del banco de rescates de Potosí', *Anuario de Estudios Americanos*, ii (1945), 723–37.
—, *El tercer Pacto de Familia* (Madrid, 1946).
PARRY, J. H., *The sale of public office in the Spanish Indies under the Hapsburgs* (Berkeley and Los Angeles, 1953).
PEREYRA, CARLOS, 'La comprobación del fraude cometido por el editor de las Noticias Secretas', *Revista de Indias*, ii (1941), 107–33.
—, 'Las Noticias Secretas de América y el enigma de su publicación', *Revista de Indias*, i (1940), 5–33.
PIERSON, WILLIAM WHATLEY, 'The establishment and early functioning of the *intendencia* of Cuba', *The James Sprunt Historical Studies*, xix (Chapel Hill, 1927), 74–133.
—, 'Some reflections on the *cabildo* as an institution', *H.A.H.R.*, v (1922), 573–96.
PINO, J. J. DEL, 'Significado de la revolución de Túpac Amaru frente al estudio de la causa de la independencia', *La causa de la emancipación del Perú* (Lima, 1960), 23–34.
PRIESTLEY, HERBERT INGRAM, *José de Gálvez, visitador general of New Spain, 1765–1771* (Berkeley, Calif., 1916).
PUENTE CANDAMO, J. A. DE LA, *Notas sobre la causa de la independencia del Perú* (Lima, 1964).
RIVA AGÜERO, JOSÉ DE LA, 'Don José Baquíjano y Carrillo', *Boletín del Museo Bolivariano*, xii (1929), 453–91.
RODRÍGUEZ CASADO, VICENTE, 'Causa seguida contra el marqués de Casa Hermosa, gobernador intendente del Puno', *Anuario de Estudios Americanos*, iii (1946), 957–68.

—, 'Política exterior de Carlos III en torno al problema indiano', *Revista de Indias*, v (1944), 227–66.
RODRÍGUEZ CASADO, VICENTE, and F. PÉREZ EMBID, *Construcciones militares del virrey Amat* (Sevilla, 1949).
ROMERO, EMILIO, 'Apuntes sobre las ideas de orden económico durante la revolución por la independencia del Perú', *Mercurio Peruano*, xxi (1939), no. 146, 35–41.
—, *Historia económica del Perú* (Buenos Aires, 1949).
ROSENBLAT, ANGEL, *La población indígena y el mestizaje en América* (2 vols., Buenos Aires, 1954).
ROUSSEAU, F., *Règne de Charles III d'Espagne* (2 vols., Paris, 1907).
ROWE, J. H., 'The Incas under Spanish colonial institutions', *H.A.H.R.*, xxxvii (1957), 155–99.
SAN CRISTÓVAL, EVARISTO, *Apendice al diccionario* (4 vols., Lima, 1935–8).
SÁNCHEZ AGESTA, LUÍS, *El pensamiento político del despotismo ilustrado* (Madrid, 1953).
SANZ, LUIS SANTIAGO, 'El proyecto de extinción del regimen de las intendencias de América y la Ordenanza General de 1803', *Revista del Instituto de Historia del Derecho*, v (1953), 123–85.
SARRAILH, JEAN, *L'Espagne éclairée de la seconde moitié du XVIII siècle* (Paris, 1954).
SHAFER, ROBERT J., *The economic societies in the Spanish world* (Norman, Okla., 1958).
VALCÁRCEL, CARLOS DANIEL, 'Como se inicio la rebelión de Túpac Amaru', *Mercurio Peruano*, xxvi (1945), 226–32.
—, 'Dos objetivos de Túpac Amaru', *Estudios Americanos*, xi (1956), 43–6.
—, 'Fidelismo y separatismo en el Perú', *Revista de Historia de América*, xxxvii–xxxviii (1954), 133–62.
—, *La rebelión de Túpac Amaru* (Mexico, 1947).
—, *Las Noticias Secretas en 1783* (Lima, 1965).
—, 'Perú borbónico y emancipación', *Revista de Historia de América*, i (1960), 315–438.
—, 'Túpac Amaru, fidelista y precursor', *Revista de Indias*, xvii (1957), 241–53.
VARGAS UGARTE, RUBEN, *Historia del Perú. Emancipación (1809–1825)* (Buenos Aires, 1958).
—, *Historia del Perú. Virreinato (Siglo XVIII) 1700–1799* (Lima, 1956).
—, *Historia del Perú. Virreinato (Siglo XVIII)* (Buenos Aires, 1957).
—, *Títulos nobiliarios en el Perú* (4th edn, Lima, 1965).
VIELLARD-BARON, ALAIN, 'L'établissement des intendants aux Indes por Charles III', *Revista de Indias*, xii (1952), 521–46.
—, 'L'intendant americain et l'intendant francais', *Revista de Indias*, xi (1951), 237–50.
VICUÑA MACKENNA, B., *La historia de la independencia del Perú, 1809–1819* (Lima, 1860).

VILLALOBOS R., SERGIO, *Comercio y contrabando en el Río de la Plata y Chile* (Buenos Aires, 1965).
WHITAKER, A. P., 'Antonio de Ulloa', *H.A.H.R.*, xv (1935), 155-94.
—, *The Huancavelica mercury mine* (Cambridge, Mass., 1941).
—, 'Jorge Juan and Antonio Ulloa's prologue to their secret report of 1749 on Peru', *H.A.H.R.*, xviii (1938), 507-13.

INTENDANCIES OF THE VICEROYALTY OF PERU

INDEX

Abancay, in intendancy of Cuzco, 87, 97
Abascal y Sousa, José Fernando de, viceroy of Perú, 148, 202, 211, 213, 214, 228, 229, 233, 234; and intendants, 73-6, 145, 196-7, 207-9, 210; accused of despotism, 75-6, 221; authority of, 77, 200, 203, 204, 206, 216, 225; criticizes peninsular authorities, 114, 204, 217; financial policies of, 121-2, 153-4, 199, 219; suppresses revolutions, 121, 153, 203-5, 226, 230; and public administration, 171; and *cabildos*, 187, 197, 216, 219, 221-3; and creoles, 206, 220, 226; and application of 1812 Constitution, 218-23, 224, 225
Acapulco, 52, 121
Africa, 148
Agriculture, in Perú, 5, 6, 7, 124, 126-30, 132, 133, 134-6, 148-9, 150-1, 157, 172, 236-7
Agüero, Juan Josef, 48
Aguilar, Gabriel, plot of, 82
Aguirre, Santiago, and intendant Salamanca, 210-11
Alcabala, 35, 37, 104, 105, 115, 122, 135, 152, 157, 199; on *repartimientos*, 15; and Areche, 18, 19, 20, 21; and riots in Arequipa, 19; and intendants, 63, 108-9, 115, 119; fall in revenue in wartime of, 121
Alcaldes ordinarios, 31, 196; elections of, 39, 58, 59, 175, 176, 186-7, 196-7; powers of 118, 189; and intendants, 63, 180, 194, 196-7
Almadén, 141, 146
Almojarifazgo, 105

Alvarado, Josef, 26
Álvarez y Jiménez, Antonio, intendant of Arequipa, 38, 41, 137; and Church, 43; and treasury ministers, 116; provincial *visita* of, 161-3, 166; and public administration, 169, 171, 184; and *cabildo* of Arequipa, 181, 184, 189-90; biog., 240
Álvarez de Ron, Antonio, 177
Amat y Junient, Manuel, viceroy of Perú, 16, 101, 235; and sale of *corregimientos*, 10; *residencia* of, 10, 54-5; and Ulloa, 11; and *repartimientos*, 15
Amazon, 148
Ampuero, Agustín, 228
Ancón, in intendancy of Arequipa, 225
Andes, 148, 167
Angaraes, in intendancy of Huancavelica, 33, 92, 159
Angulo, Vicente, and rebellion of Cuzco, 228, 229-30
Arandia, Baltasar de, *corregidor* of Chichas, 13
Aranjuez, 144
Aranzaval, Joaquin de, subdelegate of Jauja, 85
Areche, Antonio de, *visitador* of Perú, 12, 17, 28, 29, 37, 235; and creation of intendancies, 17, 30; and viceroy Guirior, 18, 19, 55; and viceroy Jáuregui, 25; and riots in 1780, 19-20; and *corregidores*, 19-20; dismissal of, 25; and superintendency, 101; and exchequer reform, 101, 104, 106, 107, 140; and *cabildo* of Lima, 175, 177, 180

INDEX

Arequipa, 7, 21, 23, 41, 51, 85, 129, 206, 214; 1780 riots in, 18–19; *cabildo* of, 181, 184, 188, 189–90, 195–6, 211, 223, 225; diocese of, 32, 33, 43; intendancy of, 30, 33, 37, 38, 49, 50, 51, 52, 64, 79, 80, 87, 152, 168, 207, 210–11, 224, 230; trade with viceroyalty of Río de la Plata of, 5, 35, 126, 133, 134–135; agriculture in, 35, 126, 134; and *audiencia* of Cuzco, 50–2; vice-patronage in, 39; exchequer machinery in, 104, 116; exchequer improvement in, 107, 108, 113; mining in, 137; public administration in, 161–3, 166, 169, 171, 184; and revolution in Upper Perú, 204, 225

Arica, in intendancy of Arequipa, 33, 79, 104, 115, 163, 166, 168

Arriaga, Antonio de, *corregidor* of Tinta, and Túpac Amaru, 21–2; and bishop Moscoso, 40

Asia, trade with, 153

Assessors, of intendancies, 61, 65, 72–3, 74, 118, 186, 189, 194, 208

Asturias, *junta* of, 202

Atun Jauja, 160; foundation of *cabildo* in, 160, 178–9

Audiencias: and viceroys, 54; demand for better creole representation in, 191

Audiencia of Buenos Aires, 46, 51, 62

— of Charcas, 51

— of Cuzco, creation of, 22, 27, 47–9, 235; jurisdiction of, 49–52, 92–3, 225; and intendants, 93; and public administration, 170, 183; anti-creole attitude of, 206, 226; and *cabildo* of Cuzco, 214, 228; and 1814 rebellion, 226–8, 231, 237

— of Lima, 37, 42, 45, 103, 163, 192, 197, 219; criticized by Amat, 11; and Indians, 14; and intendants, 47, 63; decline in prestige of, 47–8, 63; and *audiencia* of Cuzco, 49–51, 52, 225

— of Santa Fé, 143 n. 2

Avilés, Gabriel de, viceroy of Perú, and Túpac Amaru, 24, 25, 26, 29, 72; criticizes *corregidores*, 24, 26–7, 78, 99; and *audiencia* of Cuzco, 48; influence on José de Gálvez of, 27–8, 30, 72; supports firm government of Mata, 45, 62; and intendants, 71–3; and appointment of subdelegates, 86, 87–8; and financial and economic problems, 120–21, 149; and public administration, 171; viceroy of Río de la Plata, 209

Aymaraes, in intendancy of Cuzco, 83, 127

Azángaro, in intendancy of Puno, 49, 93

Bajamar, marqués de, 52
Baleato, Andrés, 167
Bancos de rescates, 139
Baquíjano y Carrillo, José, 203, 215; deputy-general of *cabildo* of Lima, 190–1
Barrena, Antonio, 197
Bayonne, 207
Bedoya, Bartolomé, 61, 74
Bejar, Gabriel, 228
Bodegaje, 181–2, 185, 188, 191
Bonaparte, Joseph, 201
Bonaparte, Napoleon, 121, 156, 201, 207
Bonet, Joaquin, and plans for salaries for subdelegates, 96, 167
Bordeaux, 149
Borja, Manuel, 227
Bourbons, 202; imperial reform programme of, 1–5, 18, 28, 53, 54, 78, 100, 125–6, 156. *See also* Philip V; Ferdinand VI; Charles III; Charles IV; Ferdinand VII
Bravo de Rivero, Tadeo, deputy-general of *cabildo* of Lima, 191, 192
Brazil, 6, 128, 190, 204

INDEX

Buenos Aires, 48, 50, 51, 56, 87, 115, 130, 149, 176, 209; effect on Peruvian economy, 128–9, 132–5, 155, 236; revolution in, 153, 202, 205, 216. See also Audiencia of Buenos Aires

Cabildos: in Perú: Escobedo's suspicion of, 31, 36, 176; decadence of in 1784, 39, 168, 170, 174–8; and corregidores, 31, 175, 176, 179; and viceroys, 56–7, 58–9, 122, 175–6, 182–3, 186–7, 188; and intendants, 36, 57, 58, 59, 63, 69–70, 118, 144, 160, 168, 170, 173, 174–200, 211, 212, 223, 224, 237; revival of, 160, 168, 173, 177–9, 183–90; and public administration, 160, 168, 178–9, 183–6; finances of, 174, 178–9, 180–3, 191–3; belligerence from 1808 of, 152–4, 173, 194, 195–200, 211, 212, 216, 221–3, 237; and election of deputy to *Junta Central*, 198–9, 213, 214, 238; and election of deputies to Cortes, 213–14, 225, 231; and Cortes, 216, 217; and 1812 Constitution, 218–19, 221–3, 227

Cabrera, Fernando, *corregidor* of Quispicanches, 26

Cádiz, 114, 133, 148, 202, 214, 215, 225

Cailloma, in intendancy of Arequipa, 104, 163

Cajamarca, in intendancy of Trujillo, 33, 79, 92, 112, 128, 166; division of subdelegacy, 80–1

Cajatambo, in intendancy of Tarma, 86, 137

Calatayud, Cipriano, 203

Callao, 62, 115, 131, 132, 147, 181, 182, 224

Callana, in intendancy of Trujillo, 34

Camaná, in intendancy of Arequipa, 80

Camborda, Anselmo, dismissal of from subtreasury of Arequipa, 116

Campillo y Cossío, José de, career of in Spain, 2; proposals for imperial reform, 2–3, 125

Campino, Josef Ignacio, *corregidor* of Chumbivilcas, 26

Cangallo, in intendancy of Huamanga, 41, 87

Canton, 152

Cañete, in intendancy of Lima, 175

Cape Horn, 129

Carabaya, in intendancy of Puno, 49, 51

Caracas, 202

Carbajal, Juan, 228

Carrillo de Albornoz y Bravo de Lagunas, Rosa María, 8

Casa de Moneda, Lima, product of, 254–5

Castedo, Ramón, 228

Castrovirreina, in intendancy of Huancavelica, 33, 159, 230

Caviedes, Alonso, 197

Cernadas, Pedro Antonio de, temporary president of Cuzco, 226

Cevallos, Pedro de, viceroy of Río de la Plata, expedition of, 4, 38; and embargo on export of bullion to Perú, 130

Chachapoyas, in intendancy of Trujillo, 168, 190, 214

Chancay, in intendancy of Lima, 94, 137; armed Negro bands in, 57

Charcas, 30. See also Audiencia of Charcas; Perú, Upper; Chuquisaca

Charles III, imperial reforms of, 1, 3, 4, 9, 157, 163, 234; enlightened paternalism of, 156, 157, 172

Charles IV, abdication of, 210

Chaves, Francisco de, *regidor*, in Huamanga, 118, 193–4

Chichas, in Upper Perú, 22

Chiguata, in intendancy of Arequipa, 162

Chile, 6, 129, 132, 155, 181, 199, 220; suppression of revolution in, 121, 203
Chiloé, intendancy of, 33 n. 1, 203; subsidised by Perú, 120
Chota, in intendancy of Trujillo, 91, 163; mines of, 138
Chucuito, in Upper Perú, 30
Chumbivilcas, in intendancy of Cuzco, 83
Chuquisaca, 204. *See also* Charcas
Church, and intendants, 31–2, 33, 36, 38–47, 55, 62–3, 67–8, 97, 157, 169; and creoles, 44, 46; and sub-delegates, 159
Cisneros, Diego, 203
Cobos, 110, 110 n. 3, 137
Cochabamba, intendancy of, 205
Coello y Doncel, Antonio, subdelegate of Azángaro, 93
Colla, in intendancy of Tarma, 169
Colombia, 155. *See also* New Granada
Concha, Martín, temporary president of Cuzco, 228
Conchucos, in intendancy of Tarma, 81, 112, 137, 161, 223
Condesuyos, in intendancy of Arequipa, 163
Constitución política de la monarquía española (1812), 201, 203, 214, 217; application in Perú of, 217–25, 227, 229, 231; withdrawal of, 231–2, 233–4
Consulado, of Lima, 89, 90, 102, 122, 191; criticizes imperial reform, 131–5
Contador general, in Spain, 95, 98, 150, 210
Contaduría de azogues, Huancavelica, 105, 116
Contaduría general de propios, Lima, 180, 181; abolition of, 191
Contaduría de tributos, Lima, 106, 114
Contraband, in viceroyalty of Rio de la Plata, 5; in Perú, 108, 109, 133, 153, 211

Coquet, José, mining commission of, 139
Corbalán, Santiago, and intendant Vives, 208–9
Coromandel, 152
Corral, Carlos de, president of Cuzco, and Church, 47; biog., 241
Corregidores, in Perú, 63, 80; appointment of, 10; corruption of, 11–14, 92; remuneration of, 12, 21, 93, 95 n. 3; and *repartimenteos*, 13–15, 20–2, 26, 34, 88; Indian discontent with, 14–17; and tribute collection, 17, 20, 112; and 1780 riots, 20; and Túpac Amaru, 21–4, 78, 235; and *habilitadores*, 26–7; and *cabildos*, 31, 175, 176, 179; abolition of, 27, 32, 33–4, 78–9; proposed restoration of, 62, 64, 69, 198. *See also Repartimientos*
Cortes, 228; summoning of, 201, 213; and Indians, 98, 114; and creoles, 206, 213–15, 231, 233; Peruvian deputies in, 152, 214–18, 221, 223–5; and Constitution, 201, 217; closure of, 233
Council of the Indies, 42, 48, 51–2, 67, 72, 95, 97, 149, 174, 188, 189; and revision of administrative reform, 64, 69–70, 235; and intendants, 75, 163, 164–5, 194, 209–10, 211, 212
Council of Regency, 75, 165, 201, 202, 212, 217, 231; and dismissal of intendants, 196, 206, 210–11, 237; and Cortes, 213, 225; and Constitution, 217; attacks absolutist regime, 213–14, 217, 226, 231, 237; criticized by Abascal, 217
Creoles, in Perú, 7–8, 19, 22–3, 26; participation in government, 8–9, 191, 199, 205–6, 220; appointment as intendants, 37–8, 47, 196, 211; appointment as subdelegates, 82–3, 94; in Cuzco, 44–6, 229–32; in *cabildos*, 174–5, 177, 186, 219;

Creoles (cont.)
  grievances of, 44–6, 152–4, 155, 190–1, 198–200, 205–6, 215, 216, 231, 233–4, 237–8; conservatism of, 202–4, 215, 222, 230–1, 233, 237; and Cortes, 213–15, 231; and revolution, 229–32, 234
Croix, Teodoro de, viceroy of Perú, 19, 26, 39, 41, 42, 49, 50, 132; and creation of intendancies, 32, 33, 38, 55; and intendants, 46, 57, 61–4, 66, 68, 69, 76, 115–16, 162–3, 188, 235; and Escobedo, 55–9, 60, 61, 76, 183, 235; and *cabildo* of Lima, 56, 57, 58–9, 177; requests restoration of *corregidores*, 62, 63, 64; and subdelegates, 92, 95; and public administration, 170; formal reception of in Lima, 182–3
Cuba, administrative reform in, 3–4; economic development of 125, 146
Cuellar, Francisco, subdelegate of Pasco, 137
Cuenca, Joaquin, 117
Cuzco, 7, 18, 22, 28, 29, 62, 85, 129, 147, 160, 203, 204, 206, 214; bishop of, 33, 49; creole strength in, 44–6, 82, 158, 183, 225–6; decline of, 49; appointment of subdelegate for, 81; *cabildo* of, 183, 214, 216, 223, 227–8; intendancy of, 32, 33, 37, 61, 64, 91, 168, 206; commerce of, with Upper Perú, 5, 126, 134–5; industry in, 5, 35, 126; agriculture in, 126, 134; mining in, 152; vice-patronage in, 36, 39, 43–7; resentment of Lima in, 45, 151–2; and appointment of Europeans as subdelegates, 82–3; corrupt local government in, 97; and 1814 rebellion, 98, 199, 203, 206–7, 210, 211, 225–32, 233, 234, 237; exchequer machinery in, 104; exchequer improvement in, 108, 112–13; economic decline of, 127–8; public administration in, 158–9, 166, 170, 183; and revolution in Upper Perú, 204, 229–31. *See also Audiencia* of Cuzco

Delgado, Gregorio, and intendant Vives, 145, 207–8
Diezmo, on silver, 110, 110 n. 3, 137

Egaña, José María, *teniente de policía* in Lima, 170, 186, 188; subdelegate of Chota, 91, 163
Encomenderos, 49
Errea, José Antonio, 234
Escobedo y Alarcón, Jorge, in Potosí, 25, 130; appointed *visitador*, 25, 102; and creation of intendancies, 29–53, 55, 79, 102, 112, 126–7, 140, 157–8, 177, 179, 235; and Túpac Amaru, 29–30, 78; intendant of Lima, 37, 43, 76, 182, 235; superintendent, 37, 59, 60, 76, 79, 92, 95, 102, 115, 116, 138–40, 141, 142, 162–3, 185, 186, 235; and viceroy Croix, 55–9, 60, 76, 183, 235; and *cabildo* of Lima, 56–9, 176, 177, 180–2, 183, 184–7, 188, 191, 198; and other *cabildos*, 31, 36, 176, 179, 182; and Council of the Indies, 59, 69–70, 72, 149; return to Spain of, 59–60; and intendants, 62, 112, 115, 116, 162–3; and subdelegates, 79, 81, 83, 90–1, 92, 93–4, 99; and *socorros*, 89–90; and exchequer, 102–7, 108, 111–12, 115; and economy, 131–3, 134, 149, 150; and public administration, 157–8, 170, 181–2; biog., 241. *See also* Superintendents; *Visita*
Escurra, Juan Miguel, subdelegate of Huanta, oppresses Indians, 87–8
Exchequer, administration of, 10, 11, 18, 34, 51, 56, 70, 100; and Túpac Amaru, 29, 101–2; and Areche, 30, 101, 104; and intendants, 32, 40, 41, 63, 65, 66, 67, 70–1, 72, 73, 100–23, 211–12, 236;

280   INDEX

Exchequer (cont.)
  and subdelegates, 81, 95-6, 103; and Escobedo, 102-7; conditions from 1810 of, 76, 114, 121-3, 151-5, 205
Eyzaguirre, Agustín de, 220
— Miguel de, and viceroy Abascal, 154, 219-20, 221

Ferdinand VI, 1; and intendants in Spain, 2
Ferdinand VII, 202, 229, 237; abdication of, 195, 201, 212, 214; restoration of, 98, 199, 202, 203, 218, 220, 231, 233; and restoration of absolutism, 231-2, 233-4, 238
Feyjóo, Miguel, 11
France, 125, 148, 207; and Spanish imperial reform, 1-2; and war with Spain, 153, 201, 202, 217

Gaceta de Gobierno, Lima, 216
Galdos, Francisco, 228
Gálvez, José de, marqués de Sonora, 17, 34, 36, 39, 43, 44, 55, 58, 94, 142; visitor-general of New Spain, 4; minister of the Indies, 4; and intendant system, 4, 11-12, 28, 30, 38, 55, 78, 99; and Túpac Amaru rebellion, 24, 26, 27, 78; effects on imperial reform of death of, 60-1, 163
— Juan María, intendant of Tarma, 37, 38, 71, 74, 81, 196; and audiencia of Lima, 47; and mining, 137; and public adminstration, 160-1, 163, 168-9, 178-9; intendant of Huancavelica, 71, 161; and mercury production, 144; and public administration in Huancavelica, 165, 166; intendant of Lima, 71-7, 161, 207, 210; death of, 76; biog., 241-2
Garate, Tadeo, intendant of Puno, 98; biog., 242
Gil de Taboada, Vicente, intendant of Trujillo, 206; nomination by uncle, 67; and viceroy Osorno, 67, 86; and public administration 147, 170; accused of despotism, 223-4; biog., 242
Gil de Taboada y Lemos, Fray Francisco, viceroy of Perú, 51; census of Perú by, 6, 167; fears intrigues in Lima, 64-5; and intendants, 65-6, 67, 68, 76, 84, 120, 165-6; and public administration, 65, 165, 167-8, 170-1; and subdelegates, 84-5, 95; and tobacco monopoly, 111; and economic affairs, 136, 138
Godoy, Manuel, 71 n. 2, 195, 207
González y Montoya, Josef, intendant of Puno, biog., 243
González de Prada, José, intendant of Tarma, 211; criticizes corrupt local government, 97-8; and cabildo of Tarma, 197; temporary intendant of Cochabamba, 205; views on revolution in viceroyalty of Río de la Plata, 205-6; biog., 242-3
Goyeneche, José Manuel de, 224; and royalist army in Upper Perú, 204, 206; appointed temporary president of Cuzco, 206, 226
Great Britain, 125; and Cuba, 3; defence of Perú against, 101, 204; effects on Peruvian economy and exchequer of war with, 102, 109, 111, 115, 120-1, 132, 136, 138, 141, 152, 155, 236
Guambas, in intendancy of Trujillo, 81
Guarocondo, in intendancy of Cuzco, 97
Guayaquil, 132, 214; transfer of to Perú, 6, 52-3
Guevara, Buenaventura, regidor in Cuzco, 183
Guirior, Manuel de, viceroy of Perú, 15, 26; and Areche, 18-19, 55; dismissal of, 19; and 1780 riots, 19; and repartimientos, 20-1

INDEX

Guisla Larrea, Juan de la, *corregidor* and subdelegate of Cajamarca, 92

Haënke, Tadeo, 148
Havana, occupation of by British, 3
Hualgayoc, in intendancy of Trujillo, 34, 80-1, 166
Huamochuco, in intendancy of Trujillo, 128
Huamalíes, in intendancy of Tarma, 137
Huamanga, 160, 208, 214, 223; *cabildo* of, 39, 40, 117-18, 152, 193-4, 196, 212, 214; society in, 117; diocese of, 33, 104-5, 159; intendancy of, 33, 37, 38, 49, 83, 87, 147, 152, 207, 211, 212, 230; vice-patronage in, 38-43; administrative disputes in, 38-43, 116-18, 193-4; corrupt local government in, 93; exchequer machinery in, 104-5; exchequer improvement in, 108; agriculture in, 126, 151; mining in, 152; public administration in, 164-5, 166, 171
Huancavelica, 223; corruption in, 10-11; traditional difficulty of government in, 35; subdelegate appointed to, 81; *cabildo* of, 144, 145, 181, 184; intendancy of, 33, 35, 37, 42, 49, 62, 71, 75, 79 n. 1, 207, 230; corrupt local government in, 92; exchequer machinery in, 104-5, 116; inefficient tribute collection in, 113-14; and mercury mining, 10-11, 33, 35, 62, 64, 139, 140-6, 166, 257; agriculture in, 126, 151; unrest in, 145, 207-10, 211; public administration in, 159, 165, 166, 171-2, 184
Huanchaco, in intendancy of Trujillo, 150, 190
Huanta, in intendancy of Huamanga, 41, 42, 87
Huánuco, in intendancy of Tarma, 7, 137, 161, 178, 214, 223
Huaras, in intendancy of Tarma, 178

Huarochirí, 33, 82; and intendancy of Lima, 74-5
Huaylas, in intendancy of Tarma, 7, 137, 168, 178
Hurtado de Mendoza, Manuel, 230

Ica, in intendancy of Lima, 7, 95; *cabildo* of, 182, 196
Incas, 49. *See also* Indians
Indians, in Perú, 66, 171, 203, 219; demographic increase of, 6, 112, 114, 167; as labour force, 15, 16, 23, 89, 127, 147, 148, 164; rebellions of, 14, 15-16, 98, 161, 203, 220, 230, 236; alcoholism of, 35, 164; and Church, 44-5, 164; and tribute, 80, 81, 82, 111-14; and subdelegates, 80, 81, 87-99, 114 n. 7, 220; and land tenure, 158; conscription of, 204; and Cortes, 98, 114, 215. *See also* Pumacahua, Mateo; *Repartimientos*; Santos de Atahualpa, Juan; Tribute; Túpac Amaru, José Gabriel
Industry, in Perú, 5, 23, 35, 120, 126, 128, 135, 149, 172, 236; in Spain, 125, 126, 153, 172
Intendants: in Spain, 2
— in Spanish America: 4; establishment of in viceroyalty of Río de la Plata, 30; establishment in Chile of, 38; preparations for in viceroyalty of New Granada, 60-1
— in Perú: plans of Areche for, 17; establishment of, 27-8, 30-53, 235; and viceroys, 31, 54-77, 83-8, 92, 93, 99, 115-16, 164, 165-6, 188, 196-7, 207-9, 210, 235, 236; and *audiencias*, 31, 47, 93, 99; and bishops, 31-2, 33, 36, 38-47, 62-3, 67-8, and exchequer, 32, 63, 65, 66, 72, 73, 100-23, 236; and treasury ministers, 40, 41, 67, 70-1, 103, 105, 113-14, 116-18, 120, 211-12; creole appointment as, 37-8, 47, 196, 211; and *cabildos*, 36, 57, 58, 59, 63,

INDEX

Intendants (*cont.*)
69–70, 118, 144, 160, 168, 170, 174–200, 211, 212, 223, 224, 237; salaries of, 48, 162; and administration of justice, 63, 134; and *guerra*, 64, 65, 71; unsuccessful reform of, 70–1, 96; dismissal and restoration after 1808 of, 75, 196, 206–13; and subdelegates, 78–99, 164, 235; and economic development, 90, 109, 124–55, 236–7. *See also* Subdelegates; Superintendents

Jalavera, Gregorio, subdelegate of Vilcashuamán, 83
Jauja, in intendancy of Tarma, 14, 30, 81, 85, 104, 137, 160, 168, 178–179; hostile Indians in, 161; *cabildo* of, 223
Jáuregui, Agustín de, viceroy of Perú, 19, 58; and abolition of *repartimientos*; and Areche, 25; and Túpac Amaru, 25–6, 29, 55; official reception in Lima of, 182
Jequetepeque, in intendancy of Trujillo, 147
Jesuits, break-up of estates of, 129; demand for restoration of, 215
Juan Jorge, *Noticias secretas* of, 9, 10, 13; enumerates Perú's resources, 124–5. *See also* Ulloa, Antonio de
Junta Central, 121, 195, 237; formation of, 201, 202; fall of, 202; and dismissal on intendants, 75, 146, 206–13, 237; restores contentious jurisdiction to treasury ministers, 118–19; and election of Peruvian deputy to, 198, 213, 214, 238
Junta de fortificaciones, 53
Junta de gobierno, in capital of each intendancy, 103
Junta municipal, in main towns and cities, 180
Junta provincial de real hacienda, 103
Junta superior de real hacienda, Lima, 34, 57, 79, 89, 103, 150, 169, 179, 180; and subdelegates, 80, 81, 83–4, 91, 95, 96
Justice, administration of, 9, 10, 11, 12, 13–14, 16, 18, 27, 47, 50–1, 63, 65, 78, 80, 81, 87, 93, 97, 98, 99

Lambayeque, in intendancy of Trujillo, 147
Lampa, in intendancy of Puno, 49, 51
La Paz, Upper Perú, 30, 204, 206, 212, 224, 230
La Rosa, Juan de, accountant of Huamanga subtreasury, 117–18
Las Heras, Bartolomé María de, bishop of Cuzco, 46
Lavalle Cortés, Antonio de, plans of to import Negroes, 148–9
— José Antonio de, conde de Premio Real, 7, 148
Lavalle y Zugasti, Juan Bautista de, intendant of Arequipa, 7; biog., 243
Leguanda, Ignacio, 40, 117; supports 'free trade', 133–4
León de Huánuco, in intendancy of Tarma, 168, 178
Lima, 7, 32, 38, 48, 61, 64, 67, 68, 85, 102, 128, 129, 138, 139, 142, 147, 148, 162, 163, 170, 202, 203, 205, 210, 214, 226, 229; decline of, 5, 52, 133, 134, 155; society of, 7–9, 37, 186, 202–3; intrigues in viceregal court of, 10–11, 64–5; and Guayaquil, 52–3; *cabildo* of, 56, 57, 58–9, 122, 152–4, 170, 175–6, 177–8, 180–3, 184–7, 188, 190–3, 198–200, 203, 214, 215–16, 218–219, 221–3, 233–4, 238; places of amusement in, 73, 122, 192; *corregidor* of, 81–2; Indians in, 81–2; public administration in, 91, 167, 168, 170, 172, 181–2, 185–6; exchequer affairs in, 95, 109, 113; merchants of, 131, 133, 135, 155, 182, 203; anti-Spanish feeling in, 152–4, 155; loyalty to Spain of,

INDEX 283

Lima (cont.)
202–3, 231; application of Constitution in, 218–23; intendancy of, 30, 37, 56, 64, 68, 71–7, 177, 207, 210, 235; vice-patronage in, 33, 43, 47, 68
Liniers, Santiago, 209
Lions, José, 208
López, Francisco Bruno, subdelegate of Paruro, praised by president of Cuzco, 91
López Sánchez, Francisco, bishop of Huamanga, 39–43

Madrid, 76, 163, 165, 189, 190, 191, 192, 199, 201, 202, 233, 235, 237
Mainas, 204; transfer to Perú of, 6, 52
Malabar, 152
Manrique de Lara, Francisco, marqués de Lara, 8
— Nicolás, 1st marqués de Lara, 8
Manrique de Lara y Carrillo de Albornoz, Nicolás, 3rd marqués de Lara, intendant of Huamanga, 8, 37–43; accused of *repartimiento*, 41; biog., 243–4
Marmol, Juan Luque, and intendant of Huancavelica, 116, 142
Márquez de la Plata, Fernando, intendant of Huancavelica, 37, 143 n. 2; investigates conduct of intendant of Huamanga, 42; and *Santa Barbara* mercury mine, 62, 140–3; and *cabildo* of Huancavelica, 184; and public adminstration, 184; biog., 244
Marroquin, Francisco, director of *Santa Barbara* mercury mine, 142–3
Martínez Compañon, Baltasar Jaime, bishop of Trujillo, 166
Martínez de la Mata, Luís, subdelegate of Chancay, 94
Mata Linares, Benito de la, intendant of Cuzco, 37; and Túpac Amaru, 29, 32; and tribute collection, 32, 112–13; and ecclesiastical authorities, 43–6, 48; hostility to creoles of, 44–6, 48, 61, 158, 183; appointed regent of *audiencia* of Buenos Aires, 46, 61–2; and *audiencia* of Cuzco, 48–9; attempts to stimulate economy, 127–8; and public administration, 158–9, 166; and *cabildo* of Cuzco, 183; biog., 244–5
Mateo Arnao, Juan de, 223
Menéndez Escalada, José, intendant of Arequipa, 37, 38, 137; intendant of Huamanga, 38, 41, 117, 164; and disputes with clergy, 43; biog., 245
Mercurio Peruano, 133, 136, 147, 168
Mestizos, 6, 7, 203, 215; and tribute, 19
Mexico. See New Spain
— *cabildo* of, 191
Mining, silver, in Perú, 16, 23, 29, 121, 122, 124–5, 136–40, 146, 155; and supply of mercury, 10–11, 33, 35, 62, 121, 138, 140–6, 155, 237; and Mining Tribunal, 57, 138–40; and intendants, 57, 63, 110, 136, 137; shortage of capital for, 63, 131, 133; at Hualgayoc, 80–1; annual production of, 110; and export of bullion, 132–6; in Upper Perú, 130
Mining Tribunal, 57, 138–40, 146, 152
Ministry of Finance, 96, 212
— of Grace and Justice, 144, 191
— of the Indies, 4, 24, 38, 94, 103, 142; division of, 60. See also Gálvez, José de
— of War, 71
Mita, 16; and Túpac Amaru, 23; abolition of, 98
Monesterio, Juan Alcensio, subdelegates of Cangallo, 87
Montenegro y Ubalde, José, intendant of Huancavelica, biog., 245
Montevideo, aid for royalists in from Perú, 121, 205

Moquegua, in intendancy of Arequipa, 7, 113, 163, 166; viticulture in, 35
Morales Duárez, Vicente, and Cortes, 215
Moreyra, Francisco, 234
Moscoso, Josef Gabriel, intendant of Arequipa, 196, 211; biog., 245
Moscoso y Peralta, Juan Manuel, bishop of Cuzco, 40; and intendant Mata, 44, 46; recalled to Spain, 46
Mozambique, 149
Muñoz, José, 40
Muñoz de San Clemente, Francisco, president of Cuzco, alleges sale of subdelegacies, 87; death of, 206, 226; biog., 245-6
Muros, José de, subdelegate of Abancay, 97

Negroes, in Perú, 6, 23, 128-9, 148-9, 151, 190
New Granada, viceroyalty of, 52, 61, 64, 203
New Ordinance of Intendants, 70-1, 72, 96, 235
New Spain, viceroyalty of, 64, 123
Nieto, Diego Antonio, intendant of Puno, 212; biog., 246
Nordenflicht, Baron von, mission in Perú of, 139-40
North America, English colonies in, 124, 125

Obrajes, and Indian labour, 16, 17, 161; destruction by Túpac Amaru of, 23
O'Higgins, Ambrosio, marqués de Osorno, viceroy of Perú, 120, 136, 138; and intendants, 67-9, 194; and appointment of subdelegates, 85-6; and public administration, 147; death of, 72
— Demetrio, intendant of Huamanga, resents viceregal control, 87-8, 113, 164, 193; and subdelegates, 87-8, 93, 117; provincial *visitas* of, 93, 164-5; and treasury ministers, 117-18; and *cabildo* of Huamanga, 118, 193-4; and public administration, 147, 166, 171; threatened with removal from office, 207, 211, 212; return to Spain of, 212; biog., 246
Ordinance of Intendants. *See* Intendants
Orue, Ignacio, *procurador general* of *cabildo* of Lima, criticizes Abascal's financial policies, 153-4
Oruro, Upper Perú, 30

Pagasa, Domingo de, subdelegate of Abancay, 97
Paita, in intendancy of Trujillo, 128
Pamplona, 207
Panamá, fleets to, 128; and subsidy from Perú, 120
Paraguay, 209
Pardo, Manuel, regent of *audiencia* of Cuzco, hostility to creoles of, 206; and Cuzco rebellion, 225-7, 229, 230, 232
Parinacochas, in intendancy of Huamanga, 40
Paruro, in intendancy of Cuzco, 35, 91
Pascamayo, in intendancy of Trujillo, 150, 190
Pasco, in intendancy of Tarma, subtreasury of, 104; and mining, 137-8, 161
Patagonia, 38
Patiño, José, 2
Patrón de Arnao, Pablo, subdelegate of Lima, 81
Patronage, royal, in Church, 38-9
Pausa, in intendancy of Huamanga, 40
Pérez, José, vicar-general of Cuzco, 44
Perú, viceroyalty of, decadence by 1784 of, 5-28, 129-30; effects of creation of viceroyalty of Río de la Plata on, 5-6, 28, 130, 155, 236;

Perú (cont.)
    trade of with Upper Perú, 5; agriculture in, 5, 6, 7, 124, 126–30, 132, 133, 134–6, 148–9, 150–1, 157, 172, 236–7; industry in, 5, 23, 35, 120, 126, 128, 135, 149, 172, 236; population of, 6–7, 96, 148, 167, 251–3; society in, 7–8; administrative corruption in, 9–17, 78, 86–7, 234; mining in, 10–11, 16, 23, 29, 33, 35, 57, 62, 63, 80–1, 110, 121, 122, 124–5, 131, 133, 136–46, 155, 237; reform of, 28, 29–53, 79, 235; relations between viceroys and intendants in, 31, 54–77, 83–8, 92, 93, 99, 115–16, 164, 165–6, 188, 196–7, 207–9, 210, 235, 236; relations between *audiencias* and intendants in, 31, 47, 93, 99; vice-patronage in, 31–2, 33, 36, 38–47, 62–3, 67–8; restoration of intendancy of Puno to, 51–2, 93, 113; economy of, 66, 90, 109, 120, 123, 124–55, 167, 234, 236–7; precarious financial state after 1810 of, 76, 114, 121–3, 151–5, 205, 237–8; local government in, 78–99, 235; exchequer of, 100–23, 236; natural resources of, 124, 126–7, 167; effects of imperial commercial reforms on, 128–9, 130–3, 155, 236; poor communications in, 146–8; anti-Spanish feeling in, 152–4, 155; public administration in, 156–73; relations between intendants and *cabildos* in, 174–200; political conservatism of, 195, 199, 202–3, 233, 230–1; and *Junta Central*, 198, 213, 214; and Cortes, 213–18, 233; instability from 1808 in, 206–32, 237; troops in, 203–4; and Constitution, 217–225, 227, 229, 231, 233
Perú, Upper, separation from Perú of, 5, 129; creation of intendancies in, 30; and Peruvian economy, 129–30, 155; mining in, 130; revolution in, 202, 203–5, 225, 230; Peruvian royalist army in, 121, 153, 204–5, 206, 229, 230; reannexed to Perú, 205
Peso, value of, 12
Pezuela, Joaquin de la, viceroy of Perú, and intendant of Lima, 76; financial problems of, 122; and public administration, 172
Philip V, reform programme of, 1, 2
Philippine Company, 148, 191, 192
Piedra, Juan de la, appointed intendant of Huamanga, 38, 40, 41
Piura, in intendancy of Trujillo, 79, 86, 92, 104, 168, 190
Porlier, Antonio, minister of Grace and Justice, 60
Portilla, Josef de la, regent-intendant of Cuzco, 49, 51; and public administration, 147; biog., 246
Portugal, 4, 204
Potosí, 5, 23, 30, 130, 139, 141, 147, 155
Press, 216, 234. See also *Gaceta de Gobierno*; *Mercurio Peruano*
Pucara, in intendancy of Tarma, 169
Puente, Vicente, 44
Pumacahua, Mateo, temporary president of Cuzco, and Túpac Amaru, 227; and Cuzco rebellion, 227, 229–32
Puno, 214, 229; intendancy of, 49, 114, 207, 211–12, 230; restoration to Perú of, 6, 49–52, 93, 113, 120, 235; *repartimientos* in, 51, 92–3; and Cortes, 98; public administration in, 165, 171; *cabildo* of, 223, 224; Constitution in, 224
Putiña, in intendancy of Puno, 51

Quimper Manuel, intendant of Puno, 165, 224; and public administration, 171; and revolution in Upper Perú, 204, 212; suspension of, 207, 211–12; intendant of Huamanga, 212; biog., 247

Quispicanches, in intendancy of Cuzco, 26, 82
Quito, kingdom of, 52, 147, 170; revolution in, 121, 202, 205

Ramírez, Juan, suppresses Cuzco rebellion, 231
Ramírez de Arellano, Rafael de, and Cuzco rebellion, 227-8
Real acuerdo, 42
Recavarren, Francisco José de, intendant of Huamanga, biog., 247
Regidores. See Cabildos
Register-ships, 9, 129
Repartimientos, in Perú, 13, 14; Arache's attempts to control, 20-1; and Túpac Amaru rebellion, 21-3, 89, 235; revival in 1783 of, 26-7, 34; and Lima merchants, 26-7, 85; abolition of, 28, 79, 96; illegal persistence of, 41, 42, 79, 83, 87-8, 90-9, 236; economic results of abolition of, 49, 51, 63, 66, 88-91, 97-8, 127, 131, 198; suggested restoration of, 64, 66, 198; proposed modification of, 88-90. *See also Corregidores; Indians; Subdelegates*
Residencias, 10, 13-14, 54
Revenue. *See* Exchequer
Revillagigedo, conde de, viceroy of New Spain, 70; defends intendant system, 64, 69
Río de la Plata, viceroyalty of, 49, 78, 88-9, 141, 174, 209; expedition of Cevallos to, 4; creation of, 4-5, 28, 130, 236; intendants in, 27, 30, 89, 119; and diocese of Cuzco, 33; and transfer of Puno to Perú, 51; economic development of, 123, 125, 128, 129; revolution in, 203, 205-6
Rivera, Nicolás de, *conquistador* of Perú, 8
Rivera y Espinosa, Lázaro de, intendant of Huancavelica, 113, 165; and public administration, 172; dismissal of, 209-10; biog., 247-248
Rivero, Antonio, subdelegate of Ancón, 225
— Manuel, 225
— Mariano, criticizes Abascal in Cortes, 225
Rosillo Velarde, Joaquin de, subdelegate of Piura, 86
Ruiz de la Vega, Miguel, alcalde of *cabildo* of Huamanga, 194; elected to Cortes, 214
Ruiz Urries de Castilla, Manuel, intendant of Huancavelica, 62; and mercury mining, 143-4; and public administration, 159, 165; president of Cuzco, 144; prefers Europeans as subdelegates, 82-3; biog., 248

Saavedra, Fernando, intendant of Trujillo, 37, 38, 67; and tobacco monopoly, 111; and public administration, 166, 170; and *cabildo* of Trujillo, 183; biog., 248
Salamanca, Bartolomé María de, intendant of Arequipa, accused of selling subdelegacy, 87; and public administration, 163, 169, 195; and *cabildo* of Arequipa, 195-6; dismissal of, 196, 210-11; biog., 248-9
Salazar y Carrillo, Francisco, 214
Salta, in viceroyalty of Río de la Plata, 205
Samper, Tomás de, intendant of Puno, biog., 249
San Marcos, university of, 198
Santa, in intendancy of Lima, 33, 112, 113
Santa Barbara, mercury mine of. *See* Huancavelica
Santa Fé de Bogota, 52
Santiago de Chile, 220
Santos de Atahualpa, Juan, rebellion of, 14, 169
Secada, Manuel de la, 197

Seven Years' War, 1
Sicaya, in intendancy of Tarma, cabildo of, 223
Silva y Olave, José de, 198
Silver. *See* Mining
Sisa, 179, 191, 192
Sociedad de Amantes del País, Lima, 168
Socorros, 89–90
Soler, Miguel Cayetano, minister of Grace and Justice, 144
Spain, decline in seventeenth century of, 1; revival under Bourbons of, 1–2
Spanish Succession, War of, 1
Stamped paper, monopoly of, 105, 199
Suárez de Castilla Valcárcel, Francisco, intendant of Tarma, provincial *visita* of, 161; biog., 249
Subdelegates, 31; appointment of, 34, 67, 69, 72, 79, 83–8, 228; remuneration of, 34, 66, 70–1, 80, 81, 82, 85–6, 90, 93–6, 98, 182, 236; continuity with *corregidores* of, 34, 79, 80, 90, 97; and *repartimientos*, 51, 91, 236; and administration of justice, 65, 93, 97, 98; and intendants, 78–99, 164, 235; powers of, 79–80, 81; creole appointment as, 82–3, 94; suspected sale of posts as, 86–7, 211; and Indians, 87–99, 114 n. 7, 190, 220; and public administration, 91, 94, 158, 159, 163; and exchequer, 103, 114, 117, 190
Sugar, production of in Perú, 5, 6, 128–9, 146, 150
Sugasti Ortiz de Foronda, Mariana de, 7
Superintendents, in Perú, 29, 37, 82, 100, 101, 103, 106; powers of, 31, 37; clash with viceroy of, 31, 54–9, 60, 76; restoration of powers to viceroy of, 31, 59, 60, 61, 70, 71, 72, 92, 115–16, 235; and intendants, 62, 115. *See also* Escobedo y Alarcón, Jorge

Superunda, conde de, viceroy of Perú, and *repartimientos*, 14–15

Tagle y Bracho, Pedro de, at Huancavelica, 64, 65, 143
Tarapacá, in intendancy of Arequipa, 163, 166; mining in, 137
Tarma, 7, 137, 144, 203, 214; and rebellion of Santos, 14; *cabildo* of, 160–1, 168, 178, 196–7, 223; intendancy of, 30, 33, 35, 37, 64, 71, 72, 81, 86, 168, 205, 207, 211; vice-patronage in, 33, 43, 47, 55, 67–8; corrupt local government in, 97–8; exchequer machinery in, 104; resources of, 124, 126, 127, 131; economic conditions in, 127, 137–8; mining in, 137–8; agriculture in, 169; public administration in, 160–1, 166, 168–9, 178–9; *cabildos* in, 160, 168, 178–9; 1812 rebellion in, 220
Tayacaja, in intendancy of Huancavelica, 33, 159
Tayo, Bernardo, 44
Tenencia de policía, Lima, 170, 186, 188; abolition of, 191
Tinta, in intendancy of Cuzco, 21, 23, 82, 168
Tobacco monopoly, 102, 105, 198; and intendants, 110–11
Trade, 122, 125, 151; liberation of, 3, 124–5, 129, 150, 190, 236
— Peruvian, with viceroyalty of Río de la Plata, 5, 6, 35, 115, 126, 128–9, 130–5, 153, 236; with Spain, 9, 35, 102, 109, 111, 115, 120–1, 129, 130, 131–6, 146–7, 236; with Chile, 6, 128, 129, 132, 134, 150, 154, 181, 199, 219; within Perú, 14–15, 29, 66, 88, 90, 93, 97–8, 108, 135, 137–8, 160; with Guayaquil, 52, 132, 150; with Chiloé, 134; with Santa Fé, 134; with Guatemala, 134; with foreigners, 152–4
Treasury. *See* Exchequer

Tribunal of accounts, Lima, 38, 63, 66–7, 95, 96, 103, 115; reform of, 101; continuing inefficiency of, 106–7, 119

Tribunal de la acordada, proposed for Lima, 57

Tribute, 17; and *mestizos*, 19; reform by Areche of collection of, 20, 111; and intendants, 32, 105–6, 111–14, 119; and subdelegates, 80, 81, 93, 94, 95, 158; abolition of, 98, 114, 121, 153; revenue of, 256

Tristán, Domingo, temporary intendant of La Paz, 206, 224; criticized by Abascal, 224–5

Trujillo, 7, 214, 223–4; diocese of, 33, 166; intendancy of, 30, 33, 37, 39, 52, 67, 79, 80, 86, 91, 212; corrupt local government in, 92; exchequer machinery in, 104; exchequer improvement in, 108; agriculture in, 126, 128–9, 150–1, 190; mining in, 138; public administration in, 147, 166, 167, 170, 183; *cabildo* of, 128, 179, 183, 190

Tucumán, 5

Tungasuca, and Túpac Amaru rebellion, 23, 25

Túpac Amaru, Andrés, 25
— Diego, 25, 26, 29
— José Gabriel, rebellion of, 13, 21–8, 49, 78, 98; aims of, 22, 48, 235; and creoles, 22–3; and Church, 22, 44, 46; and Areche, 23; crown policy towards, 23–8, 100, 234–5; economic and financial results of, 26, 29, 101–2, 112, 127, 131; suppression of, 29–30, 101–2, 227
— Mariano, 25

Ubalde, José Manuel de, plot of, 82
Ulloa, Antonio de, *Noticias Secretas* of, 9, 10, 13; governor of Huancavelica, 10–11, 140; enumerates resources of Perú, 124–5. *See also* Juan Jorge

Unanue, Hipólito, 6, 168
Urquizu, Santiago, mining commission of, 139
Urrutia y las Casas, Ramón de, intendant of Tarma, quarrels with Osorno over vice-patronage, 67–8; and *cabildo* of Tarma, 196–7; dismissal of, 211; biog., 249–50

Valdés, Antonio, minister of War and Finance, 60, 62; and transfer of superintendencies to viceroys, 60
Valdivia, 120
Valer, Martín, 228
Valle, Manuel del, 186
Vargas y Aliaga, Gaspar, 222
Venezuela, economic development of, 123, 125, 146
Vice-patronage, in Perú, 32, 33, 36, 38–47, 55, 62–3, 67–8, 70
Viceroyalties. *See* New Granada; New Spain; Perú; Río de la Plata
Viceroys, in Perú, corruption of, 9–11, 54–5, 77; and *visita general*, 18–19, 25, 101; and superintendency, 31, 54–61, 70; and vice-patronage, 36, 39, 43, 55, 62, 70; and intendants, 31, 54–77, 83–8, 92, 93, 99, 115–16, 164, 165–6, 188, 196–7, 207–9, 210, 235, 236; and *cabildos*, 56, 57, 58–9, 122, 175–6, 182–3, 186–7, 188, and appointment of subdelegates, 66, 83–8, 99; and intendancy of Lima, 71–7

Vidaurre, Manuel de, and Cuzco rebellion, 226–7
Vilcashuamán, in intendancy of Huamanga, 83
Villalta y Concha, Manuel de, 203
Visita, 3; of O'Reilly in Cuba, 3–4; of Gálvez in New Spain, 4; of Areche in Perú, 12, 17–21, 37, 55, 101, 106, 175; of Escobedo in Perú, 29–37, 55, 56, 102–7, 179, 198, 235. *See also* Areche, Antonio de; Escobedo y Alarcón, Jorge

Visitas, provincial, of intendants in Perú, 31, 48, 63, 68, 92, 93, 158–65, 167, 178; of subdelegates in Perú, 94, 158, 159, 163

Viton, Ramón, 41

Vives y Echeverría, Juan, intendant of Huancavelica, dismissal and restoration of, 75, 146, 207–10; declares policy of ending mercury production, 144–5; biog., 250

Yauyos, in intendancy of Lima, 91, 230

Zavala, José Antonio de, *corregidor* of Piura, 79

Zenteno, Pedro, *corregidor* of Calca, 26